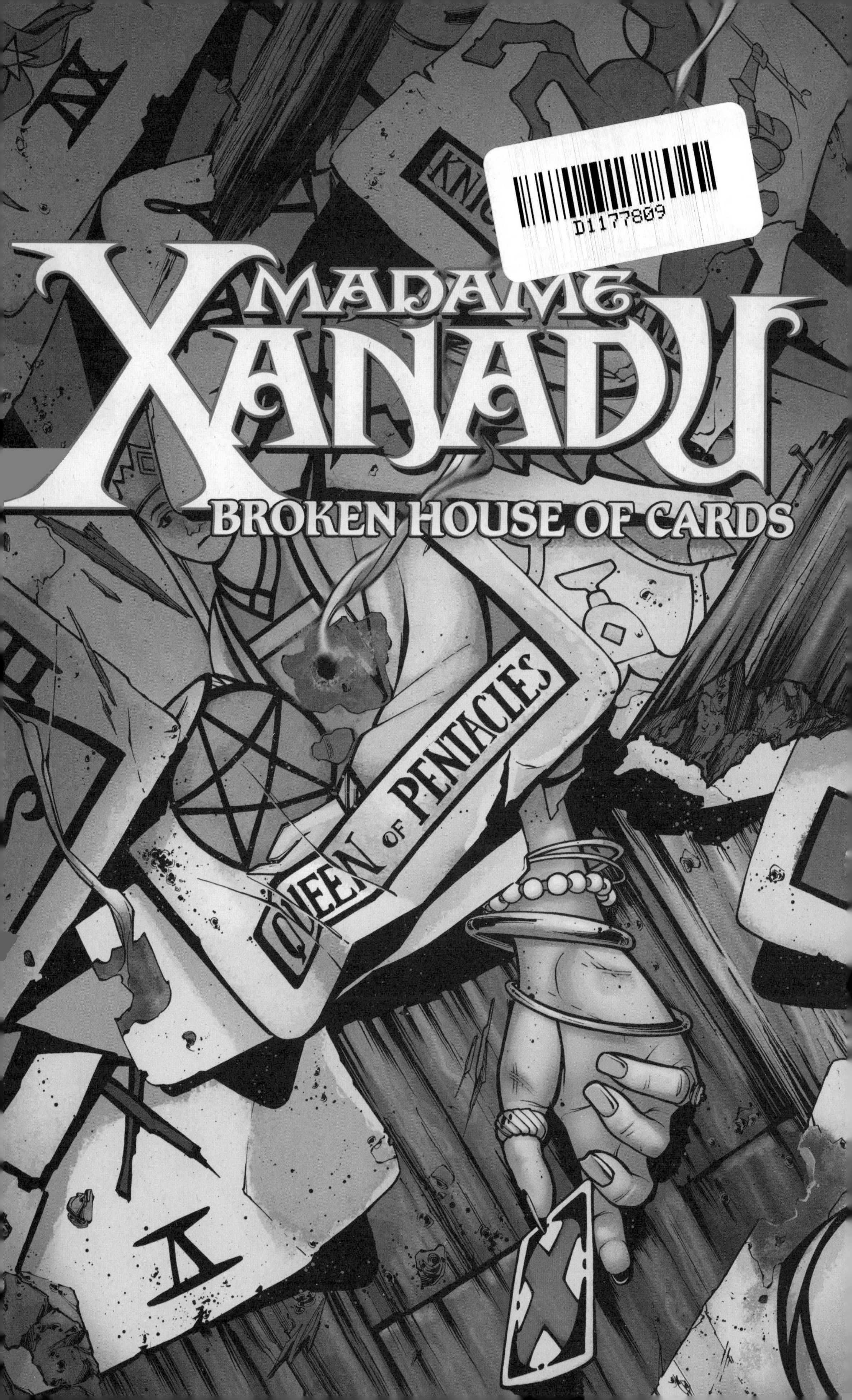
MADAME XANADU
BROKEN HOUSE OF CARDS
QUEEN OF PENTACLES

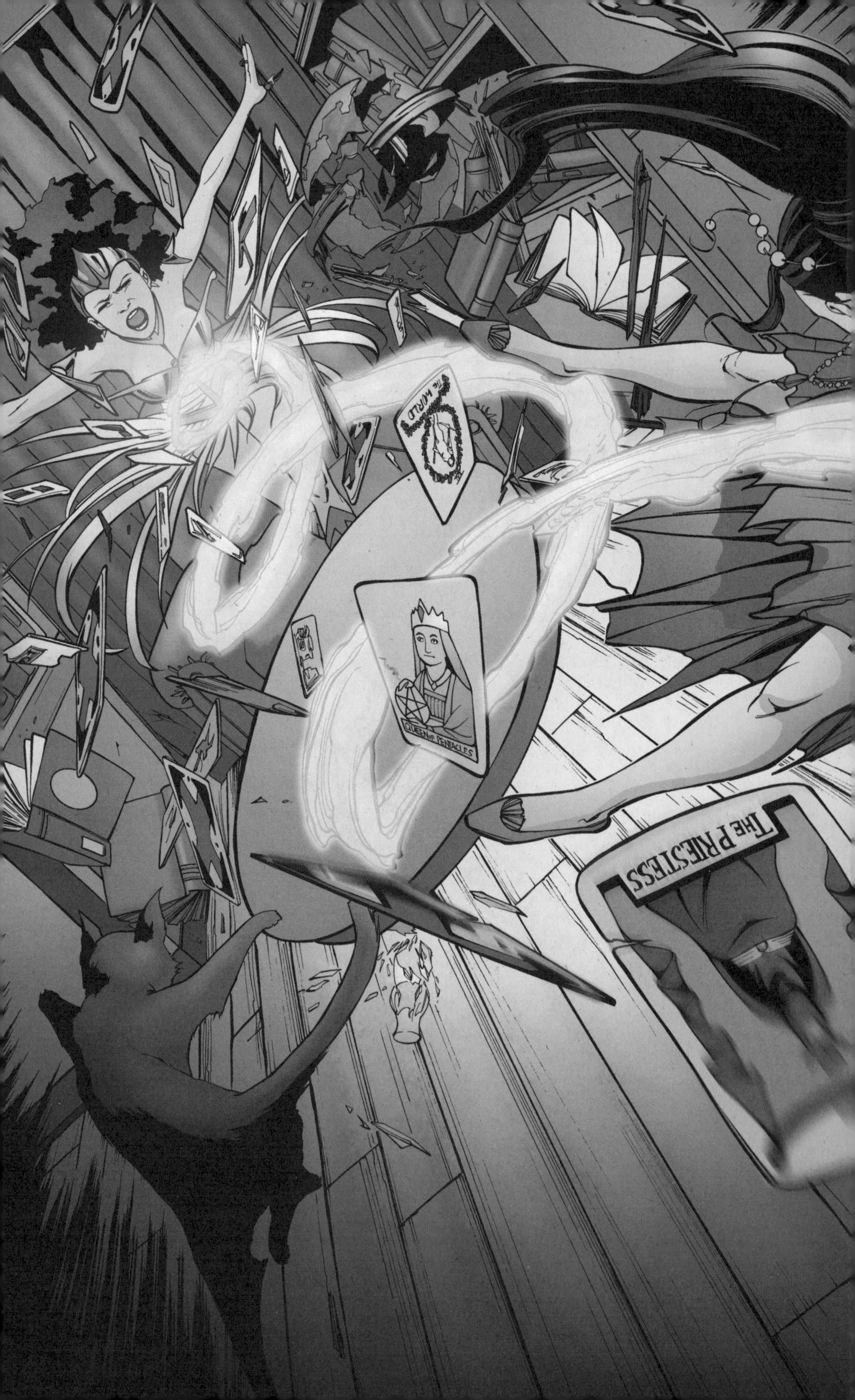
THE WORLD
QUEEN OF PENTACLES
THE PRIESTESS

MADAME XANADU
BROKEN HOUSE OF CARDS

Matt **Wagner** Writer

Amy **Reeder** and
Richard **Friend** Artists
Chapters One — Three, Six — Eight, and
the short story "Captive Audience"

Joëlle **Jones** and
David **Hahn** Artists
Chapters Four and Five

Guy **Major** Colorist

Jared K. **Fletcher** Letterer

Reeder, Friend and **Major** Covers

Karen Berger SVP-Executive Editor
Shelly Bond Editor-Original Series
Angela Rufino Associate Editor-Original Series
Brandon Montclare Assistant Editor-Original Series
Bob Harras Group Editor-Collected Editions
Robbin Brosterman Design Director-Books
Curtis King Jr. Senior Art Director

DC COMICS
Diane Nelson President / Dan DiDio and Jim Lee Co-Publishers / Geoff Johns Chief Creative Officer
Patrick Caldon EVP-Finance and Administration / John Rood EVP-Sales, Marketing and Business Development
Amy Genkins SVP-Business and Legal Affairs / Steve Rotterdam SVP-Sales and Marketing
John Cunningham VP-Marketing / Terri Cunningham VP-Managing Editor / Alison Gill VP-Manufacturing
David Hyde VP-Publicity / Sue Pohja VP-Book Trade Sales / Alysse Soll VP-Advertising and Custom Publishing
Bob Wayne VP-Sales / Mark Chiarello Art Director

DC Comics, 1700 Broadway, New York, NY 10019
A Warner Bros. Entertainment Company
Printed in the USA. First Printing.
ISBN: 978-1-4012-2881-1

SUSTAINABLE
FORESTRY
INITIATIVE

Certified Fiber
Sourcing
www.sfiprogram.org

Fiber used in this product line meets the sourcing requirements
of the SFI program. www.sfiprogram.org PWC-SFICOC-260

Chapter One: Ladies' Harm Journal

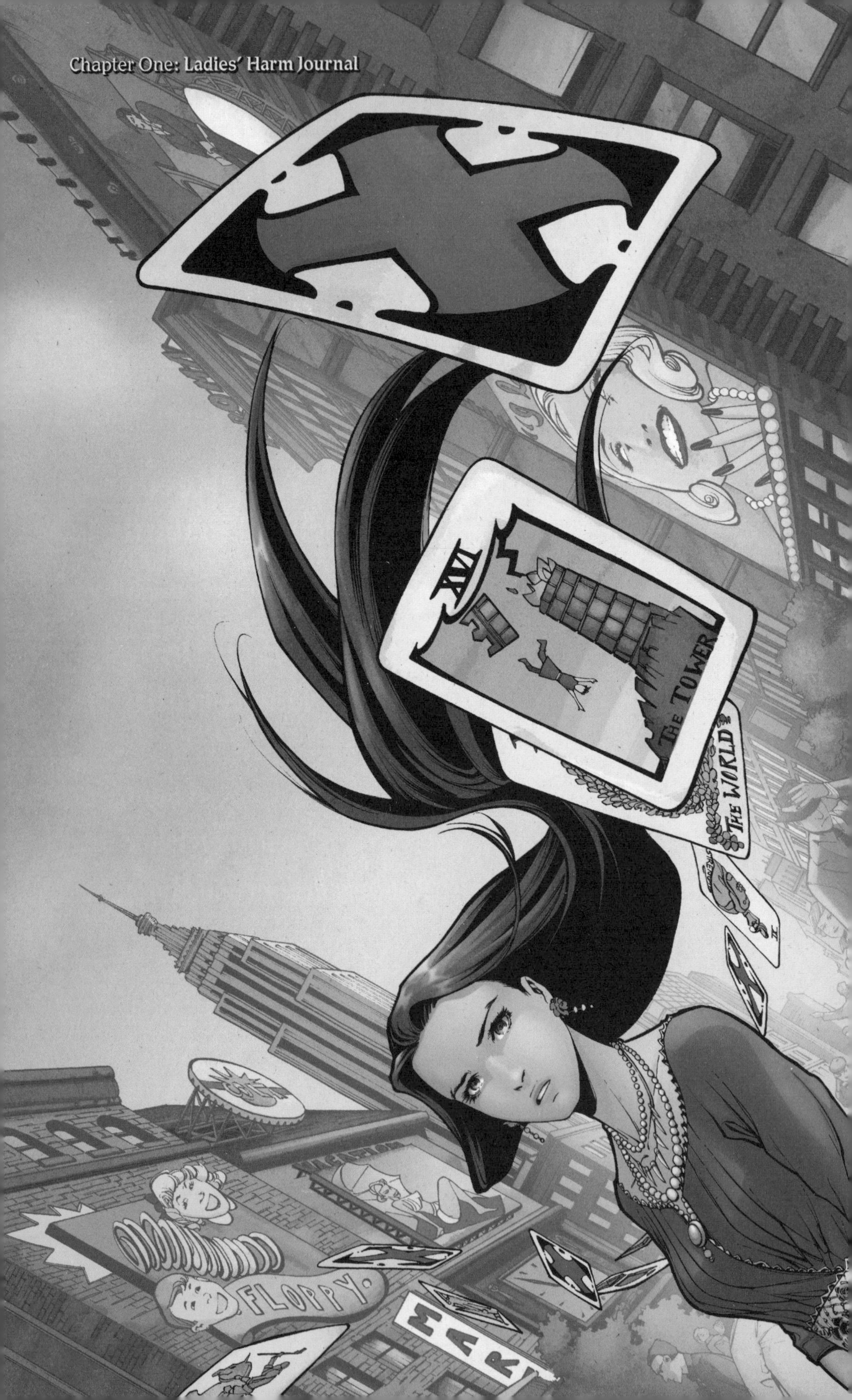
XVI
THE TOWER
THE WORLD
FLOPPY

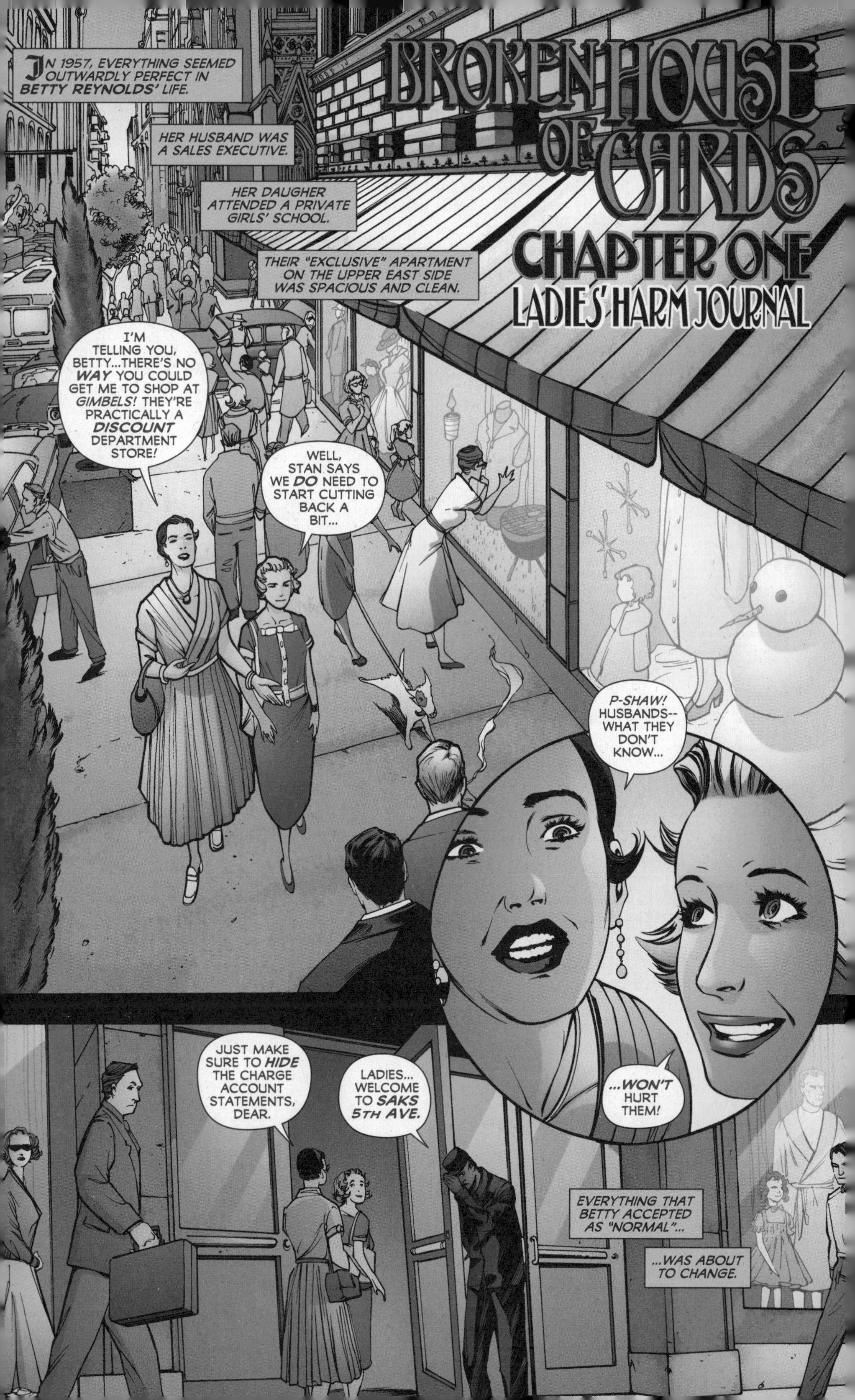
BROKEN HOUSE OF CARDS
CHAPTER ONE
LADIES' HARM JOURNAL
IN 1957, EVERYTHING SEEMED OUTWARDLY PERFECT IN BETTY REYNOLDS' LIFE.
HER HUSBAND WAS A SALES EXECUTIVE.
HER DAUGHER ATTENDED A PRIVATE GIRLS' SCHOOL.
THEIR "EXCLUSIVE" APARTMENT ON THE UPPER EAST SIDE WAS SPACIOUS AND CLEAN.
I'M TELLING YOU, BETTY...THERE'S NO WAY YOU COULD GET ME TO SHOP AT GIMBELS! THEY'RE PRACTICALLY A DISCOUNT DEPARTMENT STORE!
WELL, STAN SAYS WE DO NEED TO START CUTTING BACK A BIT...
P-SHAW! HUSBANDS--WHAT THEY DON'T KNOW...
...WON'T HURT THEM!
JUST MAKE SURE TO HIDE THE CHARGE ACCOUNT STATEMENTS, DEAR.
LADIES... WELCOME TO SAKS 5TH AVE.
EVERYTHING THAT BETTY ACCEPTED AS "NORMAL"...
...WAS ABOUT TO CHANGE.

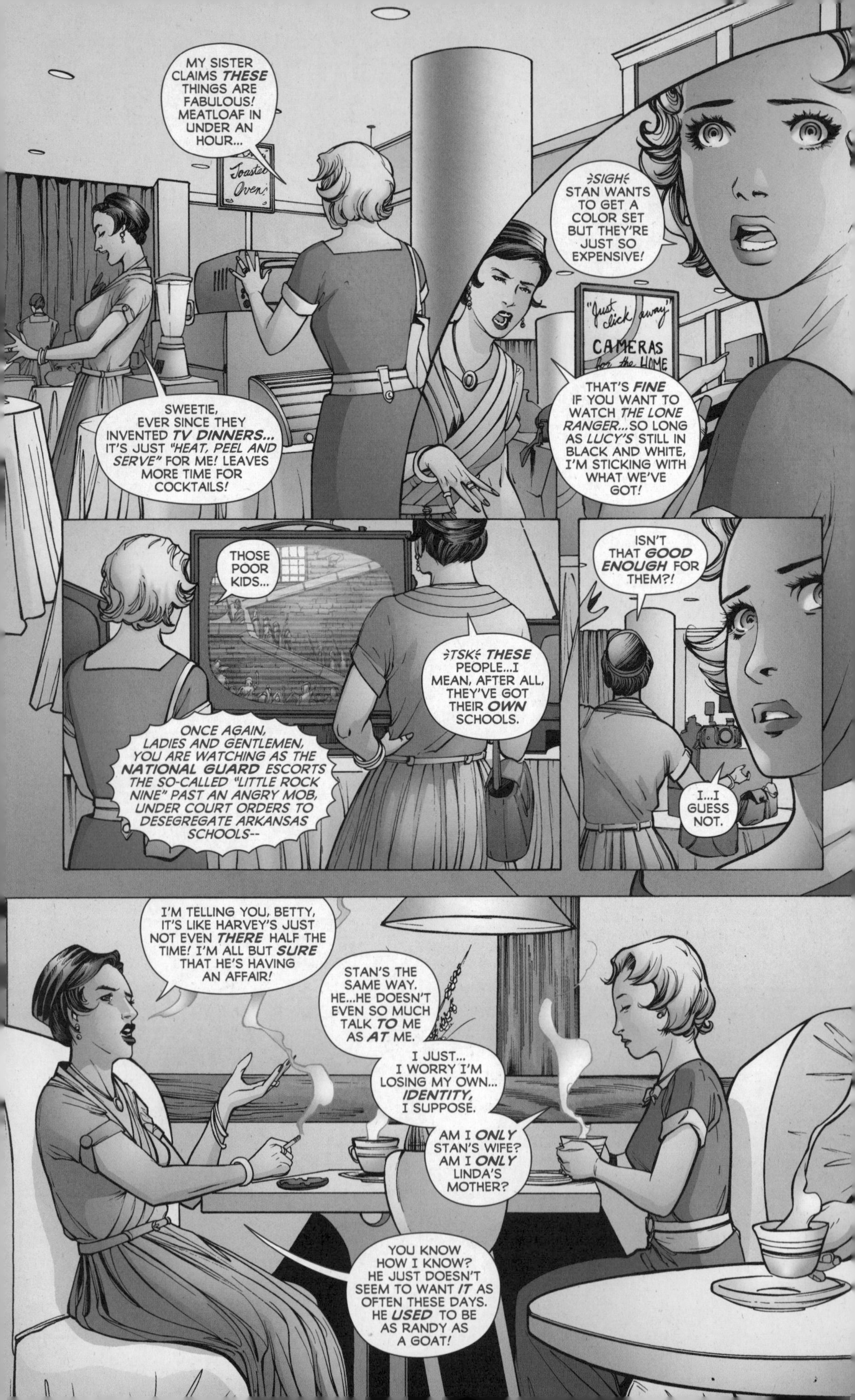
MY SISTER CLAIMS THESE THINGS ARE FABULOUS! MEATLOAF IN UNDER AN HOUR...
Toaster Oven
SWEETIE, EVER SINCE THEY INVENTED TV DINNERS... IT'S JUST "HEAT, PEEL AND SERVE" FOR ME! LEAVES MORE TIME FOR COCKTAILS!
SIGH STAN WANTS TO GET A COLOR SET BUT THEY'RE JUST SO EXPENSIVE!
"Just click away" CAMERAS for the HOME
THAT'S FINE IF YOU WANT TO WATCH THE LONE RANGER...SO LONG AS LUCY'S STILL IN BLACK AND WHITE, I'M STICKING WITH WHAT WE'VE GOT!
THOSE POOR KIDS...
TSK THESE PEOPLE...I MEAN, AFTER ALL, THEY'VE GOT THEIR OWN SCHOOLS.
ONCE AGAIN, LADIES AND GENTLEMEN, YOU ARE WATCHING AS THE NATIONAL GUARD ESCORTS THE SO-CALLED "LITTLE ROCK NINE" PAST AN ANGRY MOB, UNDER COURT ORDERS TO DESEGREGATE ARKANSAS SCHOOLS--
ISN'T THAT GOOD ENOUGH FOR THEM?!
I...I GUESS NOT.
I'M TELLING YOU, BETTY, IT'S LIKE HARVEY'S JUST NOT EVEN THERE HALF THE TIME! I'M ALL BUT SURE THAT HE'S HAVING AN AFFAIR!
STAN'S THE SAME WAY. HE...HE DOESN'T EVEN SO MUCH TALK TO ME AS AT ME.
I JUST... I WORRY I'M LOSING MY OWN... IDENTITY, I SUPPOSE.
AM I ONLY STAN'S WIFE? AM I ONLY LINDA'S MOTHER?
YOU KNOW HOW I KNOW? HE JUST DOESN'T SEEM TO WANT IT AS OFTEN THESE DAYS. HE USED TO BE AS RANDY AS A GOAT!

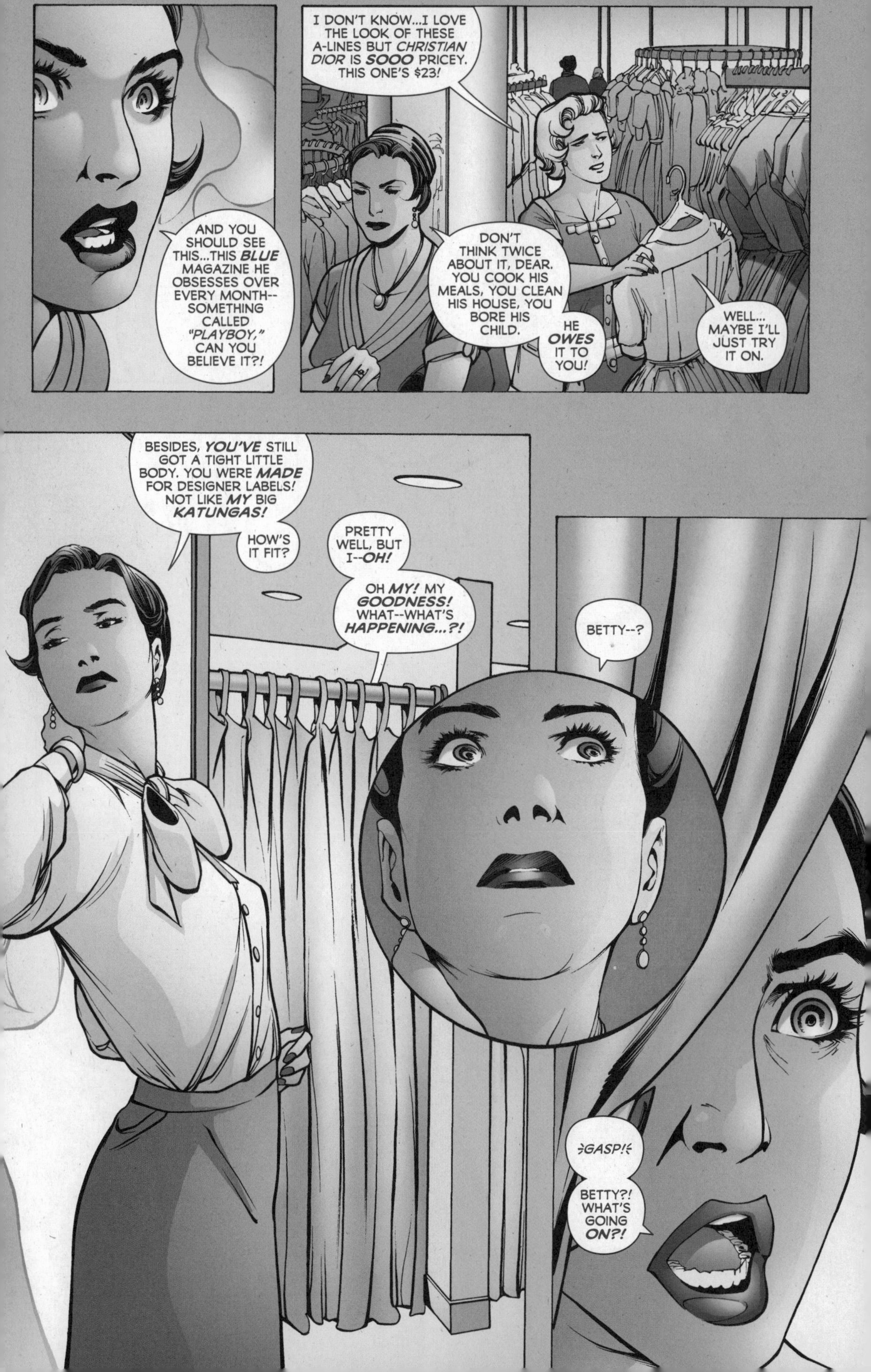
AND YOU SHOULD SEE THIS...THIS BLUE MAGAZINE HE OBSESSES OVER EVERY MONTH-- SOMETHING CALLED "PLAYBOY," CAN YOU BELIEVE IT?!
I DON'T KNOW...I LOVE THE LOOK OF THESE A-LINES BUT CHRISTIAN DIOR IS SOOO PRICEY. THIS ONE'S $23!
DON'T THINK TWICE ABOUT IT, DEAR. YOU COOK HIS MEALS, YOU CLEAN HIS HOUSE, YOU BORE HIS CHILD.
HE OWES IT TO YOU!
WELL... MAYBE I'LL JUST TRY IT ON.
BESIDES, YOU'VE STILL GOT A TIGHT LITTLE BODY. YOU WERE MADE FOR DESIGNER LABELS! NOT LIKE MY BIG KATUNGAS!
HOW'S IT FIT?
PRETTY WELL, BUT I--OH!
OH MY! MY GOODNESS! WHAT--WHAT'S HAPPENING...?!
BETTY--?
GASP!
BETTY?! WHAT'S GOING ON?!

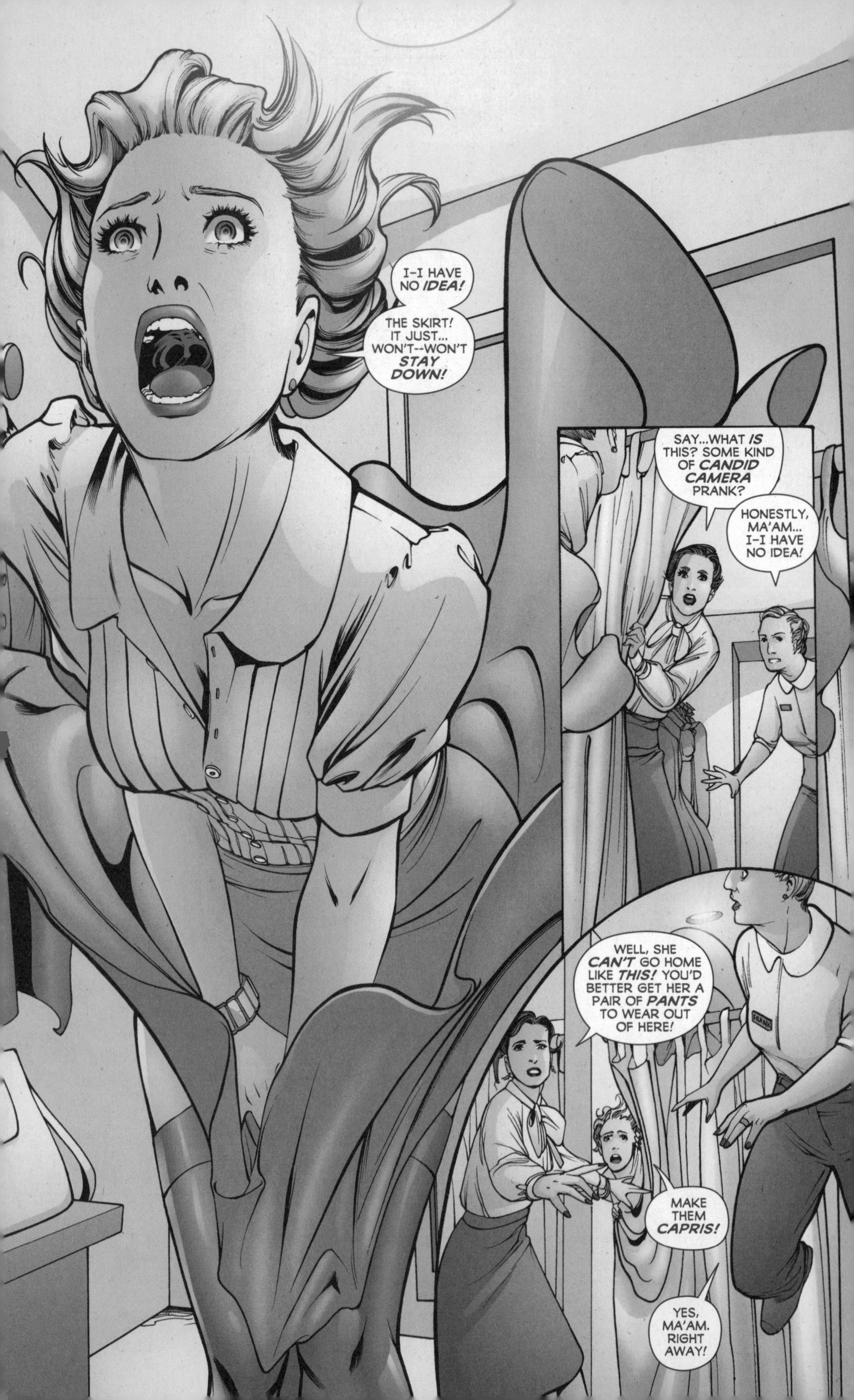
I-I HAVE NO IDEA!
THE SKIRT! IT JUST... WON'T--WON'T STAY DOWN!
SAY...WHAT IS THIS? SOME KIND OF CANDID CAMERA PRANK?
HONESTLY, MA'AM... I-I HAVE NO IDEA!
WELL, SHE CAN'T GO HOME LIKE THIS! YOU'D BETTER GET HER A PAIR OF PANTS TO WEAR OUT OF HERE!
MAKE THEM CAPRIS!
YES, MA'AM. RIGHT AWAY!

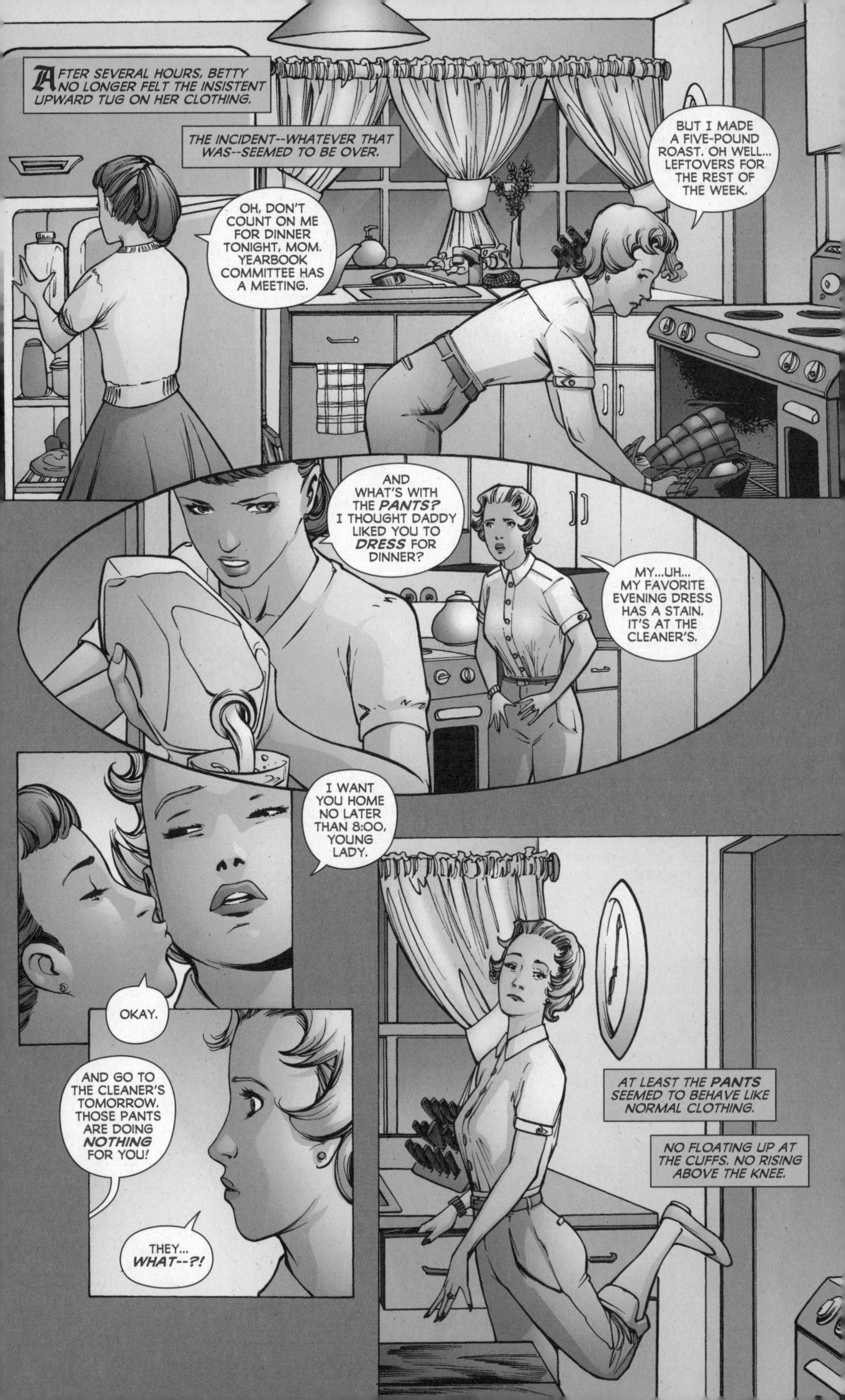
AFTER SEVERAL HOURS, BETTY NO LONGER FELT THE INSISTENT UPWARD TUG ON HER CLOTHING.
THE INCIDENT--WHATEVER THAT WAS--SEEMED TO BE OVER.
OH, DON'T COUNT ON ME FOR DINNER TONIGHT, MOM. YEARBOOK COMMITTEE HAS A MEETING.
BUT I MADE A FIVE-POUND ROAST. OH WELL... LEFTOVERS FOR THE REST OF THE WEEK.
AND WHAT'S WITH THE PANTS? I THOUGHT DADDY LIKED YOU TO DRESS FOR DINNER?
MY...UH... MY FAVORITE EVENING DRESS HAS A STAIN. IT'S AT THE CLEANER'S.
I WANT YOU HOME NO LATER THAN 8:00, YOUNG LADY.
OKAY.
AND GO TO THE CLEANER'S TOMORROW. THOSE PANTS ARE DOING NOTHING FOR YOU!
THEY... WHAT--?!
AT LEAST THE PANTS SEEMED TO BEHAVE LIKE NORMAL CLOTHING.
NO FLOATING UP AT THE CUFFS. NO RISING ABOVE THE KNEE.

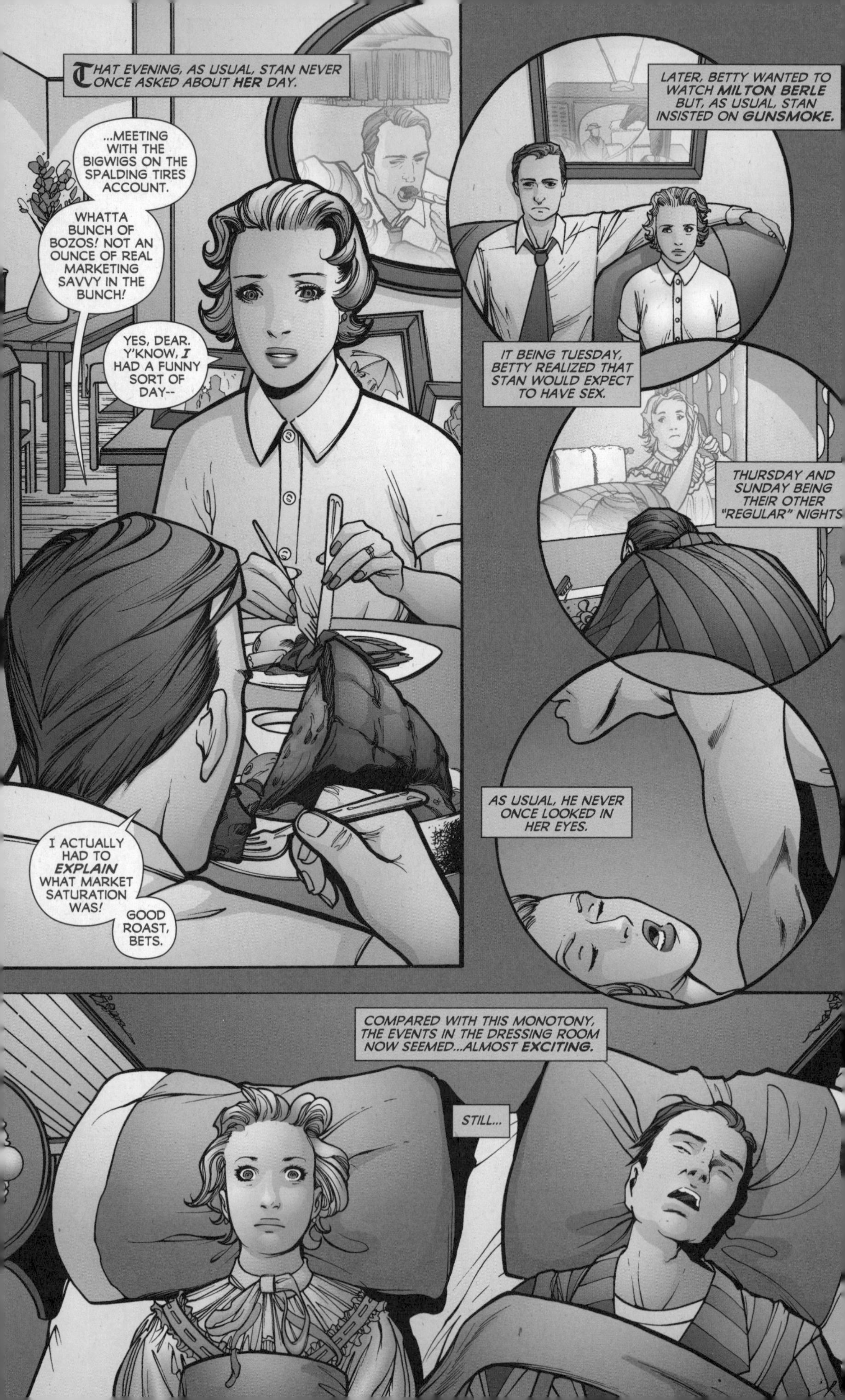
THAT EVENING, AS USUAL, STAN NEVER ONCE ASKED ABOUT HER DAY.
...MEETING WITH THE BIGWIGS ON THE SPALDING TIRES ACCOUNT.
WHATTA BUNCH OF BOZOS! NOT AN OUNCE OF REAL MARKETING SAVVY IN THE BUNCH!
YES, DEAR. Y'KNOW, I HAD A FUNNY SORT OF DAY--
I ACTUALLY HAD TO EXPLAIN WHAT MARKET SATURATION WAS!
GOOD ROAST, BETS.
LATER, BETTY WANTED TO WATCH MILTON BERLE BUT, AS USUAL, STAN INSISTED ON GUNSMOKE.
IT BEING TUESDAY, BETTY REALIZED THAT STAN WOULD EXPECT TO HAVE SEX.
THURSDAY AND SUNDAY BEING THEIR OTHER "REGULAR" NIGHTS.
AS USUAL, HE NEVER ONCE LOOKED IN HER EYES.
COMPARED WITH THIS MONOTONY, THE EVENTS IN THE DRESSING ROOM NOW SEEMED...ALMOST EXCITING.
STILL...

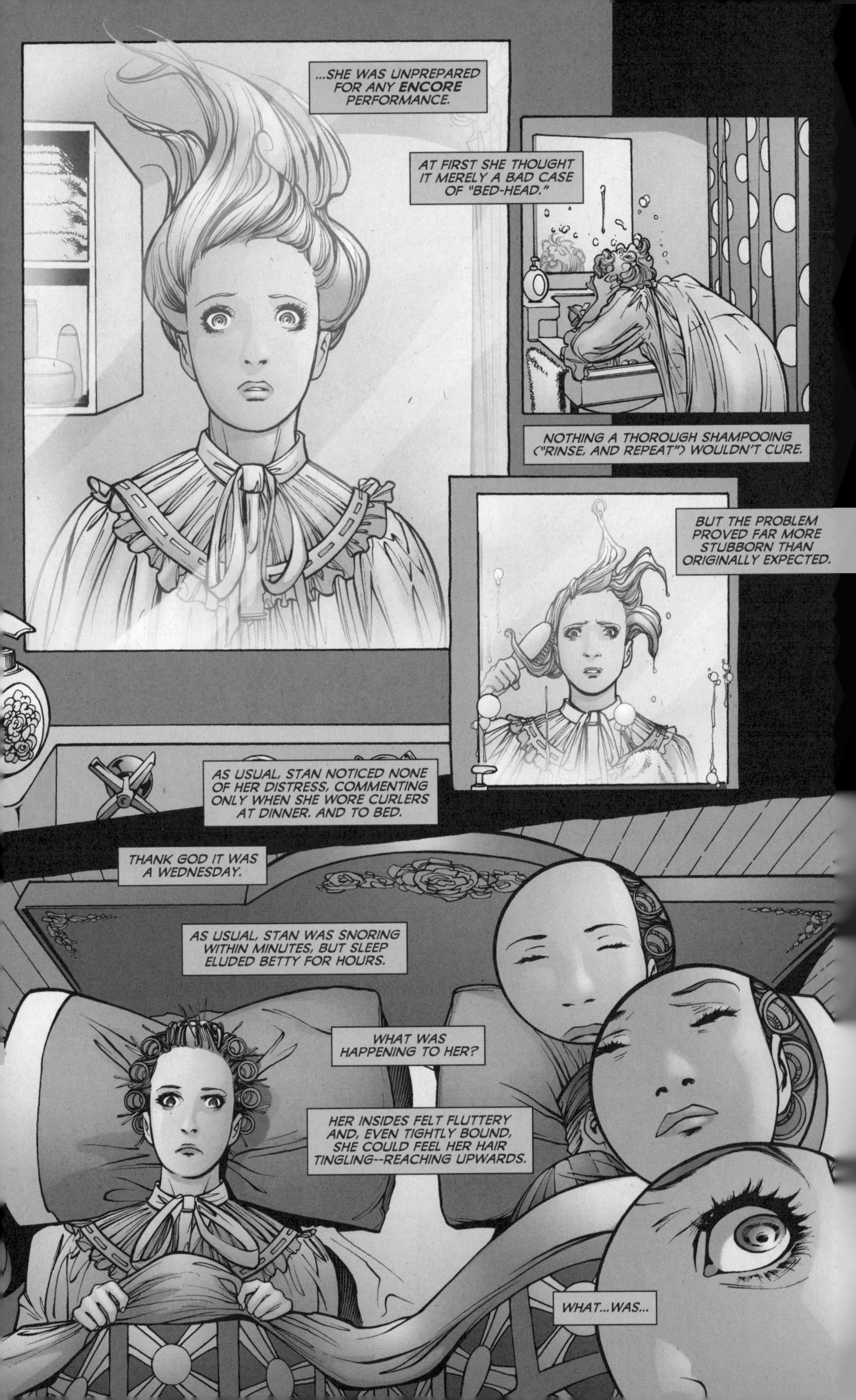
...SHE WAS UNPREPARED FOR ANY ENCORE PERFORMANCE.
AT FIRST SHE THOUGHT IT MERELY A BAD CASE OF "BED-HEAD."
NOTHING A THOROUGH SHAMPOOING ("RINSE, AND REPEAT") WOULDN'T CURE.
BUT THE PROBLEM PROVED FAR MORE STUBBORN THAN ORIGINALLY EXPECTED.
AS USUAL, STAN NOTICED NONE OF HER DISTRESS, COMMENTING ONLY WHEN SHE WORE CURLERS AT DINNER. AND TO BED.
THANK GOD IT WAS A WEDNESDAY.
AS USUAL, STAN WAS SNORING WITHIN MINUTES, BUT SLEEP ELUDED BETTY FOR HOURS.
WHAT WAS HAPPENING TO HER?
HER INSIDES FELT FLUTTERY AND, EVEN TIGHTLY BOUND, SHE COULD FEEL HER HAIR TINGLING--REACHING UPWARDS.
WHAT...WAS...

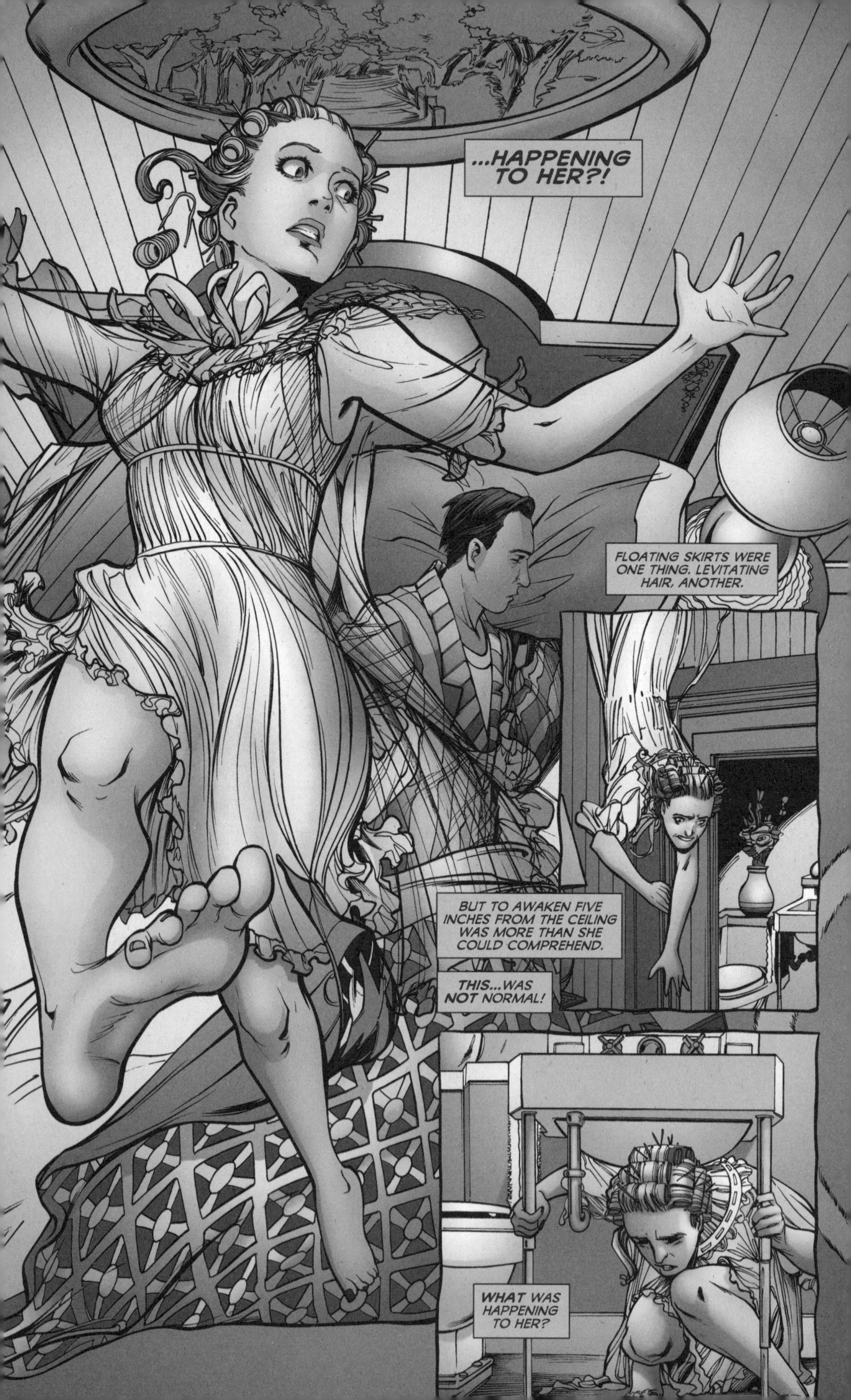
...HAPPENING TO HER?!
FLOATING SKIRTS WERE ONE THING. LEVITATING HAIR, ANOTHER.
BUT TO AWAKEN FIVE INCHES FROM THE CEILING WAS MORE THAN SHE COULD COMPREHEND.
THIS...WAS NOT NORMAL!
WHAT WAS HAPPENING TO HER?

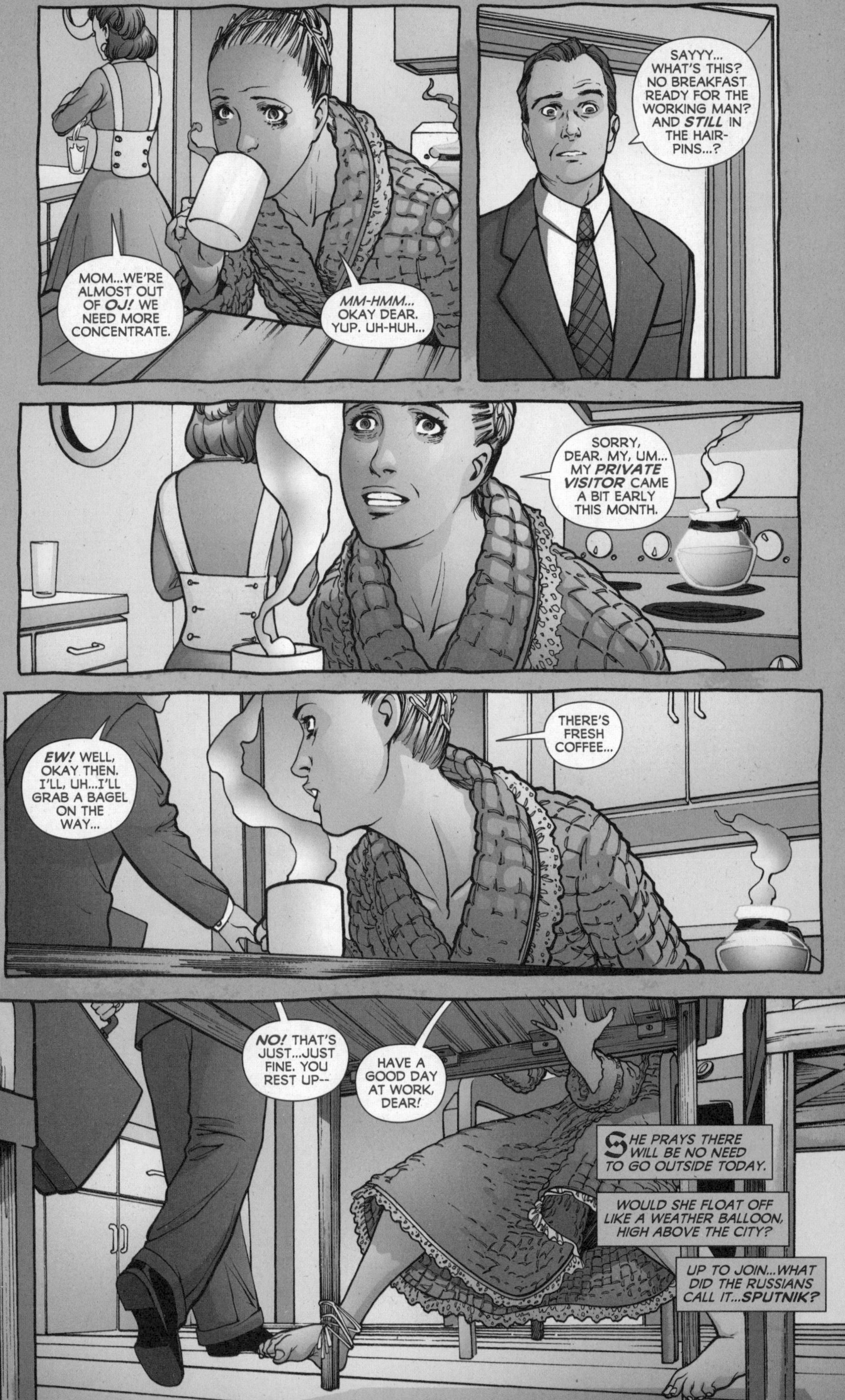
MOM...WE'RE ALMOST OUT OF OJ! WE NEED MORE CONCENTRATE.
MM-HMM... OKAY DEAR. YUP. UH-HUH...
SAYYY... WHAT'S THIS? NO BREAKFAST READY FOR THE WORKING MAN? AND STILL IN THE HAIR-PINS...?
SORRY, DEAR. MY, UM... MY PRIVATE VISITOR CAME A BIT EARLY THIS MONTH.
EW! WELL, OKAY THEN. I'LL, UH...I'LL GRAB A BAGEL ON THE WAY...
THERE'S FRESH COFFEE...
NO! THAT'S JUST...JUST FINE. YOU REST UP--
HAVE A GOOD DAY AT WORK, DEAR!
SHE PRAYS THERE WILL BE NO NEED TO GO OUTSIDE TODAY.
WOULD SHE FLOAT OFF LIKE A WEATHER BALLOON, HIGH ABOVE THE CITY?
UP TO JOIN...WHAT DID THE RUSSIANS CALL IT...SPUTNIK?

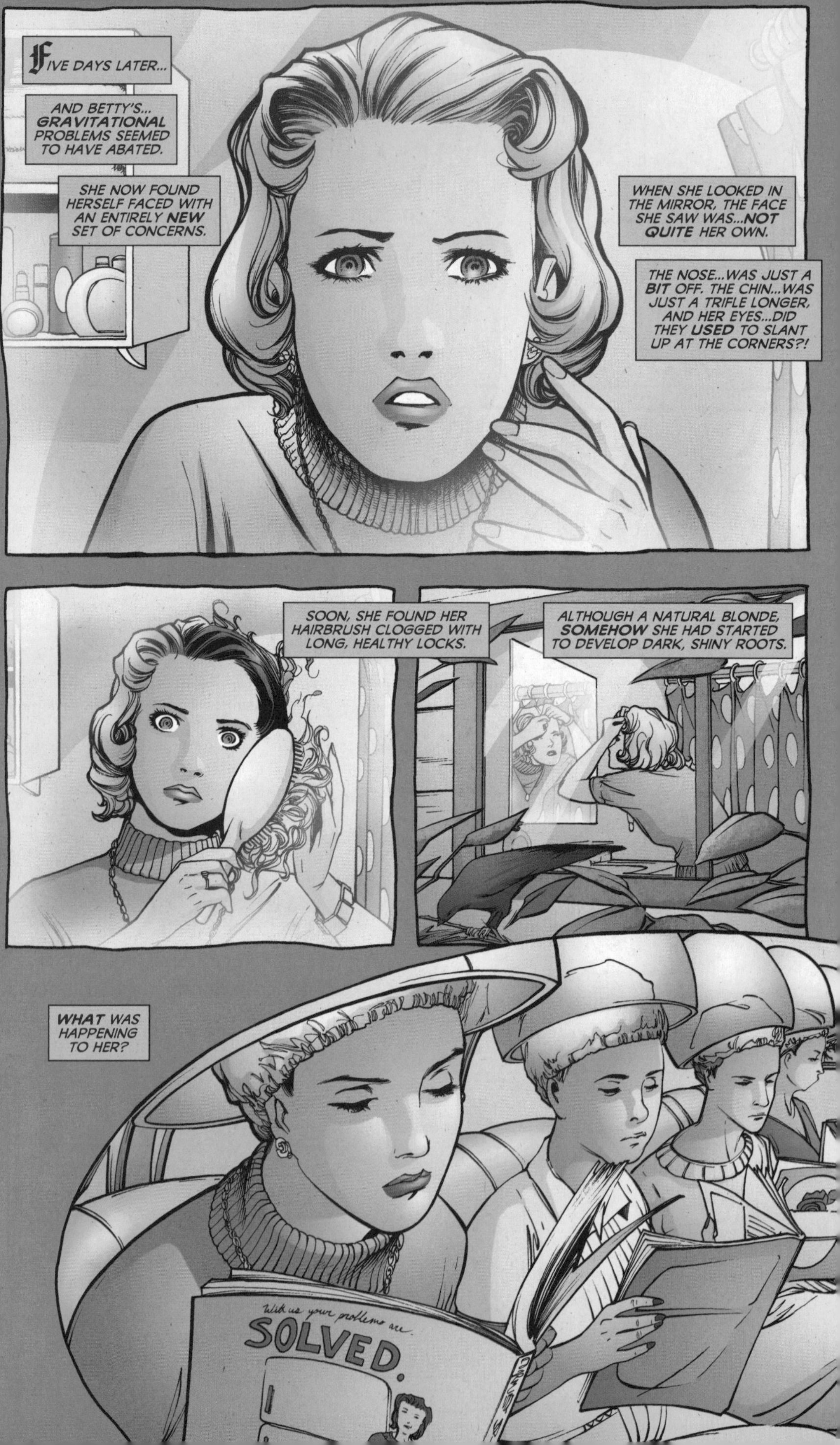
FIVE DAYS LATER...
AND BETTY'S... GRAVITATIONAL PROBLEMS SEEMED TO HAVE ABATED.
SHE NOW FOUND HERSELF FACED WITH AN ENTIRELY NEW SET OF CONCERNS.
WHEN SHE LOOKED IN THE MIRROR, THE FACE SHE SAW WAS...NOT QUITE HER OWN.
THE NOSE...WAS JUST A BIT OFF. THE CHIN...WAS JUST A TRIFLE LONGER, AND HER EYES...DID THEY USED TO SLANT UP AT THE CORNERS?!
SOON, SHE FOUND HER HAIRBRUSH CLOGGED WITH LONG, HEALTHY LOCKS.
ALTHOUGH A NATURAL BLONDE, SOMEHOW SHE HAD STARTED TO DEVELOP DARK, SHINY ROOTS.
WHAT WAS HAPPENING TO HER?
With us your problems are
SOLVED.

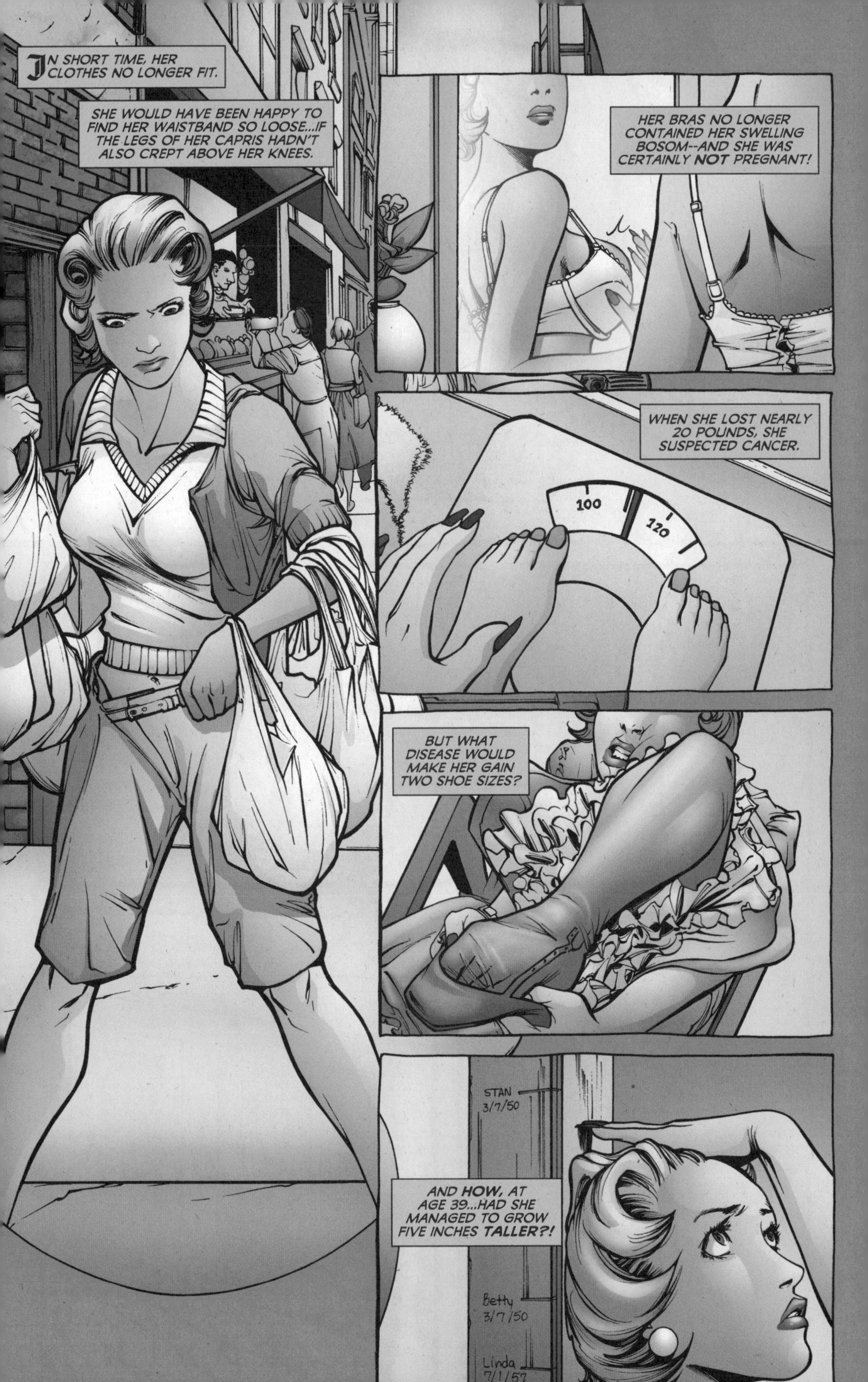

IN SHORT TIME, HER CLOTHES NO LONGER FIT.
SHE WOULD HAVE BEEN HAPPY TO FIND HER WAISTBAND SO LOOSE...IF THE LEGS OF HER CAPRIS HADN'T ALSO CREPT ABOVE HER KNEES.
HER BRAS NO LONGER CONTAINED HER SWELLING BOSOM--AND SHE WAS CERTAINLY NOT PREGNANT!
WHEN SHE LOST NEARLY 20 POUNDS, SHE SUSPECTED CANCER.
100
120
BUT WHAT DISEASE WOULD MAKE HER GAIN TWO SHOE SIZES?
STAN 3/7/50
AND HOW, AT AGE 39...HAD SHE MANAGED TO GROW FIVE INCHES TALLER?!
Betty 3/7/50
Linda 7/1/57

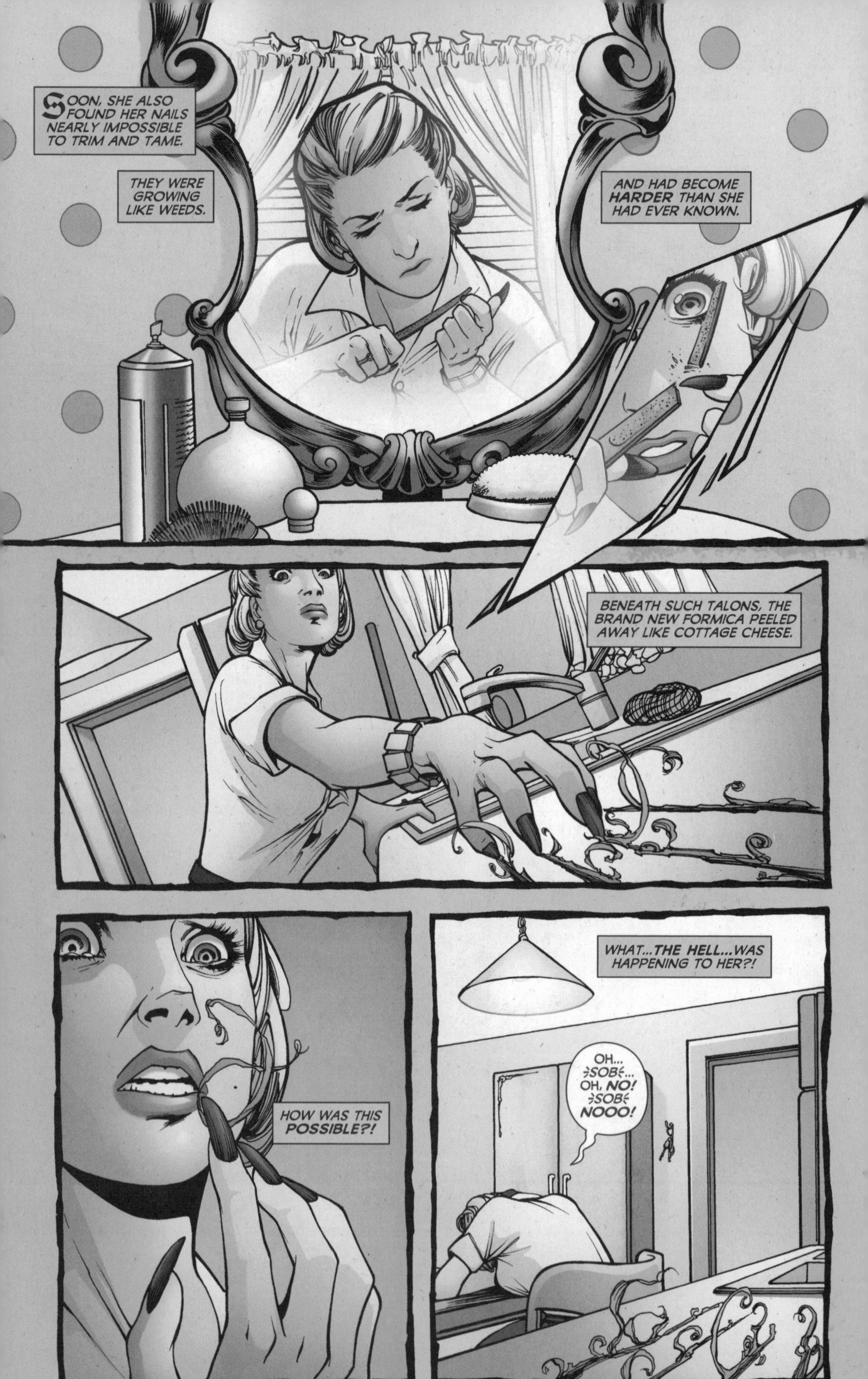
SOON, SHE ALSO FOUND HER NAILS NEARLY IMPOSSIBLE TO TRIM AND TAME.
THEY WERE GROWING LIKE WEEDS.
AND HAD BECOME HARDER THAN SHE HAD EVER KNOWN.
BENEATH SUCH TALONS, THE BRAND NEW FORMICA PEELED AWAY LIKE COTTAGE CHEESE.
HOW WAS THIS POSSIBLE?!
WHAT...THE HELL...WAS HAPPENING TO HER?!
OH... *SOB*... OH, NO! *SOB* NOOO!

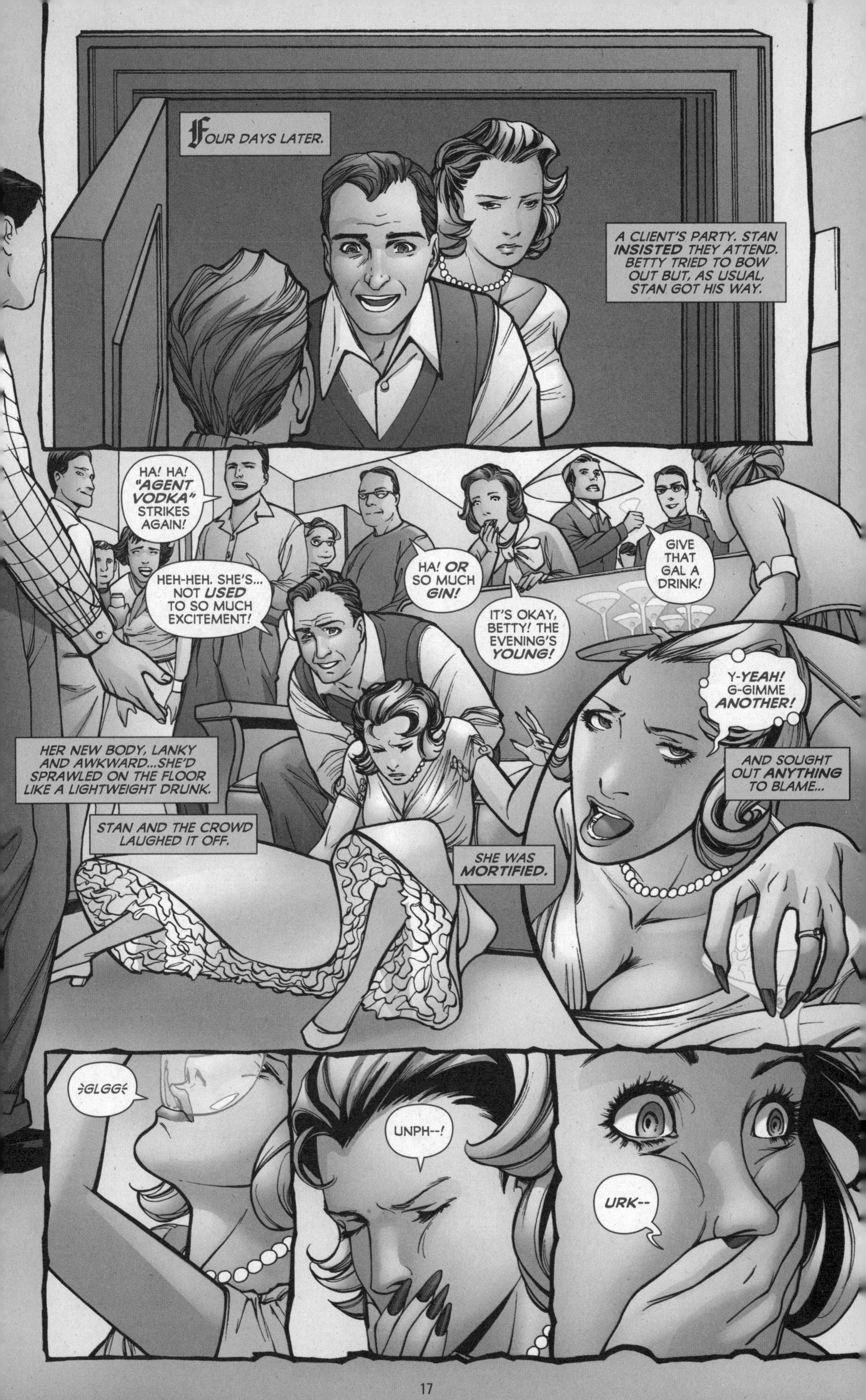
FOUR DAYS LATER.
A CLIENT'S PARTY. STAN INSISTED THEY ATTEND. BETTY TRIED TO BOW OUT BUT, AS USUAL, STAN GOT HIS WAY.
HA! HA! "AGENT VODKA" STRIKES AGAIN!
HEH-HEH. SHE'S... NOT USED TO SO MUCH EXCITEMENT!
HA! OR SO MUCH GIN!
IT'S OKAY, BETTY! THE EVENING'S YOUNG!
GIVE THAT GAL A DRINK!
Y-YEAH! G-GIMME ANOTHER!
HER NEW BODY, LANKY AND AWKWARD...SHE'D SPRAWLED ON THE FLOOR LIKE A LIGHTWEIGHT DRUNK.
STAN AND THE CROWD LAUGHED IT OFF.
SHE WAS MORTIFIED.
AND SOUGHT OUT ANYTHING TO BLAME...
GLGG
UNPH--!
URK--

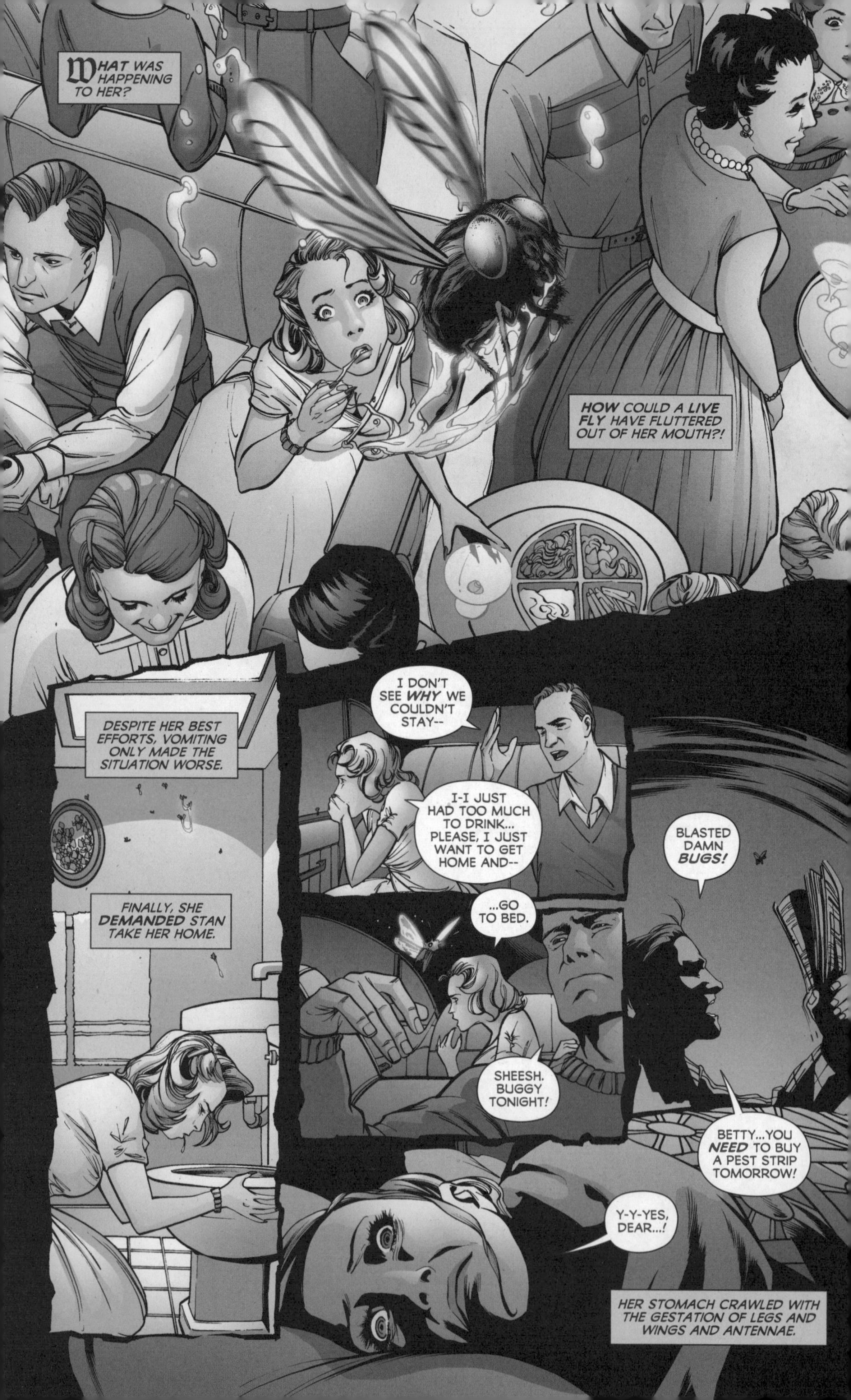
WHAT WAS HAPPENING TO HER?
HOW COULD A LIVE FLY HAVE FLUTTERED OUT OF HER MOUTH?!
DESPITE HER BEST EFFORTS, VOMITING ONLY MADE THE SITUATION WORSE.
FINALLY, SHE DEMANDED STAN TAKE HER HOME.
I DON'T SEE WHY WE COULDN'T STAY--
I-I JUST HAD TOO MUCH TO DRINK... PLEASE, I JUST WANT TO GET HOME AND--
...GO TO BED.
SHEESH. BUGGY TONIGHT!
BLASTED DAMN BUGS!
BETTY...YOU NEED TO BUY A PEST STRIP TOMORROW!
Y-Y-YES, DEAR...!
HER STOMACH CRAWLED WITH THE GESTATION OF LEGS AND WINGS AND ANTENNAE.

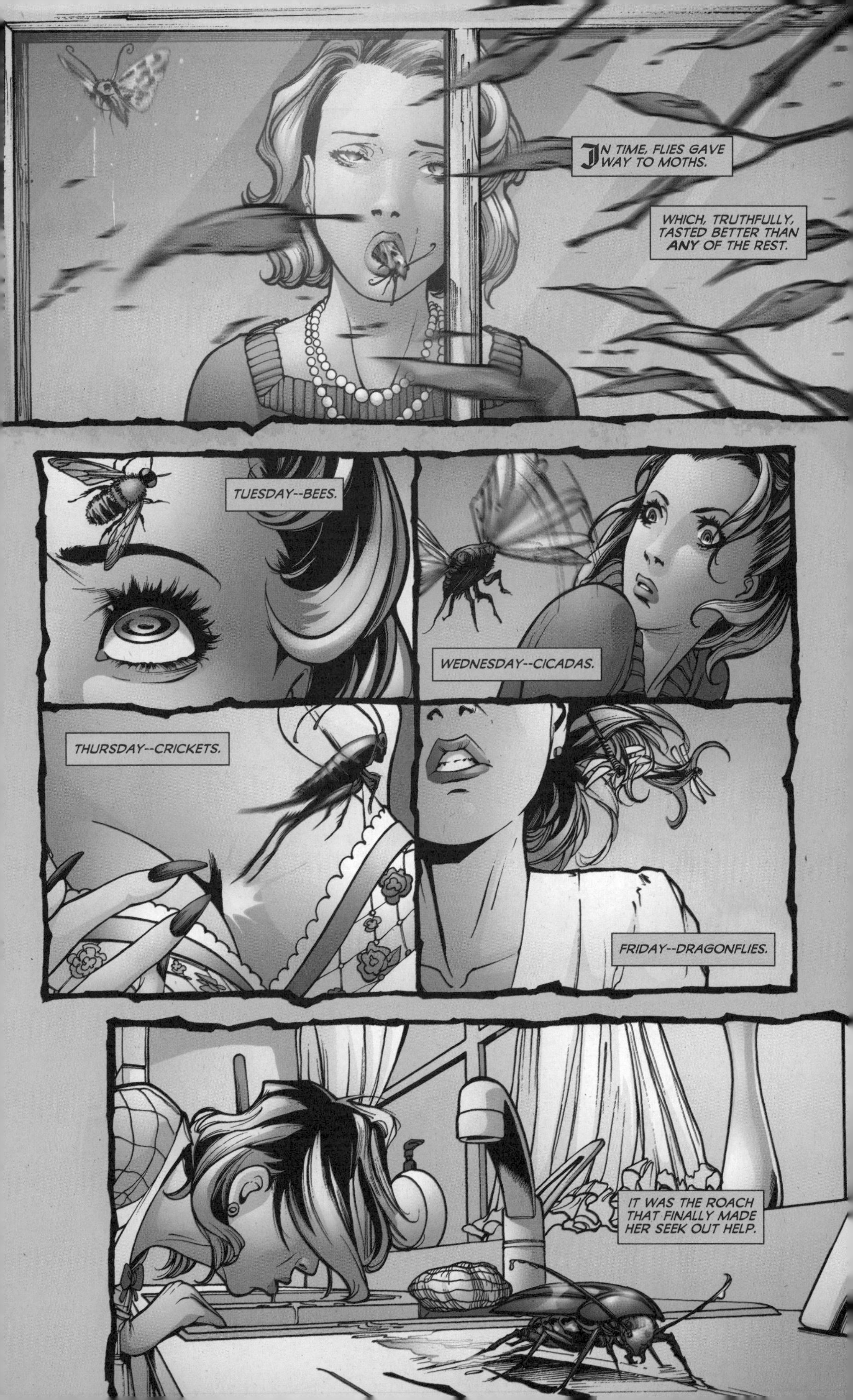
IN TIME, FLIES GAVE WAY TO MOTHS.
WHICH, TRUTHFULLY, TASTED BETTER THAN ANY OF THE REST.
TUESDAY--BEES.
WEDNESDAY--CICADAS.
THURSDAY--CRICKETS.
FRIDAY--DRAGONFLIES.
IT WAS THE ROACH THAT FINALLY MADE HER SEEK OUT HELP.

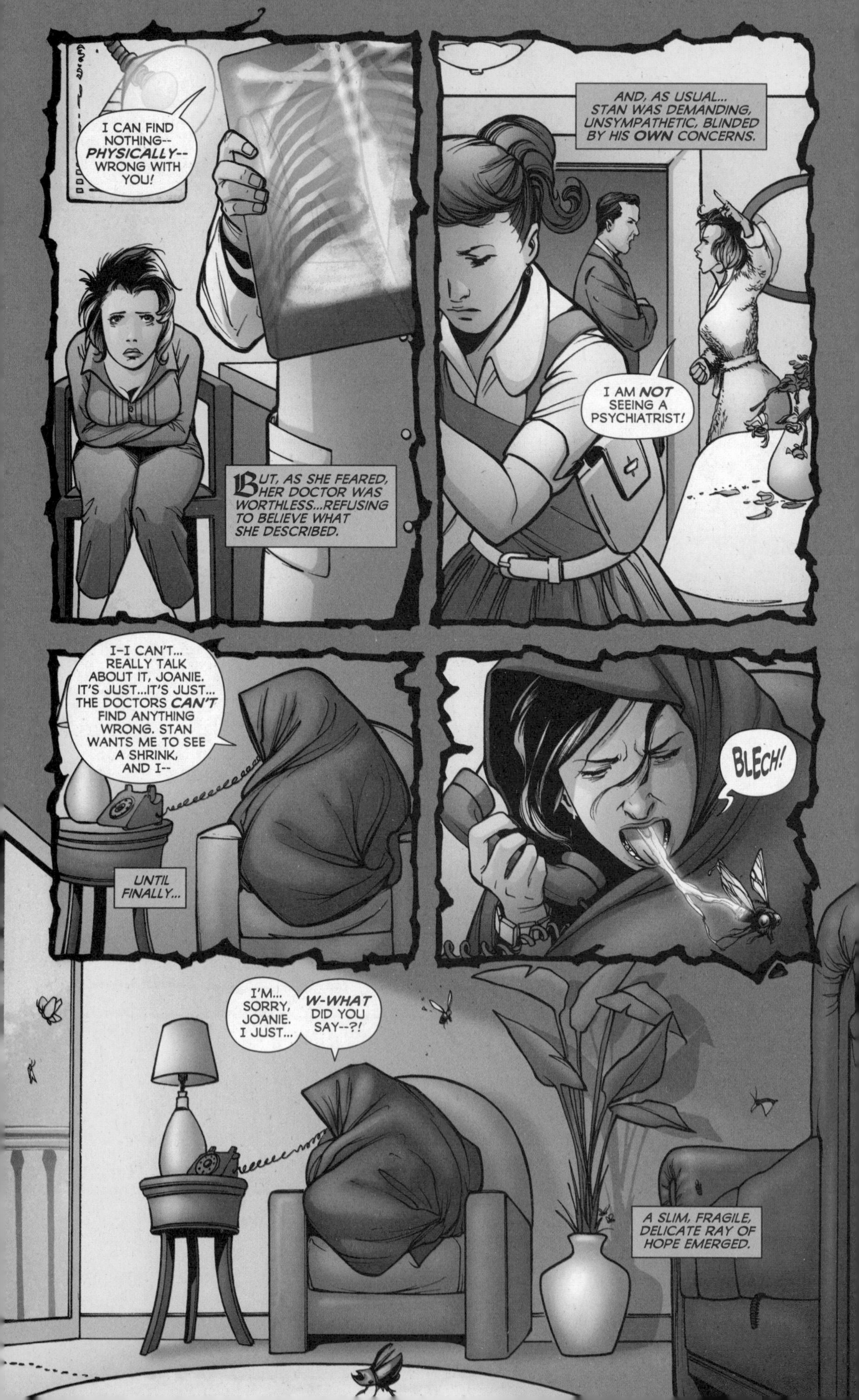
I CAN FIND NOTHING-- PHYSICALLY-- WRONG WITH YOU!
BUT, AS SHE FEARED, HER DOCTOR WAS WORTHLESS...REFUSING TO BELIEVE WHAT SHE DESCRIBED.
AND, AS USUAL... STAN WAS DEMANDING, UNSYMPATHETIC, BLINDED BY HIS OWN CONCERNS.
I AM NOT SEEING A PSYCHIATRIST!
I-I CAN'T... REALLY TALK ABOUT IT, JOANIE. IT'S JUST...IT'S JUST... THE DOCTORS CAN'T FIND ANYTHING WRONG. STAN WANTS ME TO SEE A SHRINK, AND I--
UNTIL FINALLY...
BLECH!
I'M... SORRY, JOANIE. I JUST...
W-WHAT DID YOU SAY--?!
A SLIM, FRAGILE, DELICATE RAY OF HOPE EMERGED.

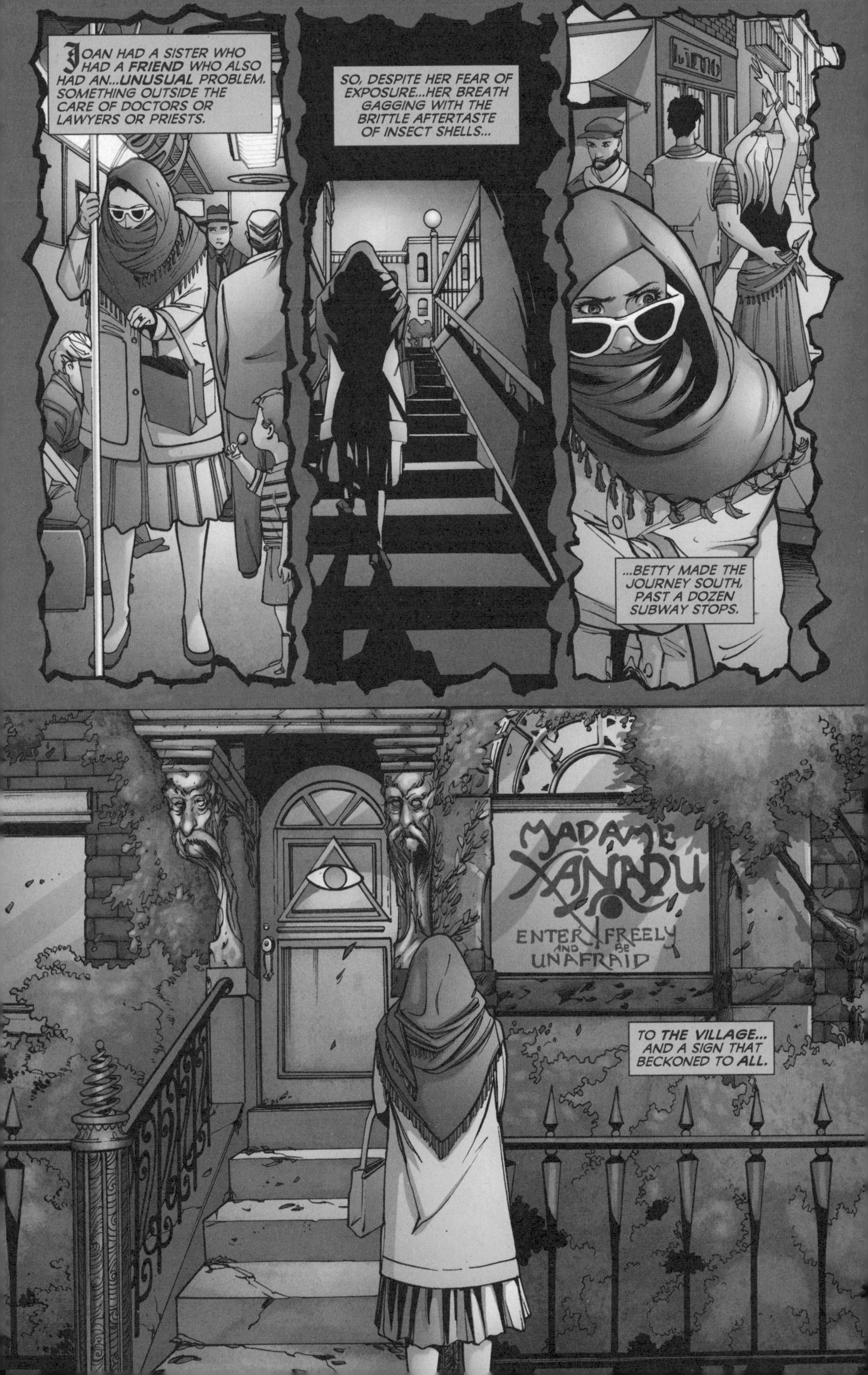
JOAN HAD A SISTER WHO HAD A FRIEND WHO ALSO HAD AN...UNUSUAL PROBLEM. SOMETHING OUTSIDE THE CARE OF DOCTORS OR LAWYERS OR PRIESTS.
SO, DESPITE HER FEAR OF EXPOSURE...HER BREATH GAGGING WITH THE BRITTLE AFTERTASTE OF INSECT SHELLS...
...BETTY MADE THE JOURNEY SOUTH, PAST A DOZEN SUBWAY STOPS.
MADAME XANADU
ENTER FREELY AND BE UNAFRAID
TO THE VILLAGE... AND A SIGN THAT BECKONED TO ALL.

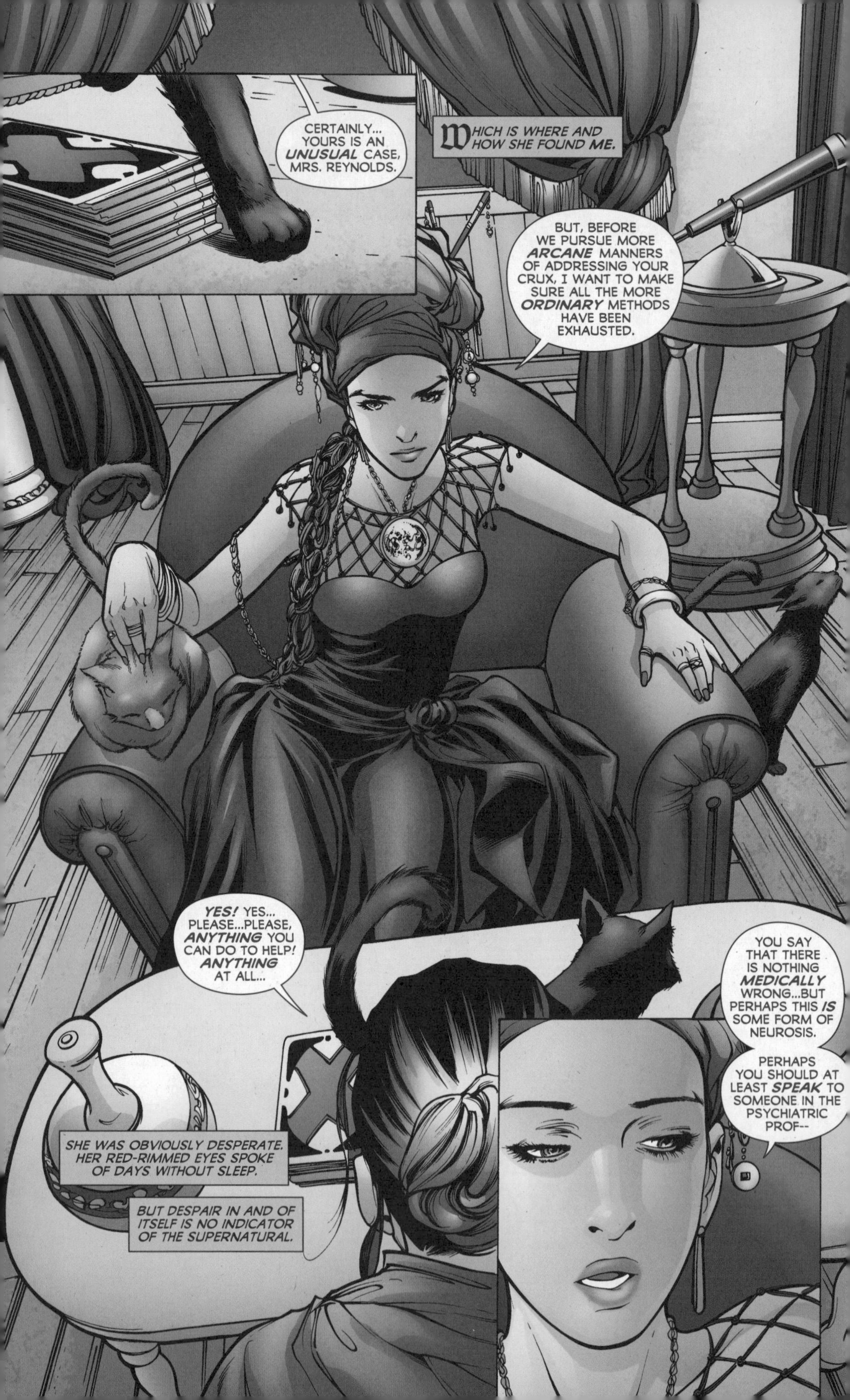
CERTAINLY... YOURS IS AN UNUSUAL CASE, MRS. REYNOLDS.
WHICH IS WHERE AND HOW SHE FOUND ME.
BUT, BEFORE WE PURSUE MORE ARCANE MANNERS OF ADDRESSING YOUR CRUX, I WANT TO MAKE SURE ALL THE MORE ORDINARY METHODS HAVE BEEN EXHAUSTED.
YES! YES... PLEASE...PLEASE, ANYTHING YOU CAN DO TO HELP! ANYTHING AT ALL...
SHE WAS OBVIOUSLY DESPERATE. HER RED-RIMMED EYES SPOKE OF DAYS WITHOUT SLEEP.
BUT DESPAIR IN AND OF ITSELF IS NO INDICATOR OF THE SUPERNATURAL.
YOU SAY THAT THERE IS NOTHING MEDICALLY WRONG...BUT PERHAPS THIS IS SOME FORM OF NEUROSIS.
PERHAPS YOU SHOULD AT LEAST SPEAK TO SOMEONE IN THE PSYCHIATRIC PROF--

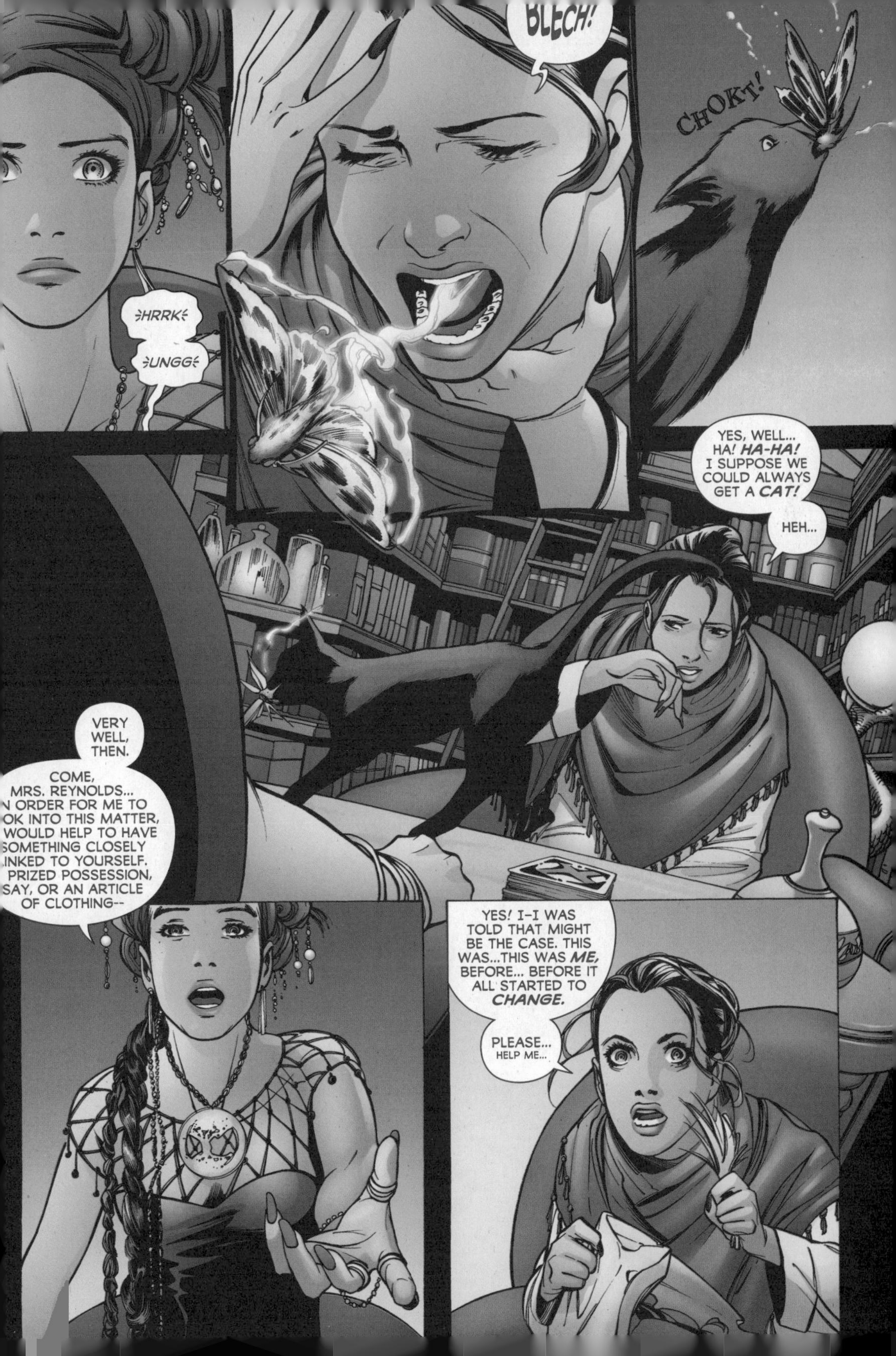
HRRK
UNGG
BLECH!
CHOKT!
YES, WELL... HA! HA-HA! I SUPPOSE WE COULD ALWAYS GET A CAT!
HEH...
VERY WELL, THEN.
COME, MRS. REYNOLDS... N ORDER FOR ME TO OK INTO THIS MATTER, WOULD HELP TO HAVE SOMETHING CLOSELY INKED TO YOURSELF. PRIZED POSSESSION, SAY, OR AN ARTICLE OF CLOTHING--
YES! I–I WAS TOLD THAT MIGHT BE THE CASE. THIS WAS...THIS WAS ME, BEFORE... BEFORE IT ALL STARTED TO CHANGE.
PLEASE... HELP ME...

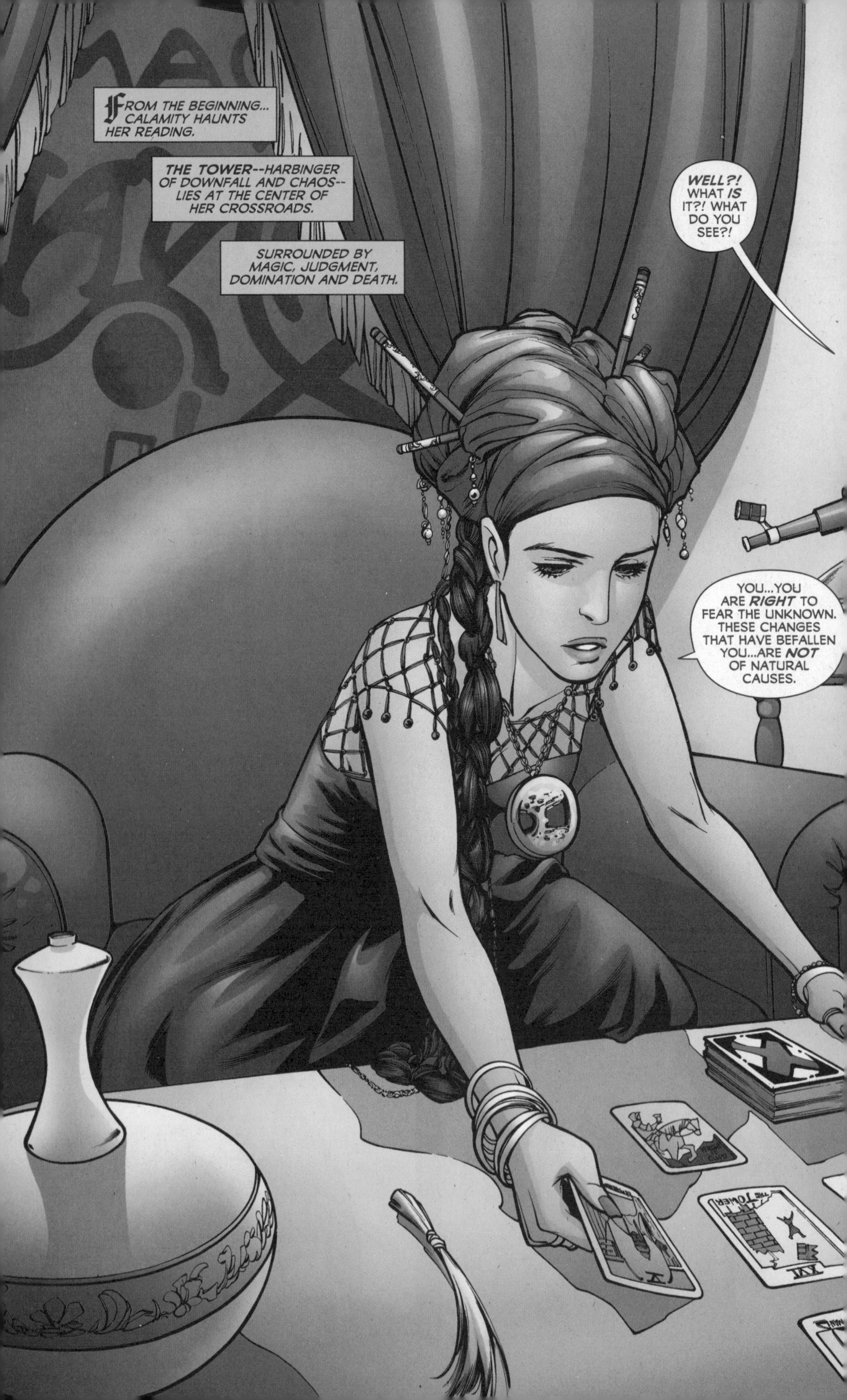
FROM THE BEGINNING... CALAMITY HAUNTS HER READING.
THE TOWER--HARBINGER OF DOWNFALL AND CHAOS--LIES AT THE CENTER OF HER CROSSROADS.
SURROUNDED BY MAGIC, JUDGMENT, DOMINATION AND DEATH.
WELL?! WHAT IS IT?! WHAT DO YOU SEE?!
YOU...YOU ARE RIGHT TO FEAR THE UNKNOWN. THESE CHANGES THAT HAVE BEFALLEN YOU...ARE NOT OF NATURAL CAUSES.
THE TOWER

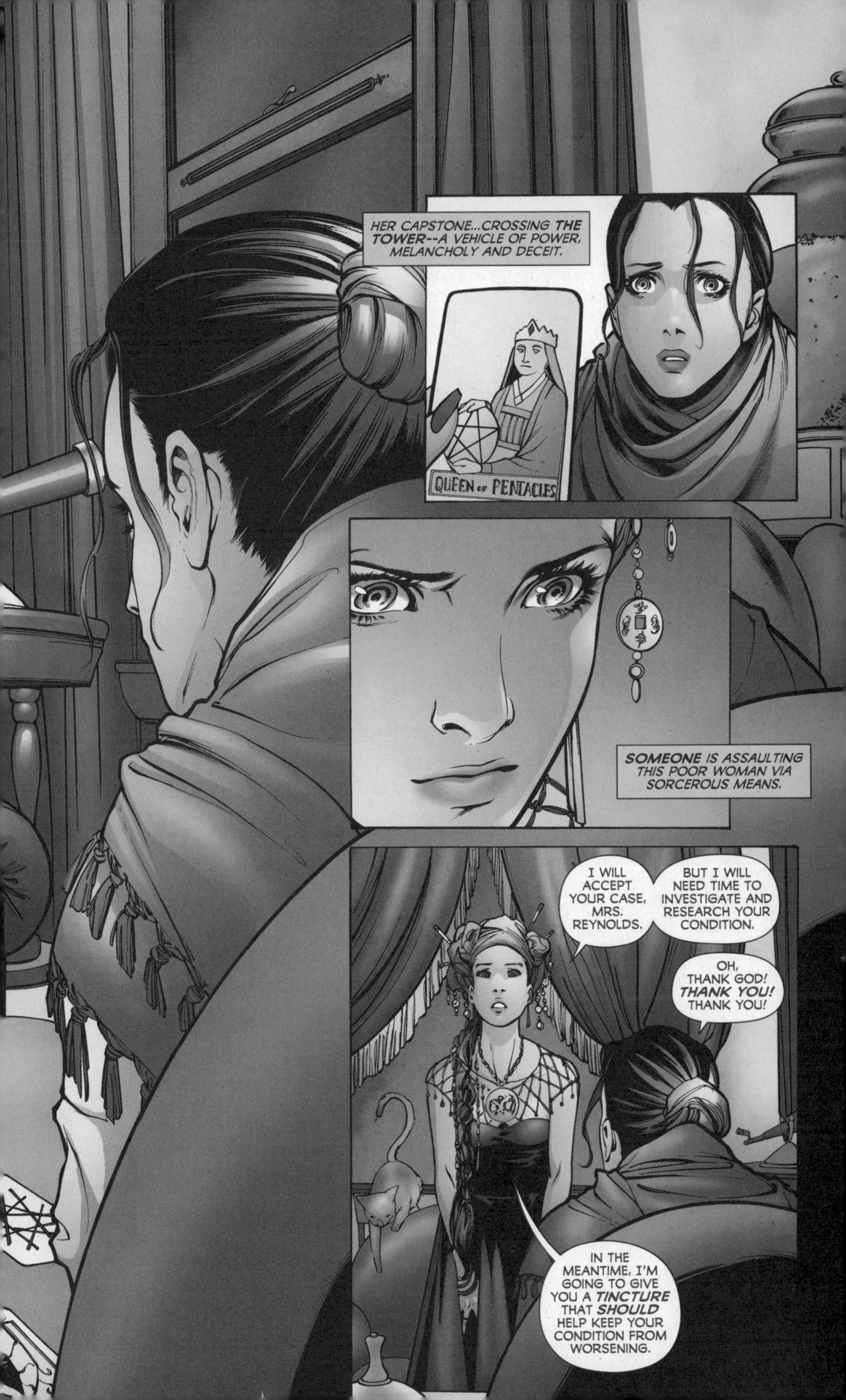
HER CAPSTONE...CROSSING THE TOWER--A VEHICLE OF POWER, MELANCHOLY AND DECEIT.
QUEEN OF PENTACLES
SOMEONE IS ASSAULTING THIS POOR WOMAN VIA SORCEROUS MEANS.
I WILL ACCEPT YOUR CASE, MRS. REYNOLDS.
BUT I WILL NEED TIME TO INVESTIGATE AND RESEARCH YOUR CONDITION.
OH, THANK GOD! THANK YOU! THANK YOU!
IN THE MEANTIME, I'M GOING TO GIVE YOU A TINCTURE THAT SHOULD HELP KEEP YOUR CONDITION FROM WORSENING.

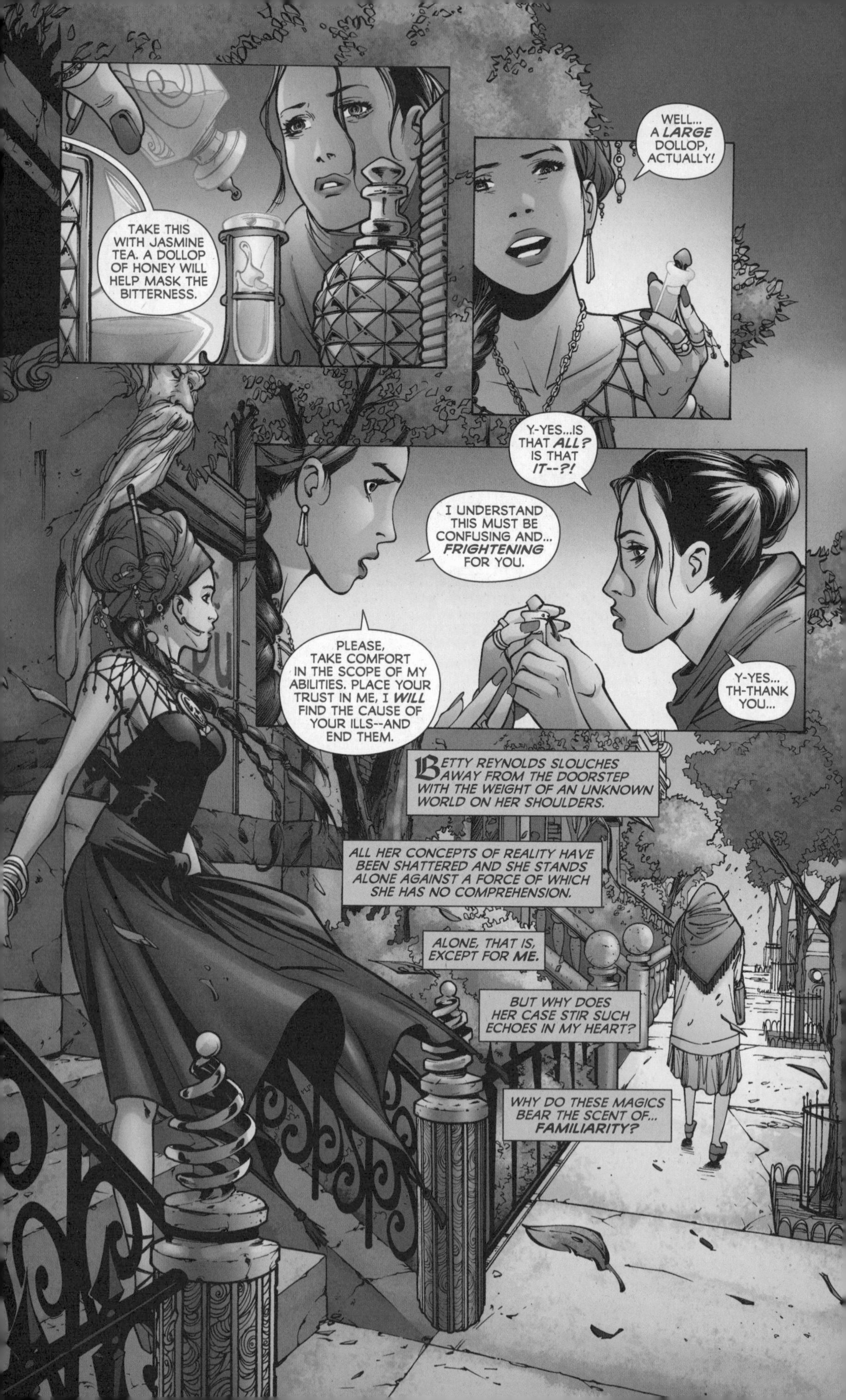
TAKE THIS WITH JASMINE TEA. A DOLLOP OF HONEY WILL HELP MASK THE BITTERNESS.
WELL... A LARGE DOLLOP, ACTUALLY!
Y-YES...IS THAT ALL? IS THAT IT--?!
I UNDERSTAND THIS MUST BE CONFUSING AND... FRIGHTENING FOR YOU.
PLEASE, TAKE COMFORT IN THE SCOPE OF MY ABILITIES. PLACE YOUR TRUST IN ME, I WILL FIND THE CAUSE OF YOUR ILLS--AND END THEM.
Y-YES... TH-THANK YOU...
BETTY REYNOLDS SLOUCHES AWAY FROM THE DOORSTEP WITH THE WEIGHT OF AN UNKNOWN WORLD ON HER SHOULDERS.
ALL HER CONCEPTS OF REALITY HAVE BEEN SHATTERED AND SHE STANDS ALONE AGAINST A FORCE OF WHICH SHE HAS NO COMPREHENSION.
ALONE, THAT IS, EXCEPT FOR ME.
BUT WHY DOES HER CASE STIR SUCH ECHOES IN MY HEART?
WHY DO THESE MAGICS BEAR THE SCENT OF... FAMILIARITY?

Chapter Two: **Popular Satanics**

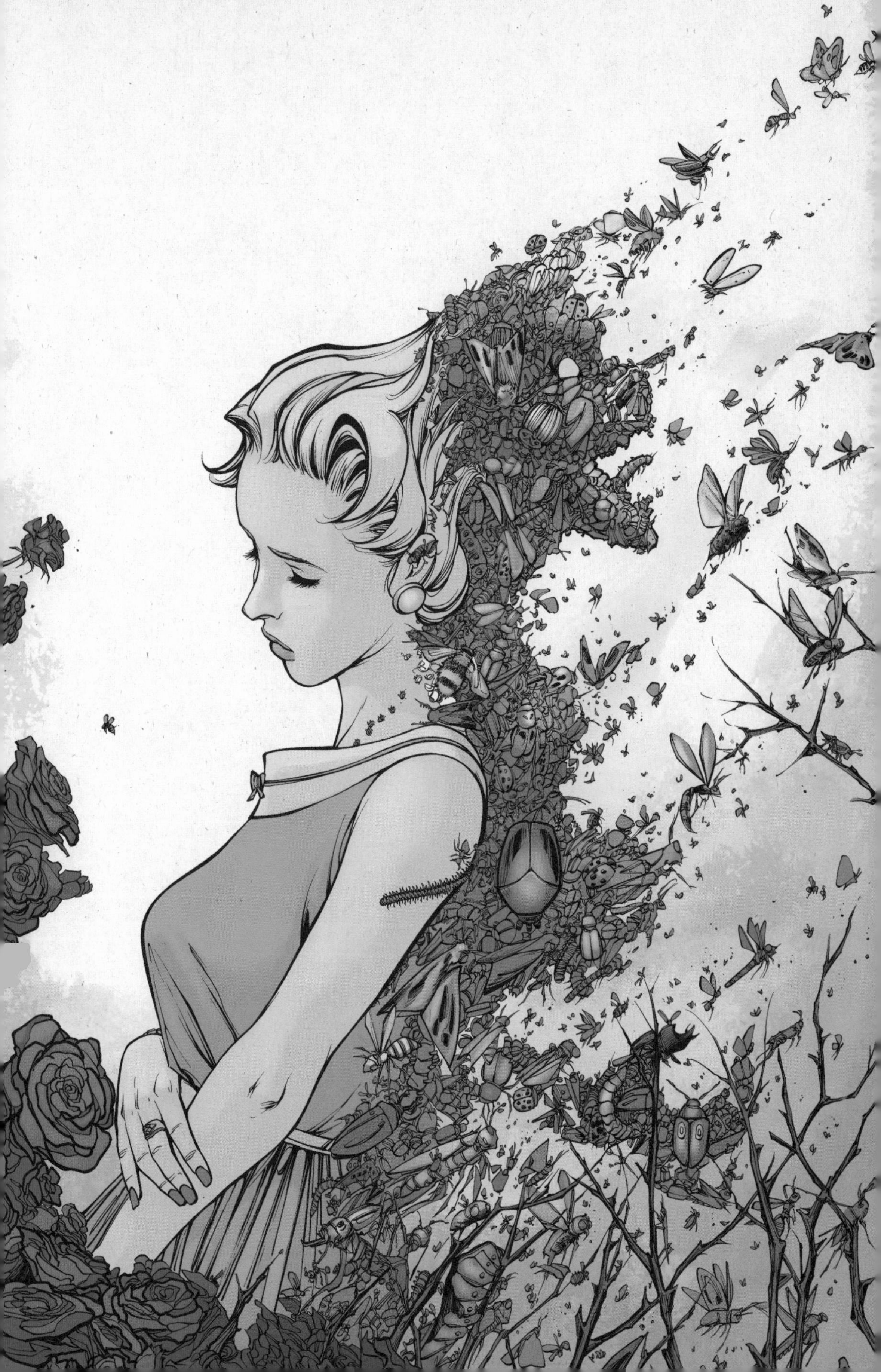

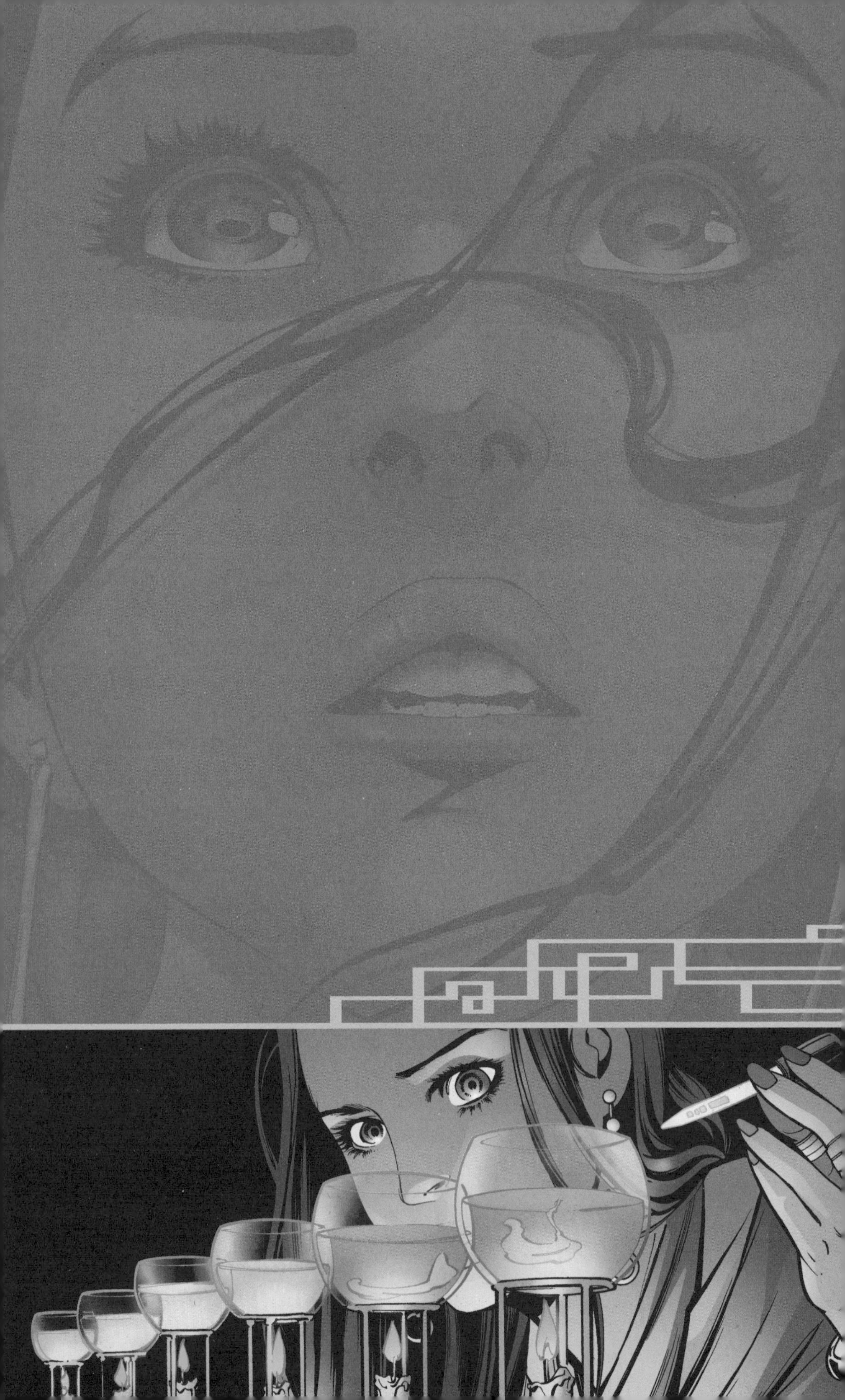

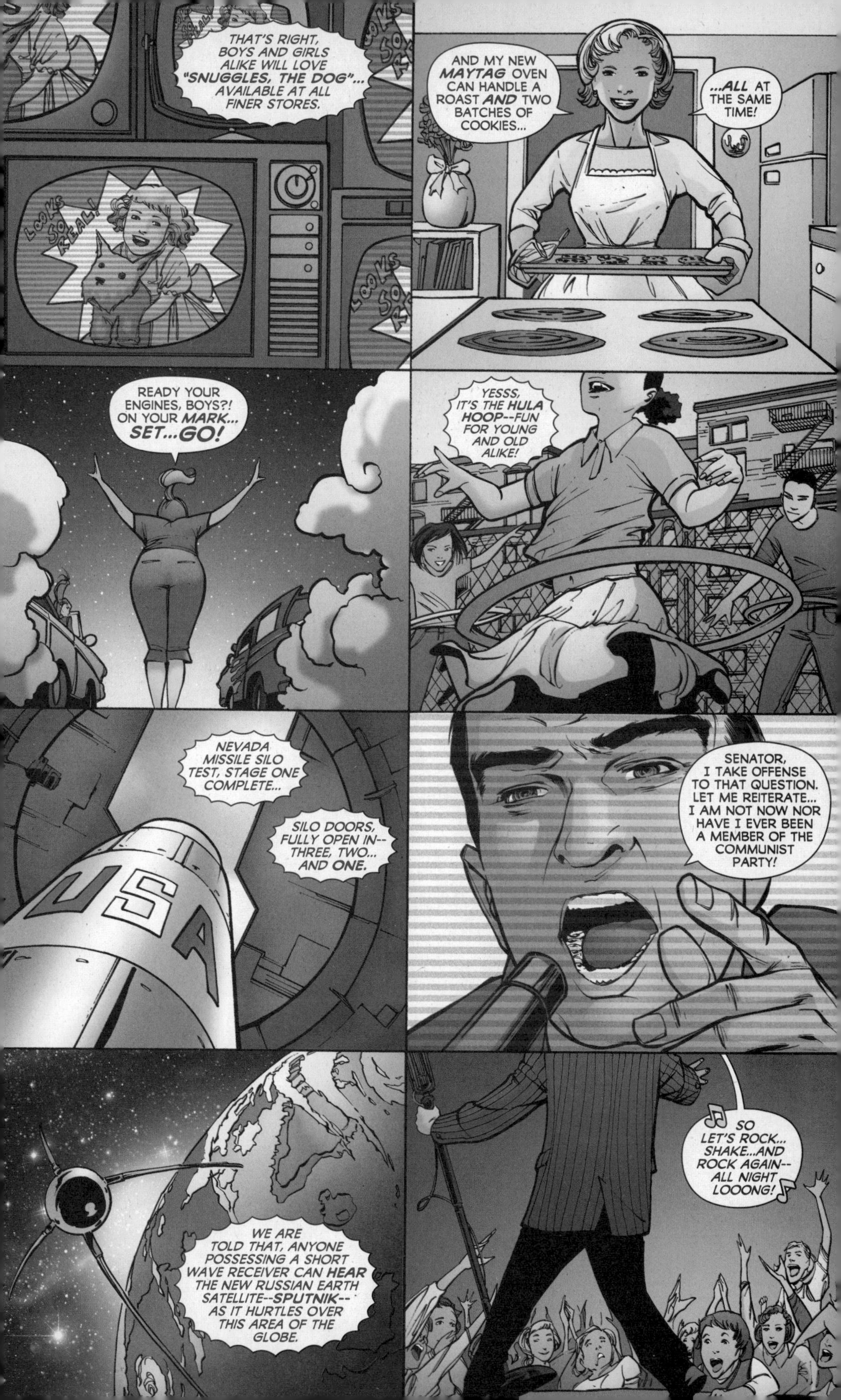
THAT'S RIGHT, BOYS AND GIRLS ALIKE WILL LOVE "SNUGGLES, THE DOG"... AVAILABLE AT ALL FINER STORES.
LOOKS SO REAL!
AND MY NEW MAYTAG OVEN CAN HANDLE A ROAST AND TWO BATCHES OF COOKIES...
...ALL AT THE SAME TIME!
READY YOUR ENGINES, BOYS?! ON YOUR MARK... SET...GO!
YESSS, IT'S THE HULA HOOP--FUN FOR YOUNG AND OLD ALIKE!
NEVADA MISSILE SILO TEST, STAGE ONE COMPLETE...
SILO DOORS, FULLY OPEN IN--THREE, TWO... AND ONE.
USA
SENATOR, I TAKE OFFENSE TO THAT QUESTION. LET ME REITERATE... I AM NOT NOW NOR HAVE I EVER BEEN A MEMBER OF THE COMMUNIST PARTY!
WE ARE TOLD THAT, ANYONE POSSESSING A SHORT WAVE RECEIVER CAN HEAR THE NEW RUSSIAN EARTH SATELLITE--SPUTNIK--AS IT HURTLES OVER THIS AREA OF THE GLOBE.
SO LET'S ROCK... SHAKE...AND ROCK AGAIN--ALL NIGHT LOOONG!

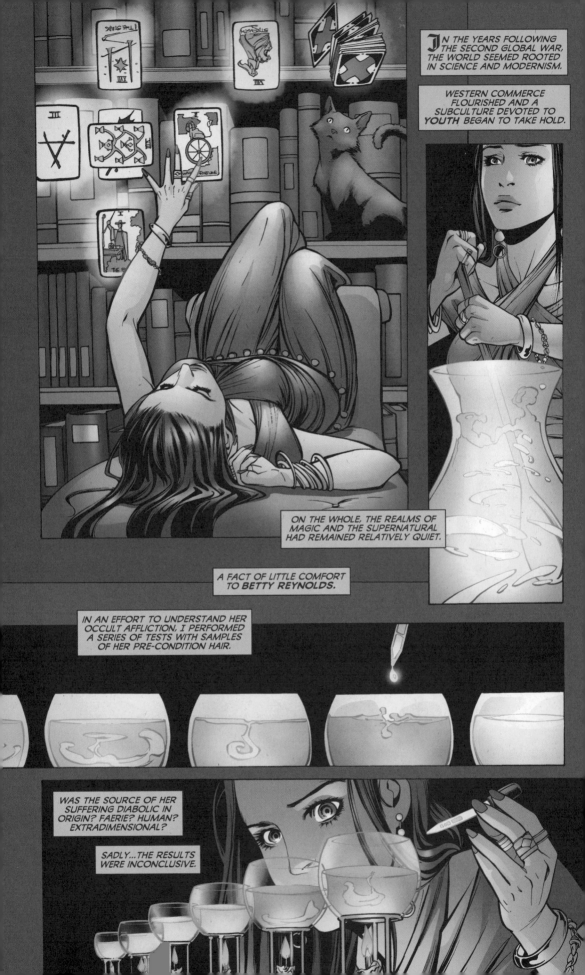

IN THE YEARS FOLLOWING THE SECOND GLOBAL WAR, THE WORLD SEEMED ROOTED IN SCIENCE AND MODERNISM.

WESTERN COMMERCE FLOURISHED AND A SUBCULTURE DEVOTED TO YOUTH BEGAN TO TAKE HOLD.

ON THE WHOLE, THE REALMS OF MAGIC AND THE SUPERNATURAL HAD REMAINED RELATIVELY QUIET.

A FACT OF LITTLE COMFORT TO BETTY REYNOLDS.

IN AN EFFORT TO UNDERSTAND HER OCCULT AFFLICTION, I PERFORMED A SERIES OF TESTS WITH SAMPLES OF HER PRE-CONDITION HAIR.

WAS THE SOURCE OF HER SUFFERING DIABOLIC IN ORIGIN? FAERIE? HUMAN? EXTRADIMENSIONAL?

SADLY...THE RESULTS WERE INCONCLUSIVE.

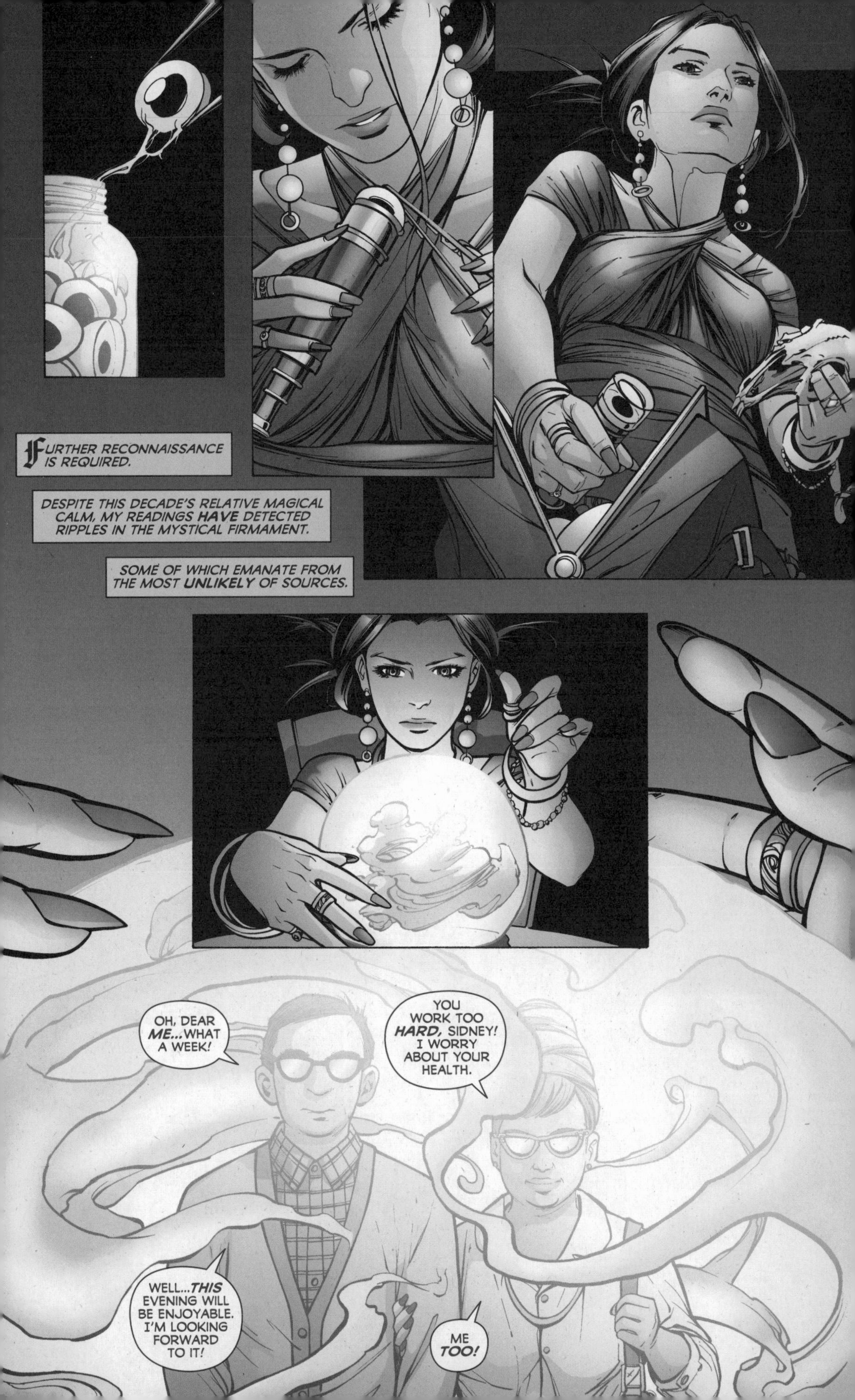
FURTHER RECONNAISSANCE IS REQUIRED.
DESPITE THIS DECADE'S RELATIVE MAGICAL CALM, MY READINGS HAVE DETECTED RIPPLES IN THE MYSTICAL FIRMAMENT.
SOME OF WHICH EMANATE FROM THE MOST UNLIKELY OF SOURCES.
OH, DEAR ME...WHAT A WEEK!
YOU WORK TOO HARD, SIDNEY! I WORRY ABOUT YOUR HEALTH.
WELL...THIS EVENING WILL BE ENJOYABLE. I'M LOOKING FORWARD TO IT!
ME TOO!

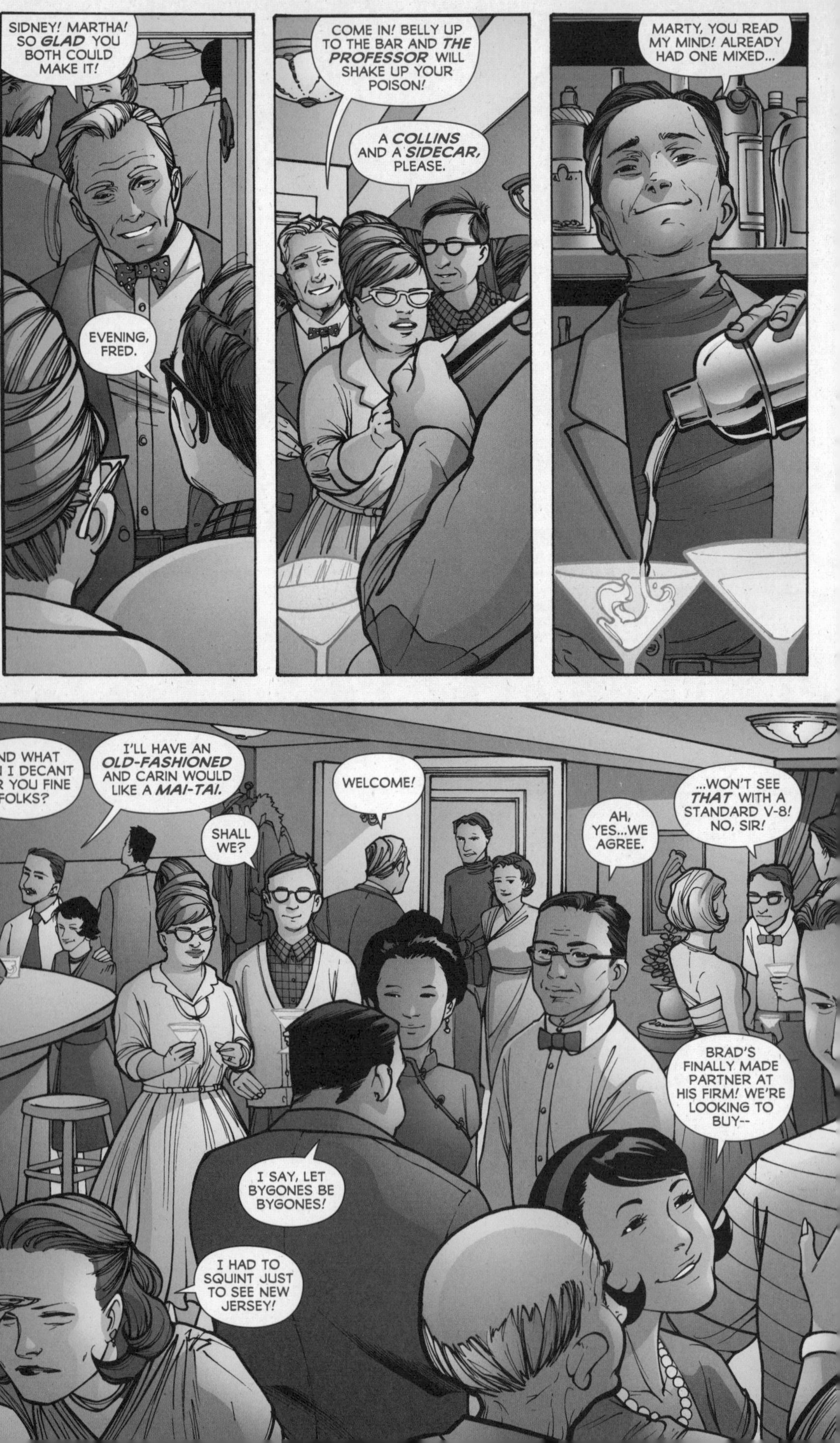
SIDNEY! MARTHA! SO GLAD YOU BOTH COULD MAKE IT!
EVENING, FRED.
COME IN! BELLY UP TO THE BAR AND THE PROFESSOR WILL SHAKE UP YOUR POISON!
A COLLINS AND A SIDECAR, PLEASE.
MARTY, YOU READ MY MIND! ALREADY HAD ONE MIXED...
AND WHAT CAN I DECANT FOR YOU FINE FOLKS?
I'LL HAVE AN OLD-FASHIONED AND CARIN WOULD LIKE A MAI-TAI.
SHALL WE?
WELCOME!
AH, YES...WE AGREE.
...WON'T SEE THAT WITH A STANDARD V-8! NO, SIR!
BRAD'S FINALLY MADE PARTNER AT HIS FIRM! WE'RE LOOKING TO BUY--
I SAY, LET BYGONES BE BYGONES!
I HAD TO SQUINT JUST TO SEE NEW JERSEY!

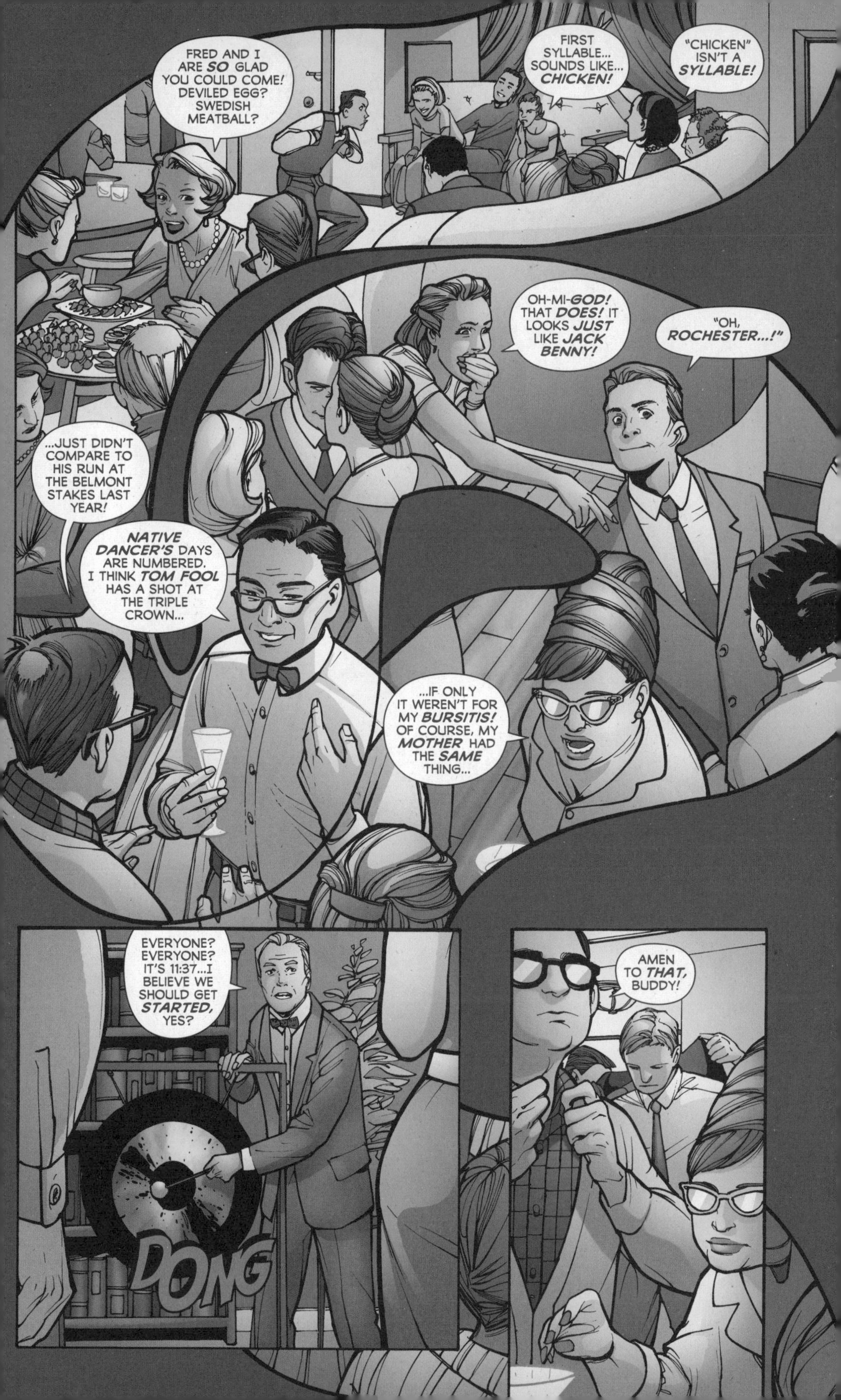
FRED AND I ARE SO GLAD YOU COULD COME! DEVILED EGG? SWEDISH MEATBALL?
FIRST SYLLABLE... SOUNDS LIKE... CHICKEN!
"CHICKEN" ISN'T A SYLLABLE!
OH-MI-GOD! THAT DOES! IT LOOKS JUST LIKE JACK BENNY!
"OH, ROCHESTER...!"
...JUST DIDN'T COMPARE TO HIS RUN AT THE BELMONT STAKES LAST YEAR!
NATIVE DANCER'S DAYS ARE NUMBERED. I THINK TOM FOOL HAS A SHOT AT THE TRIPLE CROWN...
...IF ONLY IT WEREN'T FOR MY BURSITIS! OF COURSE, MY MOTHER HAD THE SAME THING...
EVERYONE? EVERYONE? IT'S 11:37...I BELIEVE WE SHOULD GET STARTED, YES?
DONG
AMEN TO THAT, BUDDY!

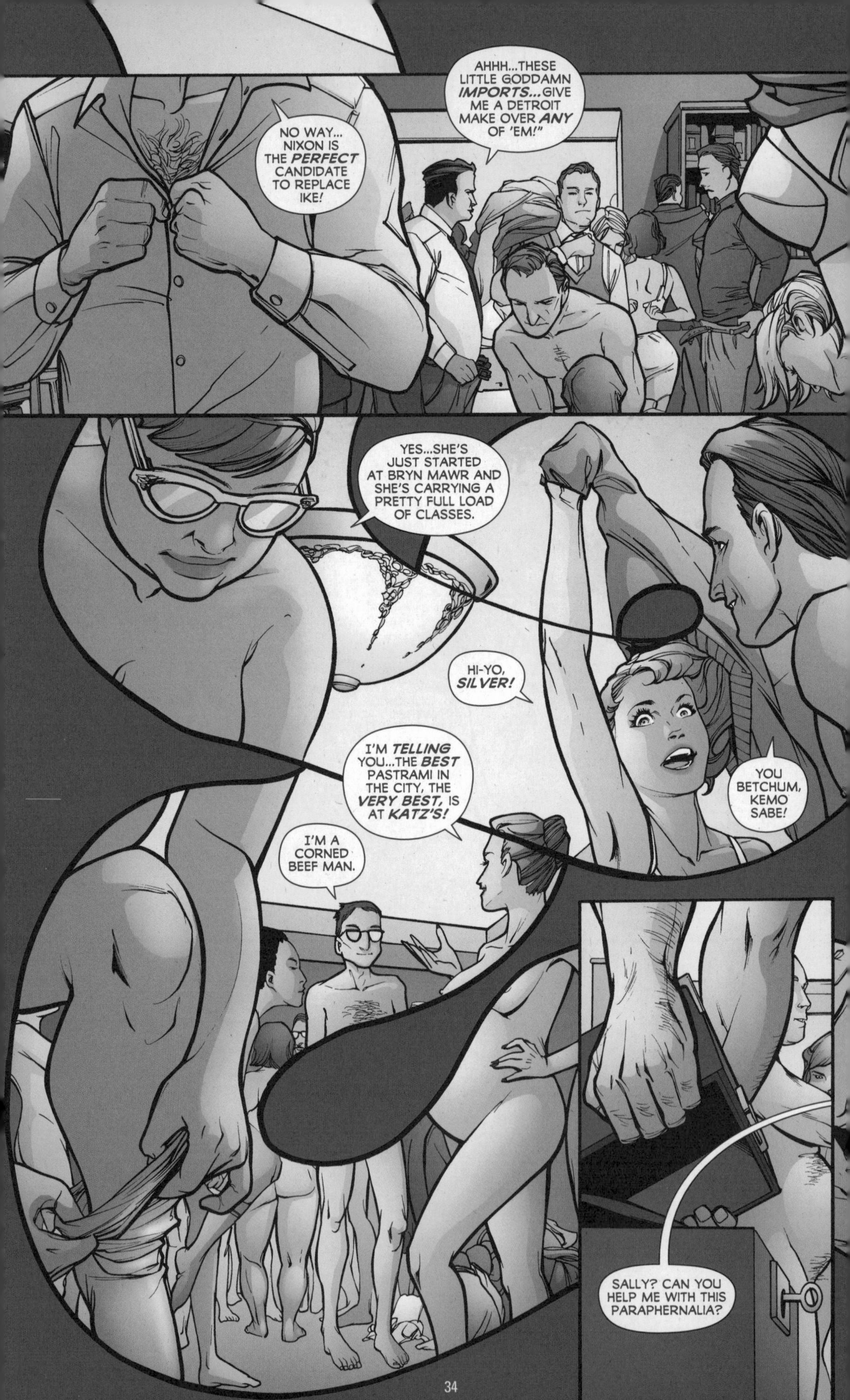
NO WAY... NIXON IS THE PERFECT CANDIDATE TO REPLACE IKE!
AHHH...THESE LITTLE GODDAMN IMPORTS...GIVE ME A DETROIT MAKE OVER ANY OF 'EM!"
YES...SHE'S JUST STARTED AT BRYN MAWR AND SHE'S CARRYING A PRETTY FULL LOAD OF CLASSES.
HI-YO, SILVER!
I'M TELLING YOU...THE BEST PASTRAMI IN THE CITY, THE VERY BEST, IS AT KATZ'S!
YOU BETCHUM, KEMO SABE!
I'M A CORNED BEEF MAN.
SALLY? CAN YOU HELP ME WITH THIS PARAPHERNALIA?

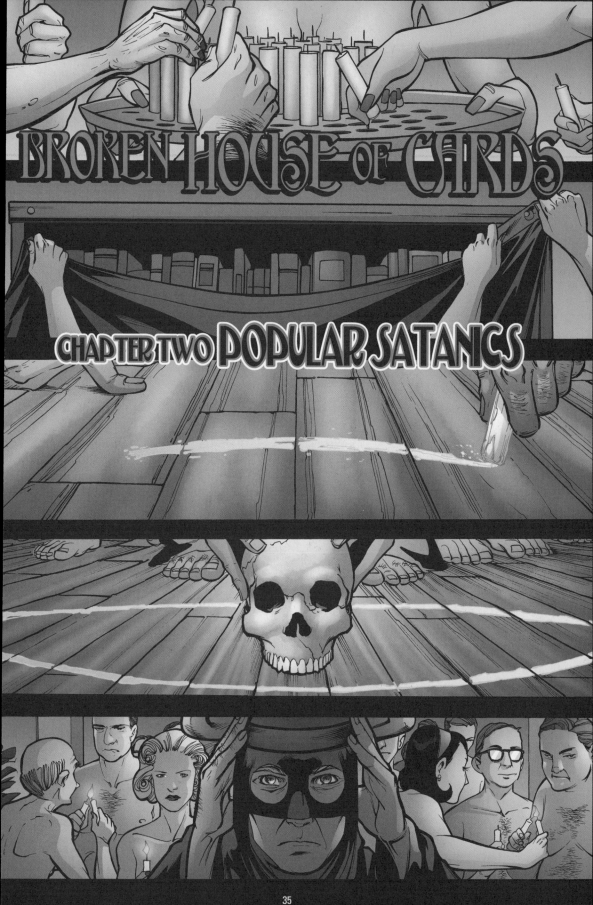

BROKEN HOUSE OF CARDS

CHAPTER TWO POPULAR SATANICS

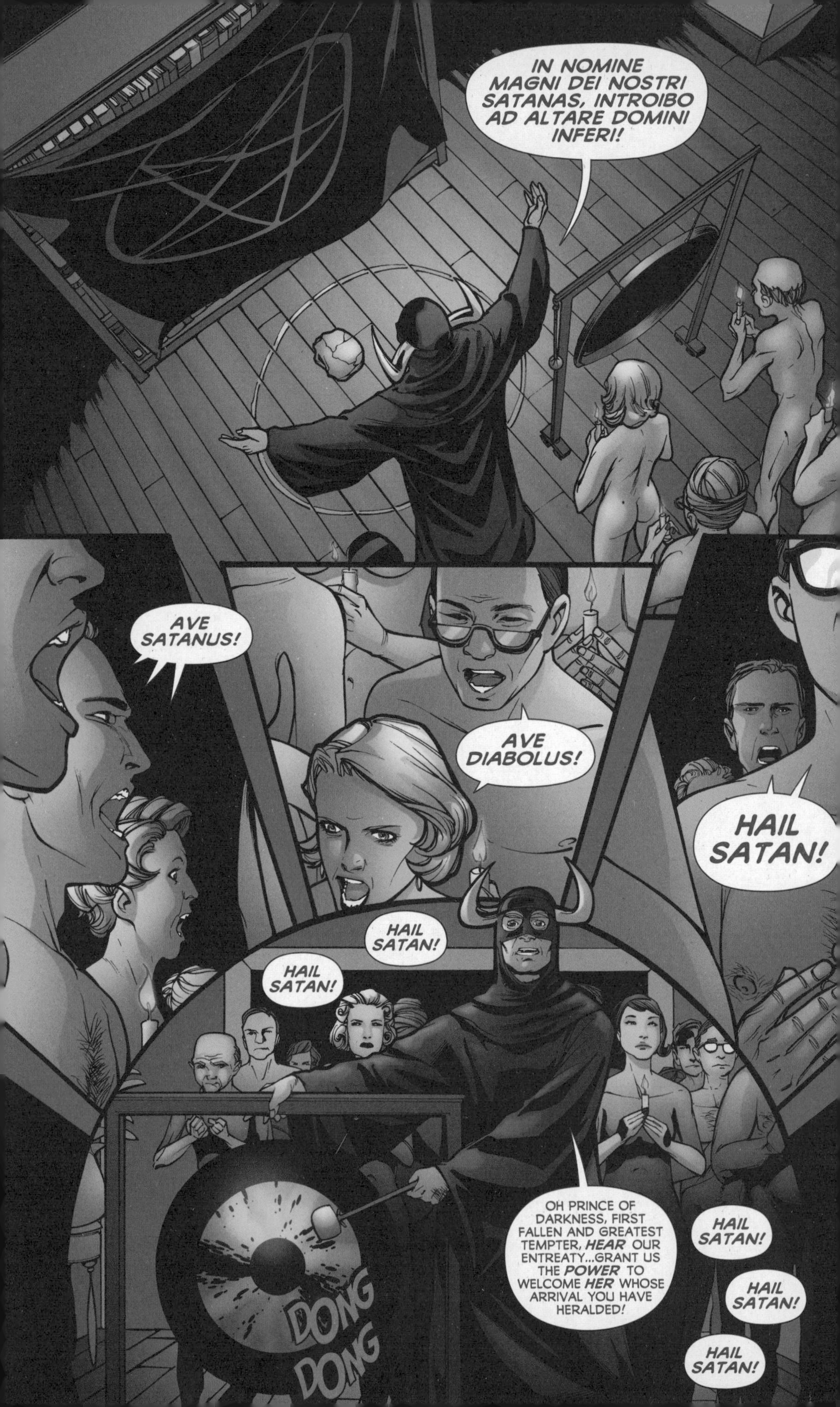
IN NOMINE MAGNI DEI NOSTRI SATANAS, INTROIBO AD ALTARE DOMINI INFERI!
AVE SATANUS!
AVE DIABOLUS!
HAIL SATAN!
HAIL SATAN!
HAIL SATAN!
OH PRINCE OF DARKNESS, FIRST FALLEN AND GREATEST TEMPTER, HEAR OUR ENTREATY...GRANT US THE POWER TO WELCOME HER WHOSE ARRIVAL YOU HAVE HERALDED!
DONG
DONG
HAIL SATAN!
HAIL SATAN!
HAIL SATAN!

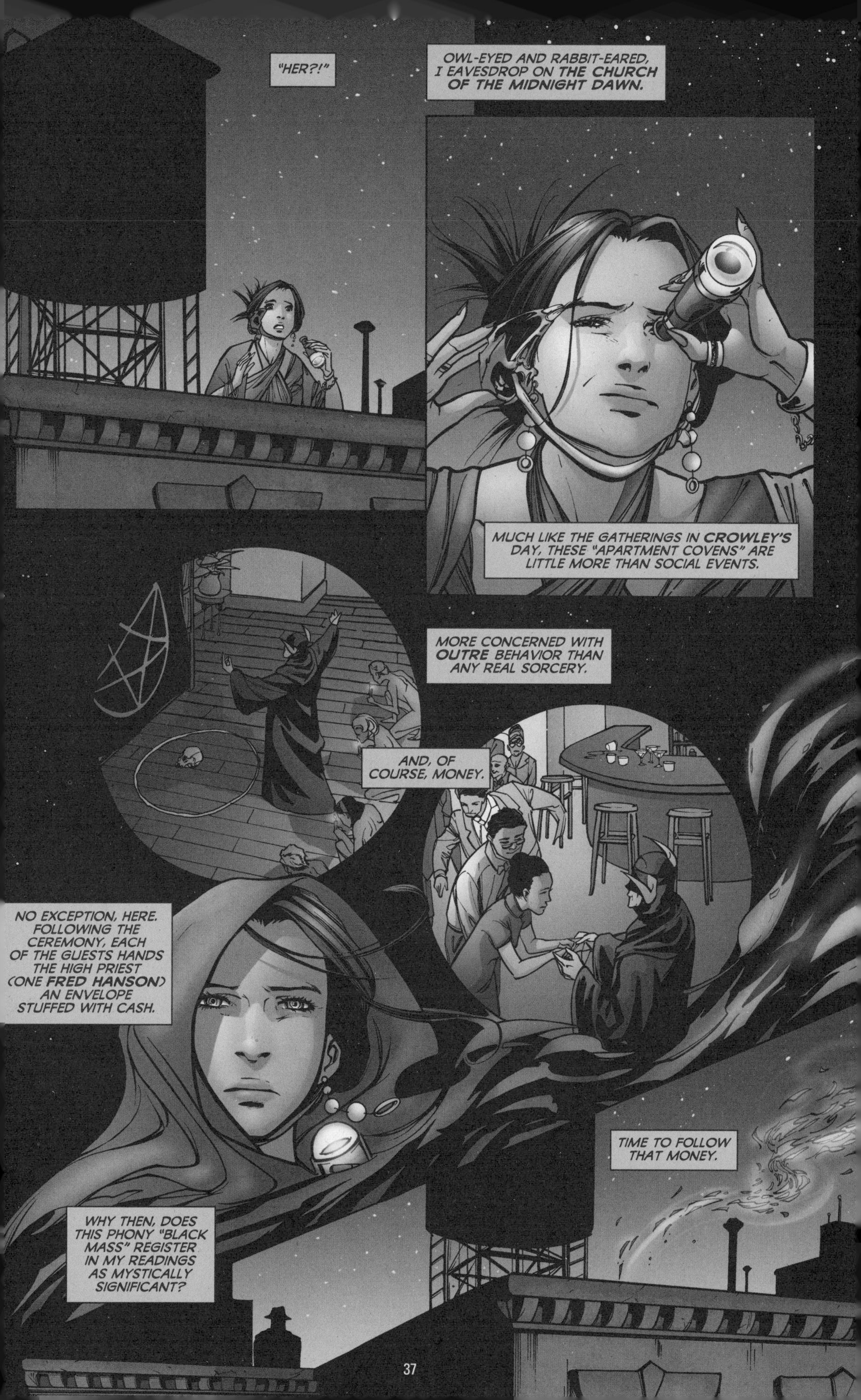
"HER?!"
OWL-EYED AND RABBIT-EARED, I EAVESDROP ON THE CHURCH OF THE MIDNIGHT DAWN.
MUCH LIKE THE GATHERINGS IN CROWLEY'S DAY, THESE "APARTMENT COVENS" ARE LITTLE MORE THAN SOCIAL EVENTS.
MORE CONCERNED WITH OUTRE BEHAVIOR THAN ANY REAL SORCERY.
AND, OF COURSE, MONEY.
NO EXCEPTION, HERE. FOLLOWING THE CEREMONY, EACH OF THE GUESTS HANDS THE HIGH PRIEST (ONE FRED HANSON) AN ENVELOPE STUFFED WITH CASH.
WHY THEN, DOES THIS PHONY "BLACK MASS" REGISTER IN MY READINGS AS MYSTICALLY SIGNIFICANT?
TIME TO FOLLOW THAT MONEY.

LATER...

THE HIGH PRIEST AND HIS CLOSEST ACOLYTE--"THE PROFESSOR" (ONE *CHARLES KOWALSKI*) HEAD OUT WITH AN *OBVIOUSLY* HEAVY BRIEFCASE.

IN A LOCAL ITALIAN EATERY, THEY MEET UP WITH AN *OBVIOUS* GANGSTER.

HERE'S YOUR TEA, MISS.

THANK YOU.

THEIR HOST ESCORTS THEM TO A BACK ROOM.

LEAVING ME NO CHOICE BUT TO OBSERVE THEIR CONFERENCE...

LÉASSCÉAWERE!

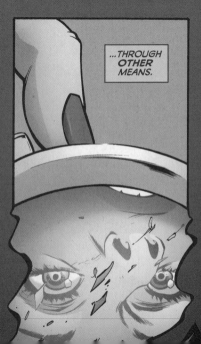

...THROUGH OTHER MEANS.

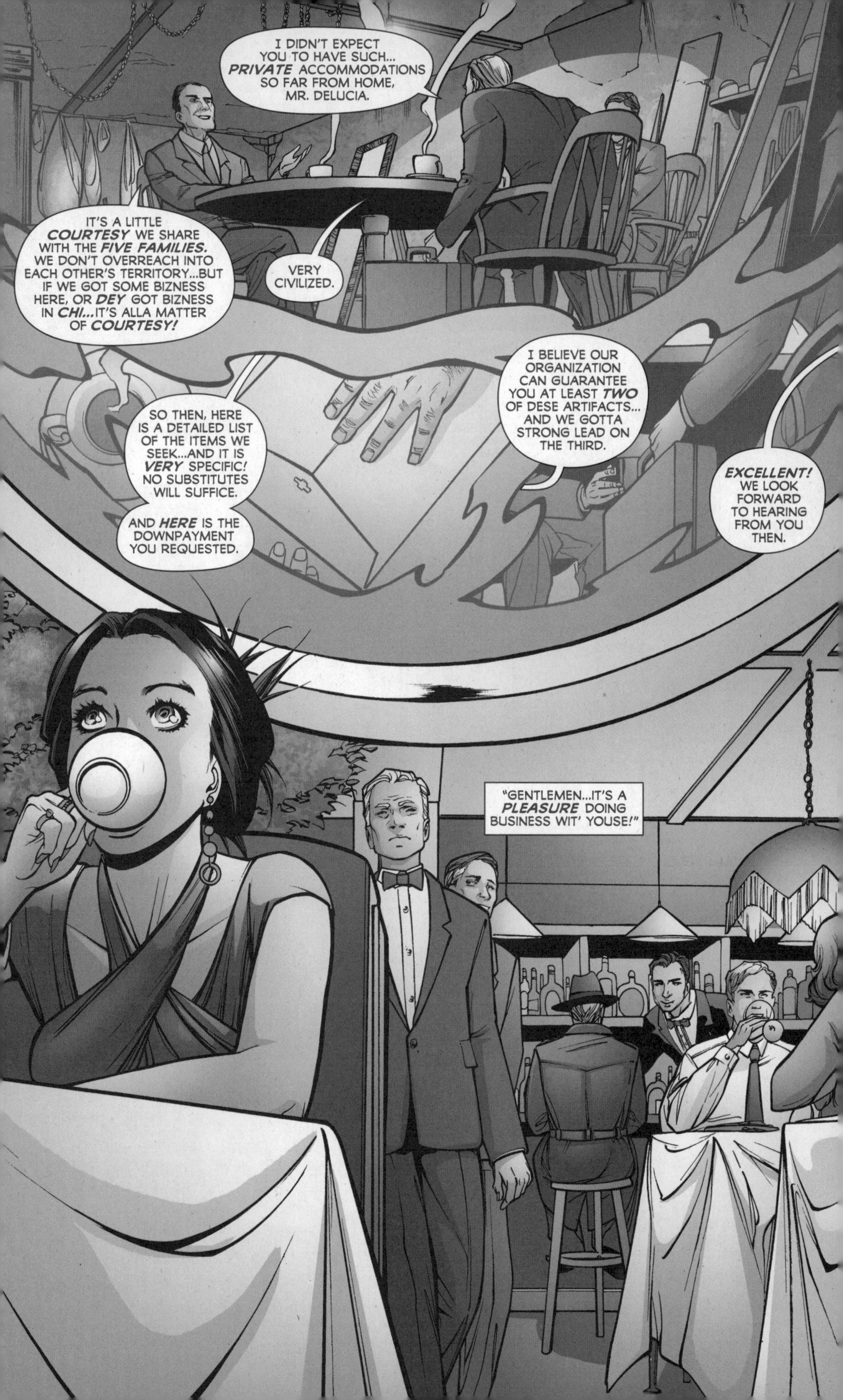

I DIDN'T EXPECT YOU TO HAVE SUCH... PRIVATE ACCOMMODATIONS SO FAR FROM HOME, MR. DELUCIA.
IT'S A LITTLE COURTESY WE SHARE WITH THE FIVE FAMILIES. WE DON'T OVERREACH INTO EACH OTHER'S TERRITORY...BUT IF WE GOT SOME BIZNESS HERE, OR DEY GOT BIZNESS IN CHI...IT'S ALLA MATTER OF COURTESY!
VERY CIVILIZED.
SO THEN, HERE IS A DETAILED LIST OF THE ITEMS WE SEEK...AND IT IS VERY SPECIFIC! NO SUBSTITUTES WILL SUFFICE.
AND HERE IS THE DOWNPAYMENT YOU REQUESTED.
I BELIEVE OUR ORGANIZATION CAN GUARANTEE YOU AT LEAST TWO OF DESE ARTIFACTS... AND WE GOTTA STRONG LEAD ON THE THIRD.
EXCELLENT! WE LOOK FORWARD TO HEARING FROM YOU THEN.
"GENTLEMEN...IT'S A PLEASURE DOING BUSINESS WIT' YOUSE!"

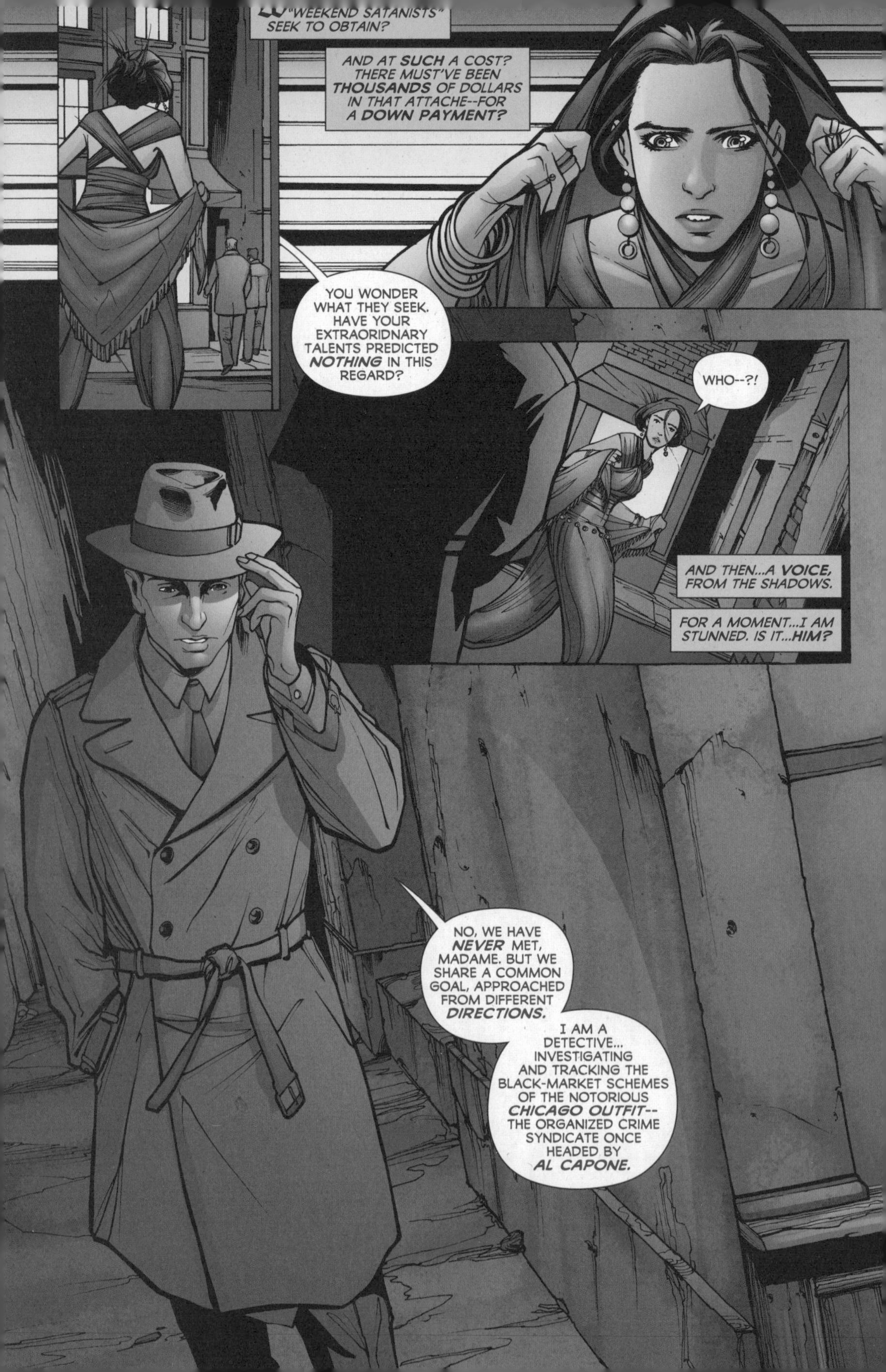
"WEEKEND SATANISTS" SEEK TO OBTAIN?
AND AT SUCH A COST? THERE MUST'VE BEEN THOUSANDS OF DOLLARS IN THAT ATTACHE--FOR A DOWN PAYMENT?
YOU WONDER WHAT THEY SEEK. HAVE YOUR EXTRAORIDNARY TALENTS PREDICTED NOTHING IN THIS REGARD?
WHO--?!
AND THEN...A VOICE, FROM THE SHADOWS.
FOR A MOMENT...I AM STUNNED. IS IT...HIM?
NO, WE HAVE NEVER MET, MADAME. BUT WE SHARE A COMMON GOAL, APPROACHED FROM DIFFERENT DIRECTIONS.
I AM A DETECTIVE... INVESTIGATING AND TRACKING THE BLACK-MARKET SCHEMES OF THE NOTORIOUS CHICAGO OUTFIT-- THE ORGANIZED CRIME SYNDICATE ONCE HEADED BY AL CAPONE.

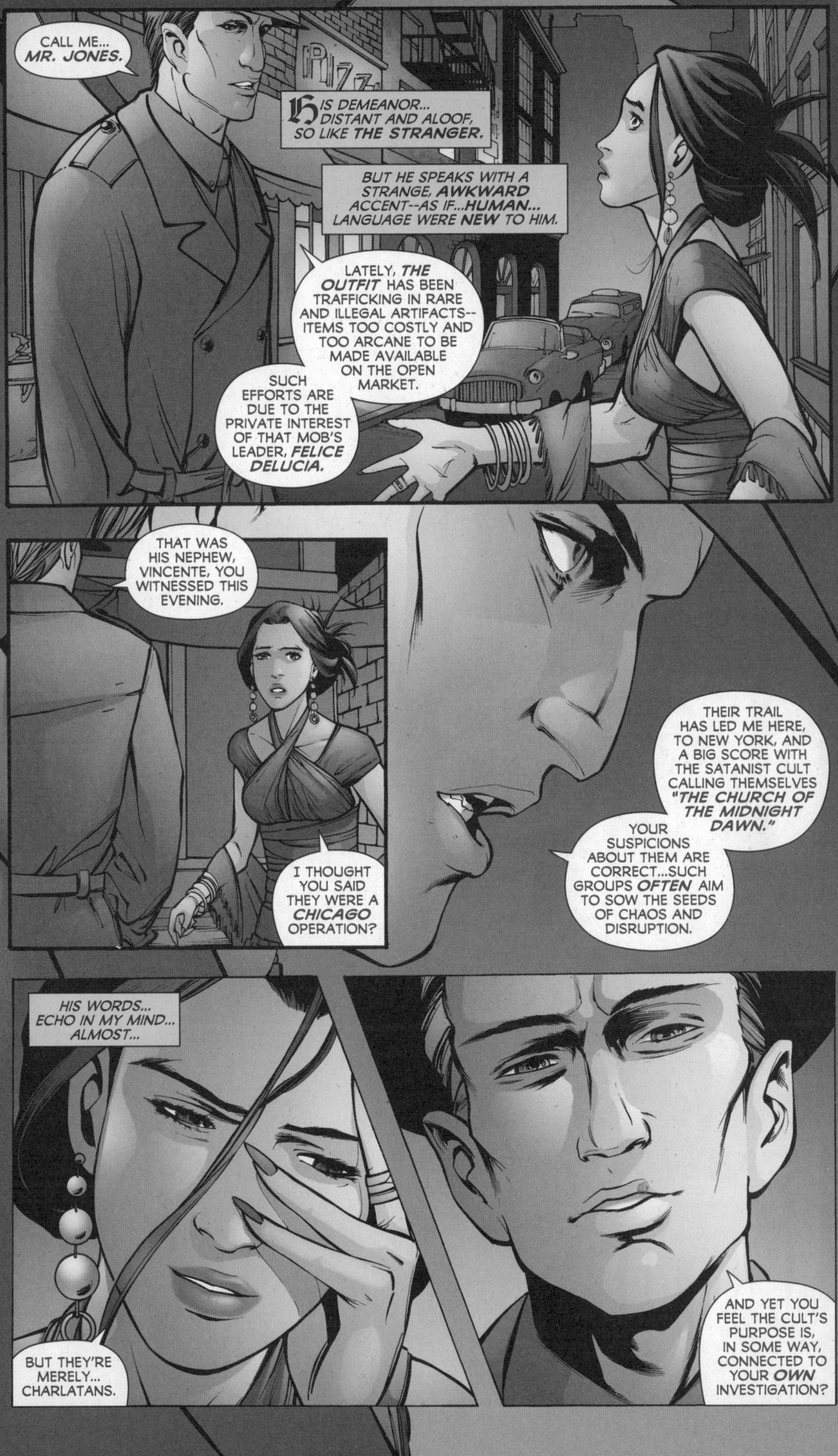

CALL ME... MR. JONES.
HIS DEMEANOR... DISTANT AND ALOOF, SO LIKE THE STRANGER.
BUT HE SPEAKS WITH A STRANGE, AWKWARD ACCENT--AS IF...HUMAN... LANGUAGE WERE NEW TO HIM.
LATELY, THE OUTFIT HAS BEEN TRAFFICKING IN RARE AND ILLEGAL ARTIFACTS--ITEMS TOO COSTLY AND TOO ARCANE TO BE MADE AVAILABLE ON THE OPEN MARKET.
SUCH EFFORTS ARE DUE TO THE PRIVATE INTEREST OF THAT MOB'S LEADER, FELICE DELUCIA.
THAT WAS HIS NEPHEW, VINCENTE, YOU WITNESSED THIS EVENING.
I THOUGHT YOU SAID THEY WERE A CHICAGO OPERATION?
THEIR TRAIL HAS LED ME HERE, TO NEW YORK, AND A BIG SCORE WITH THE SATANIST CULT CALLING THEMSELVES "THE CHURCH OF THE MIDNIGHT DAWN."
YOUR SUSPICIONS ABOUT THEM ARE CORRECT...SUCH GROUPS OFTEN AIM TO SOW THE SEEDS OF CHAOS AND DISRUPTION.
HIS WORDS... ECHO IN MY MIND... ALMOST...
BUT THEY'RE MERELY... CHARLATANS.
AND YET YOU FEEL THE CULT'S PURPOSE IS, IN SOME WAY, CONNECTED TO YOUR OWN INVESTIGATION?

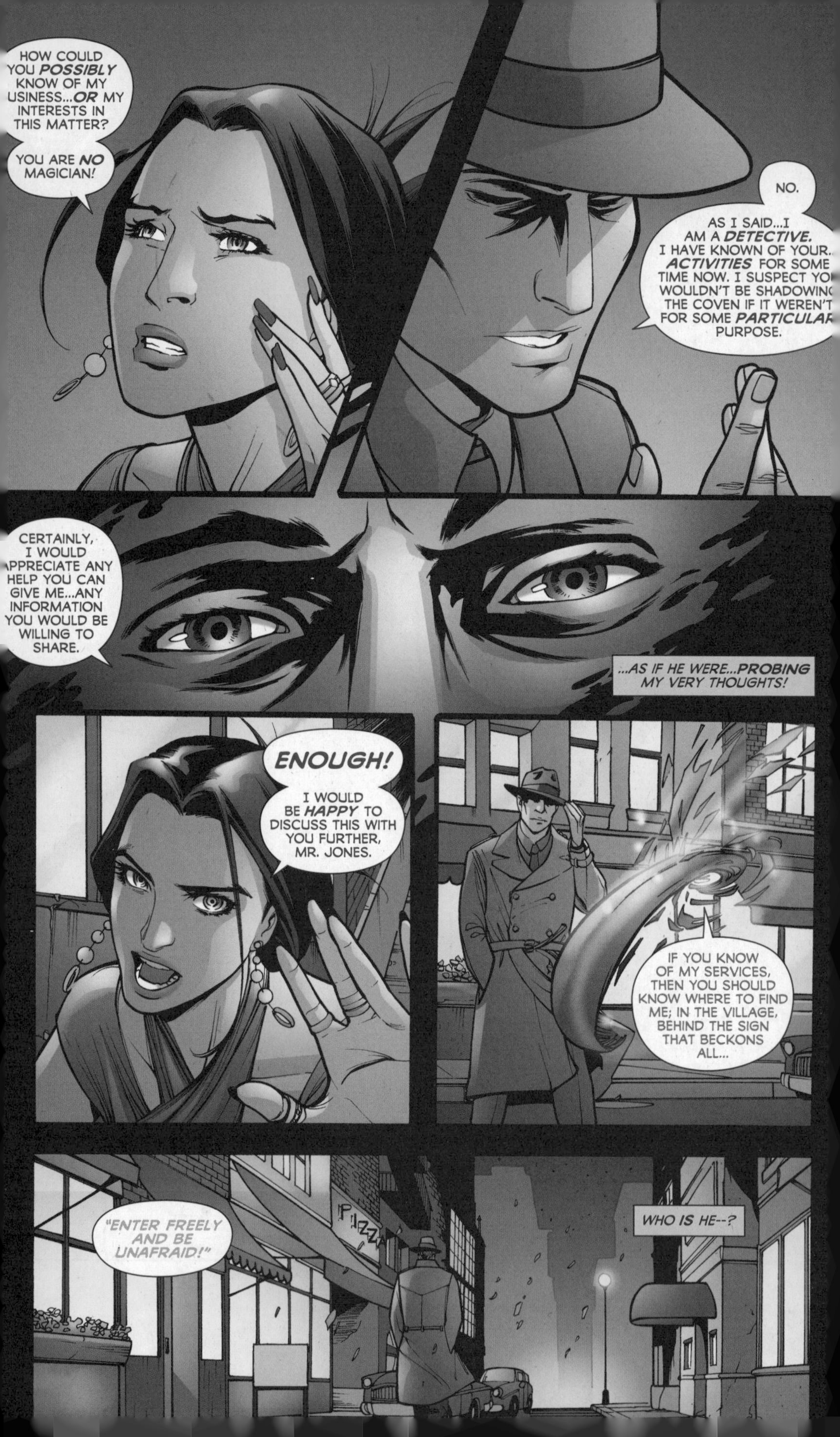

HOW COULD YOU POSSIBLY KNOW OF MY USINESS...OR MY INTERESTS IN THIS MATTER?
YOU ARE NO MAGICIAN!
NO.
AS I SAID...I AM A DETECTIVE. I HAVE KNOWN OF YOUR... ACTIVITIES FOR SOME TIME NOW. I SUSPECT YOU WOULDN'T BE SHADOWING THE COVEN IF IT WEREN'T FOR SOME PARTICULAR PURPOSE.
CERTAINLY, I WOULD APPRECIATE ANY HELP YOU CAN GIVE ME...ANY INFORMATION YOU WOULD BE WILLING TO SHARE.
...AS IF HE WERE...PROBING MY VERY THOUGHTS!
ENOUGH!
I WOULD BE HAPPY TO DISCUSS THIS WITH YOU FURTHER, MR. JONES.
IF YOU KNOW OF MY SERVICES, THEN YOU SHOULD KNOW WHERE TO FIND ME; IN THE VILLAGE, BEHIND THE SIGN THAT BECKONS ALL...
"ENTER FREELY AND BE UNAFRAID!"
PIZZA
WHO IS HE--?

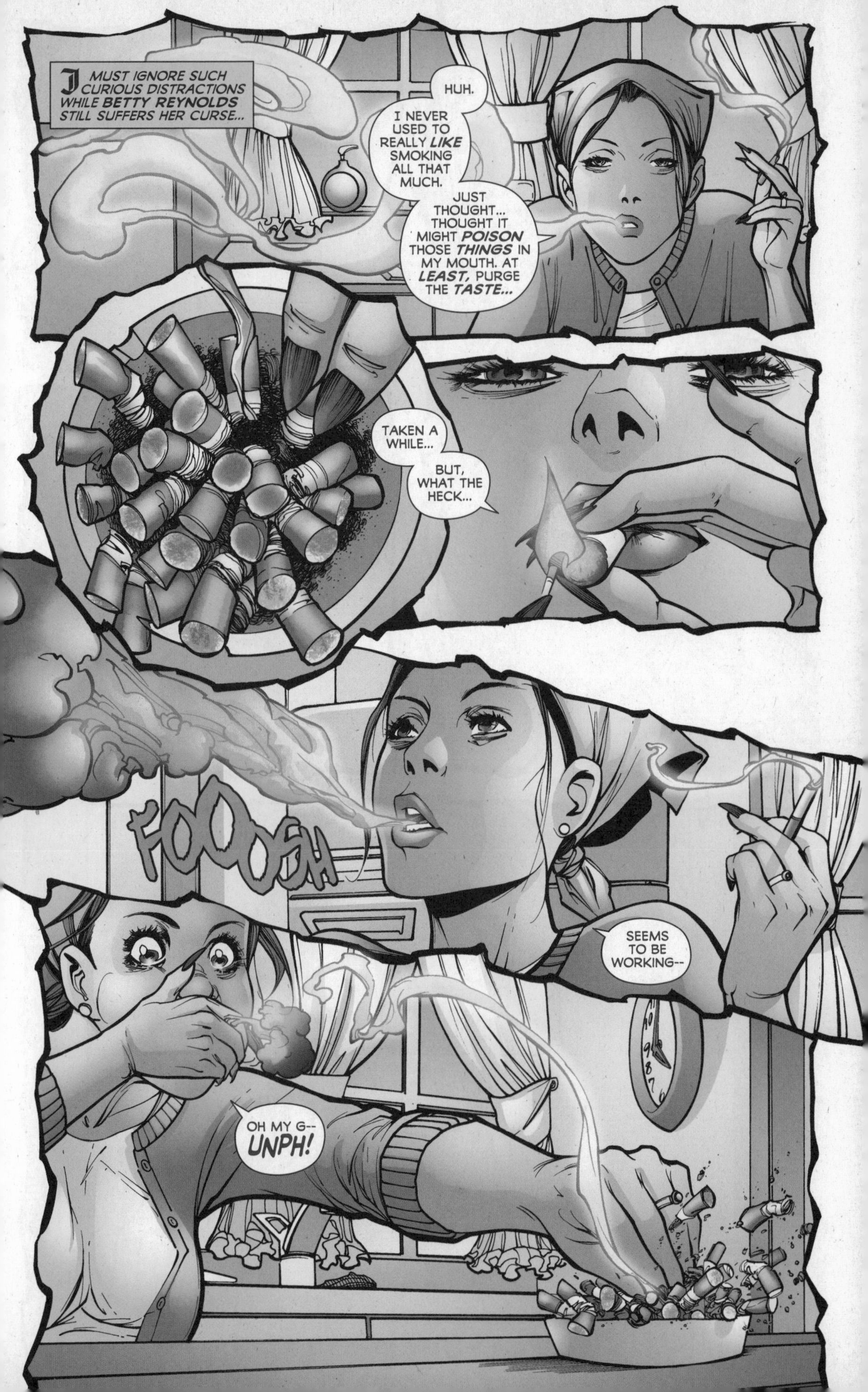
I MUST IGNORE SUCH CURIOUS DISTRACTIONS WHILE BETTY REYNOLDS STILL SUFFERS HER CURSE...
HUH.
I NEVER USED TO REALLY LIKE SMOKING ALL THAT MUCH.
JUST THOUGHT... THOUGHT IT MIGHT POISON THOSE THINGS IN MY MOUTH. AT LEAST, PURGE THE TASTE...
TAKEN A WHILE...
BUT, WHAT THE HECK...
FOOOSH
SEEMS TO BE WORKING--
OH MY G-- UNPH!

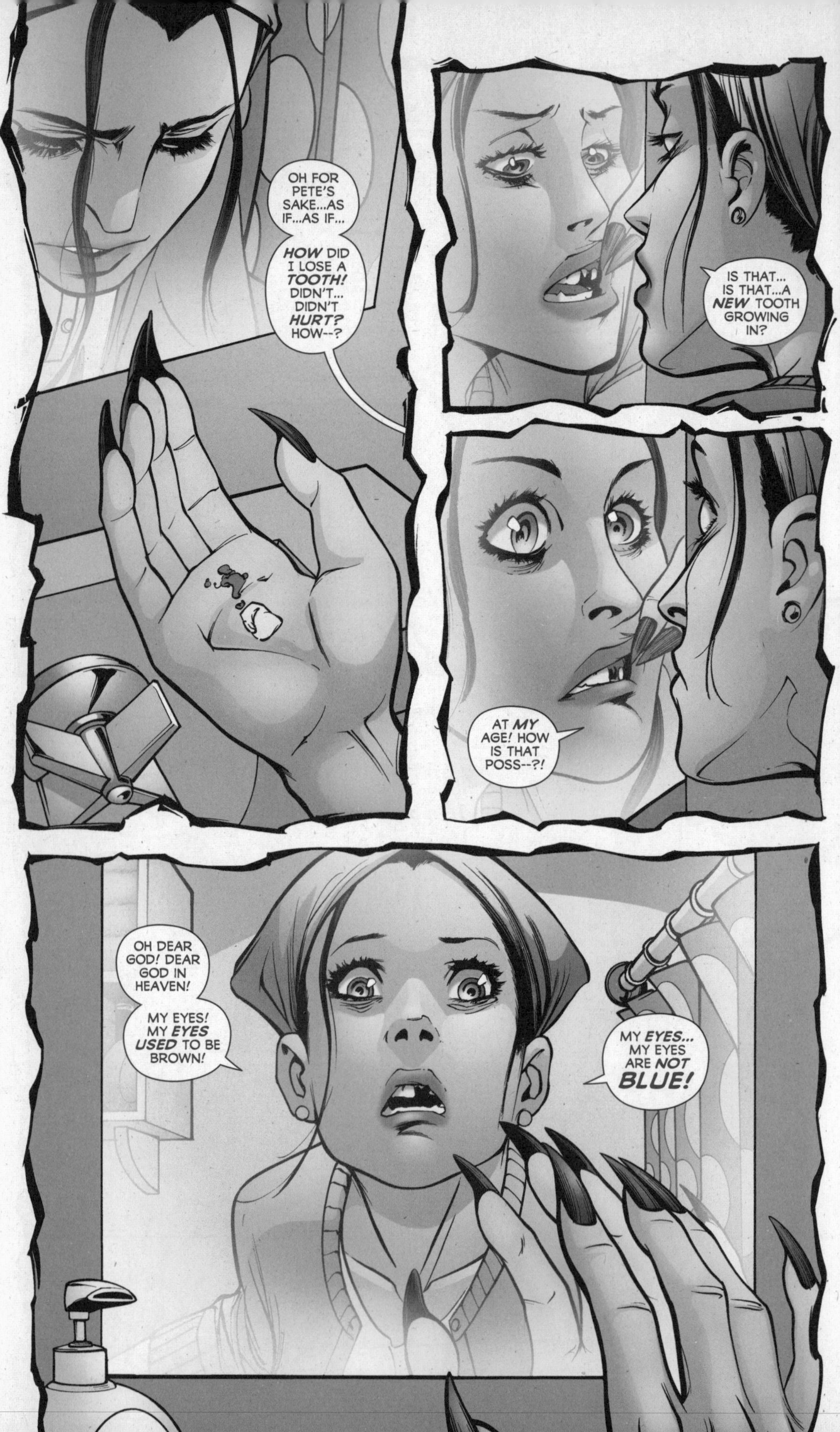

OH FOR PETE'S SAKE...AS IF...AS IF...
HOW DID I LOSE A TOOTH! DIDN'T... DIDN'T HURT? HOW--?
IS THAT... IS THAT...A NEW TOOTH GROWING IN?
AT MY AGE! HOW IS THAT POSS--?!
OH DEAR GOD! DEAR GOD IN HEAVEN!
MY EYES! MY EYES USED TO BE BROWN!
MY EYES... MY EYES ARE NOT BLUE!

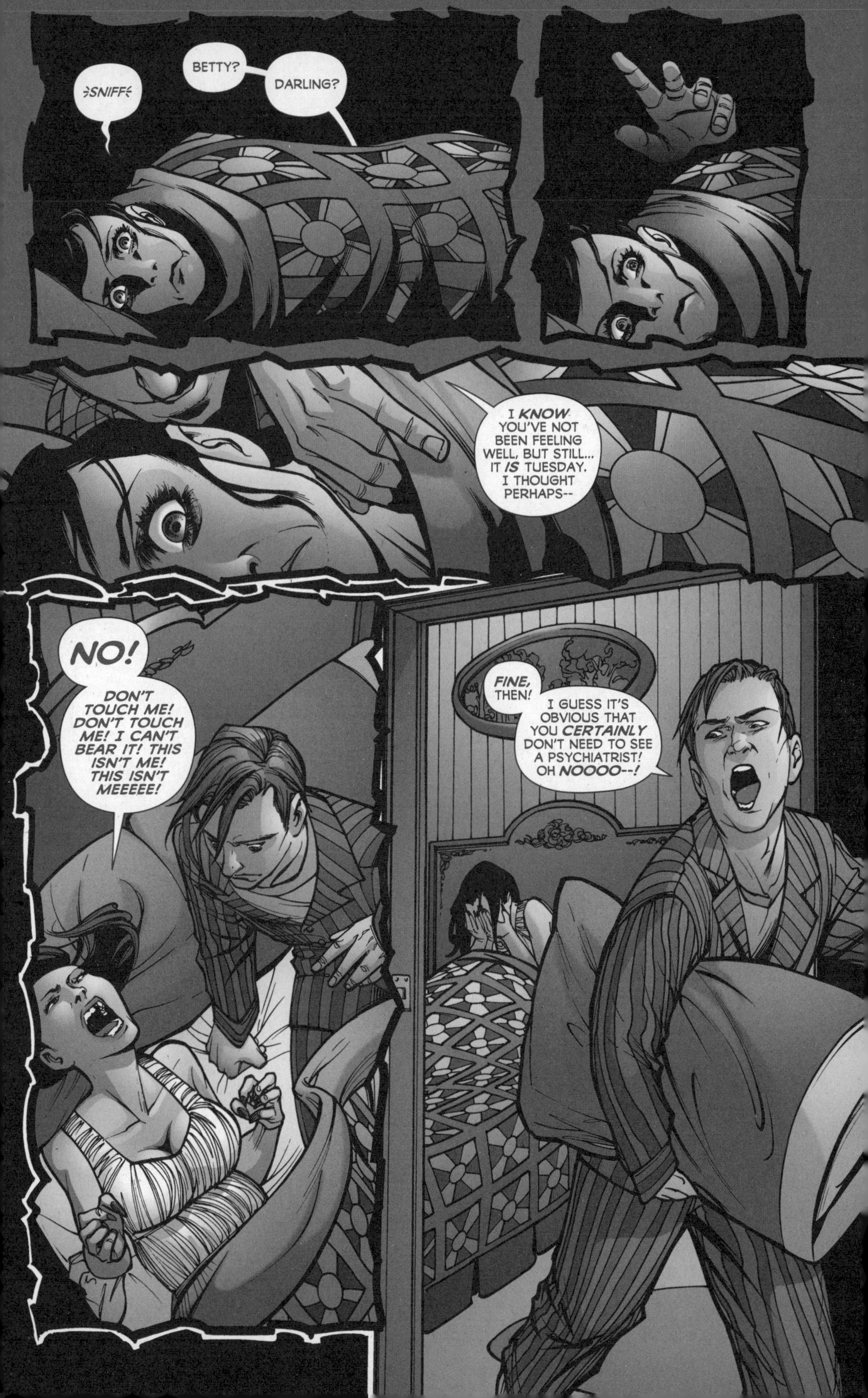

SNIFF
BETTY?
DARLING?
I KNOW YOU'VE NOT BEEN FEELING WELL, BUT STILL... IT IS TUESDAY. I THOUGHT PERHAPS--
NO!
DON'T TOUCH ME! DON'T TOUCH ME! I CAN'T BEAR IT! THIS ISN'T ME! THIS ISN'T MEEEEE!
FINE, THEN!
I GUESS IT'S OBVIOUS THAT YOU CERTAINLY DON'T NEED TO SEE A PSYCHIATRIST! OH NOOOO--!

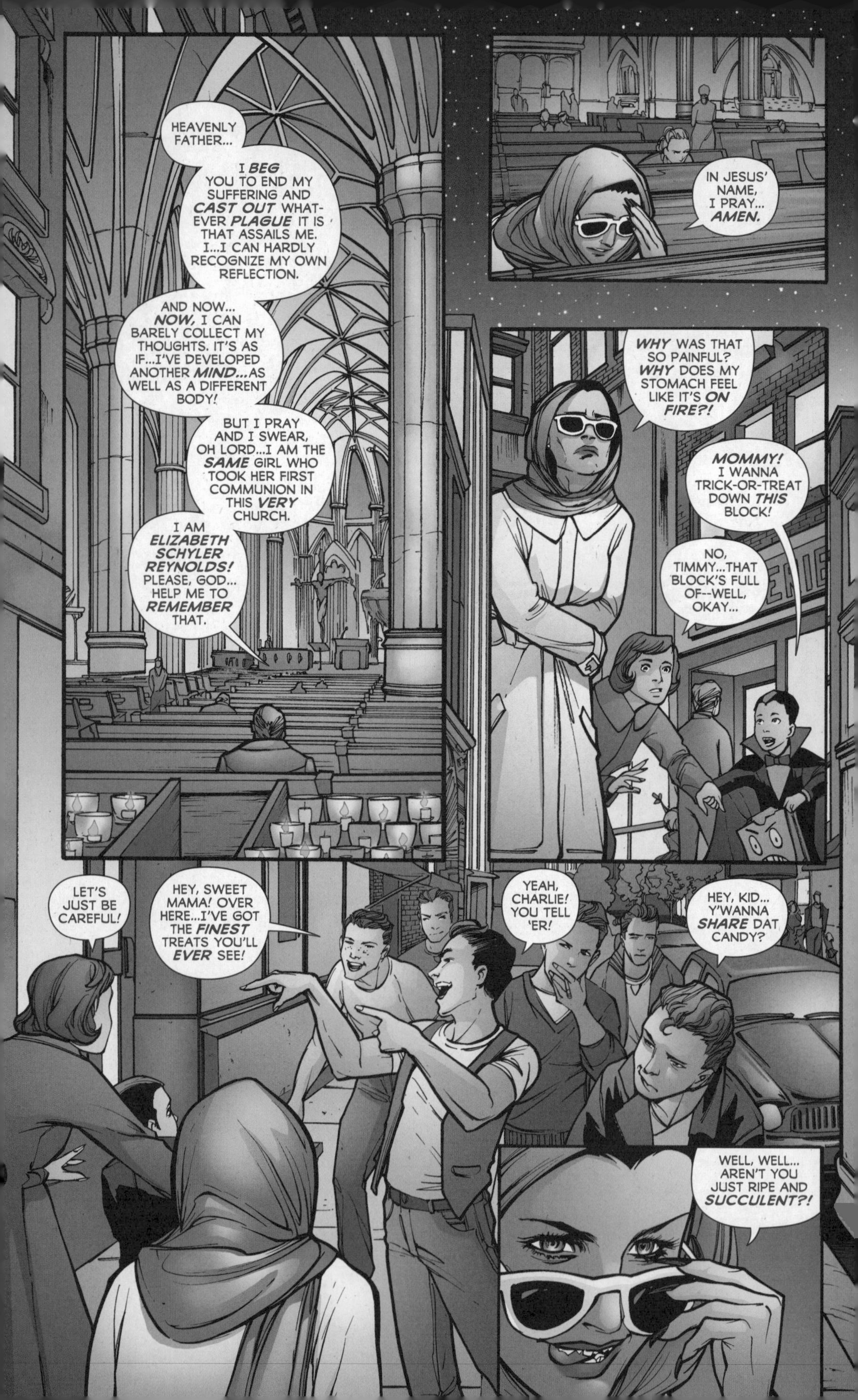
HEAVENLY FATHER...
I BEG YOU TO END MY SUFFERING AND CAST OUT WHAT-EVER PLAGUE IT IS THAT ASSAILS ME. I...I CAN HARDLY RECOGNIZE MY OWN REFLECTION.
AND NOW... NOW, I CAN BARELY COLLECT MY THOUGHTS. IT'S AS IF...I'VE DEVELOPED ANOTHER MIND...AS WELL AS A DIFFERENT BODY!
BUT I PRAY AND I SWEAR, OH LORD...I AM THE SAME GIRL WHO TOOK HER FIRST COMMUNION IN THIS VERY CHURCH.
I AM ELIZABETH SCHYLER REYNOLDS! PLEASE, GOD... HELP ME TO REMEMBER THAT.
IN JESUS' NAME, I PRAY... AMEN.
WHY WAS THAT SO PAINFUL? WHY DOES MY STOMACH FEEL LIKE IT'S ON FIRE?!
MOMMY! I WANNA TRICK-OR-TREAT DOWN THIS BLOCK!
NO, TIMMY...THAT BLOCK'S FULL OF--WELL, OKAY...
LET'S JUST BE CAREFUL!
HEY, SWEET MAMA! OVER HERE...I'VE GOT THE FINEST TREATS YOU'LL EVER SEE!
YEAH, CHARLIE! YOU TELL 'ER!
HEY, KID... Y'WANNA SHARE DAT CANDY?
WELL, WELL... AREN'T YOU JUST RIPE AND SUCCULENT?!

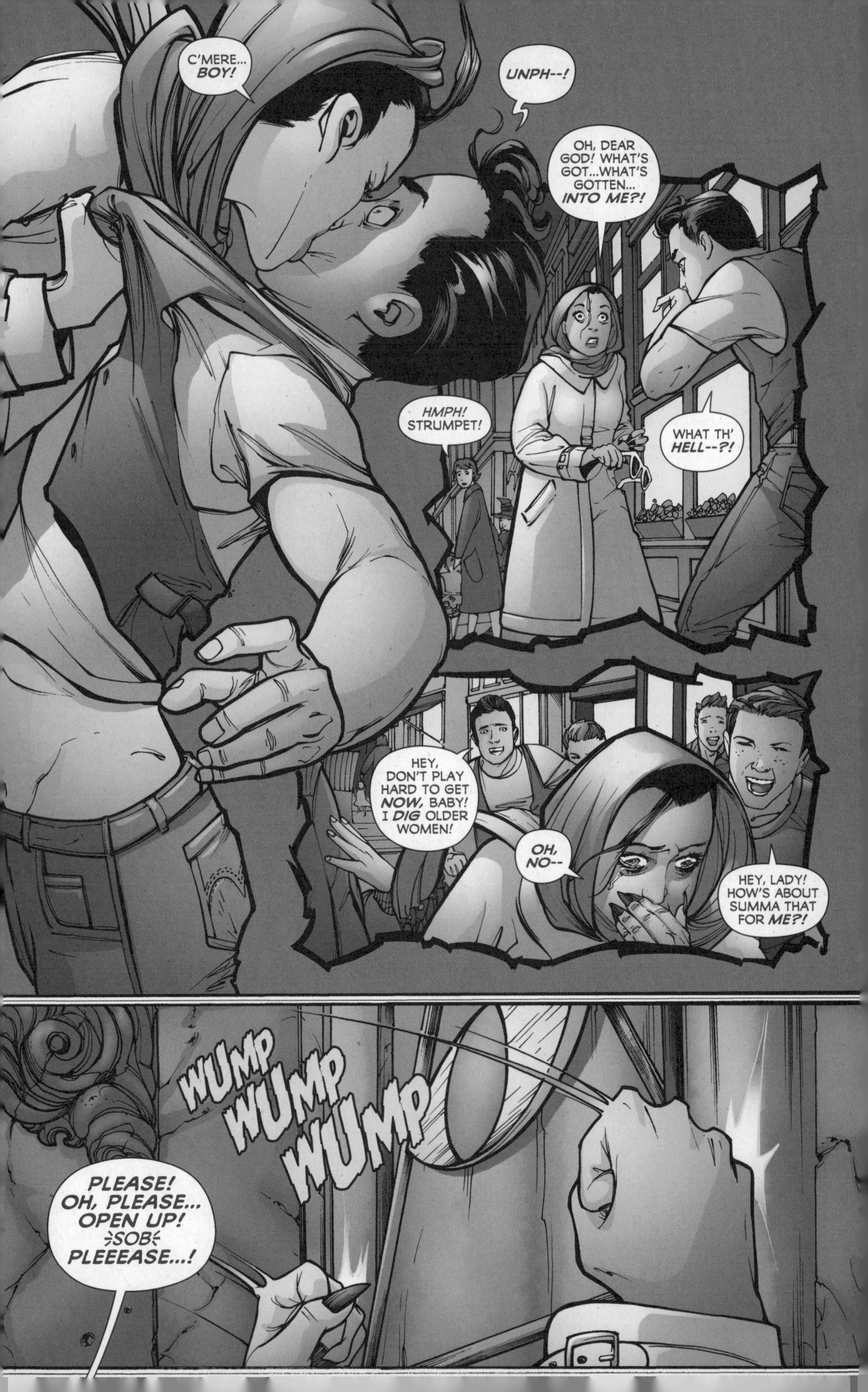
C'MERE... BOY!
UNPH--!
OH, DEAR GOD! WHAT'S GOT...WHAT'S GOTTEN... INTO ME?!
HMPH! STRUMPET!
WHAT TH' HELL--?!
HEY, DON'T PLAY HARD TO GET NOW, BABY! I DIG OLDER WOMEN!
OH, NO--
HEY, LADY! HOW'S ABOUT SUMMA THAT FOR ME?!
WUMP WUMP WUMP
PLEASE! OH, PLEASE... OPEN UP! SOB PLEEEASE...!

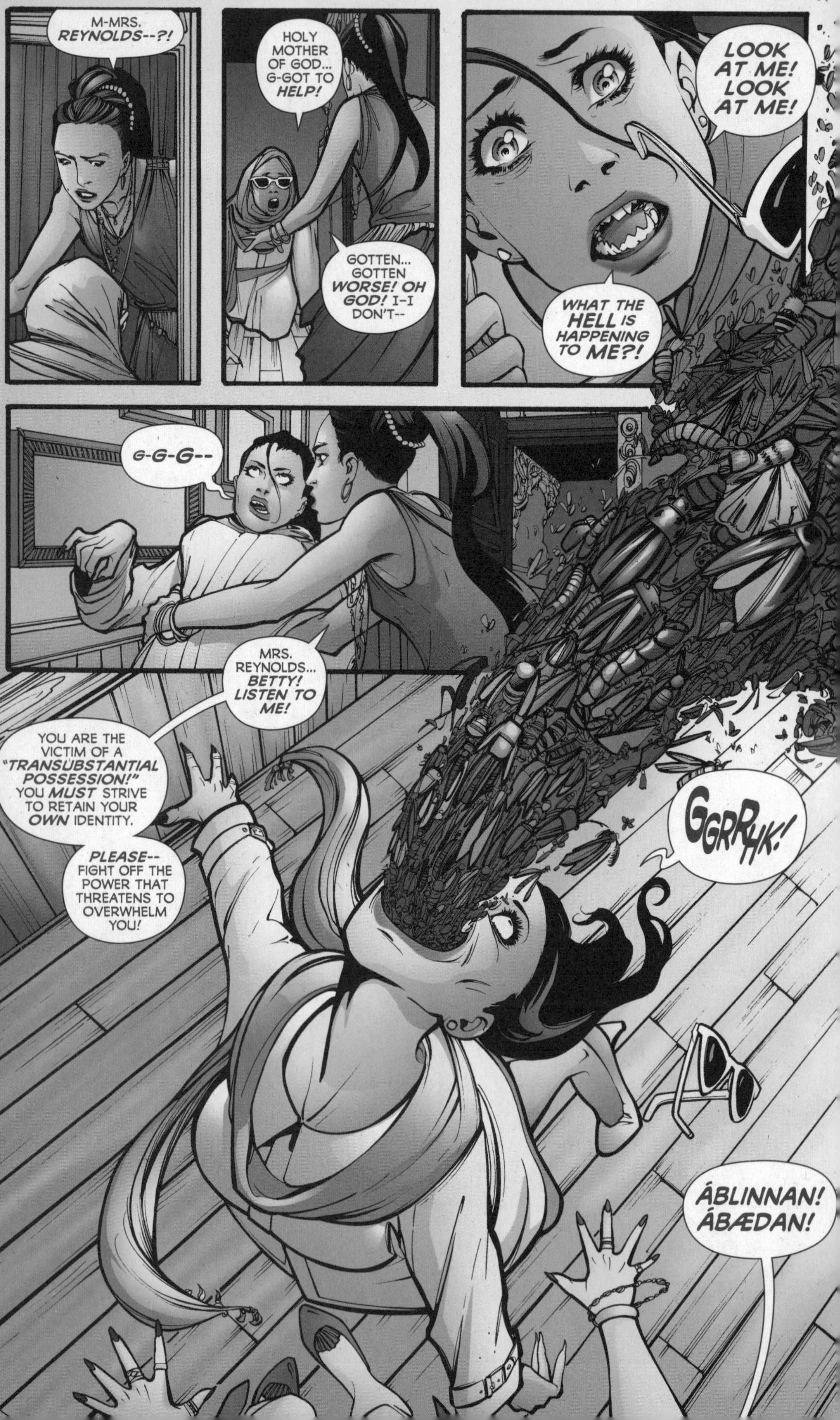
M-MRS. REYNOLDS--?!
HOLY MOTHER OF GOD... G-GOT TO HELP!
GOTTEN... GOTTEN WORSE! OH GOD! I-I DON'T--
LOOK AT ME! LOOK AT ME!
WHAT THE HELL IS HAPPENING TO ME?!
G-G-G--
MRS. REYNOLDS... BETTY! LISTEN TO ME!
YOU ARE THE VICTIM OF A "TRANSUBSTANTIAL POSSESSION!" YOU MUST STRIVE TO RETAIN YOUR OWN IDENTITY.
PLEASE-- FIGHT OFF THE POWER THAT THREATENS TO OVERWHELM YOU!
GGRRHK!
ÁBLINNAN! ÁBÆDAN!

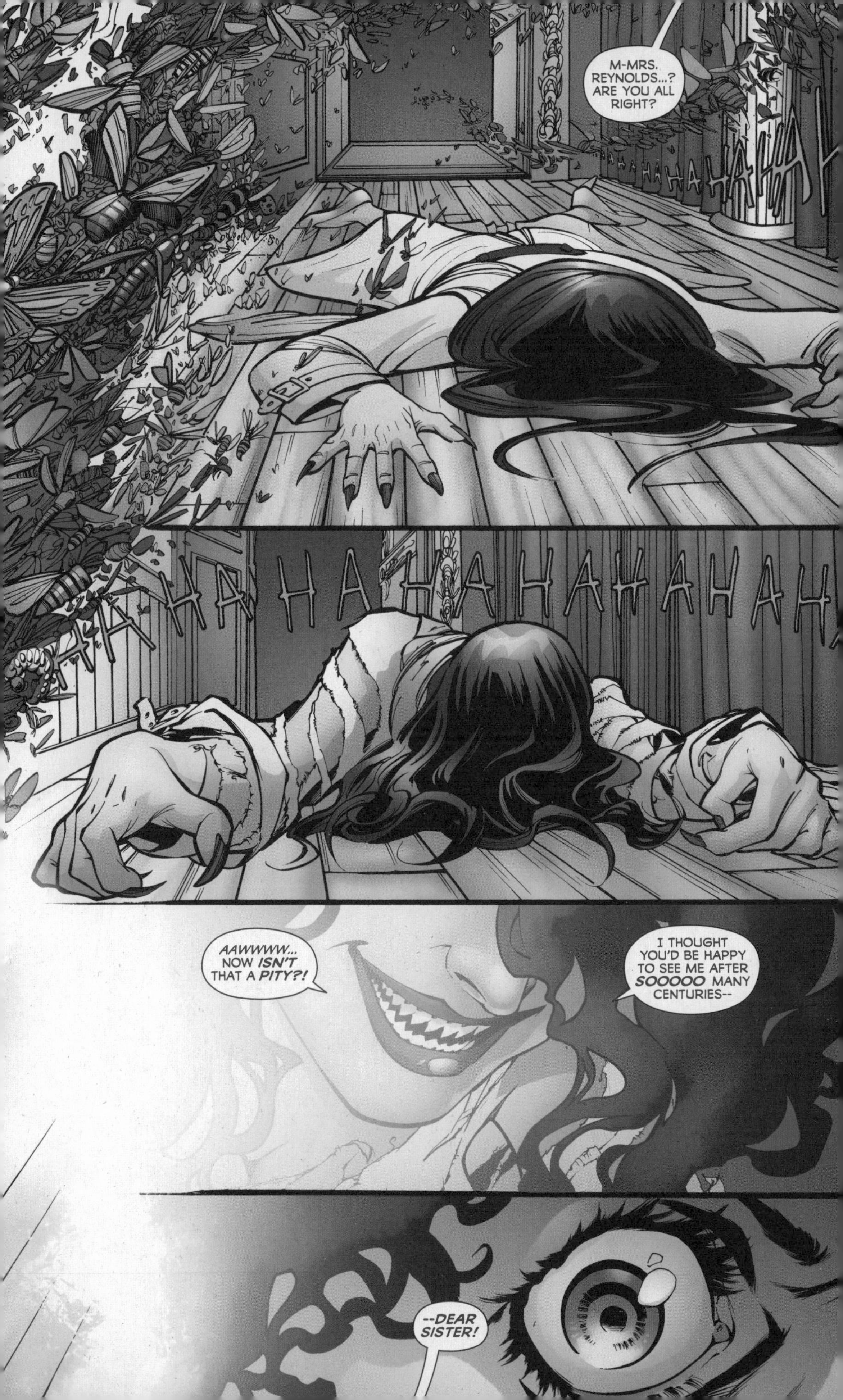
M-MRS. REYNOLDS...? ARE YOU ALL RIGHT?
HAHAHAHAHAHAHAH
HAHAHAHAHAHAHAHAHA
AAWWWW... NOW ISN'T THAT A PITY?!
I THOUGHT YOU'D BE HAPPY TO SEE ME AFTER SOOOOO MANY CENTURIES--
--DEAR SISTER!

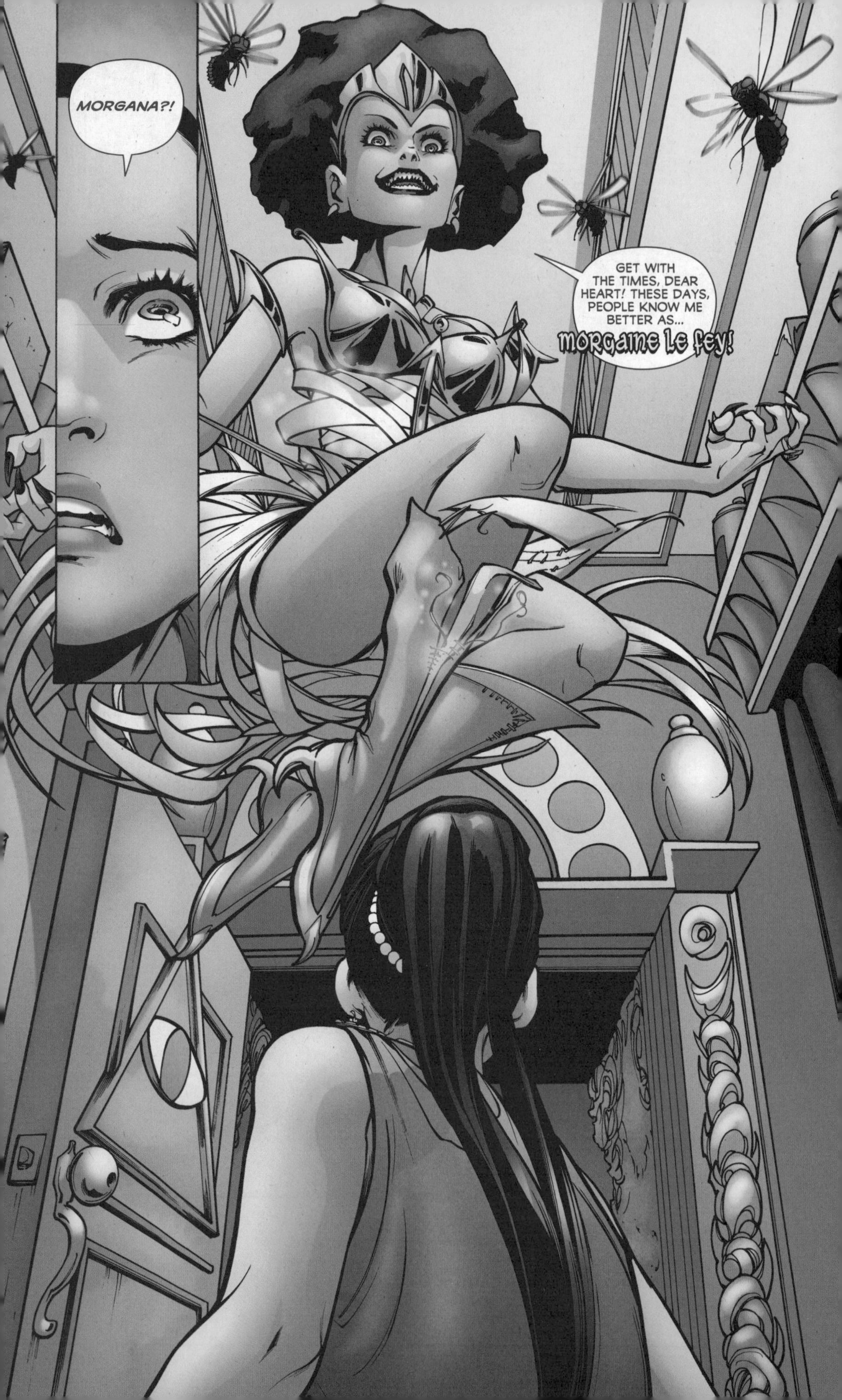
MORGANA?!
GET WITH THE TIMES, DEAR HEART! THESE DAYS, PEOPLE KNOW ME BETTER AS...
MORGAINE LE FEY!

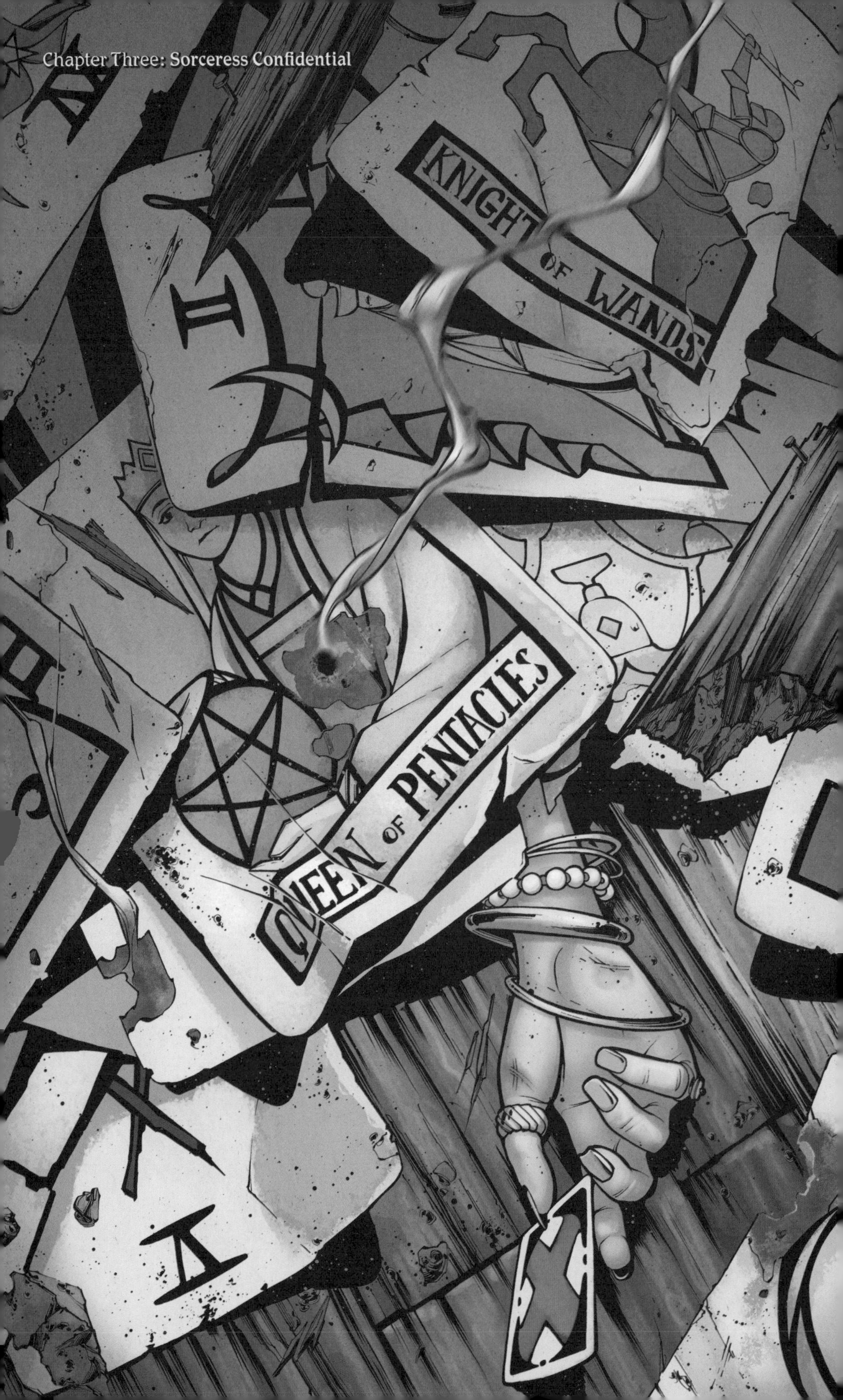
Chapter Three: Sorceress Confidential
KNIGHT OF WANDS
QUEEN OF PENTACLES

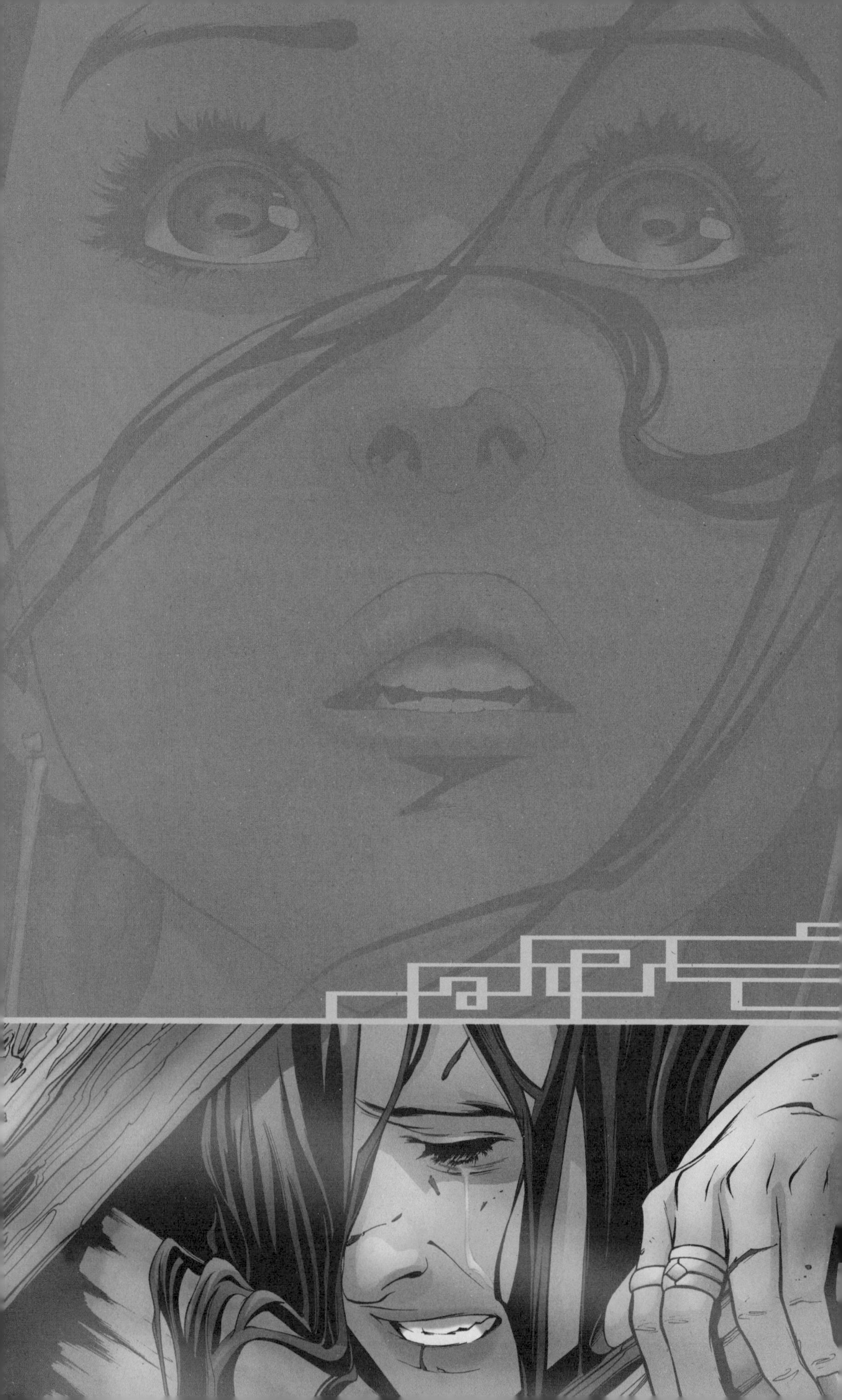

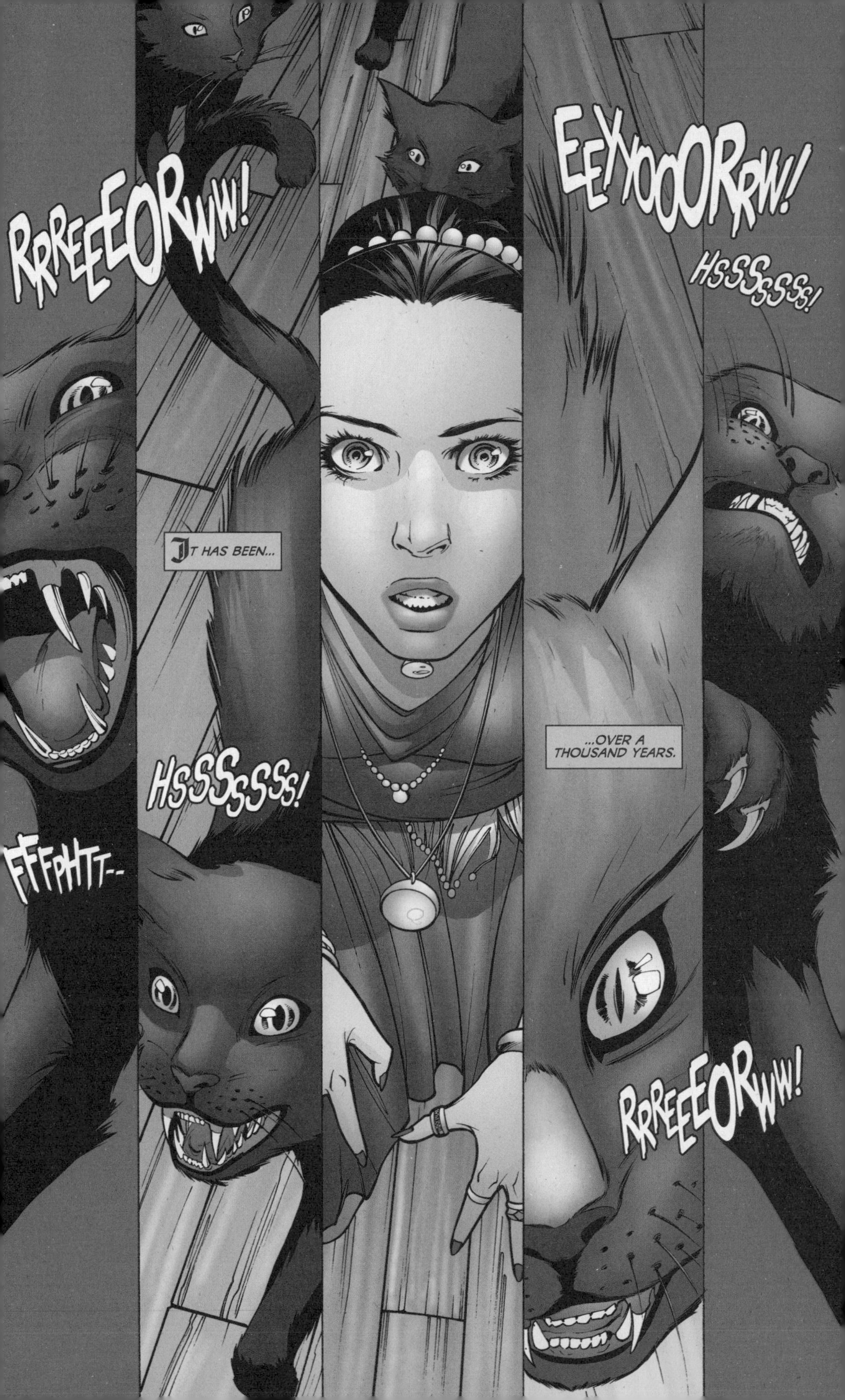
RRRREEEEORWW!
IT HAS BEEN...
HSSSSSSSS!
FFFPHTT--
EEYYOOORRRW!
HSSSSSSSS!
...OVER A THOUSAND YEARS.
RRREEEORWW!

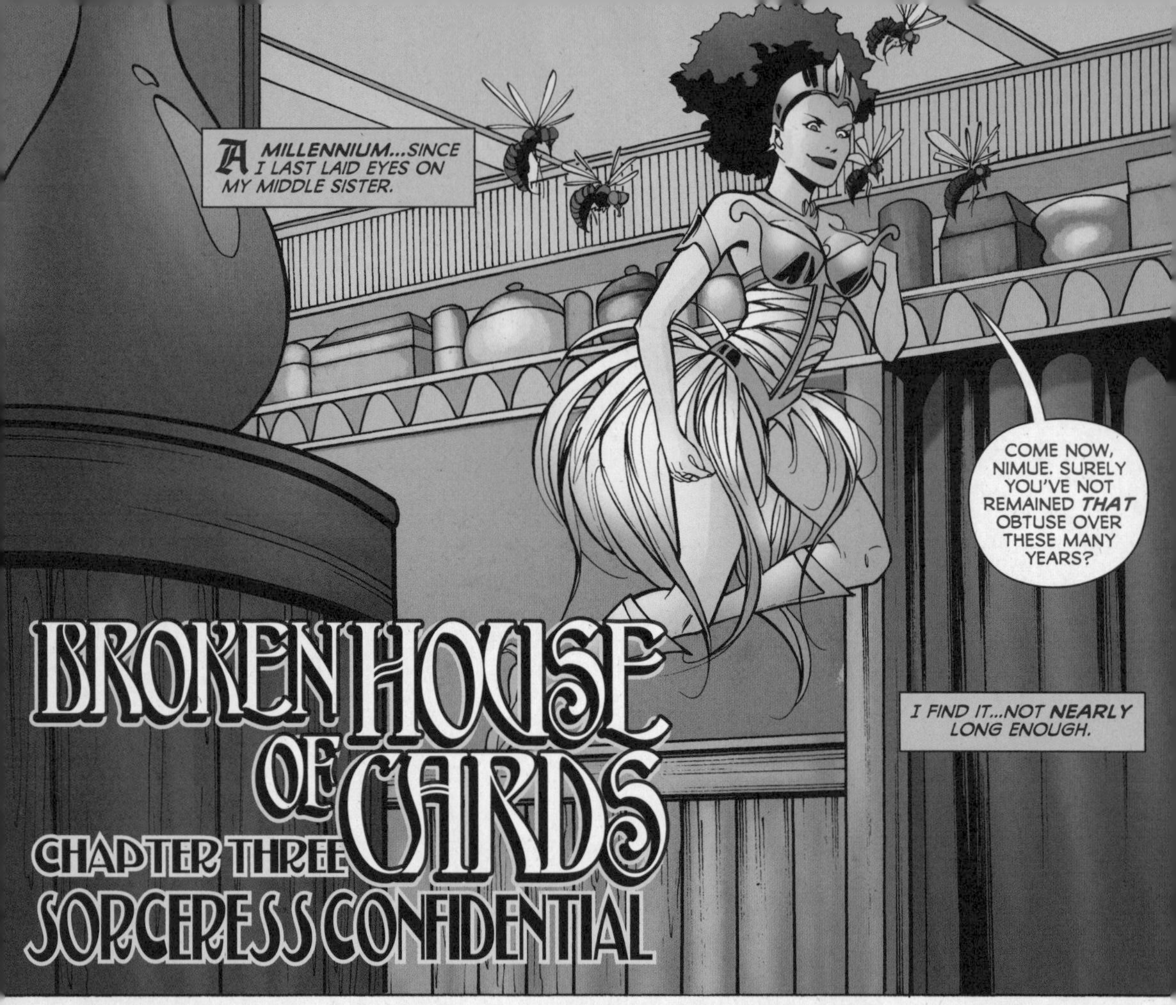
A MILLENNIUM...SINCE I LAST LAID EYES ON MY MIDDLE SISTER.
COME NOW, NIMUE. SURELY YOU'VE NOT REMAINED THAT OBTUSE OVER THESE MANY YEARS?
I FIND IT...NOT NEARLY LONG ENOUGH.
BROKEN HOUSE OF CARDS
CHAPTER THREE
SORCERESS CONFIDENTIAL

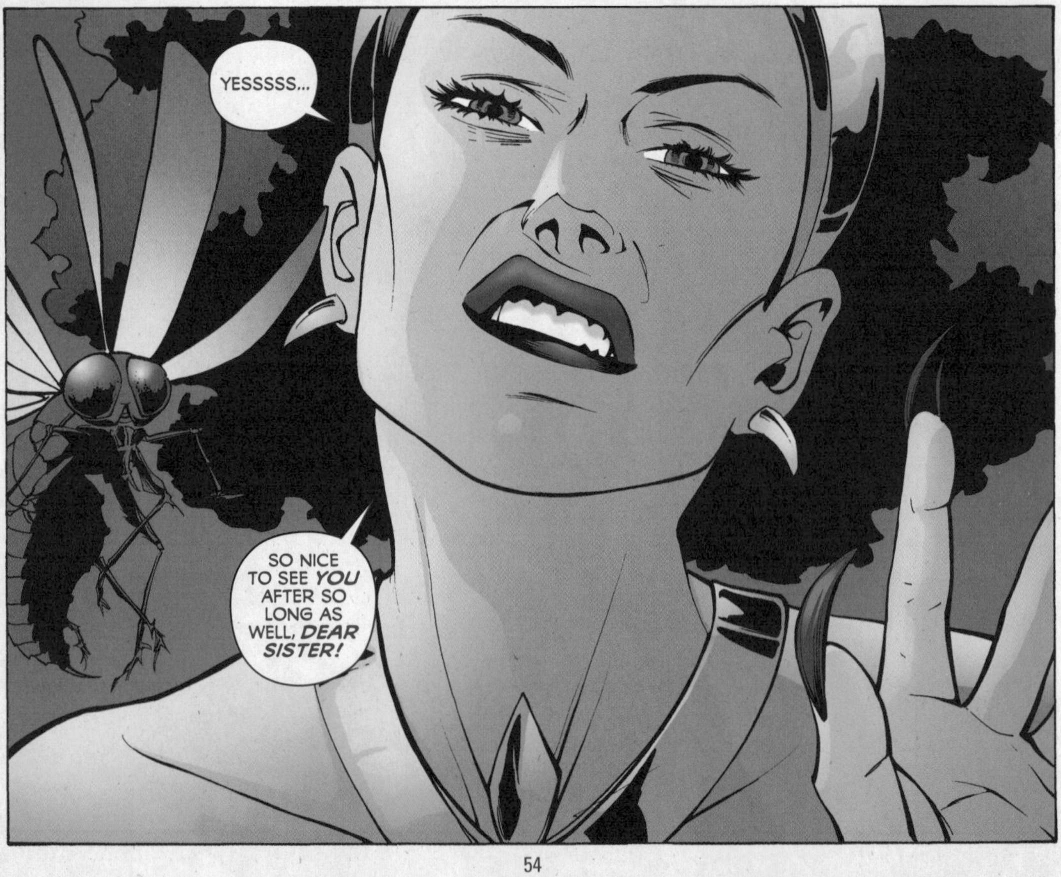
YESSSSS...
SO NICE TO SEE YOU AFTER SO LONG AS WELL, DEAR SISTER!

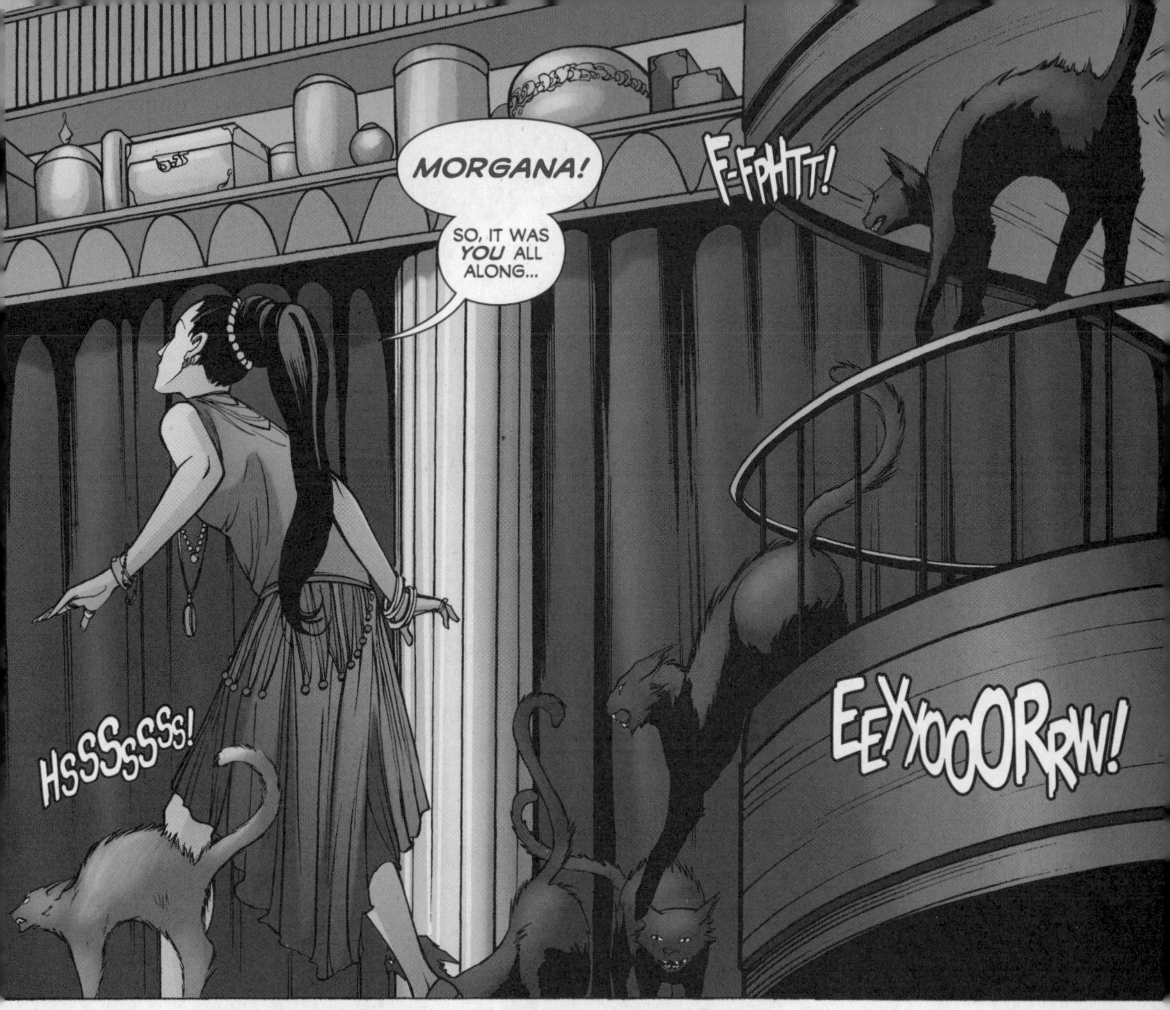
MORGANA!
SO, IT WAS YOU ALL ALONG...
F-FPHTT!
HSSSSSSS!
EEYYOOORRRW!

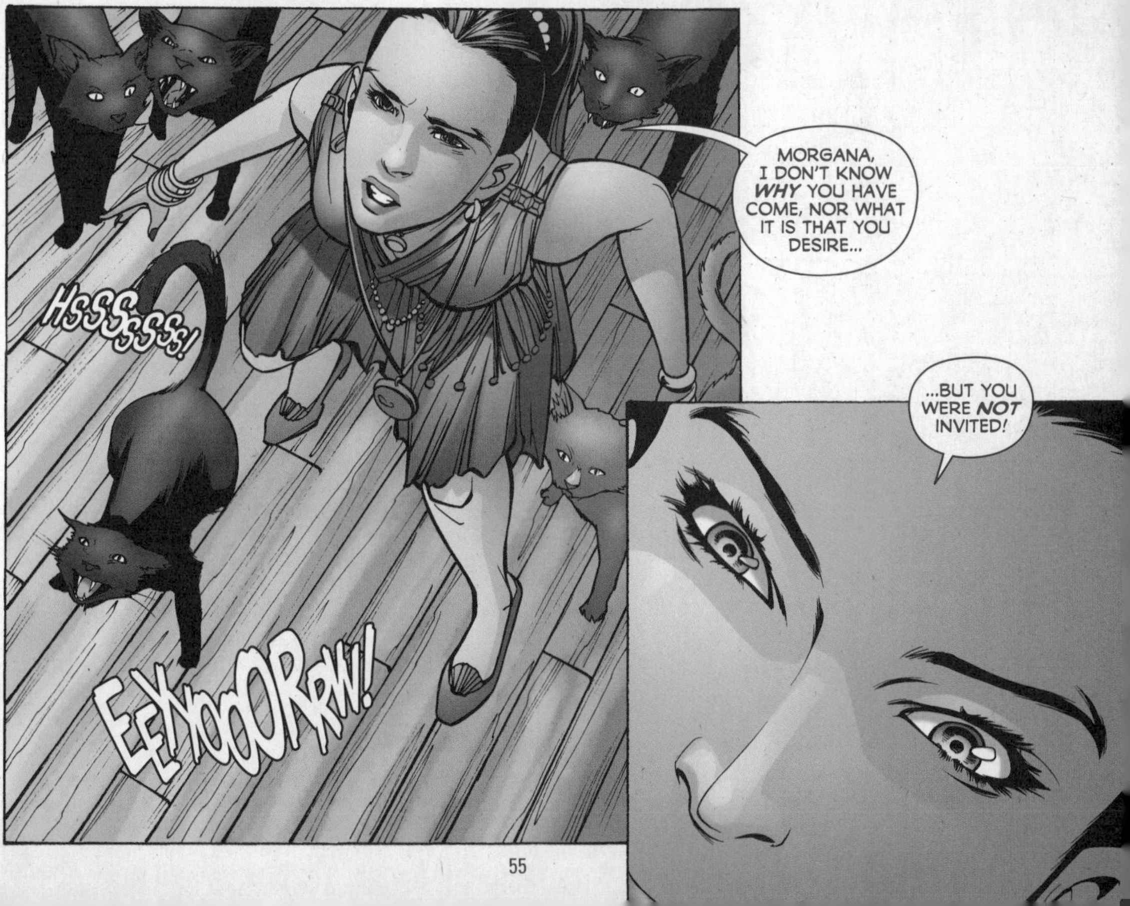
MORGANA, I DON'T KNOW WHY YOU HAVE COME, NOR WHAT IT IS THAT YOU DESIRE...
HSSSSSSS!
EEYYOOORRRW!
...BUT YOU WERE NOT INVITED!

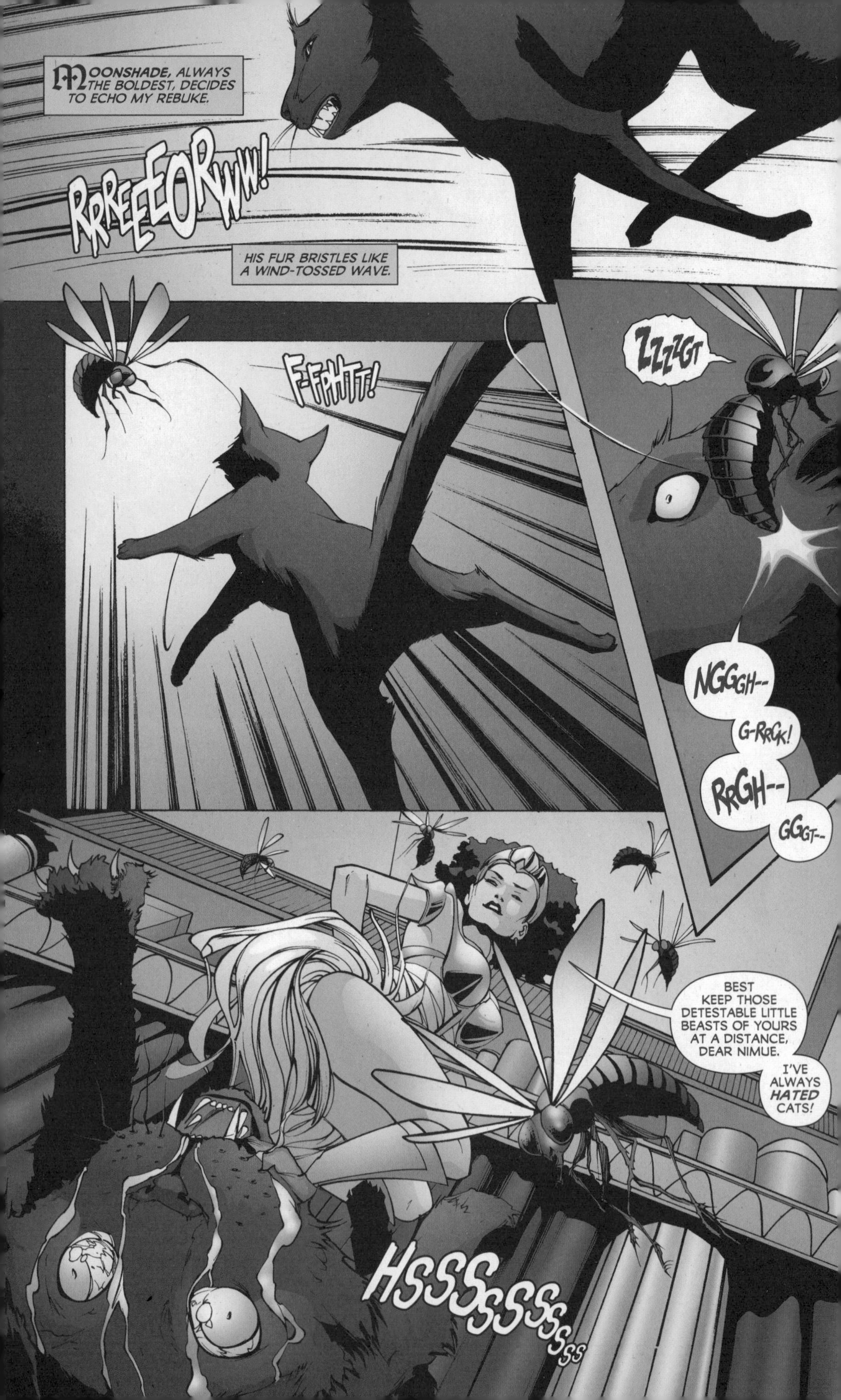

MOONSHADE, ALWAYS THE BOLDEST, DECIDES TO ECHO MY REBUKE.
RRREEEORWW!
HIS FUR BRISTLES LIKE A WIND-TOSSED WAVE.
F-FPHTT!
ZZZZGT
NGGGH--
G-RRCK!
RRGH--
GGGT--
BEST KEEP THOSE DETESTABLE LITTLE BEASTS OF YOURS AT A DISTANCE, DEAR NIMUE.
I'VE ALWAYS *HATED* CATS!
HSSSSSSSSSS

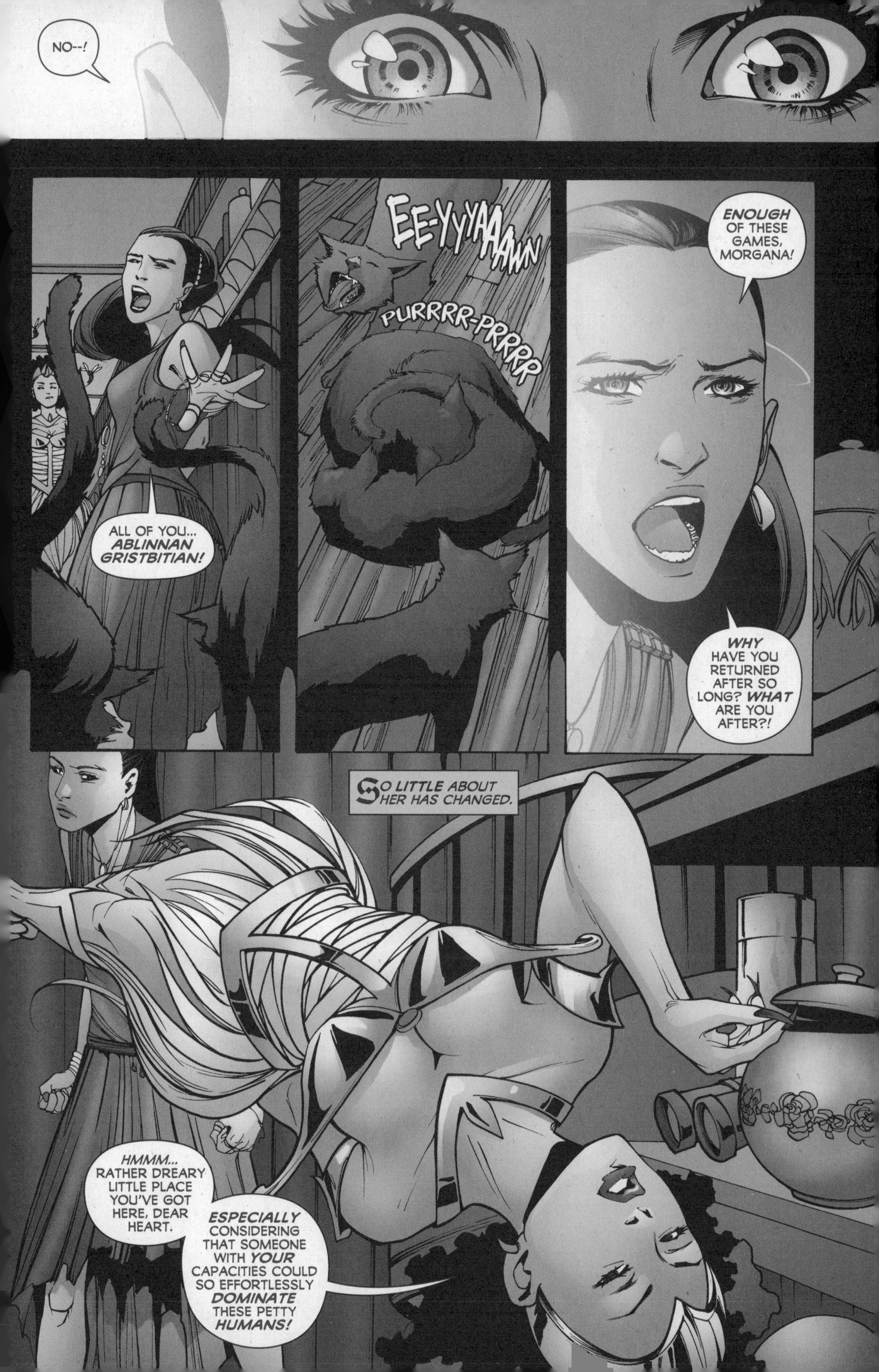
NO--!
ALL OF YOU... ABLINNAN GRISTBITIAN!
EE-YYYAAAAWN
PURRRR-PRRRR
ENOUGH OF THESE GAMES, MORGANA!
WHY HAVE YOU RETURNED AFTER SO LONG? WHAT ARE YOU AFTER?!
SO LITTLE ABOUT HER HAS CHANGED.
HMMM... RATHER DREARY LITTLE PLACE YOU'VE GOT HERE, DEAR HEART.
ESPECIALLY CONSIDERING THAT SOMEONE WITH YOUR CAPACITIES COULD SO EFFORTLESSLY DOMINATE THESE PETTY HUMANS!

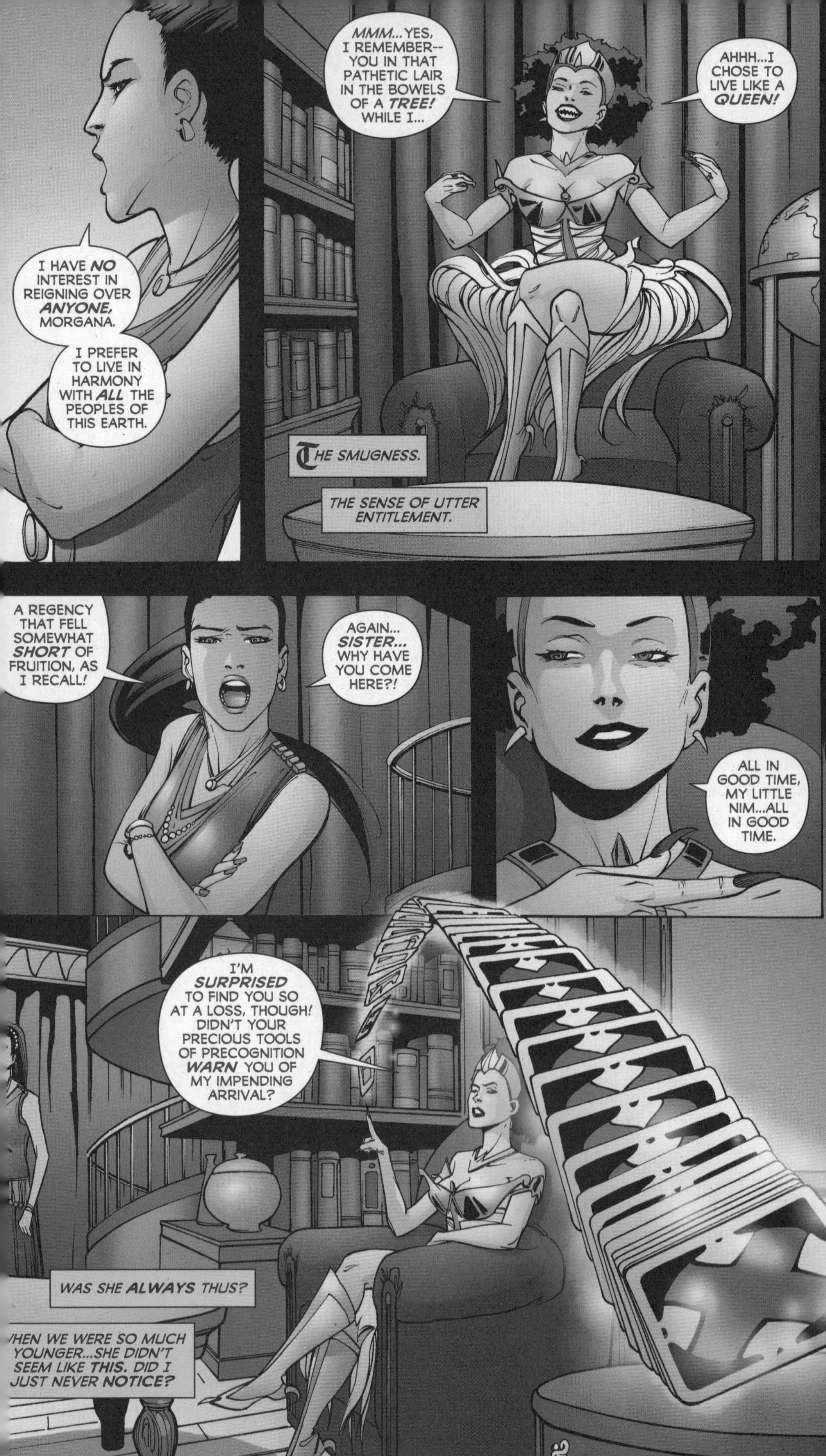

MMM...YES, I REMEMBER--YOU IN THAT PATHETIC LAIR IN THE BOWELS OF A TREE! WHILE I...
AHHH...I CHOSE TO LIVE LIKE A QUEEN!
I HAVE NO INTEREST IN REIGNING OVER ANYONE, MORGANA.
I PREFER TO LIVE IN HARMONY WITH ALL THE PEOPLES OF THIS EARTH.
THE SMUGNESS.
THE SENSE OF UTTER ENTITLEMENT.
A REGENCY THAT FELL SOMEWHAT SHORT OF FRUITION, AS I RECALL!
AGAIN... SISTER... WHY HAVE YOU COME HERE?!
ALL IN GOOD TIME, MY LITTLE NIM...ALL IN GOOD TIME.
I'M SURPRISED TO FIND YOU SO AT A LOSS, THOUGH! DIDN'T YOUR PRECIOUS TOOLS OF PRECOGNITION WARN YOU OF MY IMPENDING ARRIVAL?
WAS SHE ALWAYS THUS?
WHEN WE WERE SO MUCH YOUNGER...SHE DIDN'T SEEM LIKE THIS. DID I JUST NEVER NOTICE?

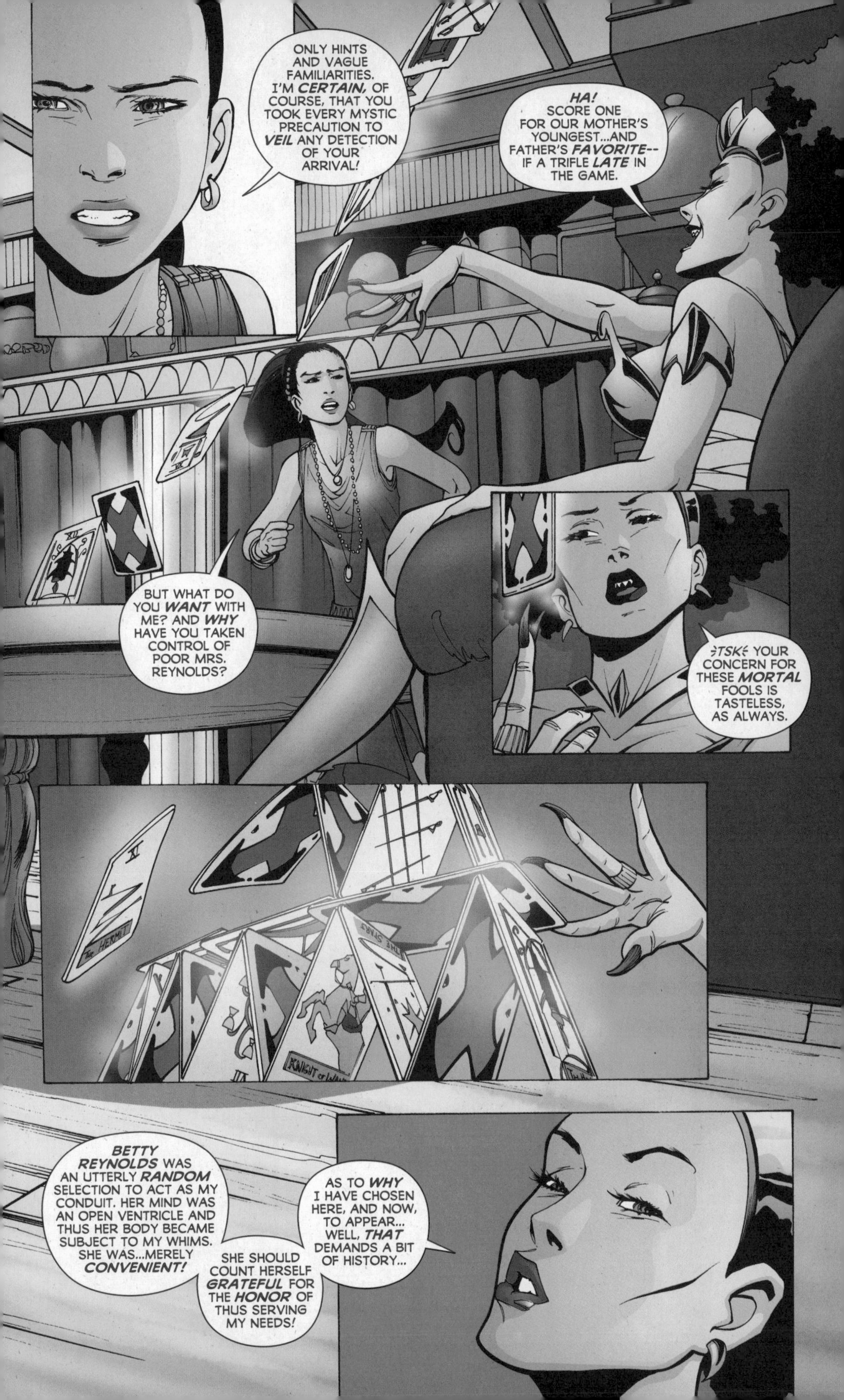
ONLY HINTS AND VAGUE FAMILIARITIES. I'M *CERTAIN,* OF COURSE, THAT YOU TOOK EVERY MYSTIC PRECAUTION TO *VEIL* ANY DETECTION OF YOUR ARRIVAL!
HA! SCORE ONE FOR OUR MOTHER'S YOUNGEST...AND FATHER'S *FAVORITE*-- IF A TRIFLE *LATE* IN THE GAME.
BUT WHAT DO YOU *WANT* WITH ME? AND *WHY* HAVE YOU TAKEN CONTROL OF POOR MRS. REYNOLDS?
TSK YOUR CONCERN FOR THESE *MORTAL* FOOLS IS TASTELESS, AS ALWAYS.
THE HERMIT
THE STARS
KNIGHT of WANDS
BETTY REYNOLDS WAS AN UTTERLY *RANDOM* SELECTION TO ACT AS MY CONDUIT. HER MIND WAS AN OPEN VENTRICLE AND THUS HER BODY BECAME SUBJECT TO MY WHIMS. SHE WAS...MERELY *CONVENIENT!*
SHE SHOULD COUNT HERSELF *GRATEFUL* FOR THE *HONOR* OF THUS SERVING MY NEEDS!
AS TO *WHY* I HAVE CHOSEN HERE, AND NOW, TO APPEAR... WELL, *THAT* DEMANDS A BIT OF HISTORY...

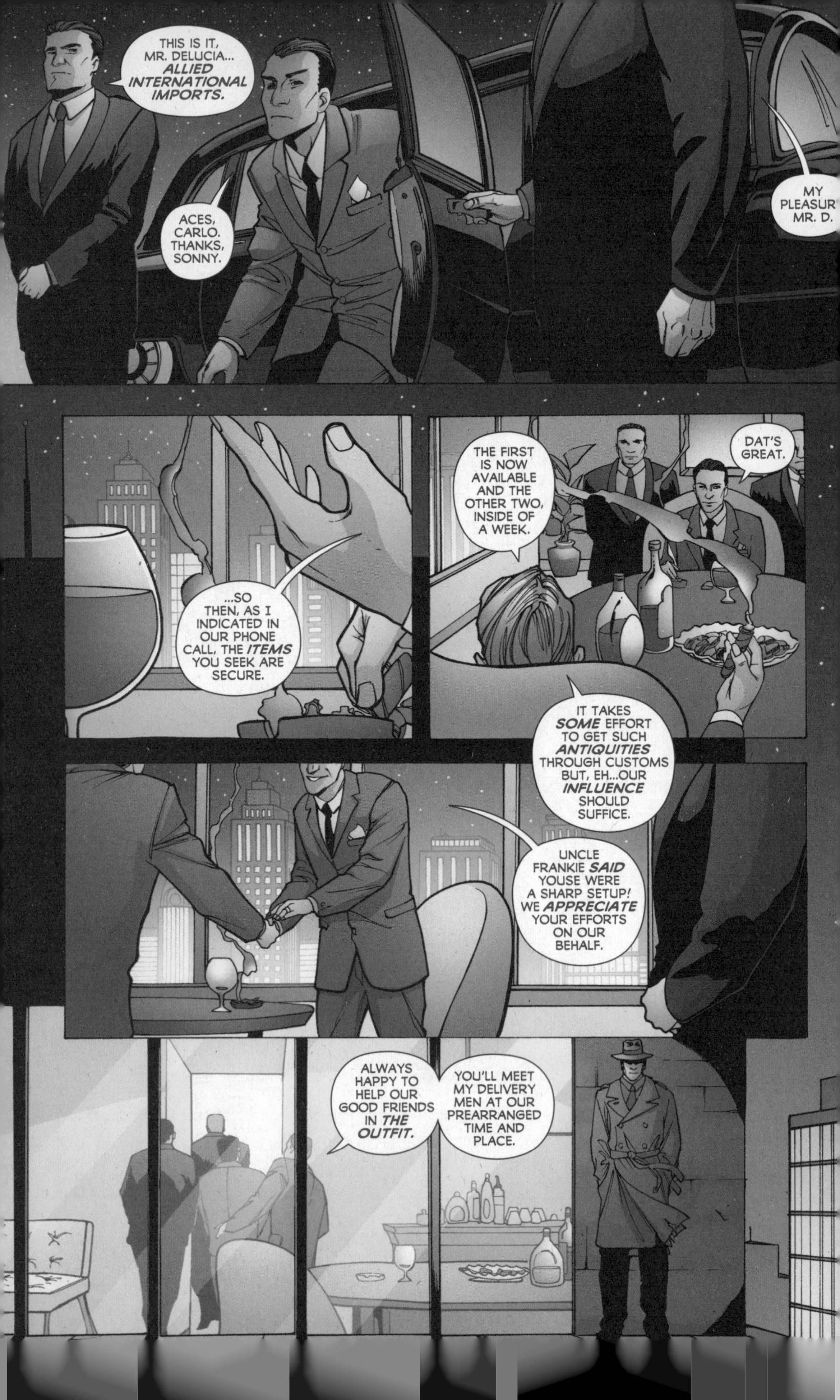
THIS IS IT, MR. DELUCIA... ALLIED INTERNATIONAL IMPORTS.
ACES, CARLO. THANKS, SONNY.
MY PLEASUR MR. D.
...SO THEN, AS I INDICATED IN OUR PHONE CALL, THE ITEMS YOU SEEK ARE SECURE.
THE FIRST IS NOW AVAILABLE AND THE OTHER TWO, INSIDE OF A WEEK.
DAT'S GREAT.
IT TAKES SOME EFFORT TO GET SUCH ANTIQUITIES THROUGH CUSTOMS BUT, EH...OUR INFLUENCE SHOULD SUFFICE.
UNCLE FRANKIE SAID YOUSE WERE A SHARP SETUP! WE APPRECIATE YOUR EFFORTS ON OUR BEHALF.
ALWAYS HAPPY TO HELP OUR GOOD FRIENDS IN THE OUTFIT.
YOU'LL MEET MY DELIVERY MEN AT OUR PREARRANGED TIME AND PLACE.

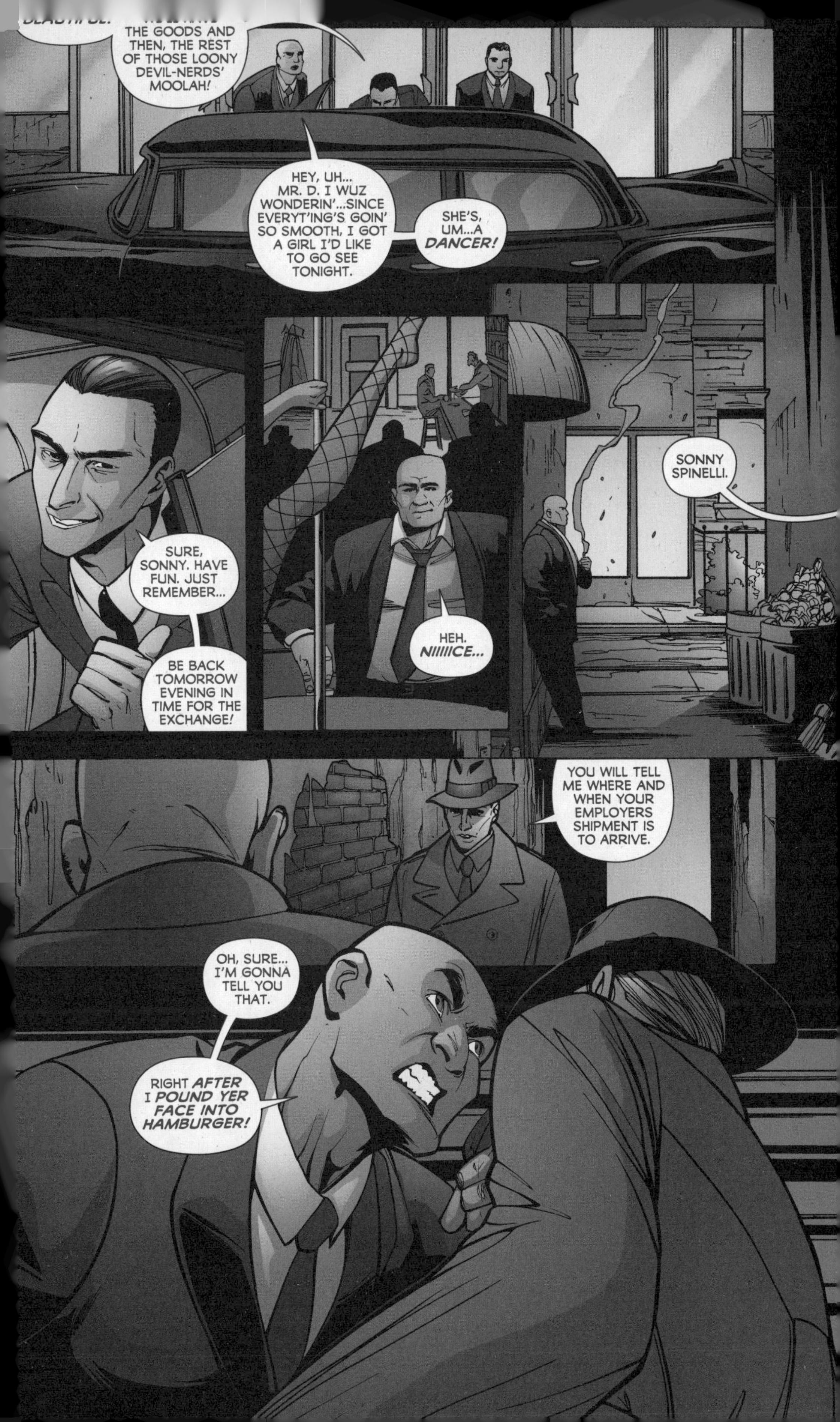
THE GOODS AND THEN, THE REST OF THOSE LOONY DEVIL-NERDS' MOOLAH!
HEY, UH... MR. D. I WUZ WONDERIN'...SINCE EVERYT'ING'S GOIN' SO SMOOTH, I GOT A GIRL I'D LIKE TO GO SEE TONIGHT.
SHE'S, UM...A *DANCER!*
SURE, SONNY. HAVE FUN. JUST REMEMBER...
BE BACK TOMORROW EVENING IN TIME FOR THE EXCHANGE!
HEH. *NIIIIICE...*
SONNY SPINELLI.
YOU WILL TELL ME WHERE AND WHEN YOUR EMPLOYERS SHIPMENT IS TO ARRIVE.
OH, SURE... I'M GONNA TELL YOU THAT.
RIGHT *AFTER* I *POUND YER FACE INTO HAMBURGER!*

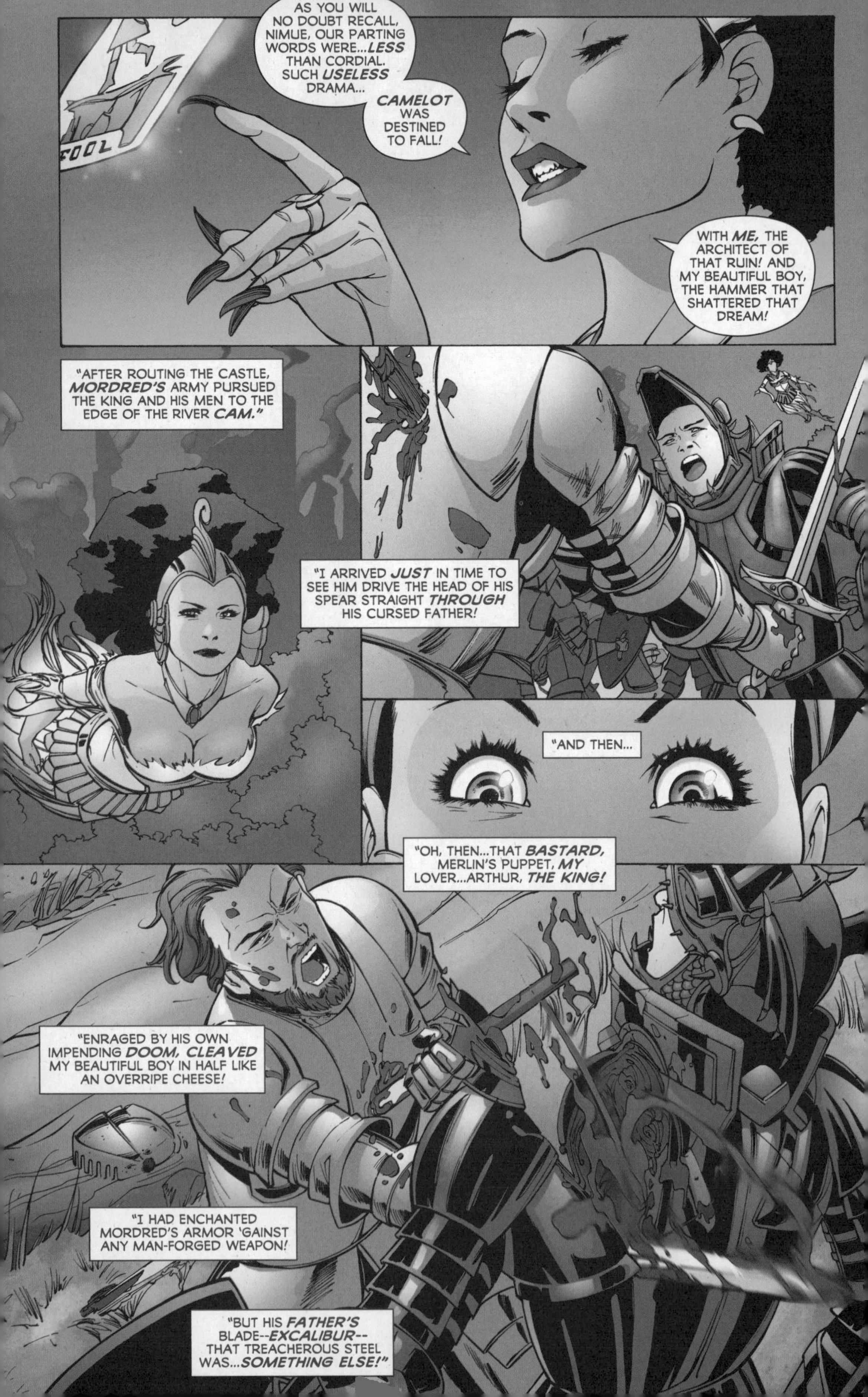

FOOL
AS YOU WILL NO DOUBT RECALL, NIMUE, OUR PARTING WORDS WERE...LESS THAN CORDIAL. SUCH USELESS DRAMA...
CAMELOT WAS DESTINED TO FALL!
WITH ME, THE ARCHITECT OF THAT RUIN! AND MY BEAUTIFUL BOY, THE HAMMER THAT SHATTERED THAT DREAM!
"AFTER ROUTING THE CASTLE, MORDRED'S ARMY PURSUED THE KING AND HIS MEN TO THE EDGE OF THE RIVER CAM."
"I ARRIVED JUST IN TIME TO SEE HIM DRIVE THE HEAD OF HIS SPEAR STRAIGHT THROUGH HIS CURSED FATHER!
"AND THEN...
"OH, THEN...THAT BASTARD, MERLIN'S PUPPET, MY LOVER...ARTHUR, THE KING!
"ENRAGED BY HIS OWN IMPENDING DOOM, CLEAVED MY BEAUTIFUL BOY IN HALF LIKE AN OVERRIPE CHEESE!
"I HAD ENCHANTED MORDRED'S ARMOR 'GAINST ANY MAN-FORGED WEAPON!
"BUT HIS FATHER'S BLADE--EXCALIBUR--THAT TREACHEROUS STEEL WAS...SOMETHING ELSE!"

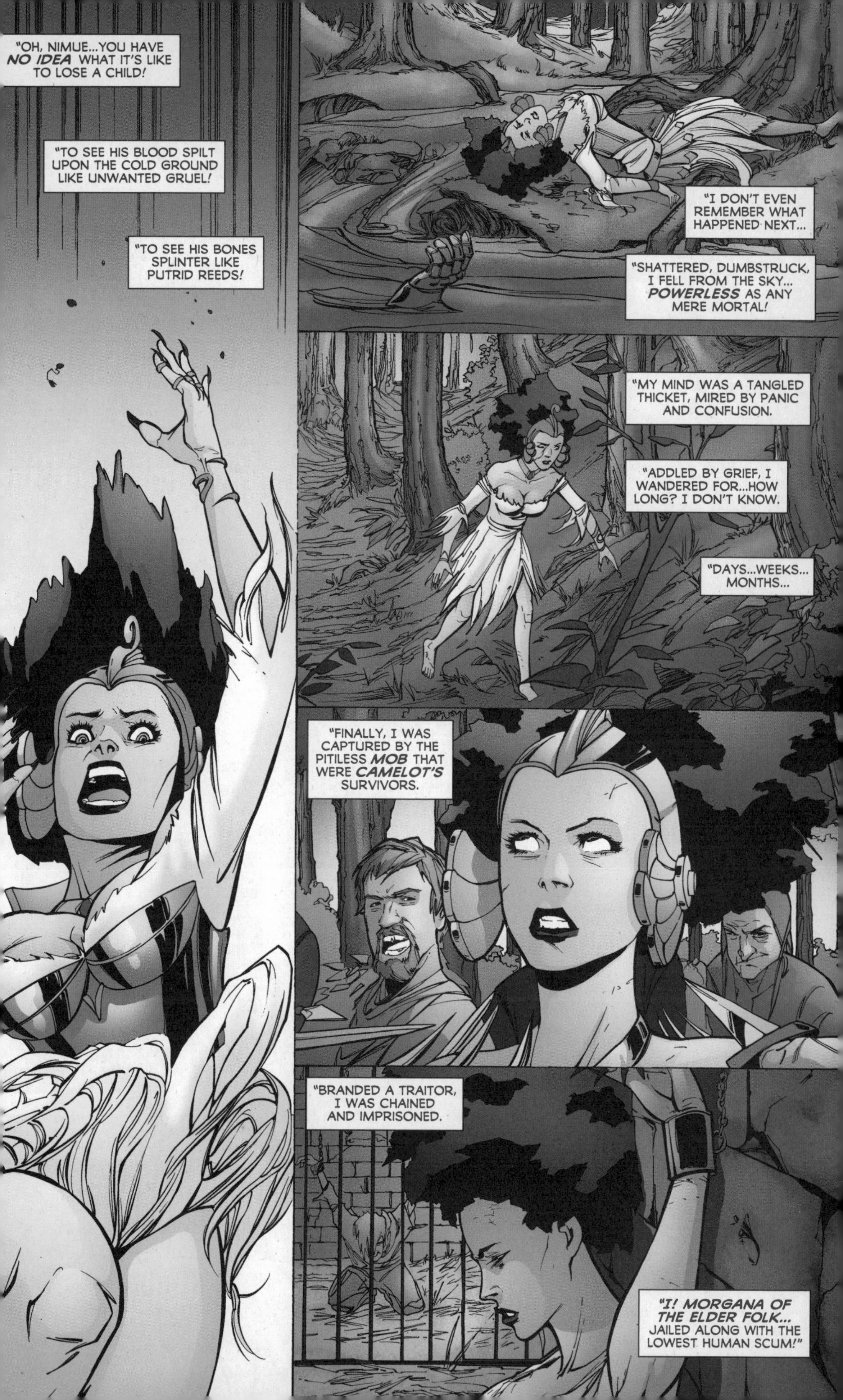
"OH, NIMUE...YOU HAVE NO IDEA WHAT IT'S LIKE TO LOSE A CHILD!
"TO SEE HIS BLOOD SPILT UPON THE COLD GROUND LIKE UNWANTED GRUEL!
"TO SEE HIS BONES SPLINTER LIKE PUTRID REEDS!
"I DON'T EVEN REMEMBER WHAT HAPPENED NEXT...
"SHATTERED, DUMBSTRUCK, I FELL FROM THE SKY... POWERLESS AS ANY MERE MORTAL!
"MY MIND WAS A TANGLED THICKET, MIRED BY PANIC AND CONFUSION.
"ADDLED BY GRIEF, I WANDERED FOR...HOW LONG? I DON'T KNOW.
"DAYS...WEEKS... MONTHS...
"FINALLY, I WAS CAPTURED BY THE PITILESS MOB THAT WERE CAMELOT'S SURVIVORS.
"BRANDED A TRAITOR, I WAS CHAINED AND IMPRISONED.
"I! MORGANA OF THE ELDER FOLK... JAILED ALONG WITH THE LOWEST HUMAN SCUM!"

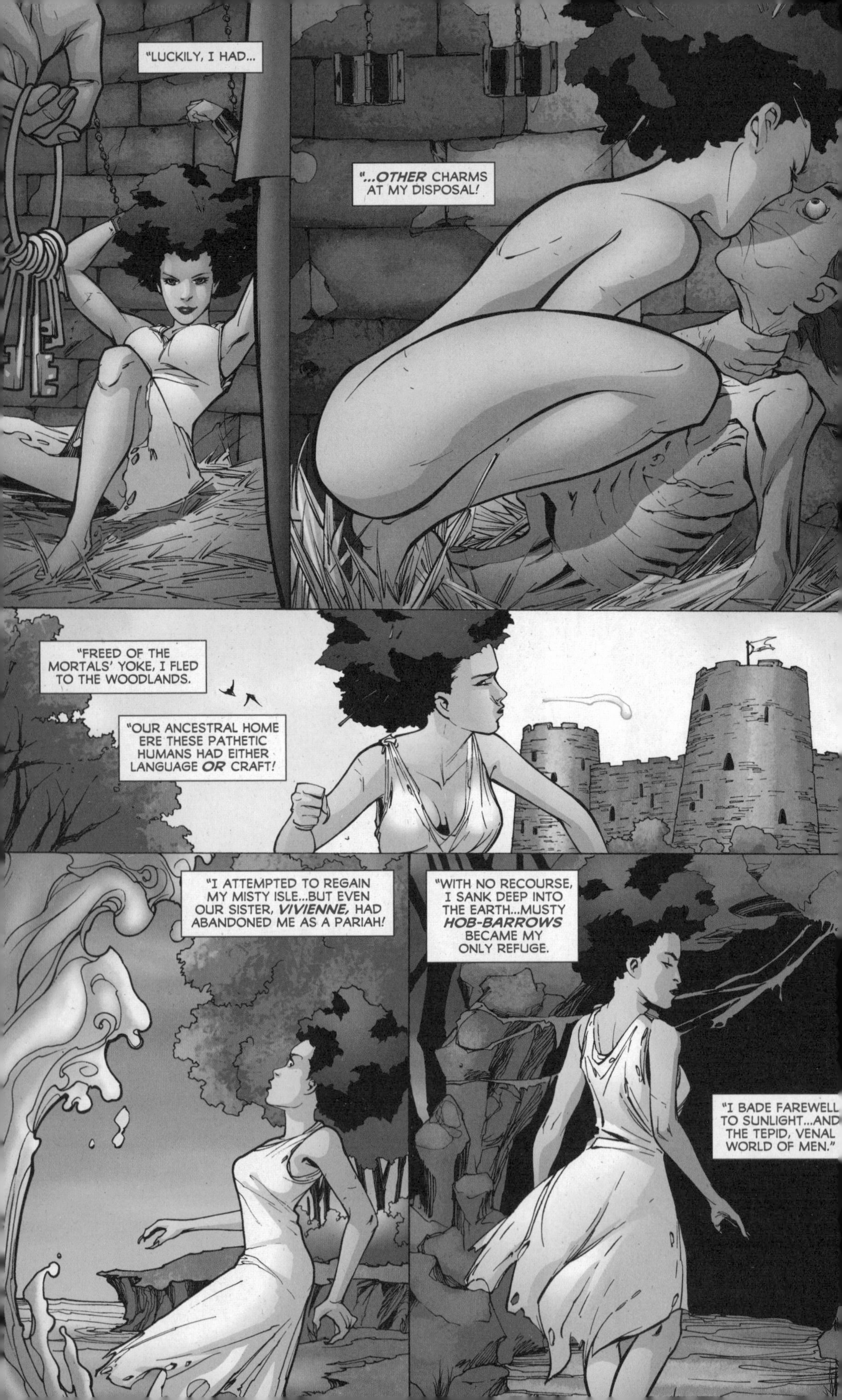
"LUCKILY, I HAD...
"...OTHER CHARMS AT MY DISPOSAL!
"FREED OF THE MORTALS' YOKE, I FLED TO THE WOODLANDS.
"OUR ANCESTRAL HOME ERE THESE PATHETIC HUMANS HAD EITHER LANGUAGE OR CRAFT!
"I ATTEMPTED TO REGAIN MY MISTY ISLE...BUT EVEN OUR SISTER, VIVIENNE, HAD ABANDONED ME AS A PARIAH!
"WITH NO RECOURSE, I SANK DEEP INTO THE EARTH...MUSTY HOB-BARROWS BECAME MY ONLY REFUGE.
"I BADE FAREWELL TO SUNLIGHT...AND THE TEPID, VENAL WORLD OF MEN."

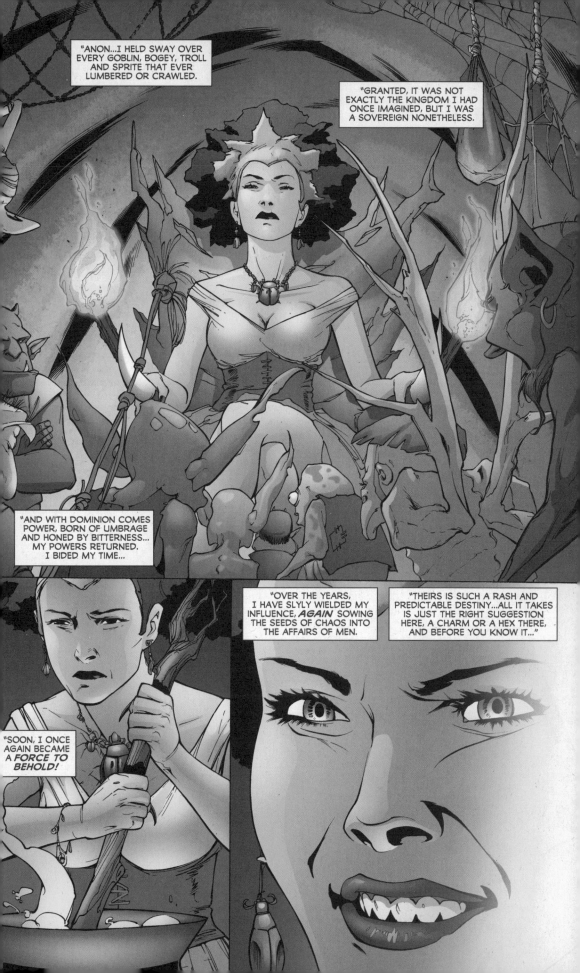

"ANON...I HELD SWAY OVER EVERY GOBLIN, BOGEY, TROLL AND SPRITE THAT EVER LUMBERED OR CRAWLED.

"GRANTED, IT WAS NOT EXACTLY THE KINGDOM I HAD ONCE IMAGINED, BUT I WAS A SOVEREIGN NONETHELESS.

"AND WITH DOMINION COMES POWER, BORN OF UMBRAGE AND HONED BY BITTERNESS... MY POWERS RETURNED. I BIDED MY TIME...

"OVER THE YEARS, I HAVE SLYLY WIELDED MY INFLUENCE, *AGAIN* SOWING THE SEEDS OF CHAOS INTO THE AFFAIRS OF MEN.

"THEIRS IS SUCH A RASH AND PREDICTABLE DESTINY...ALL IT TAKES IS JUST THE RIGHT SUGGESTION HERE, A CHARM OR A HEX THERE, AND BEFORE YOU KNOW IT..."

"SOON, I ONCE AGAIN BECAME A *FORCE TO BEHOLD!*

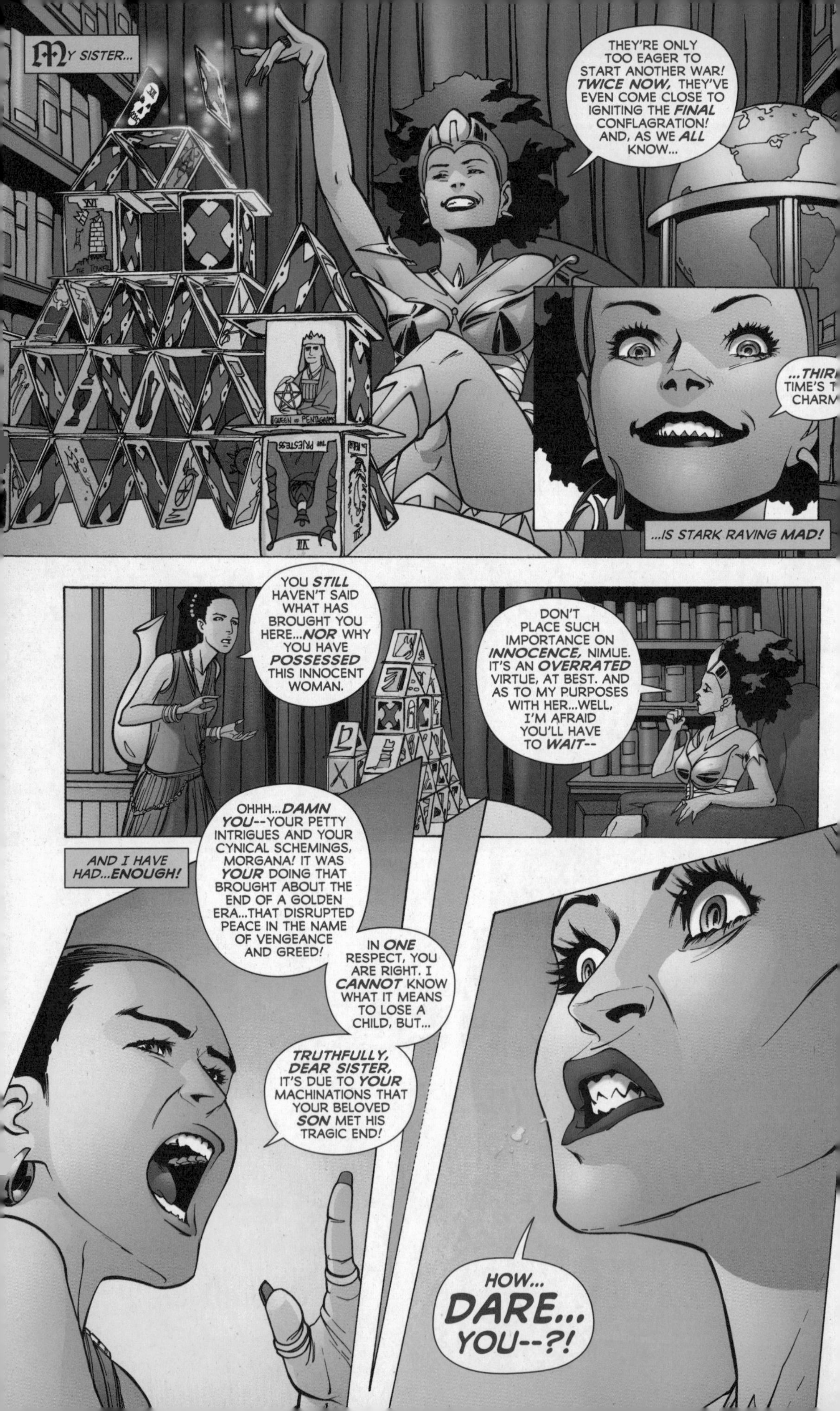
MY SISTER...
THEY'RE ONLY TOO EAGER TO START ANOTHER WAR! TWICE NOW, THEY'VE EVEN COME CLOSE TO IGNITING THE FINAL CONFLAGRATION! AND, AS WE ALL KNOW...
...THIR TIME'S T CHARM
...IS STARK RAVING MAD!
YOU STILL HAVEN'T SAID WHAT HAS BROUGHT YOU HERE...NOR WHY YOU HAVE POSSESSED THIS INNOCENT WOMAN.
DON'T PLACE SUCH IMPORTANCE ON INNOCENCE, NIMUE. IT'S AN OVERRATED VIRTUE, AT BEST. AND AS TO MY PURPOSES WITH HER...WELL, I'M AFRAID YOU'LL HAVE TO WAIT--
AND I HAVE HAD...ENOUGH!
OHHH...DAMN YOU--YOUR PETTY INTRIGUES AND YOUR CYNICAL SCHEMINGS, MORGANA! IT WAS YOUR DOING THAT BROUGHT ABOUT THE END OF A GOLDEN ERA...THAT DISRUPTED PEACE IN THE NAME OF VENGEANCE AND GREED!
IN ONE RESPECT, YOU ARE RIGHT. I CANNOT KNOW WHAT IT MEANS TO LOSE A CHILD, BUT...
TRUTHFULLY, DEAR SISTER, IT'S DUE TO YOUR MACHINATIONS THAT YOUR BELOVED SON MET HIS TRAGIC END!
HOW... DARE... YOU--?!

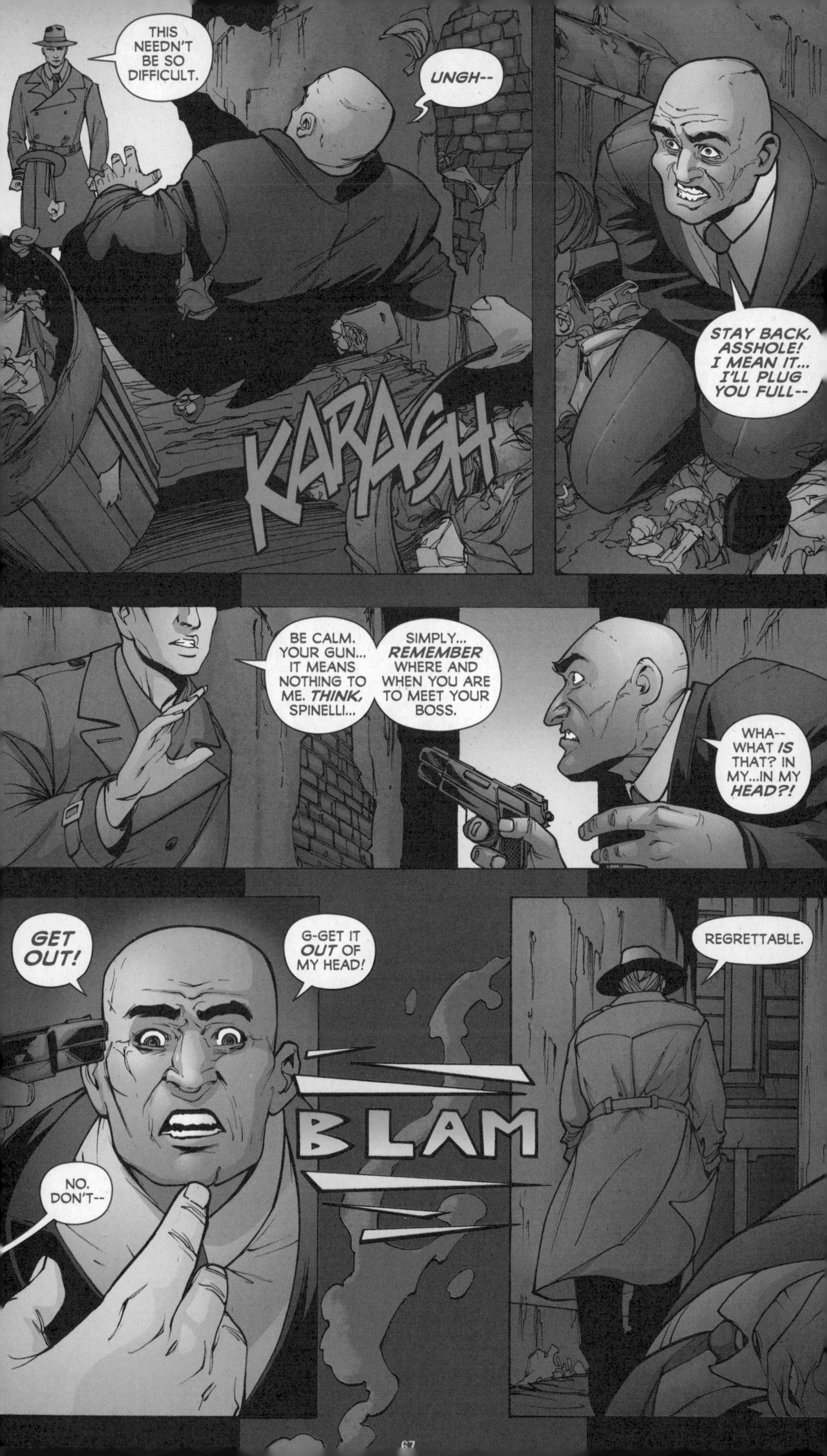
THIS NEEDN'T BE SO DIFFICULT.
UNGH--
KARASH
STAY BACK, ASSHOLE! I MEAN IT... I'LL PLUG YOU FULL--
BE CALM. YOUR GUN... IT MEANS NOTHING TO ME. THINK, SPINELLI...
SIMPLY... REMEMBER WHERE AND WHEN YOU ARE TO MEET YOUR BOSS.
WHA-- WHAT IS THAT? IN MY...IN MY HEAD?!
GET OUT!
G-GET IT OUT OF MY HEAD!
NO. DON'T--
BLAM
REGRETTABLE.

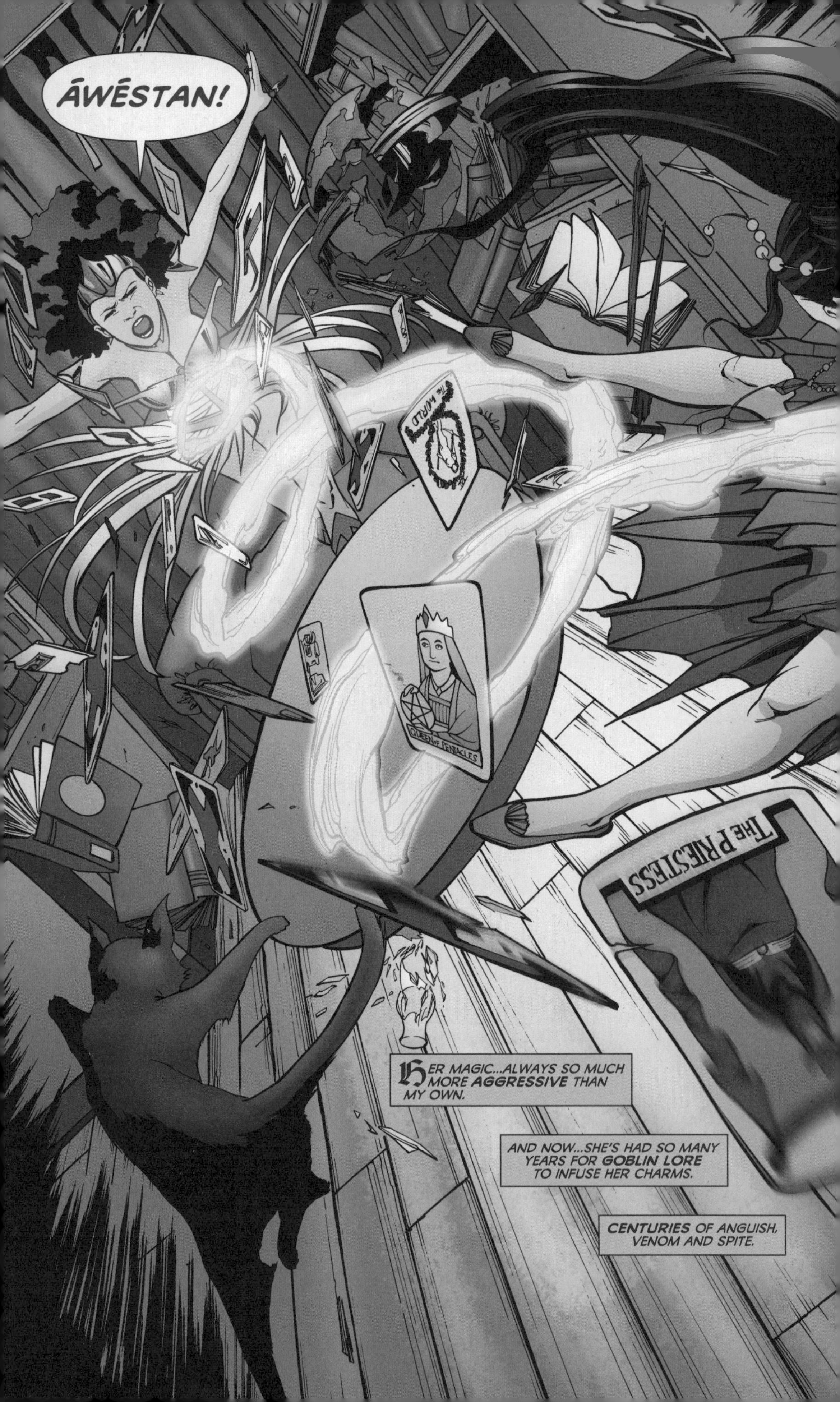
ĀWĒSTAN!
THE WORLD
QUEEN OF PENTACLES
THE PRIESTESS
HER MAGIC...ALWAYS SO MUCH MORE AGGRESSIVE THAN MY OWN.
AND NOW...SHE'S HAD SO MANY YEARS FOR GOBLIN LORE TO INFUSE HER CHARMS.
CENTURIES OF ANGUISH, VENOM AND SPITE.

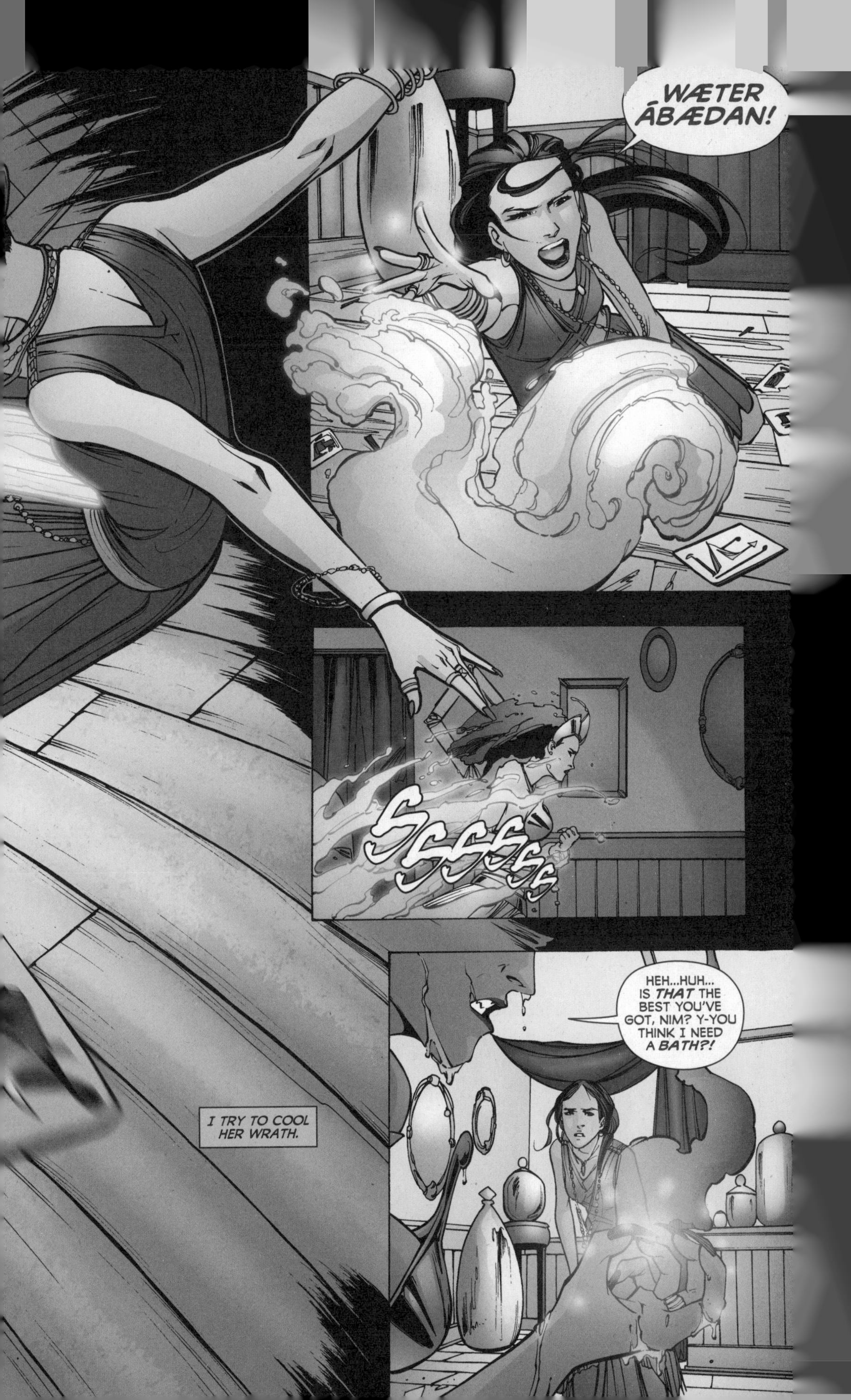
WÆTER ĀBÆDAN!
SSSSSSS
I TRY TO COOL HER WRATH.
HEH...HUH... IS THAT THE BEST YOU'VE GOT, NIM? Y-YOU THINK I NEED A BATH?!

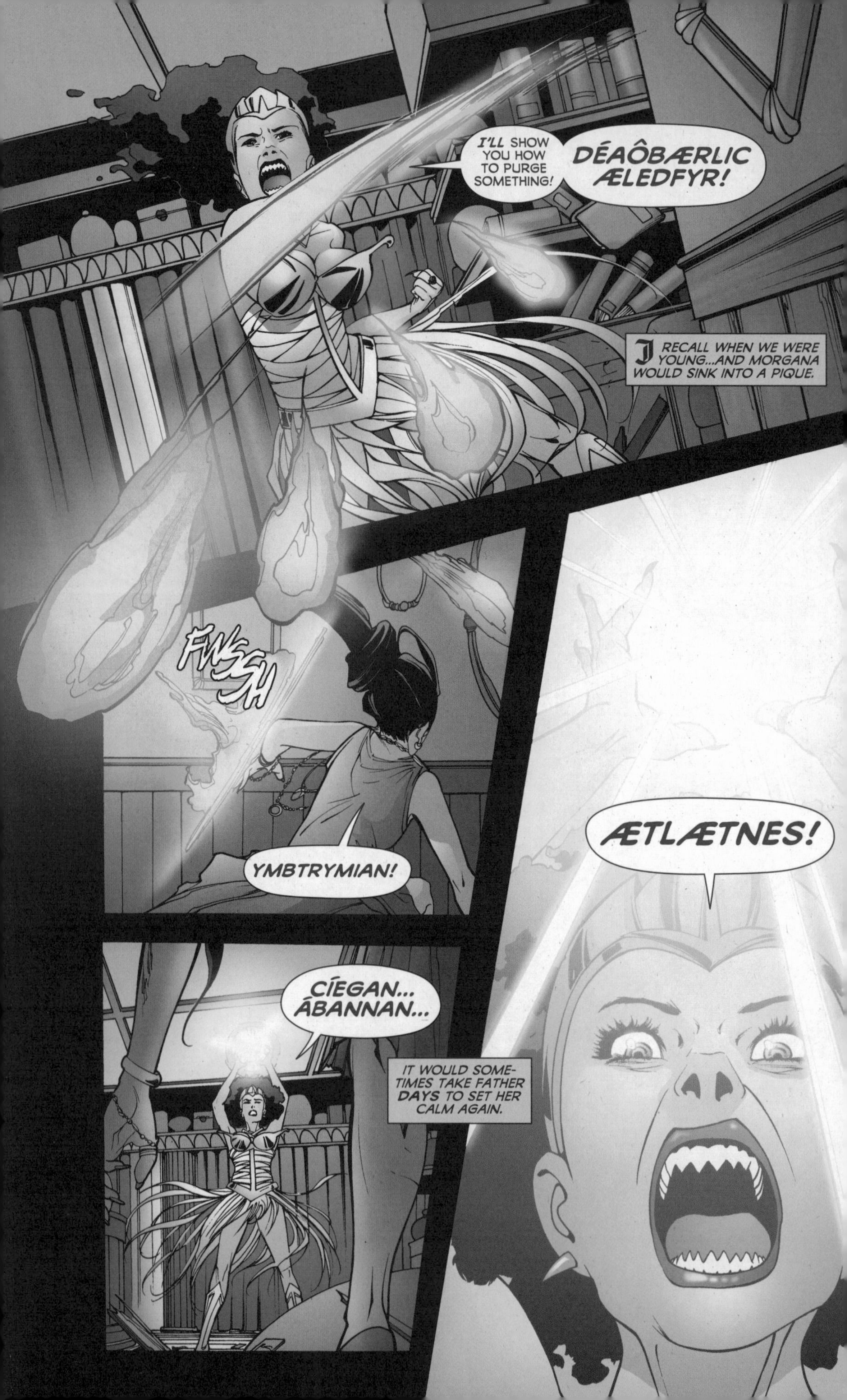
I'LL SHOW YOU HOW TO PURGE SOMETHING!
DÉAÔBÆRLIC ÆLEDFYR!
I RECALL WHEN WE WERE YOUNG...AND MORGANA WOULD SINK INTO A PIQUE.
FWSSH
YMBTRYMIAN!
ÆTLÆTNES!
CÍEGAN... ÁBANNAN...
IT WOULD SOMETIMES TAKE FATHER DAYS TO SET HER CALM AGAIN.

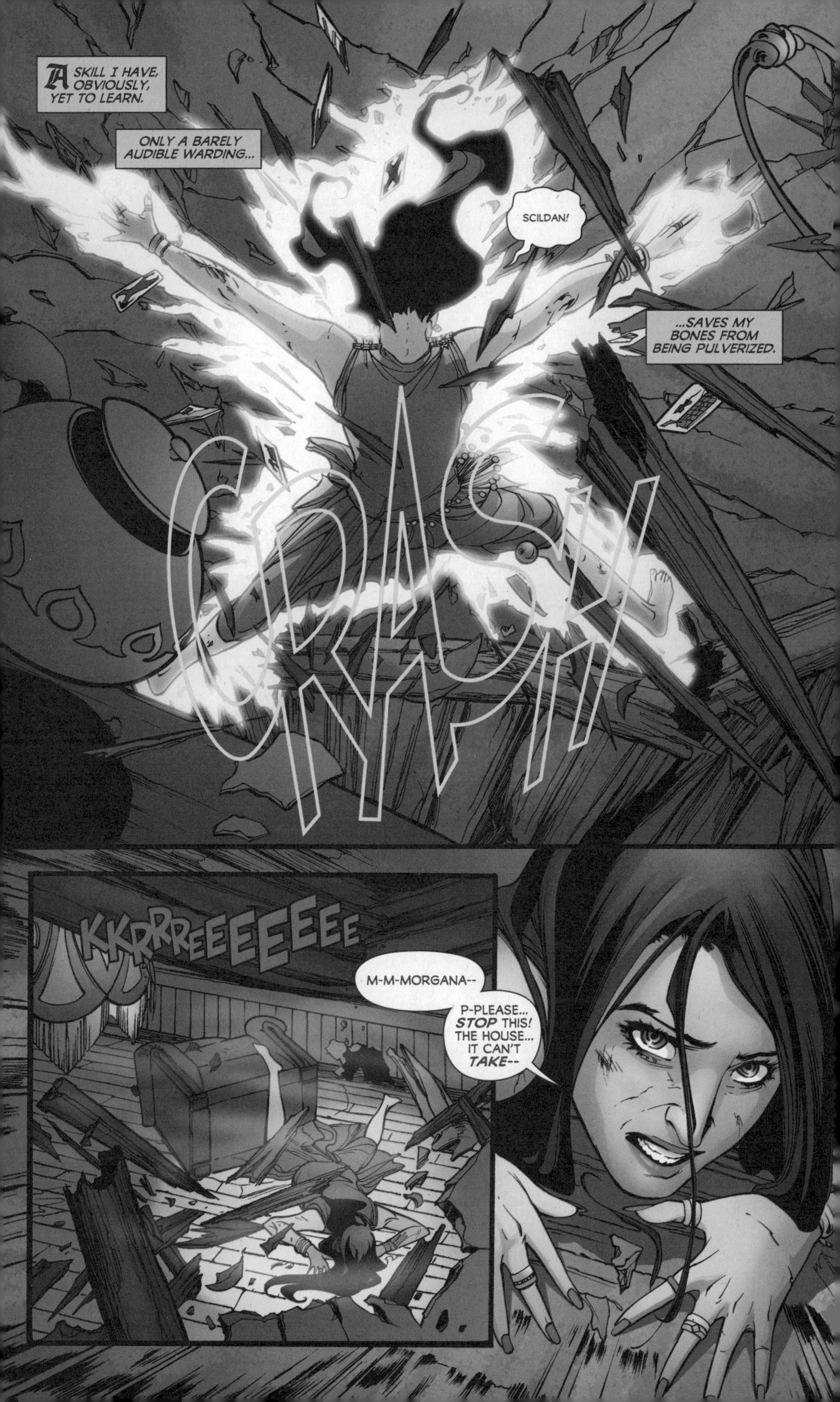
A SKILL I HAVE, OBVIOUSLY, YET TO LEARN.
ONLY A BARELY AUDIBLE WARDING...
SCILDAN!
...SAVES MY BONES FROM BEING PULVERIZED.
CRASH
KKRRREEEEEEe
M-M-MORGANA--
P-PLEASE... STOP THIS! THE HOUSE... IT CAN'T TAKE--

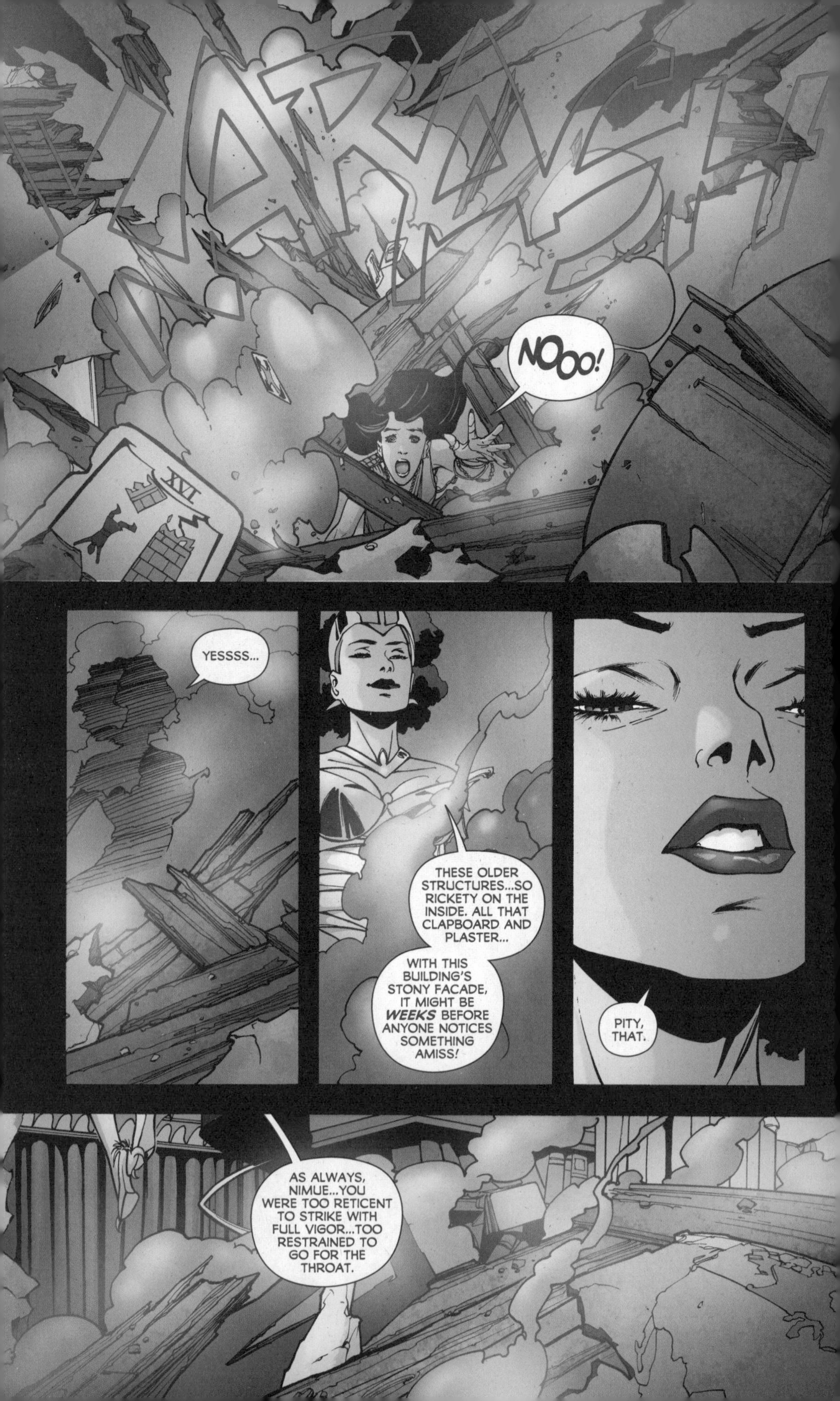
KRAASH
NOOO!
YESSSS...
THESE OLDER STRUCTURES...SO RICKETY ON THE INSIDE. ALL THAT CLAPBOARD AND PLASTER...
WITH THIS BUILDING'S STONY FACADE, IT MIGHT BE *WEEKS* BEFORE ANYONE NOTICES SOMETHING AMISS!
PITY, THAT.
AS ALWAYS, NIMUE...YOU WERE TOO RETICENT TO STRIKE WITH FULL VIGOR...TOO RESTRAINED TO GO FOR THE THROAT.

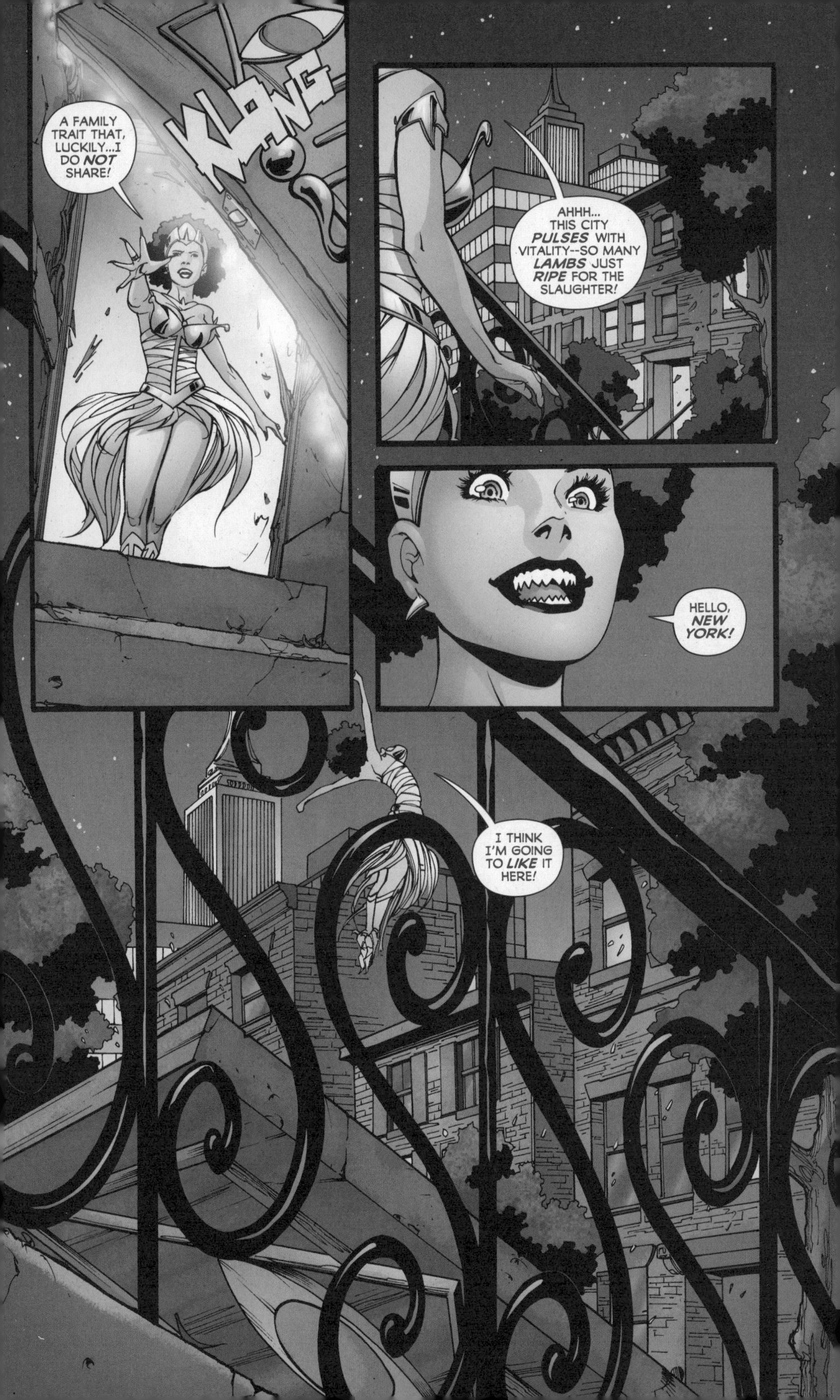
KLANG
A FAMILY TRAIT THAT, LUCKILY...I DO NOT SHARE!
AHHH... THIS CITY PULSES WITH VITALITY--SO MANY LAMBS JUST RIPE FOR THE SLAUGHTER!
HELLO, NEW YORK!
I THINK I'M GOING TO LIKE IT HERE!

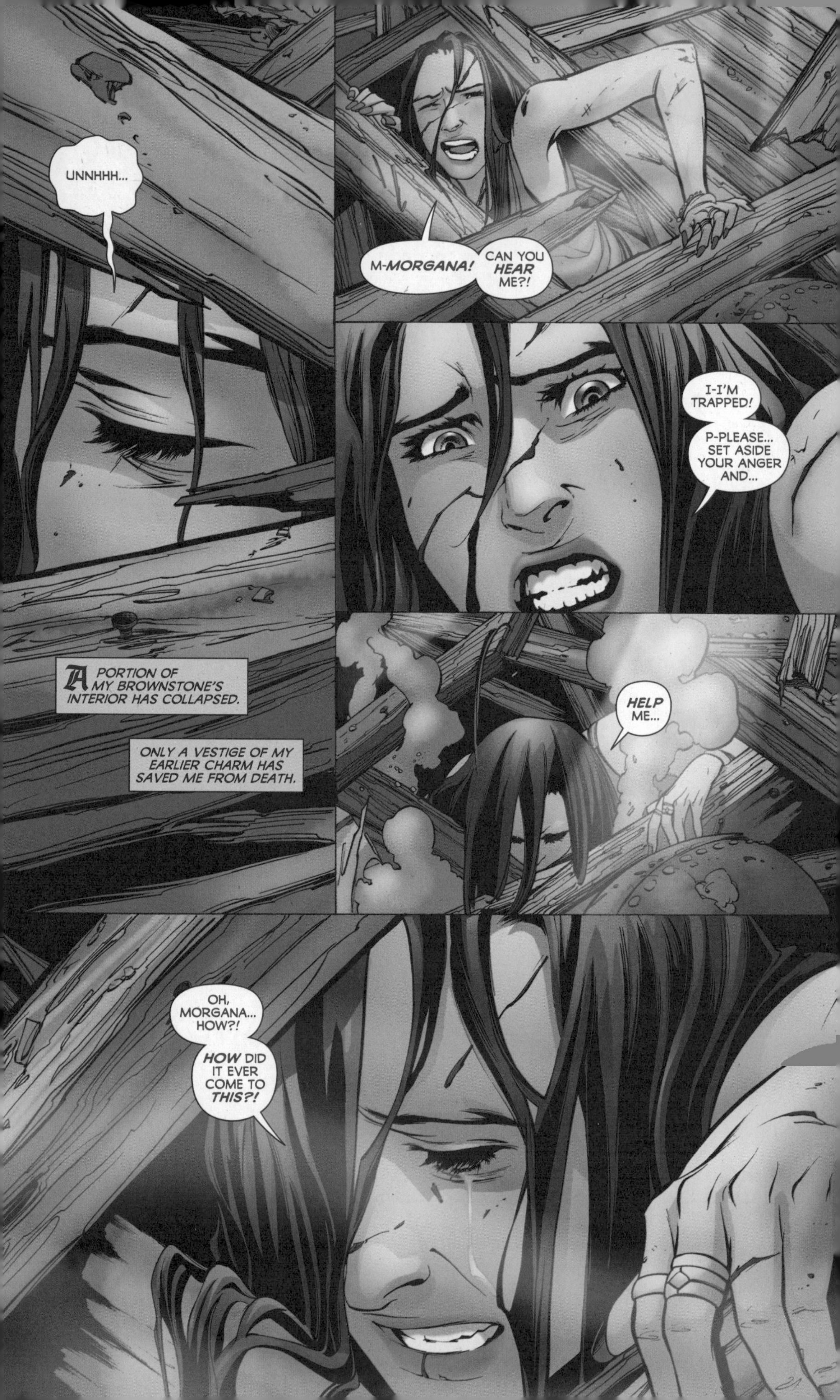

UNNHHH...
M-MORGANA!
CAN YOU HEAR ME?!
I-I'M TRAPPED!
P-PLEASE... SET ASIDE YOUR ANGER AND...
A PORTION OF MY BROWNSTONE'S INTERIOR HAS COLLAPSED.
ONLY A VESTIGE OF MY EARLIER CHARM HAS SAVED ME FROM DEATH.
HELP ME...
OH, MORGANA... HOW?!
HOW DID IT EVER COME TO THIS?!

Chapter Four: Squabbles and Spells

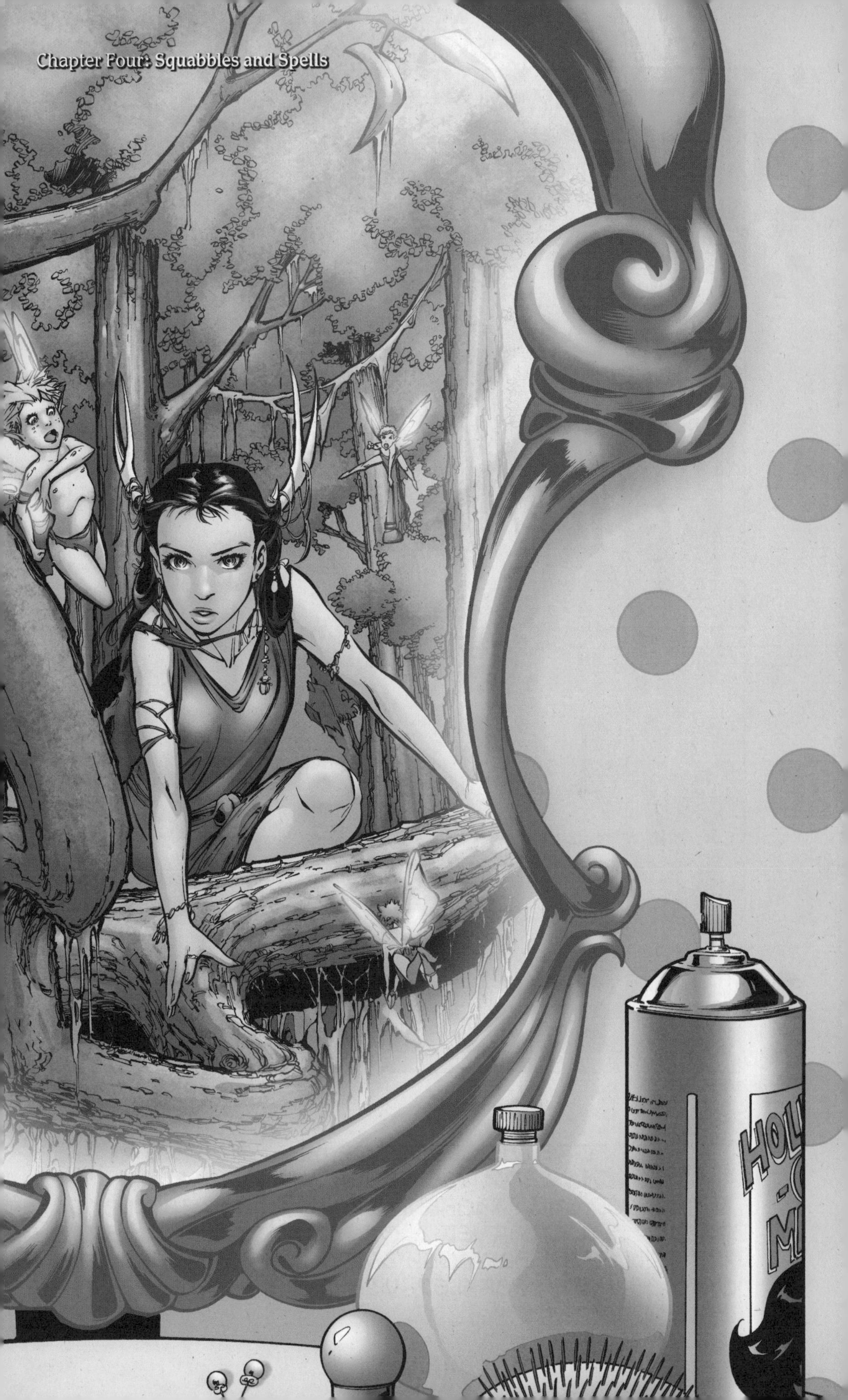

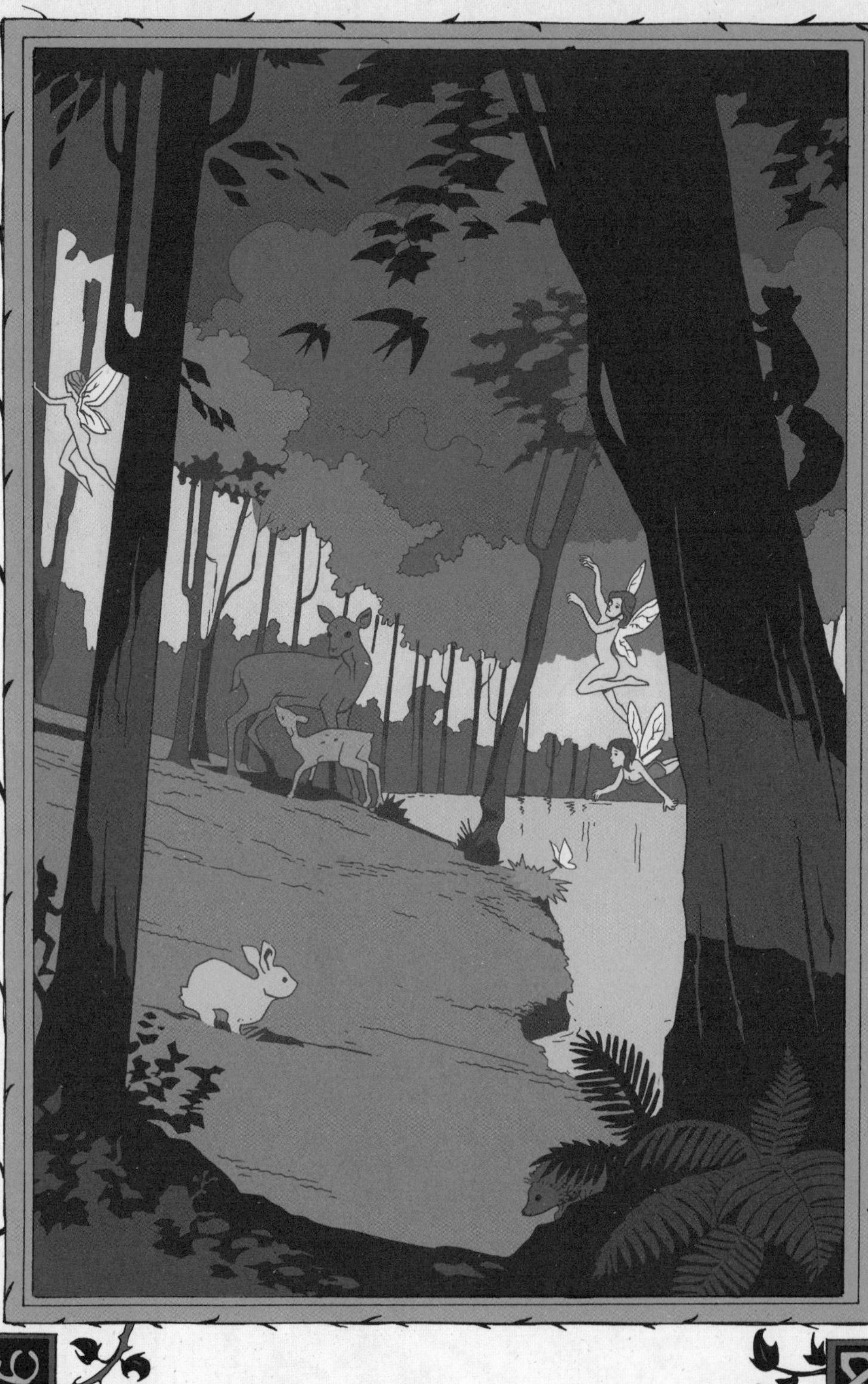

AFORE THE ADVENT OF MAGI OR MAN, **THE LAND** WAS GREEN AND PLEASANT, SUN-KISSED AND FRAGRANT, TRANQUIL AND ABUNDANT. BIRD AND BEAST THRIVED ALONGSIDE FAIRY-KIND AS THE WIND TRILLED ITS HARMONY AMONG THE TREES AND THE MORNINGS WERE SPARKLED WITH THE BLESSINGS OF DEW.

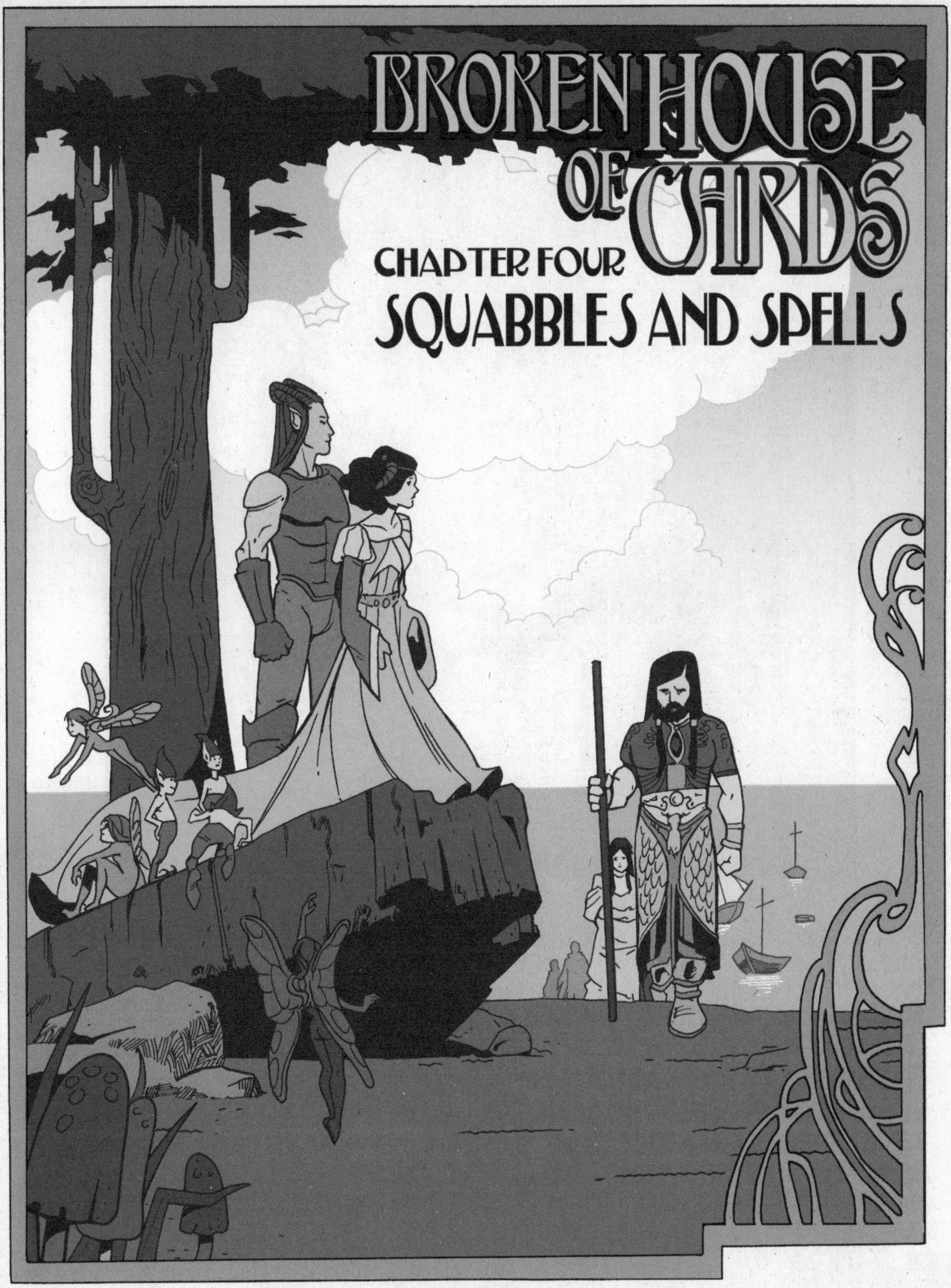
BROKEN HOUSE OF CARDS
CHAPTER FOUR
SQUABBLES AND SPELLS

But anon came the great cataclysm and the isle of *Atlantis*, mystical helix of arcane energies, sank into the sea. The refugees, magicians all, were welcomed of great *Oberon* and fair *Titania*. Thus *The Land*, timeless and chaste, at last felt the terrible footfalls of history.

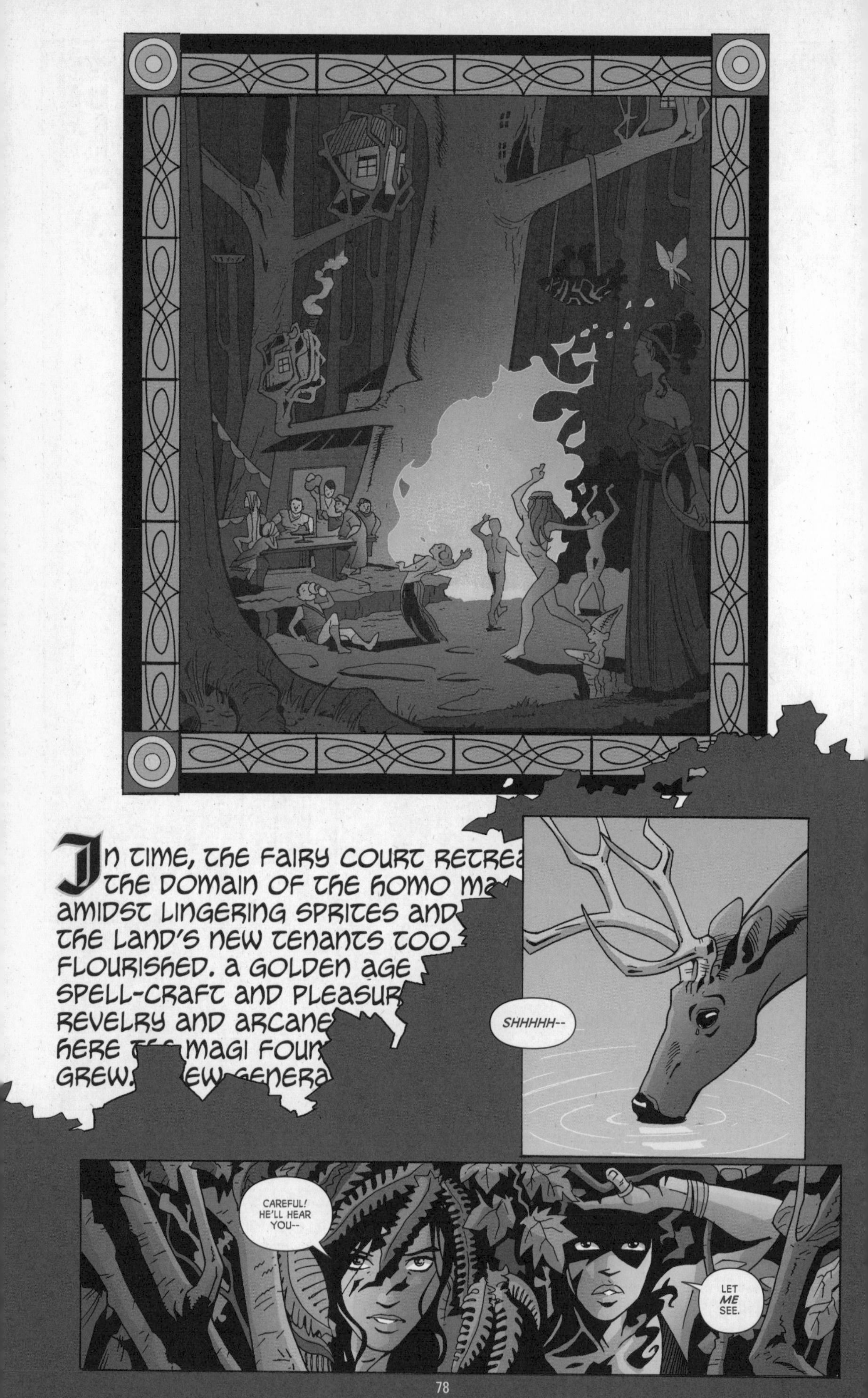
IN TIME, THE FAIRY COURT RETREA
THE DOMAIN OF THE HOMO MA
AMIDST LINGERING SPRITES AND
THE LAND'S NEW TENANTS TOO
FLOURISHED. A GOLDEN AGE
SPELL-CRAFT AND PLEASUR
REVELRY AND ARCANE
HERE MAGI FOUN
GREW.
SHHHHH--
CAREFUL! HE'LL HEAR YOU--
LET *ME* SEE.

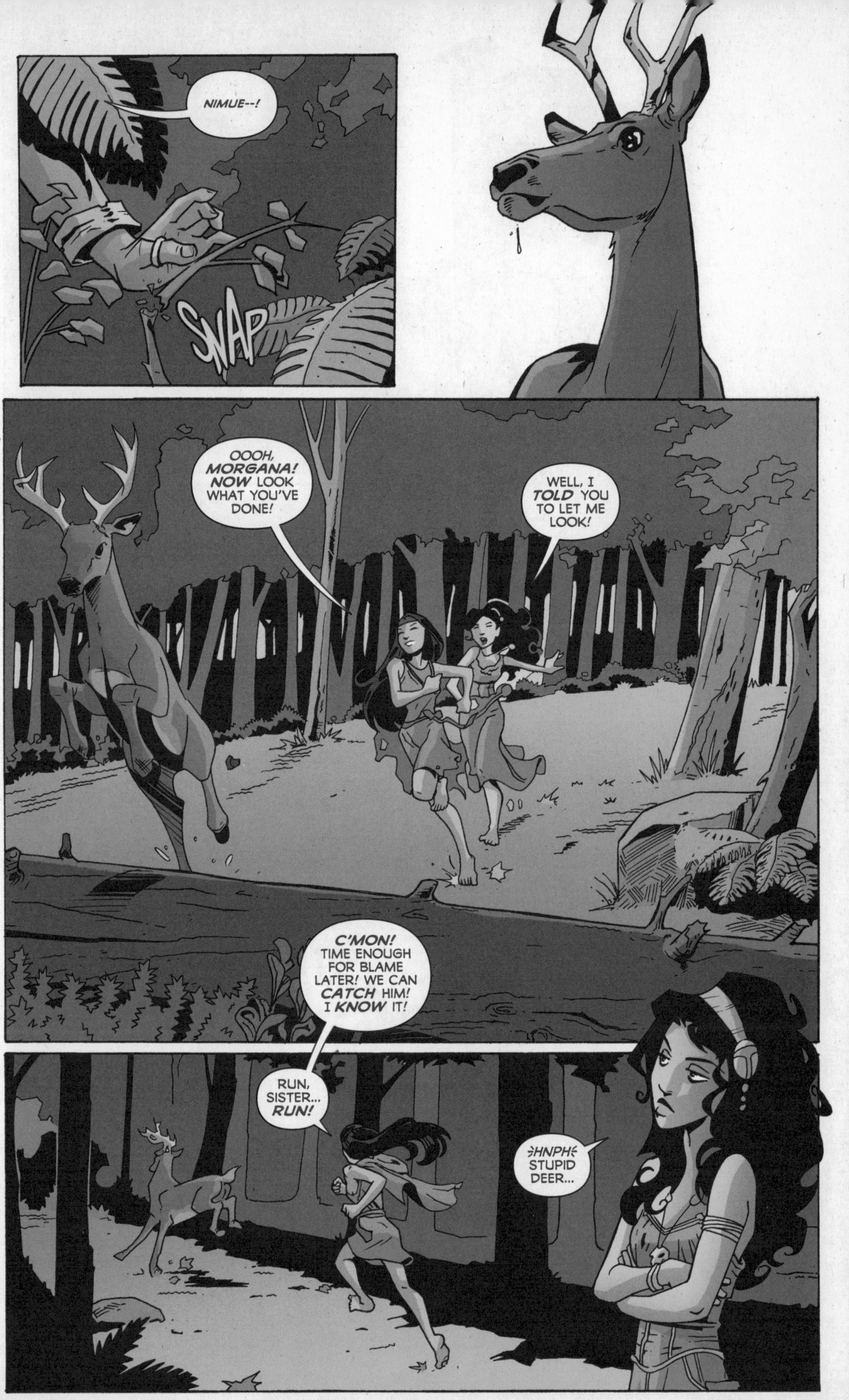
NIMUE--!
SNAP
OOOH, MORGANA! NOW LOOK WHAT YOU'VE DONE!
WELL, I TOLD YOU TO LET ME LOOK!
C'MON! TIME ENOUGH FOR BLAME LATER! WE CAN CATCH HIM! I KNOW IT!
RUN, SISTER... RUN!
HNPH STUPID DEER...

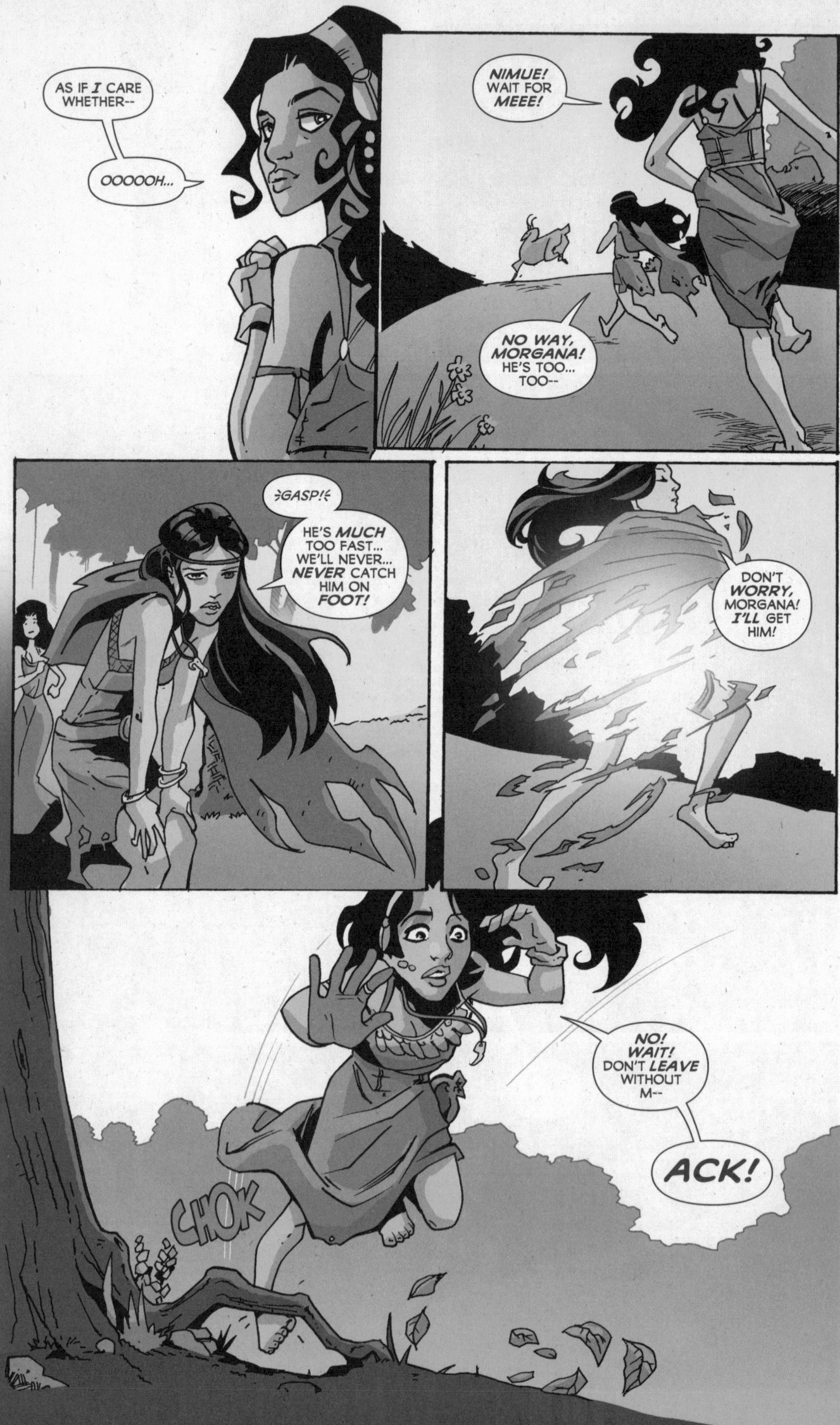

AS IF *I* CARE WHETHER--
OOOOOH...
NIMUE! WAIT FOR *MEEE!*
NO WAY, MORGANA! HE'S TOO... TOO--
GASP!
HE'S *MUCH* TOO FAST... WE'LL NEVER... *NEVER* CATCH HIM ON *FOOT!*
DON'T *WORRY,* MORGANA! *I'LL* GET HIM!
NO! WAIT! DON'T *LEAVE* WITHOUT M--
ACK!
CHOK

BLESSED MOON! WHERE HAS SHE GONE--?!

YESSSS... JUST LOOK AT *YOU*, DEAR NIMUE.

MORGANA! LOOK AT HIM! LOOK AT ME!

OHHH... ISN'T HE *BEAUTIFUL?!*

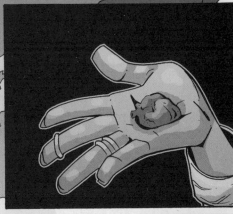

UPSTAGING YOUR *ELDER* SISTER.

NÍEDNÆM!

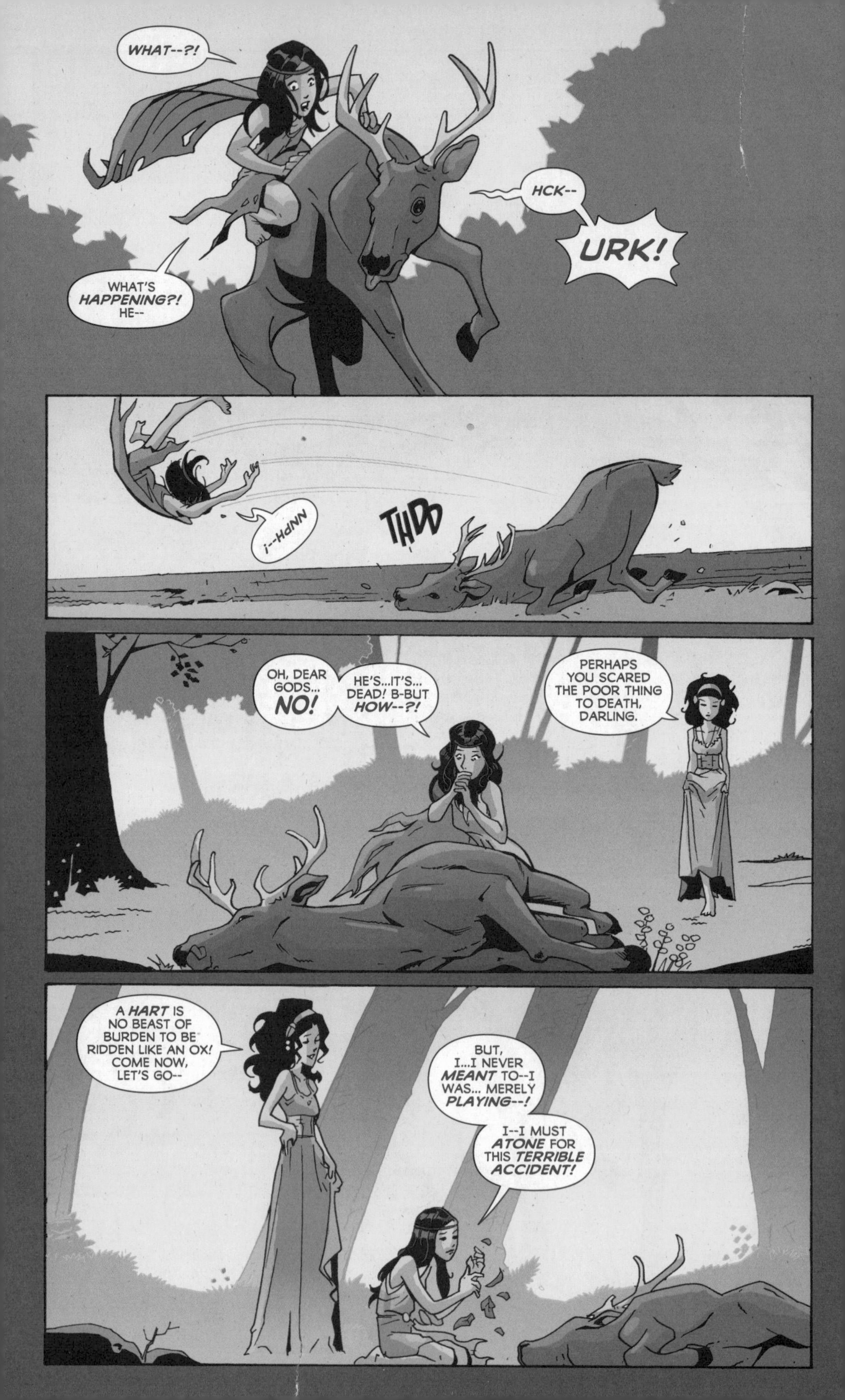
WHAT--?!
HCK--
URK!
WHAT'S HAPPENING?! HE--
NNGH--!
THDD
OH, DEAR GODS... NO!
HE'S...IT'S... DEAD! B-BUT HOW--?!
PERHAPS YOU SCARED THE POOR THING TO DEATH, DARLING.
A HART IS NO BEAST OF BURDEN TO BE RIDDEN LIKE AN OX! COME NOW, LET'S GO--
BUT, I...I NEVER MEANT TO--I WAS... MERELY PLAYING--!
I--I MUST ATONE FOR THIS TERRIBLE ACCIDENT!

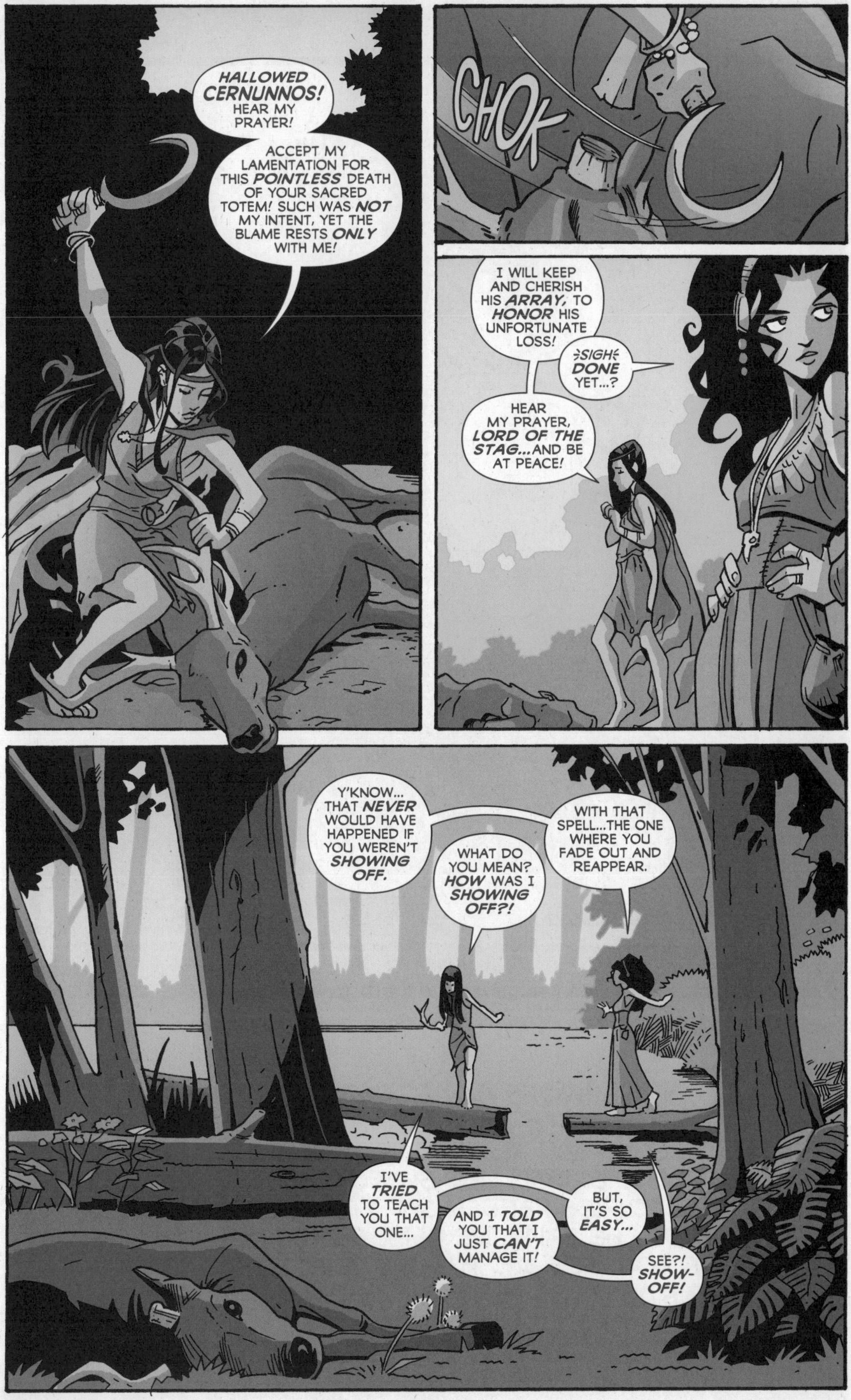
HALLOWED CERNUNNOS! HEAR MY PRAYER!
ACCEPT MY LAMENTATION FOR THIS POINTLESS DEATH OF YOUR SACRED TOTEM! SUCH WAS NOT MY INTENT, YET THE BLAME RESTS ONLY WITH ME!
CHOK
I WILL KEEP AND CHERISH HIS ARRAY, TO HONOR HIS UNFORTUNATE LOSS!
SIGH DONE YET...?
HEAR MY PRAYER, LORD OF THE STAG...AND BE AT PEACE!
Y'KNOW... THAT NEVER WOULD HAVE HAPPENED IF YOU WEREN'T SHOWING OFF.
WHAT DO YOU MEAN? HOW WAS I SHOWING OFF?!
WITH THAT SPELL...THE ONE WHERE YOU FADE OUT AND REAPPEAR.
I'VE TRIED TO TEACH YOU THAT ONE...
AND I TOLD YOU THAT I JUST CAN'T MANAGE IT!
BUT, IT'S SO EASY...
SEE?! SHOW-OFF!

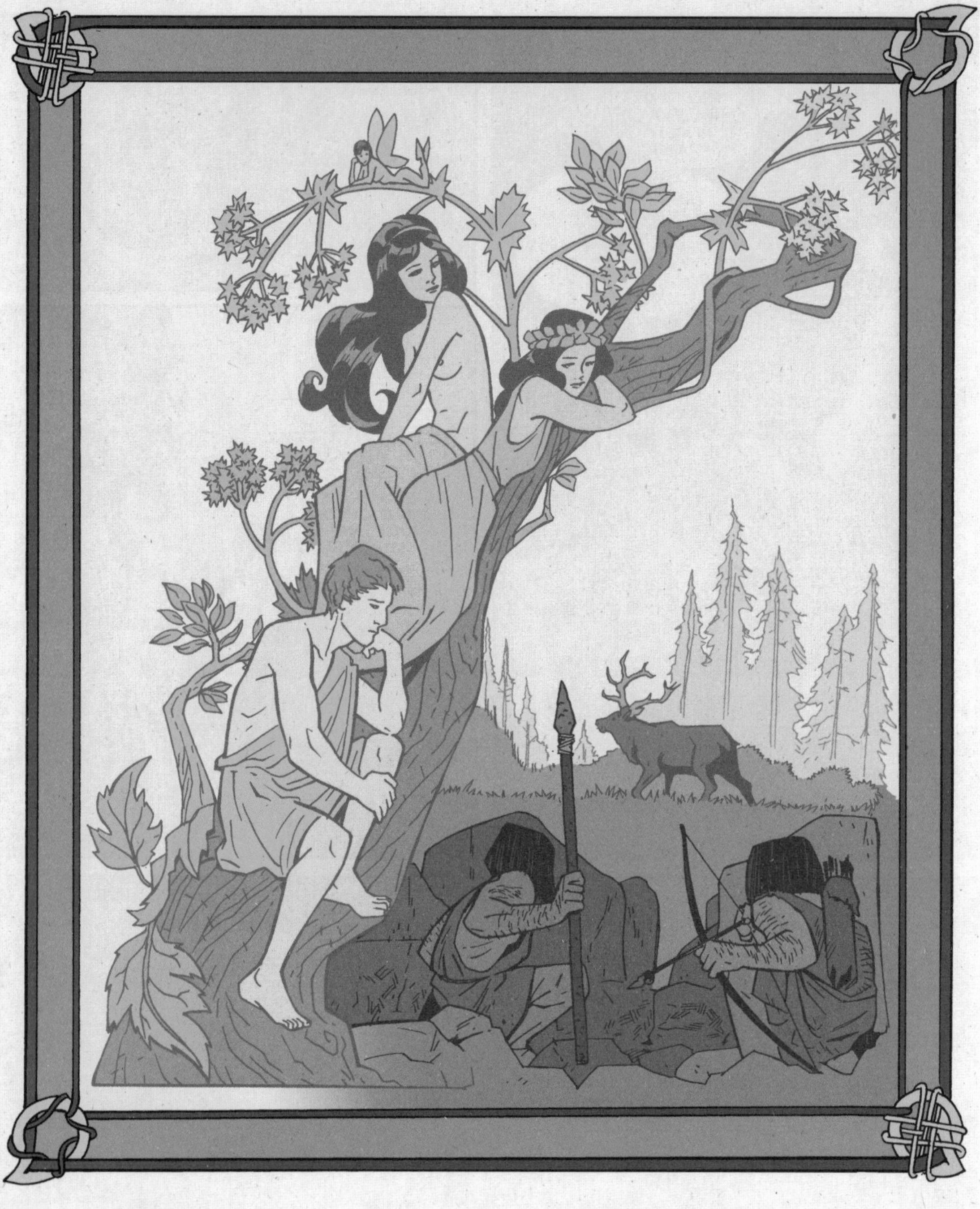

The wayworn *Homo Magi* wallowed in *The Land's* enchanting embrace. Their elixired youth and ready sorcery bred a perennial languor, a life unsullied by woefulness, worry or want. Centuries passed and they took but little notice of the primitive beings that now ran o'er the forests and hills, dwelling in caves, striking up fires. "*Man*" had also arrived.

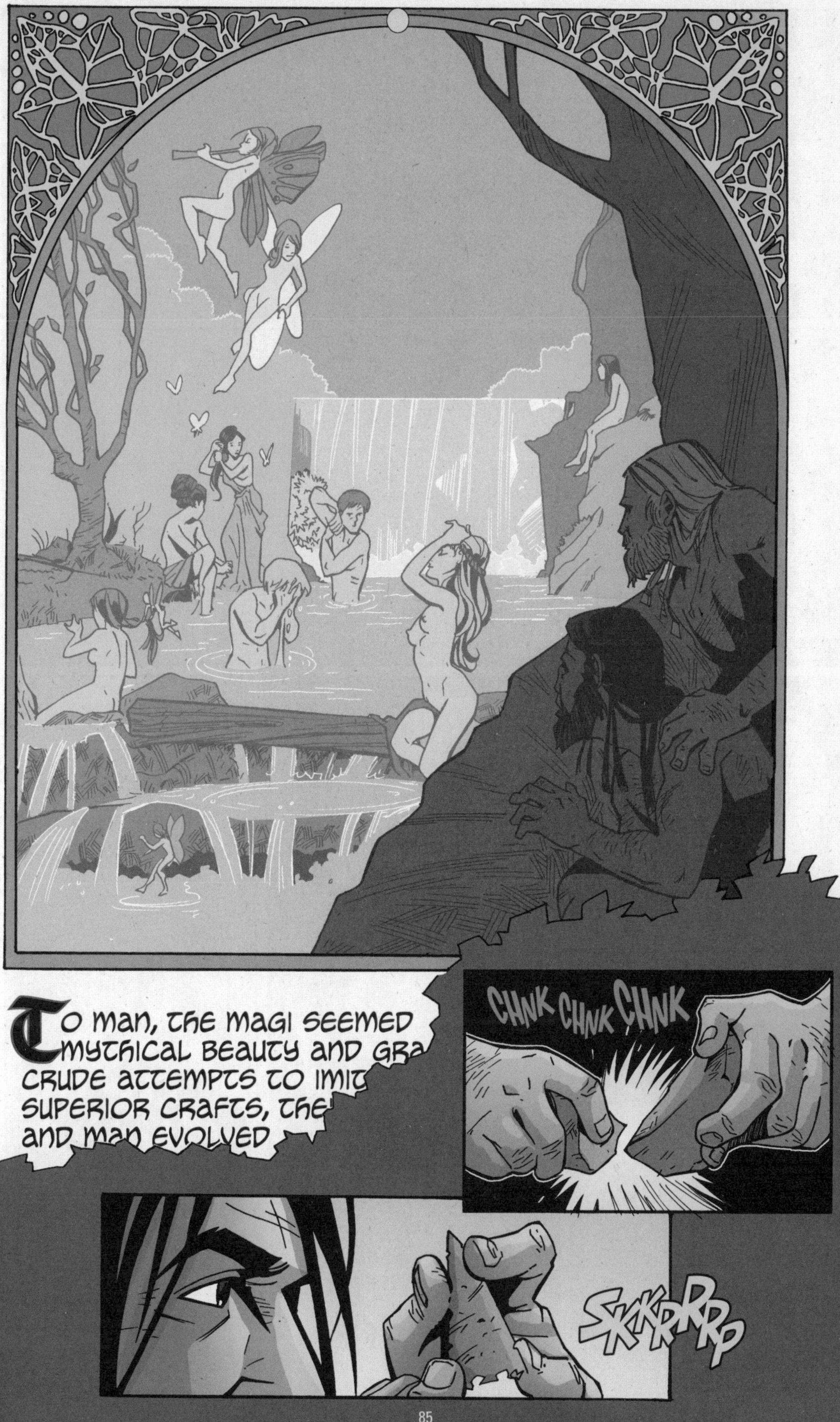

TO MAN, THE MAGI SEEMED
MYTHICAL BEAUTY AND GRA
CRUDE ATTEMPTS TO IMIT
SUPERIOR CRAFTS, THE
AND MAN EVOLVED
CHNK CHNK CHNK
SKKRRRP

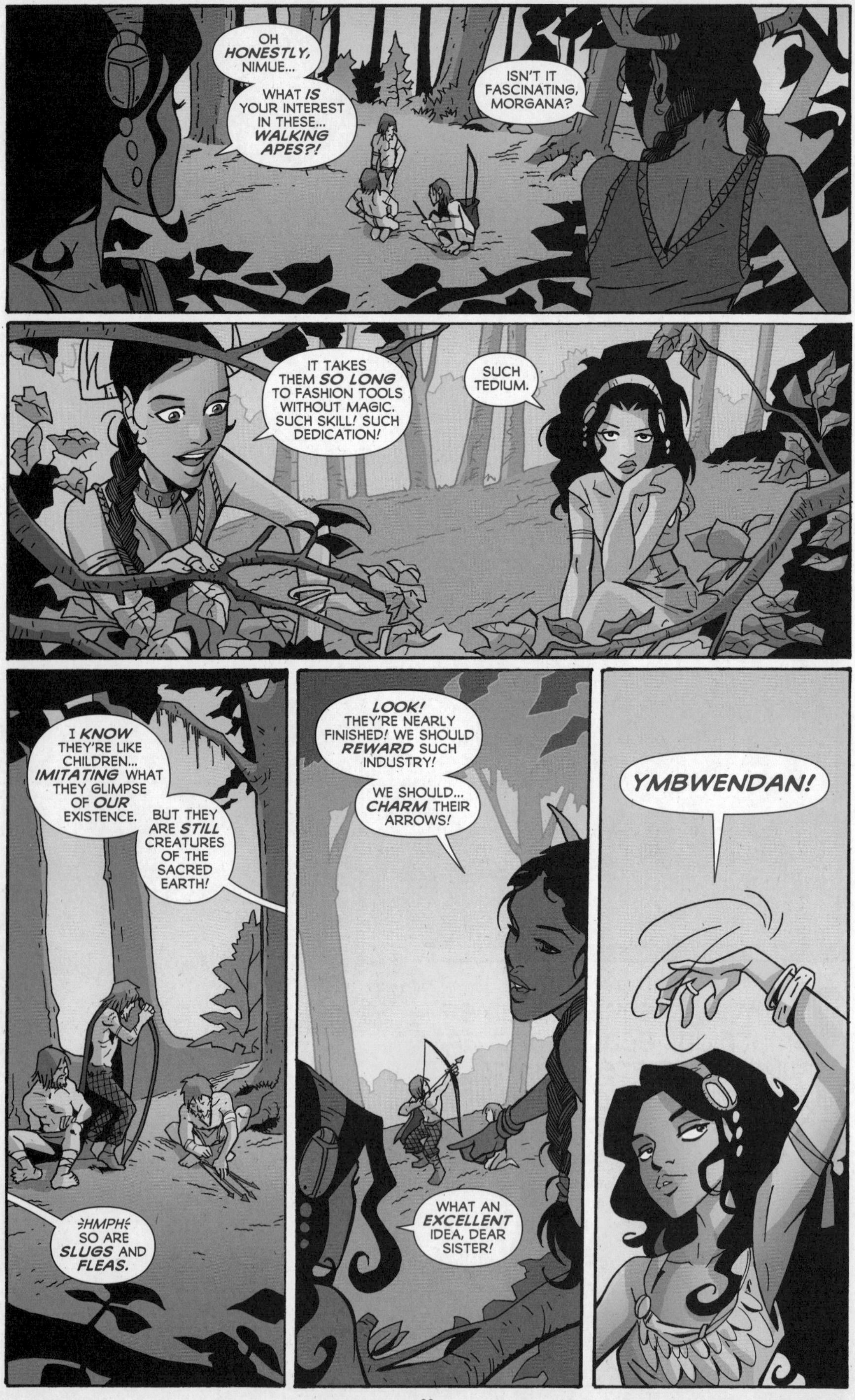
OH HONESTLY, NIMUE...
WHAT IS YOUR INTEREST IN THESE... WALKING APES?!
ISN'T IT FASCINATING, MORGANA?
IT TAKES THEM SO LONG TO FASHION TOOLS WITHOUT MAGIC. SUCH SKILL! SUCH DEDICATION!
SUCH TEDIUM.
I KNOW THEY'RE LIKE CHILDREN... IMITATING WHAT THEY GLIMPSE OF OUR EXISTENCE.
BUT THEY ARE STILL CREATURES OF THE SACRED EARTH!
HMPH SO ARE SLUGS AND FLEAS.
LOOK! THEY'RE NEARLY FINISHED! WE SHOULD REWARD SUCH INDUSTRY!
WE SHOULD... CHARM THEIR ARROWS!
WHAT AN EXCELLENT IDEA, DEAR SISTER!
YMBWENDAN!

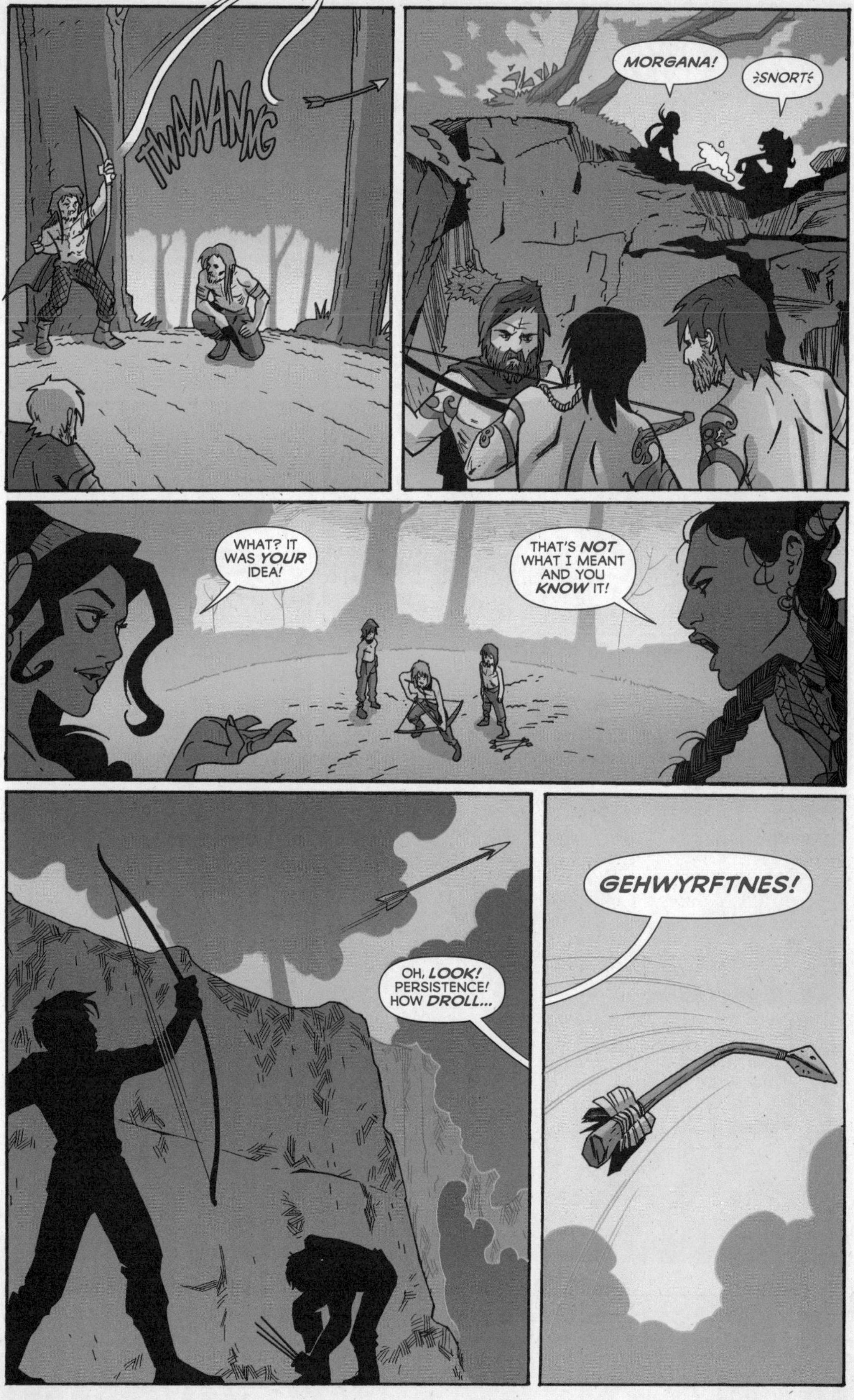
TWAAANNG
MORGANA!
SNORT
WHAT? IT WAS YOUR IDEA!
THAT'S NOT WHAT I MEANT AND YOU KNOW IT!
OH, LOOK! PERSISTENCE! HOW DROLL...
GEHWYRFTNES!

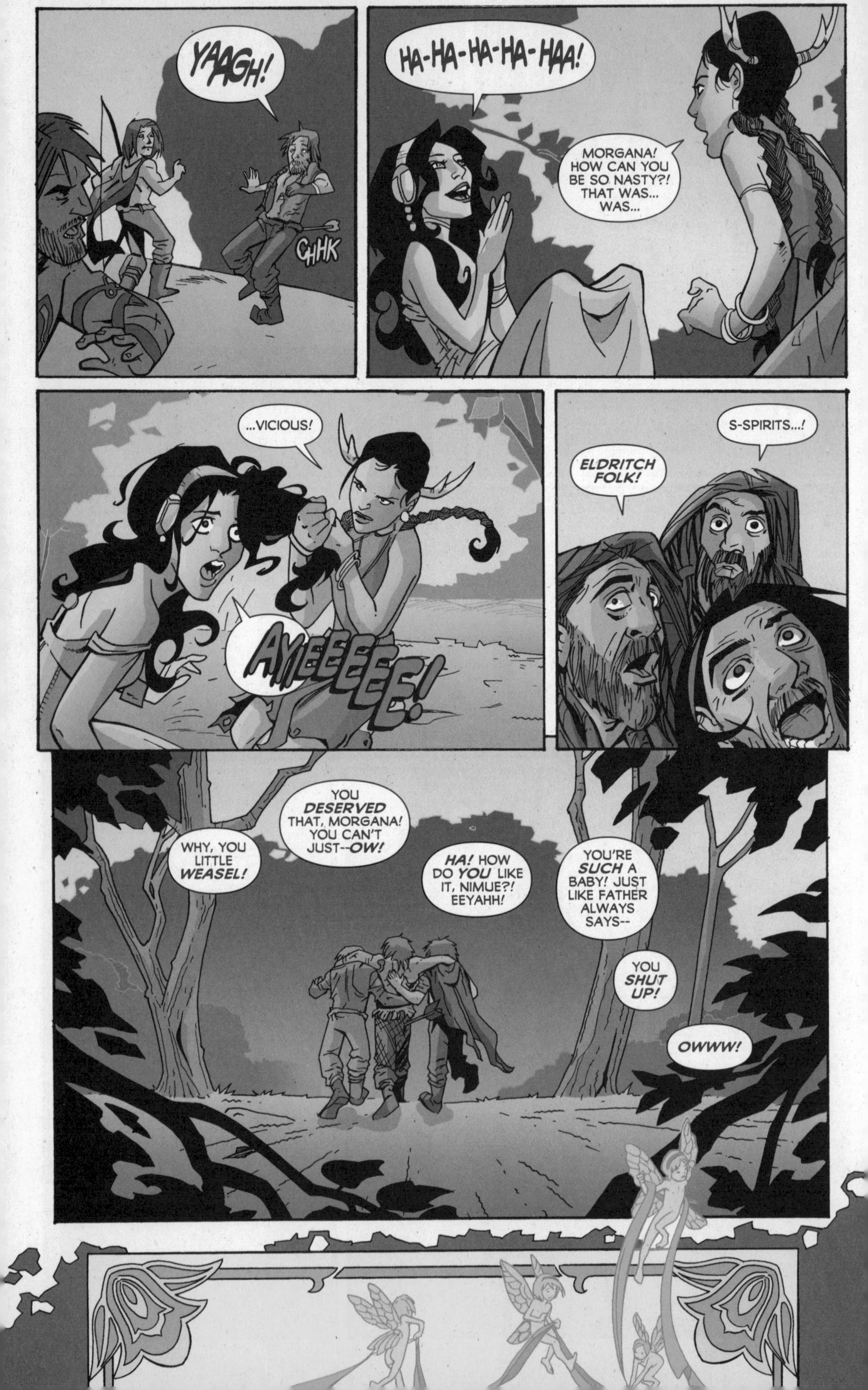
YAAGH!
CHHK
HA-HA-HA-HA-HAA!
MORGANA! HOW CAN YOU BE SO NASTY?! THAT WAS... WAS...
...VICIOUS!
AYIEEEEEE!
ELDRITCH FOLK!
S-SPIRITS...!
WHY, YOU LITTLE WEASEL!
YOU DESERVED THAT, MORGANA! YOU CAN'T JUST--OW!
HA! HOW DO YOU LIKE IT, NIMUE?! EEYAHH!
YOU'RE SUCH A BABY! JUST LIKE FATHER ALWAYS SAYS--
YOU SHUT UP!
OWWW!

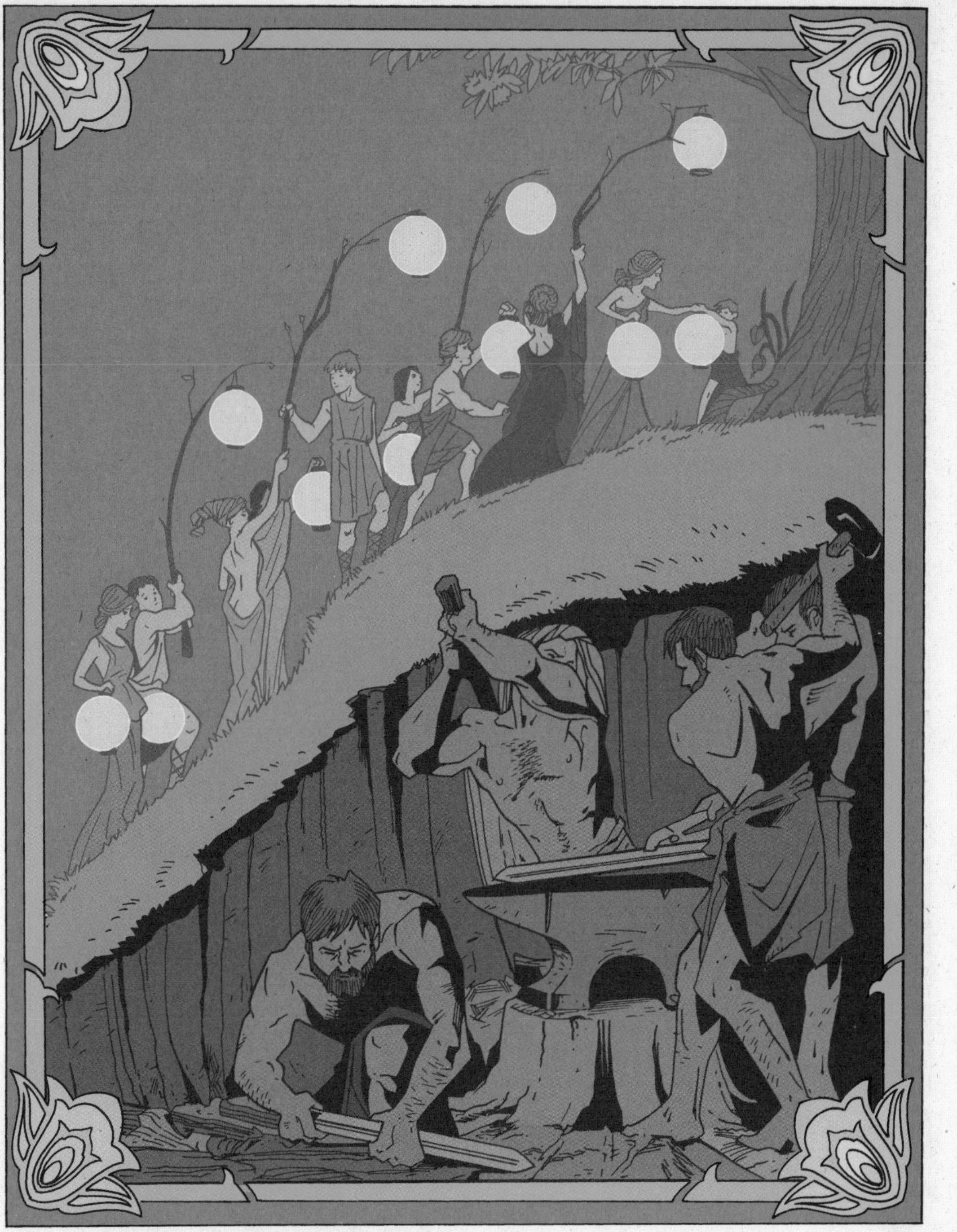

DRIVEN BY NEED, HAMPERED BY THEIR OWN LIMITATIONS, ***MANKIND*** PERSISTED IN THEIR QUEST FOR PROGRESS. THROUGH THE AGES OF STONE AND BRONZE UNTO THE SMELTING OF IRON--BANE OF ALL MAGIC AND HARDEST OF ALL CREATIONS--THEY BUILT AND BRED, NO LONGER SO FEARFUL OF THEIR MYSTIC COUSINS. AS ***THE ELDER FOLK*** FROLICKED AND DREAMT, ***MAN*** CONQUERED ***THE LAND***.

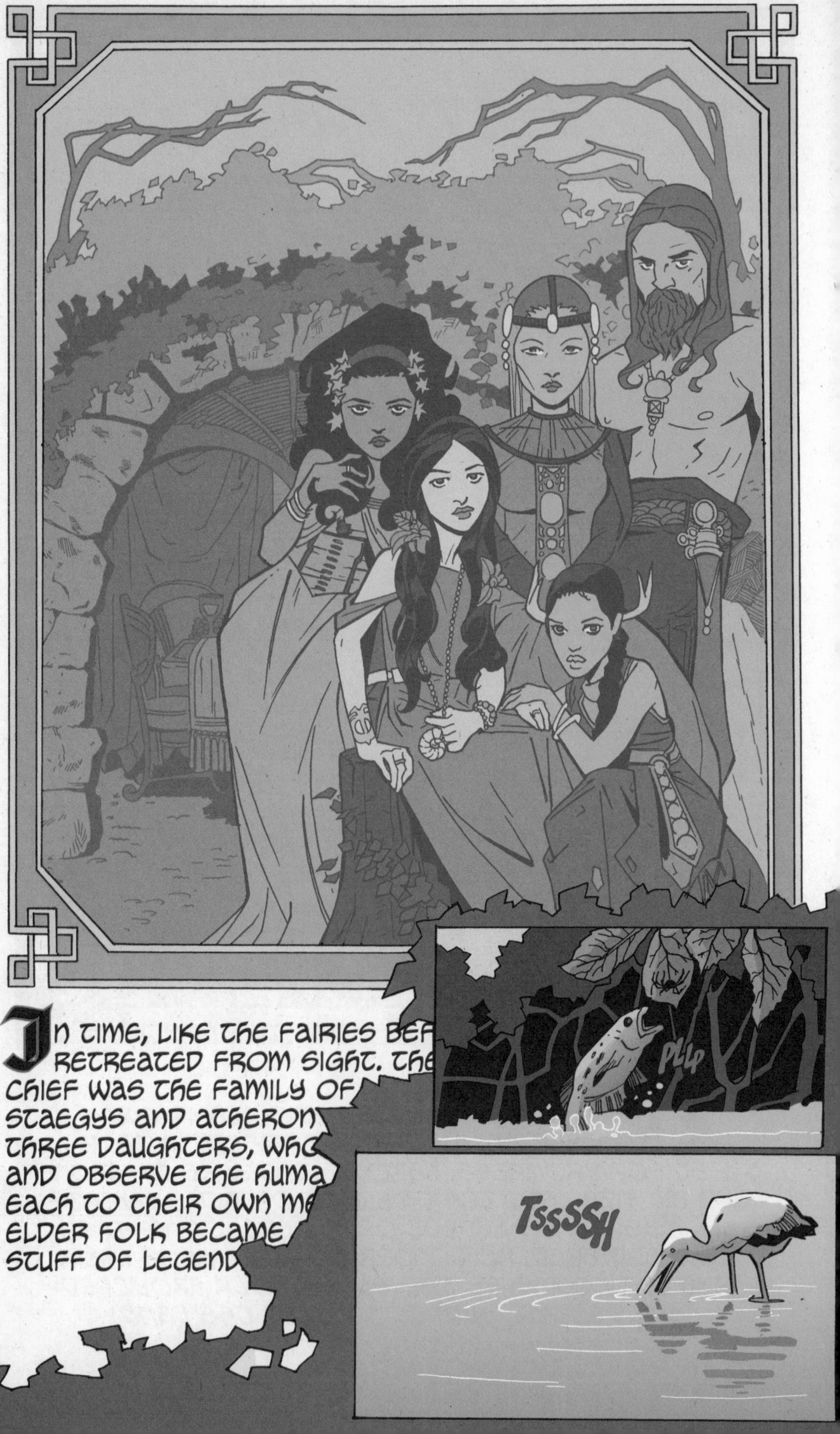
IN TIME, LIKE THE FAIRIES BEF
RETREATED FROM SIGHT. THE
CHIEF WAS THE FAMILY OF
STAEGYS AND ATHERON
THREE DAUGHTERS, WHO
AND OBSERVE THE HUMA
EACH TO THEIR OWN ME
ELDER FOLK BECAME
STUFF OF LEGEND
PLLP
TsSSSH

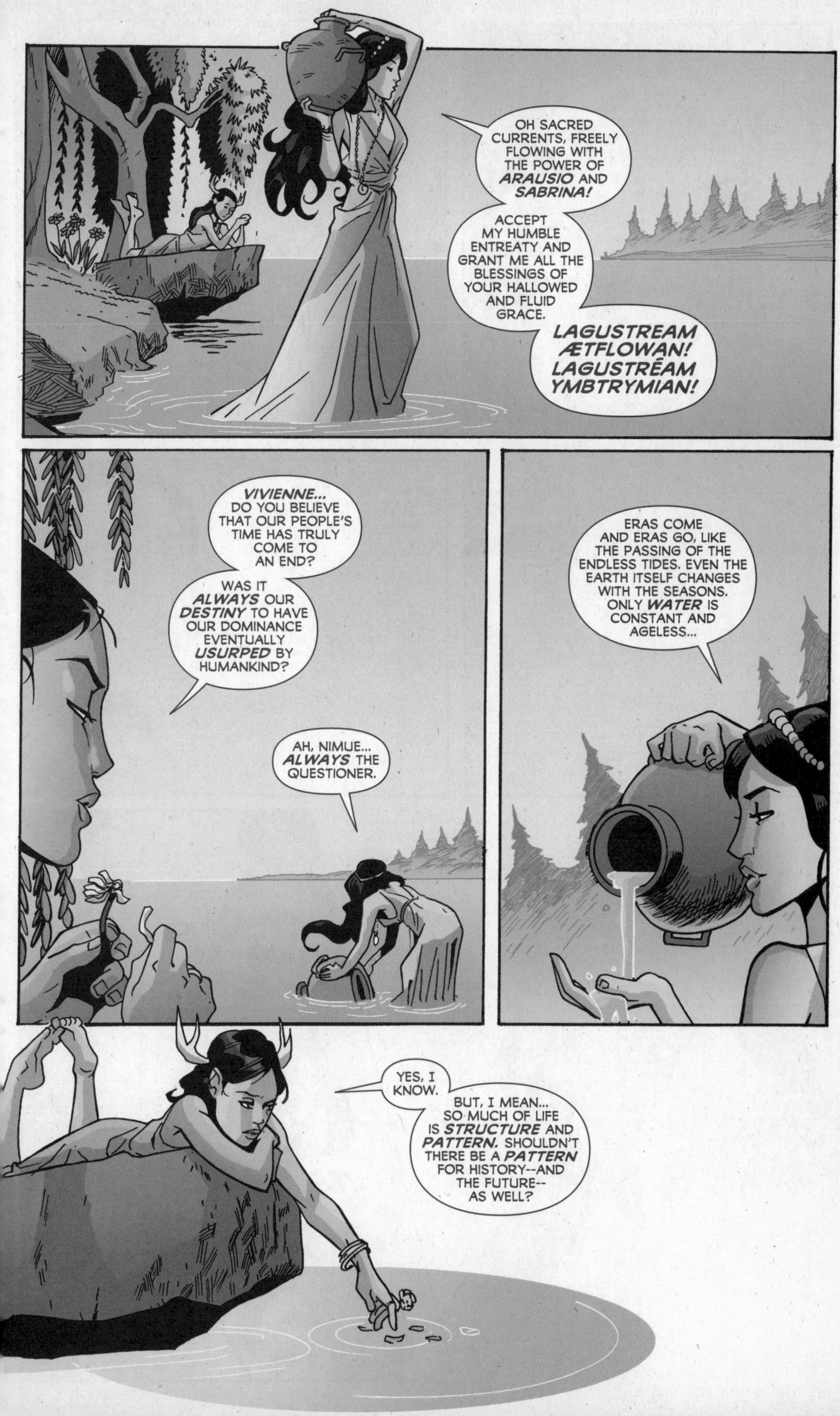

OH SACRED CURRENTS, FREELY FLOWING WITH THE POWER OF ARAUSIO AND SABRINA!
ACCEPT MY HUMBLE ENTREATY AND GRANT ME ALL THE BLESSINGS OF YOUR HALLOWED AND FLUID GRACE.
LAGUSTREAM ÆTFLOWAN! LAGUSTRÉAM YMBTRYMIAN!
VIVIENNE... DO YOU BELIEVE THAT OUR PEOPLE'S TIME HAS TRULY COME TO AN END?
WAS IT ALWAYS OUR DESTINY TO HAVE OUR DOMINANCE EVENTUALLY USURPED BY HUMANKIND?
AH, NIMUE... ALWAYS THE QUESTIONER.
ERAS COME AND ERAS GO, LIKE THE PASSING OF THE ENDLESS TIDES. EVEN THE EARTH ITSELF CHANGES WITH THE SEASONS. ONLY WATER IS CONSTANT AND AGELESS...
YES, I KNOW.
BUT, I MEAN... SO MUCH OF LIFE IS STRUCTURE AND PATTERN. SHOULDN'T THERE BE A PATTERN FOR HISTORY--AND THE FUTURE-- AS WELL?

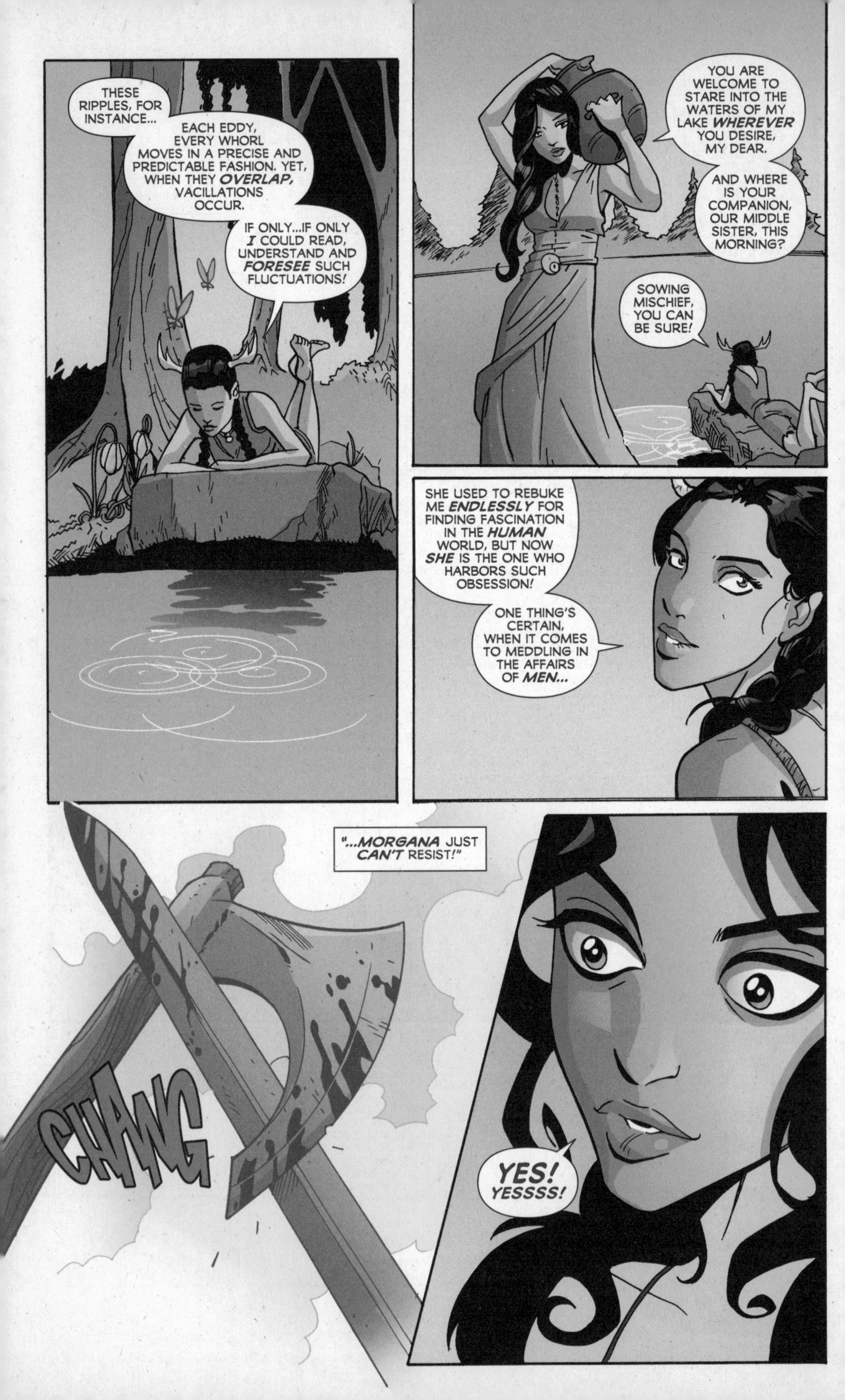
THESE RIPPLES, FOR INSTANCE...
EACH EDDY, EVERY WHORL MOVES IN A PRECISE AND PREDICTABLE FASHION. YET, WHEN THEY OVERLAP, VACILLATIONS OCCUR.
IF ONLY...IF ONLY I COULD READ, UNDERSTAND AND FORESEE SUCH FLUCTUATIONS!
YOU ARE WELCOME TO STARE INTO THE WATERS OF MY LAKE WHEREVER YOU DESIRE, MY DEAR.
AND WHERE IS YOUR COMPANION, OUR MIDDLE SISTER, THIS MORNING?
SOWING MISCHIEF, YOU CAN BE SURE!
SHE USED TO REBUKE ME ENDLESSLY FOR FINDING FASCINATION IN THE HUMAN WORLD, BUT NOW SHE IS THE ONE WHO HARBORS SUCH OBSESSION!
ONE THING'S CERTAIN, WHEN IT COMES TO MEDDLING IN THE AFFAIRS OF MEN...
"...MORGANA JUST CAN'T RESIST!"
CHANG
YES! YESSSS!

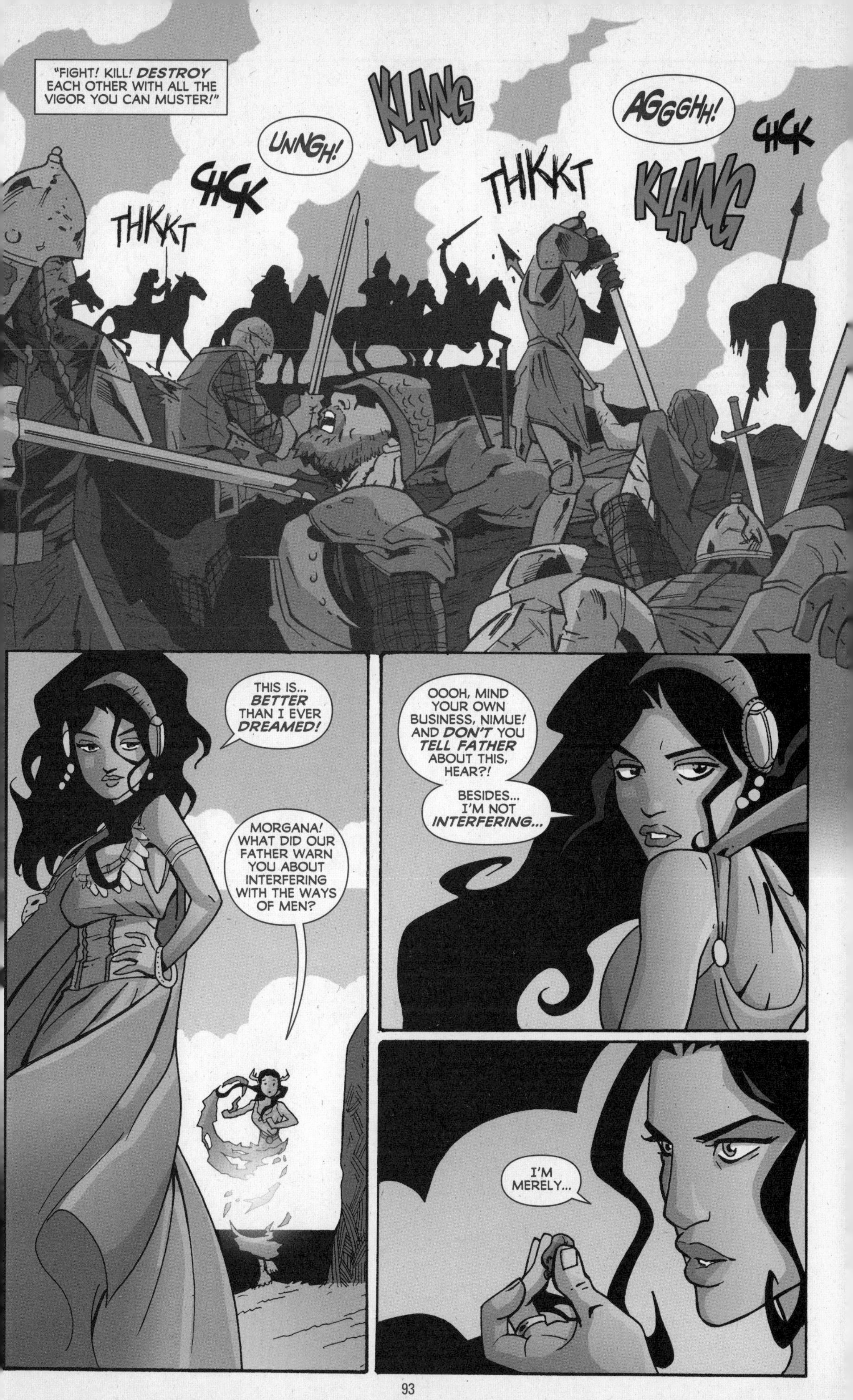
"FIGHT! KILL! DESTROY EACH OTHER WITH ALL THE VIGOR YOU CAN MUSTER!"
KLANG
UNNGH!
CHCK
THKKKT
AGGGHH!
THKKKT
CHCK
KLANG
THIS IS... BETTER THAN I EVER DREAMED!
MORGANA! WHAT DID OUR FATHER WARN YOU ABOUT INTERFERING WITH THE WAYS OF MEN?
OOOH, MIND YOUR OWN BUSINESS, NIMUE! AND DON'T YOU TELL FATHER ABOUT THIS, HEAR?!
BESIDES... I'M NOT INTERFERING...
I'M MERELY...

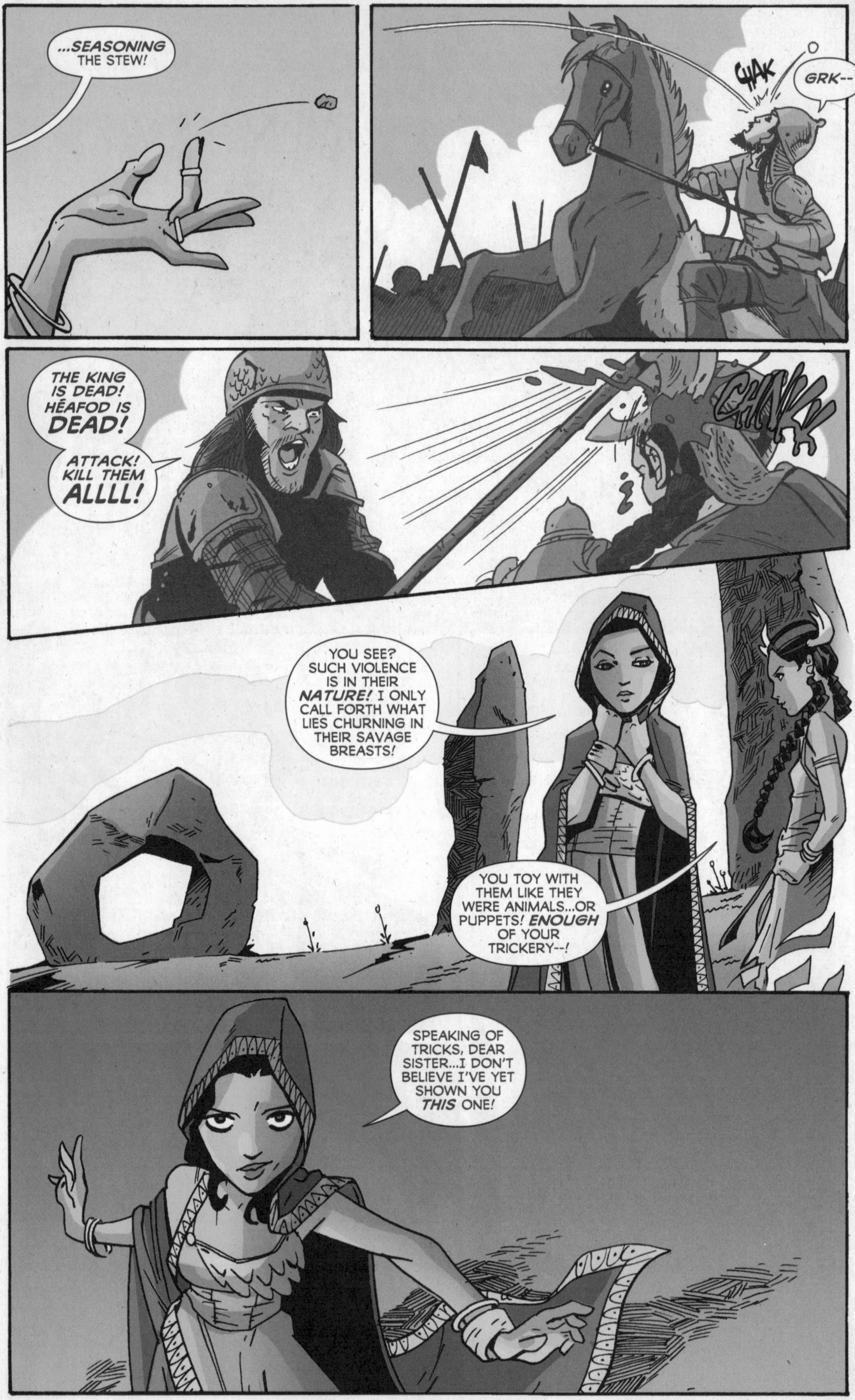
...SEASONING THE STEW!
CHAK
GRK--
THE KING IS DEAD! HÊAFOD IS DEAD!
ATTACK! KILL THEM ALLLL!
CHUNK!
YOU SEE? SUCH VIOLENCE IS IN THEIR NATURE! I ONLY CALL FORTH WHAT LIES CHURNING IN THEIR SAVAGE BREASTS!
YOU TOY WITH THEM LIKE THEY WERE ANIMALS...OR PUPPETS! ENOUGH OF YOUR TRICKERY--!
SPEAKING OF TRICKS, DEAR SISTER...I DON'T BELIEVE I'VE YET SHOWN YOU THIS ONE!

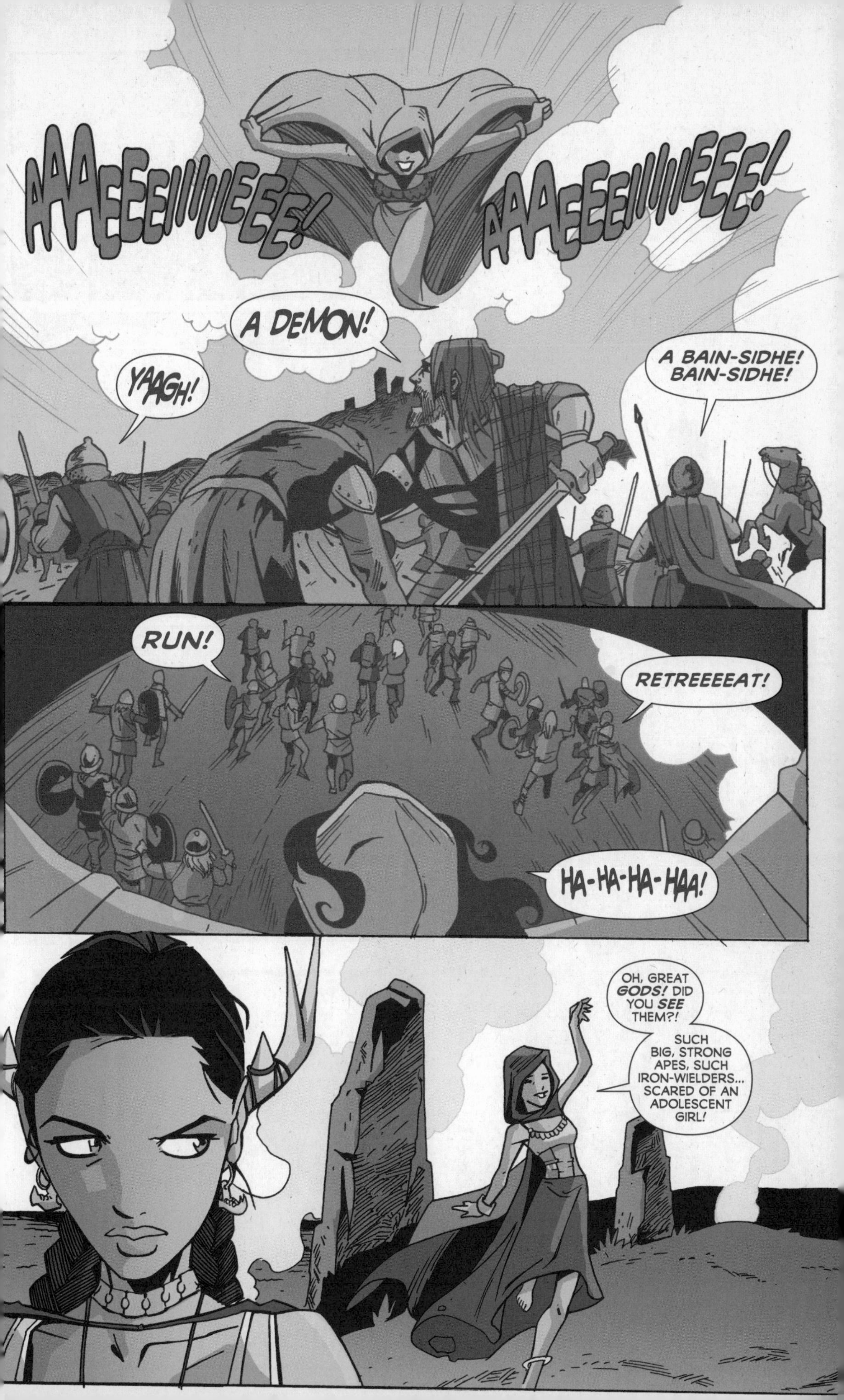
AAAEEEIIIIIIEEEE!
AAAEEEIIIIIIEEEE!
A DEMON!
YAAGH!
A BAIN-SIDHE! BAIN-SIDHE!
RUN!
RETREEEEAT!
HA-HA-HA-HAA!
OH, GREAT GODS! DID YOU SEE THEM?!
SUCH BIG, STRONG APES, SUCH IRON-WIELDERS... SCARED OF AN ADOLESCENT GIRL!

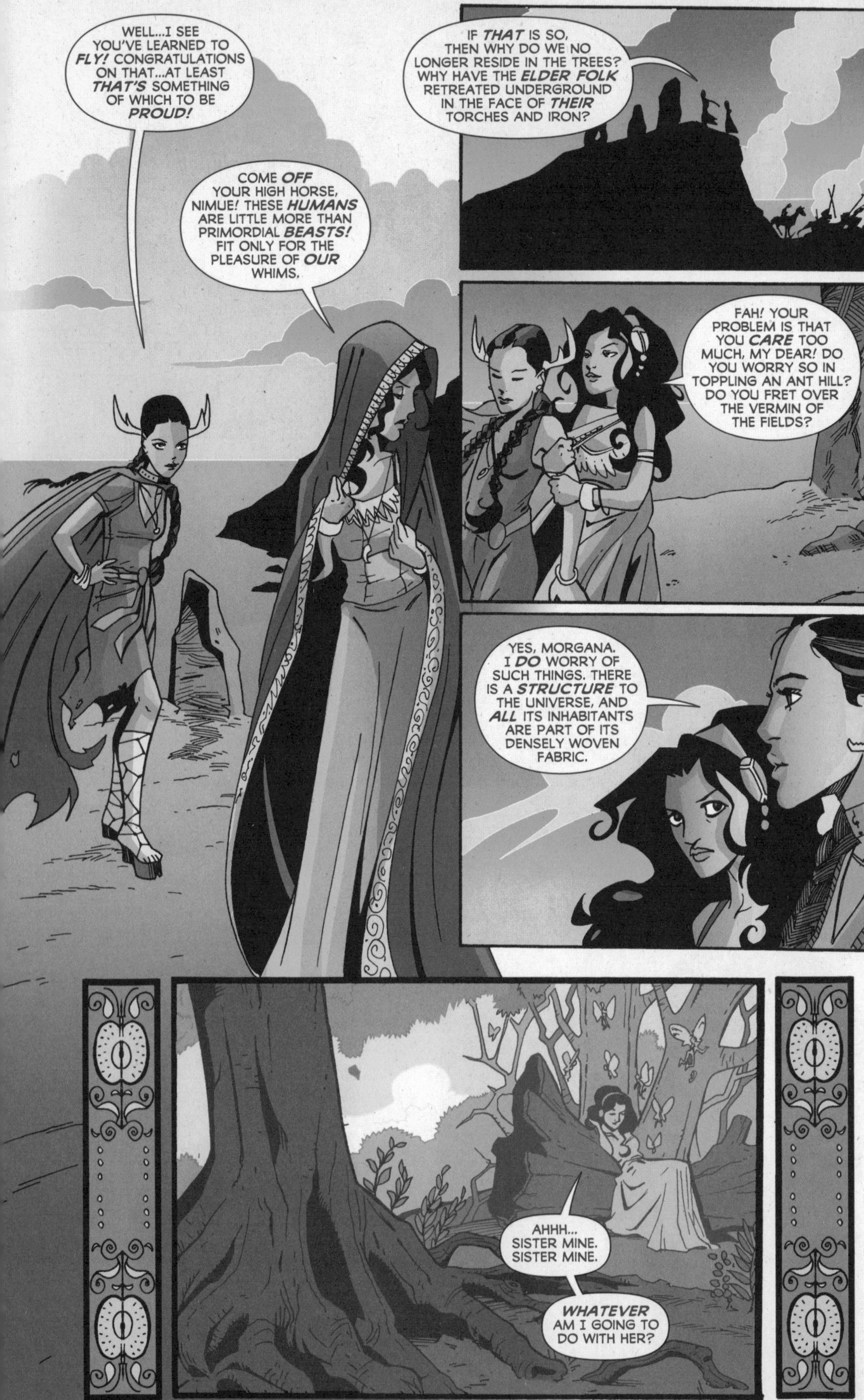
WELL...I SEE YOU'VE LEARNED TO *FLY!* CONGRATULATIONS ON THAT...AT LEAST *THAT'S* SOMETHING OF WHICH TO BE *PROUD!*
COME *OFF* YOUR HIGH HORSE, NIMUE! THESE *HUMANS* ARE LITTLE MORE THAN PRIMORDIAL *BEASTS!* FIT ONLY FOR THE PLEASURE OF *OUR* WHIMS.
IF *THAT* IS SO, THEN WHY DO WE NO LONGER RESIDE IN THE TREES? WHY HAVE THE *ELDER FOLK* RETREATED UNDERGROUND IN THE FACE OF *THEIR* TORCHES AND IRON?
FAH! YOUR PROBLEM IS THAT YOU *CARE* TOO MUCH, MY DEAR! DO YOU WORRY SO IN TOPPLING AN ANT HILL? DO YOU FRET OVER THE VERMIN OF THE FIELDS?
YES, MORGANA. I *DO* WORRY OF SUCH THINGS. THERE IS A *STRUCTURE* TO THE UNIVERSE, AND *ALL* ITS INHABITANTS ARE PART OF ITS DENSELY WOVEN FABRIC.
AHHH... SISTER MINE. SISTER MINE.
WHATEVER AM I GOING TO DO WITH HER?

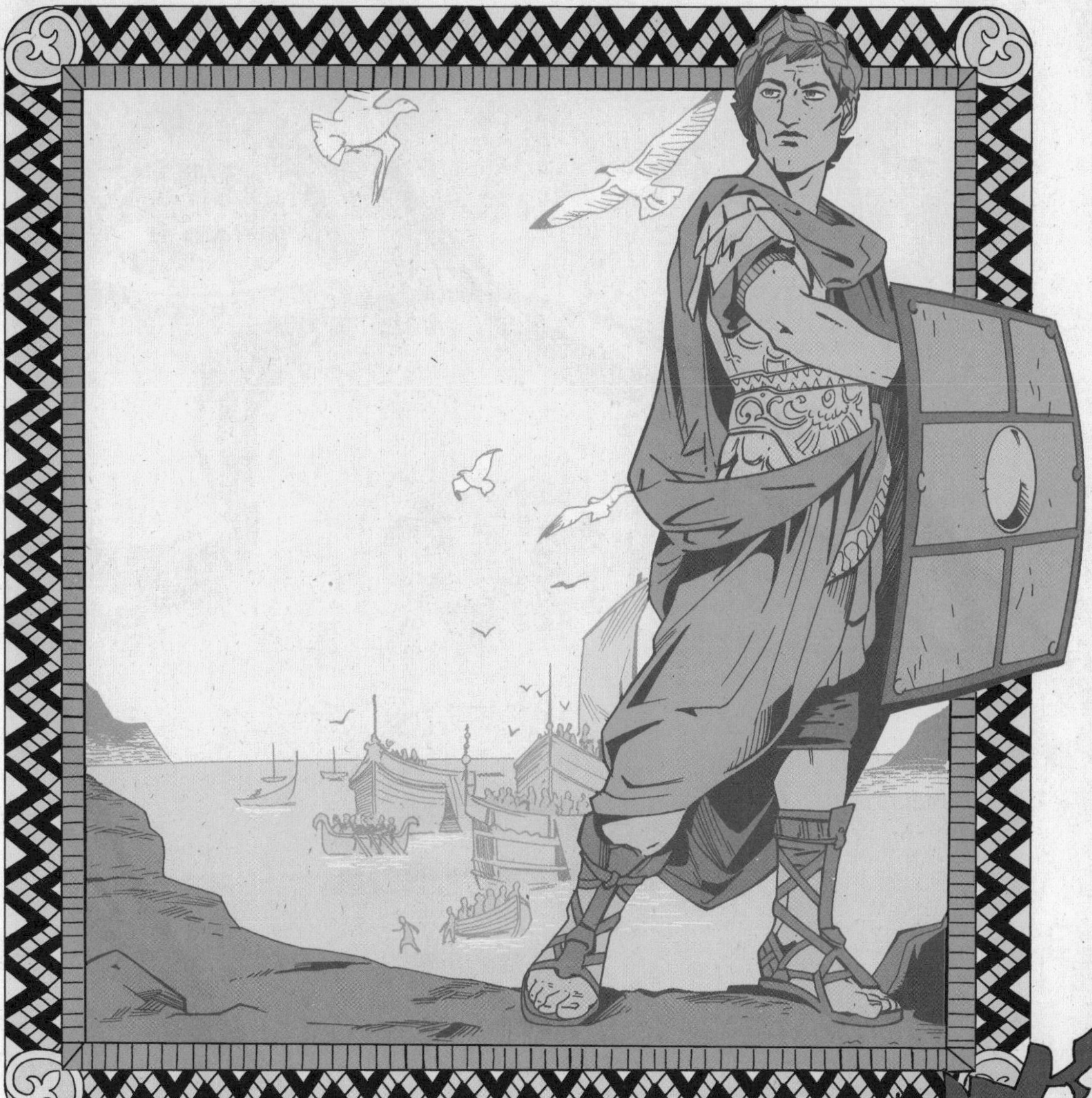

EVEN AS THE ELDER FOLK CA
TRIBES OF MAN SPREAD OV
AND EMPIRES AROSE THAT SPR
MANY LANDS AND PEOPLE UNTO
THE MIGHTIEST OF THESE WAS
LARGER THAN ANY OTHER REA
THE SHORES OF THE LAND.
IMPERIAL ROME LAID ITS CLA
ARMOR SHINING IN THE BLAZE O
WEAPONS HELD READY, BANNE
NOTHING COULD RESIST THE
PAX ROMANA.

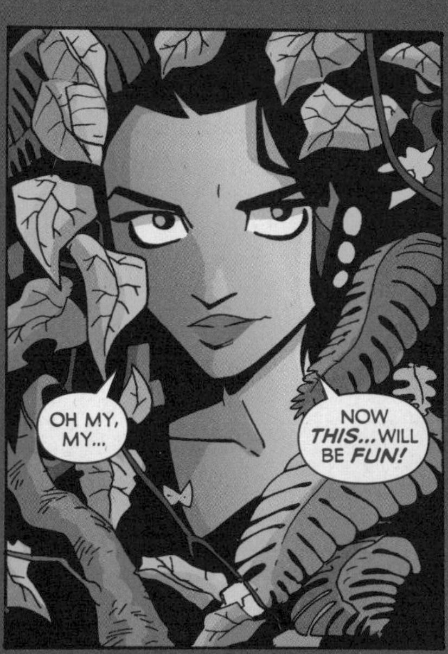
OH MY, MY...
NOW *THIS...* WILL BE *FUN!*

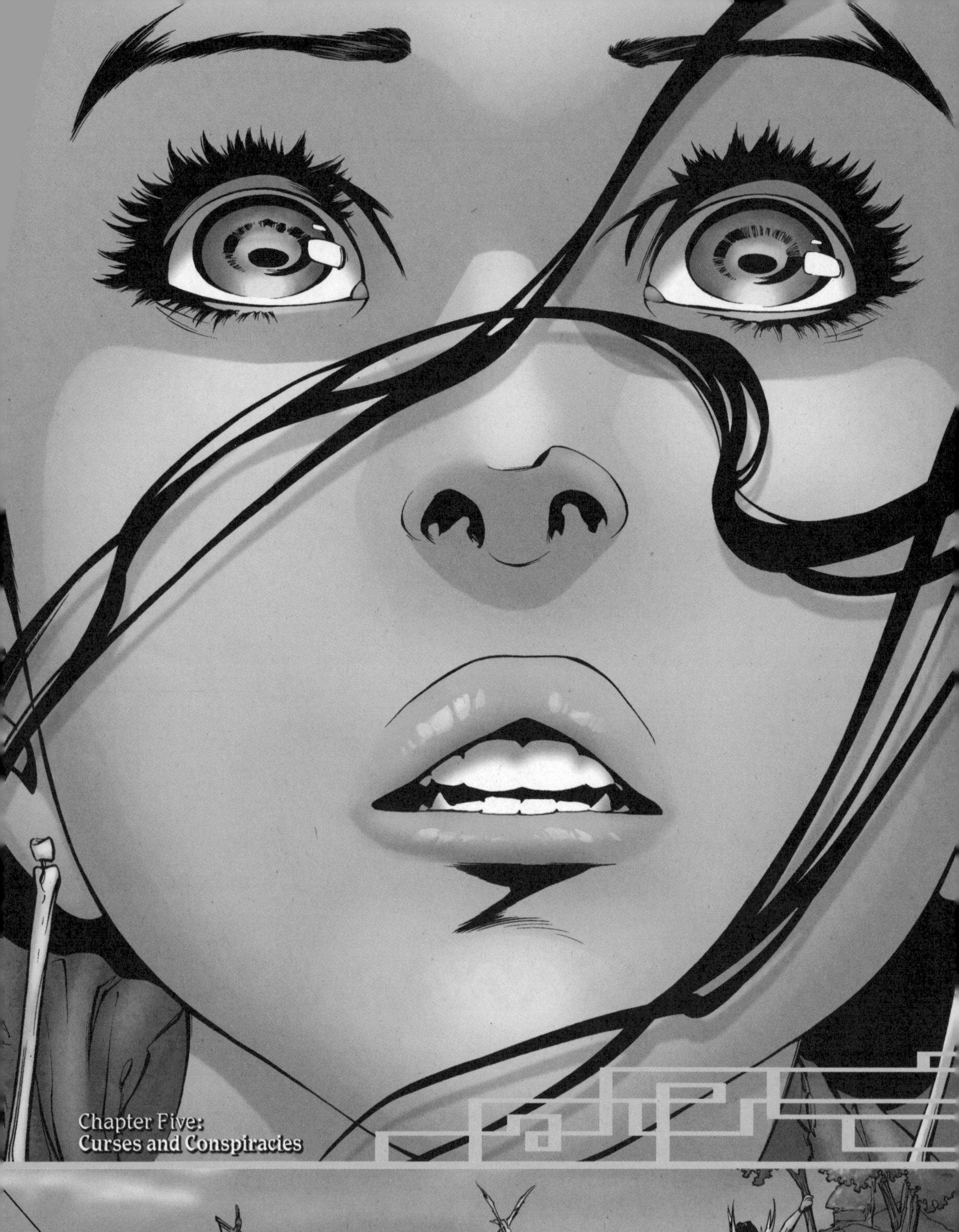
Chapter Five:
Curses and Conspiracies

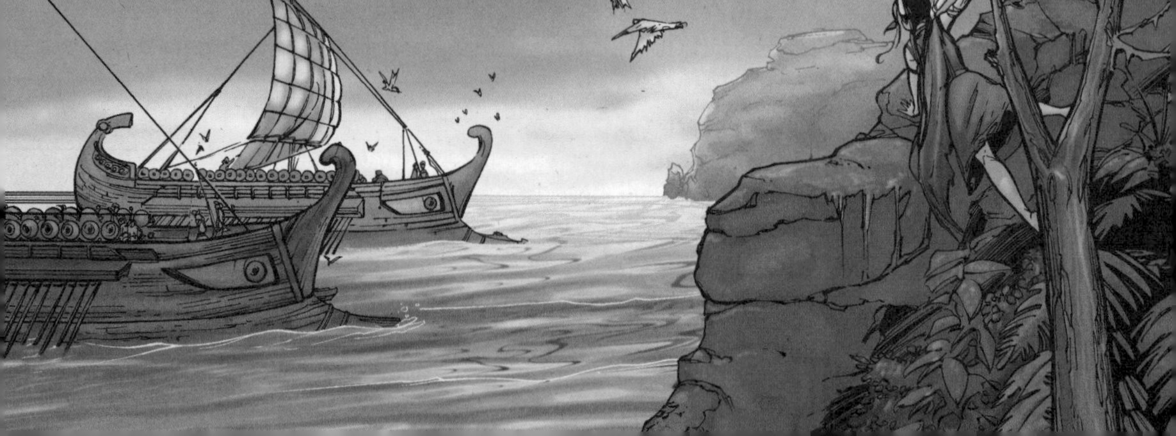

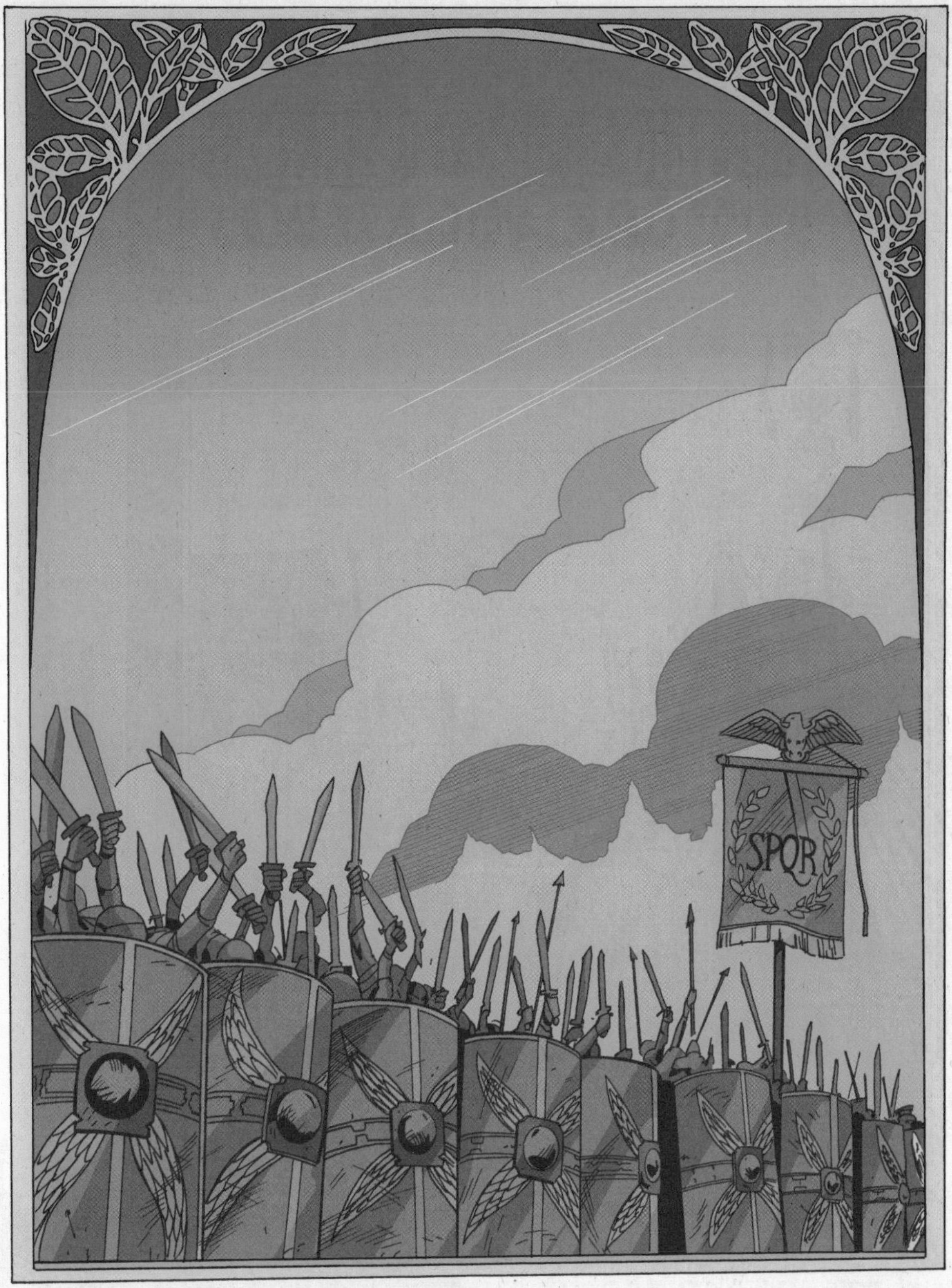
SPQR

Thus Rome, *mighty Rome*, farcast the net of its insatiable lust for conquest and came unto *the Land*. Their fearsome war machines and regimented legions were a force such as the native tribes had never seen. 'Neath eagle standard, via shielded blockade, the Romans sought to tame the misty valleys and hills.

BROKEN HOUSE OF CARDS
CHAPTER FIVE CURSES AND CONSPIRACIES

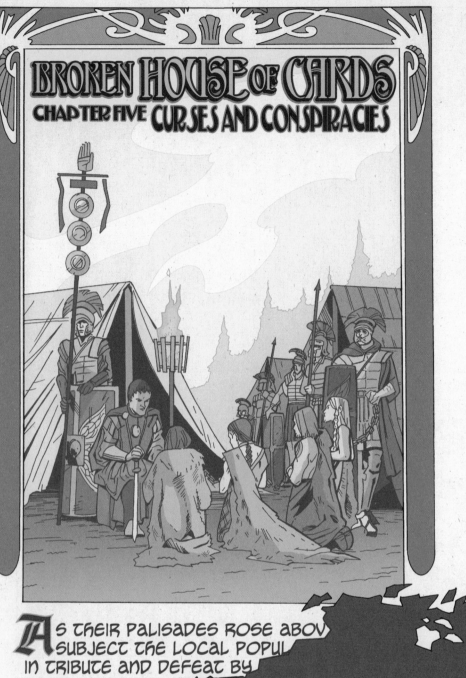

As their palisades rose abov
subject the local popu
in tribute and defeat by
their commander
unequaled by an
name would ring
tragic history
military tact
consul and
ambition by
conquest for
CAESER, first

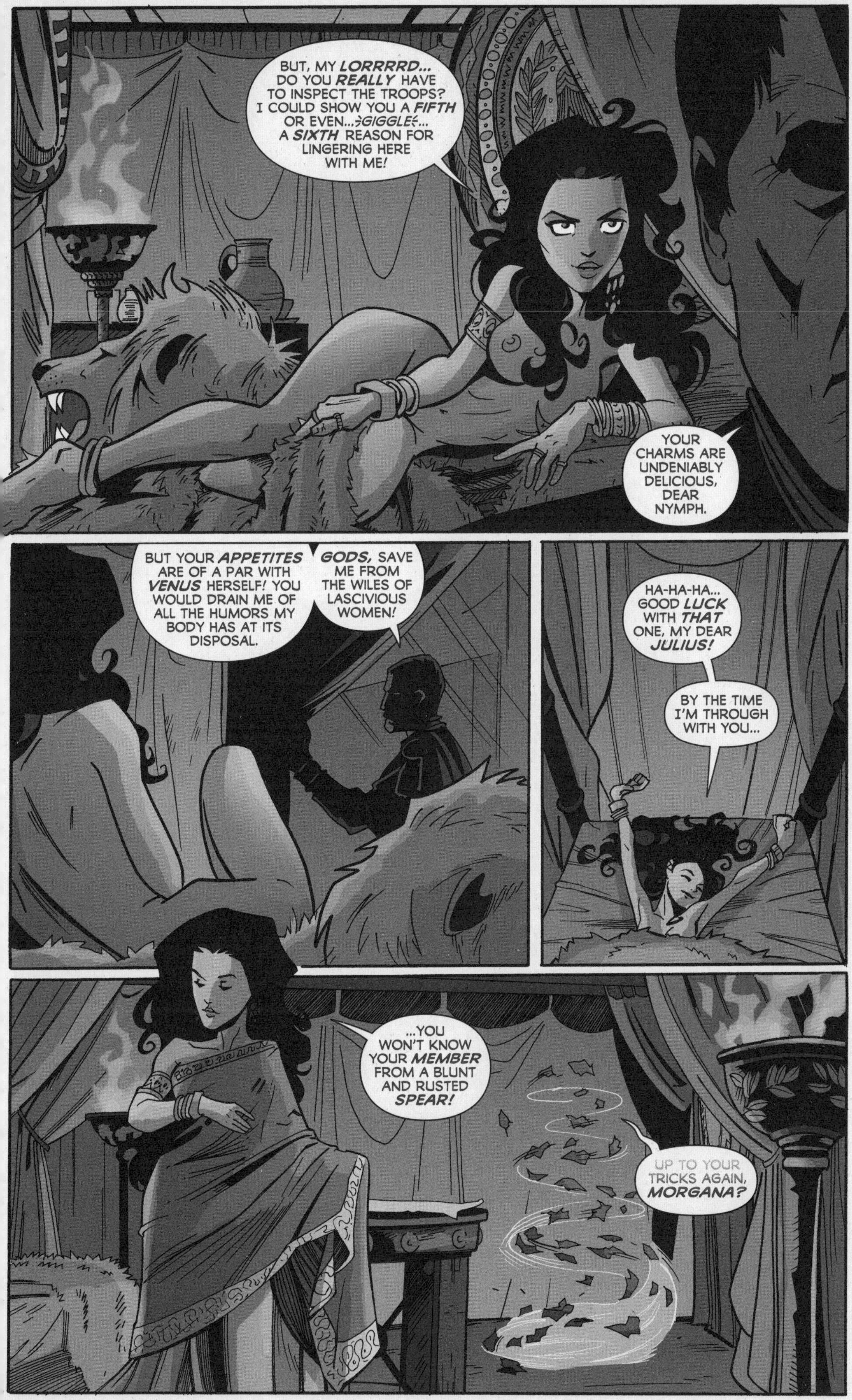
BUT, MY LORRRRD... DO YOU REALLY HAVE TO INSPECT THE TROOPS? I COULD SHOW YOU A FIFTH OR EVEN...ﾉGIGGLEﾉ... A SIXTH REASON FOR LINGERING HERE WITH ME!
YOUR CHARMS ARE UNDENIABLY DELICIOUS, DEAR NYMPH.
BUT YOUR APPETITES ARE OF A PAR WITH VENUS HERSELF! YOU WOULD DRAIN ME OF ALL THE HUMORS MY BODY HAS AT ITS DISPOSAL.
GODS, SAVE ME FROM THE WILES OF LASCIVIOUS WOMEN!
HA-HA-HA... GOOD LUCK WITH THAT ONE, MY DEAR JULIUS!
BY THE TIME I'M THROUGH WITH YOU...
...YOU WON'T KNOW YOUR MEMBER FROM A BLUNT AND RUSTED SPEAR!
UP TO YOUR TRICKS AGAIN, MORGANA?

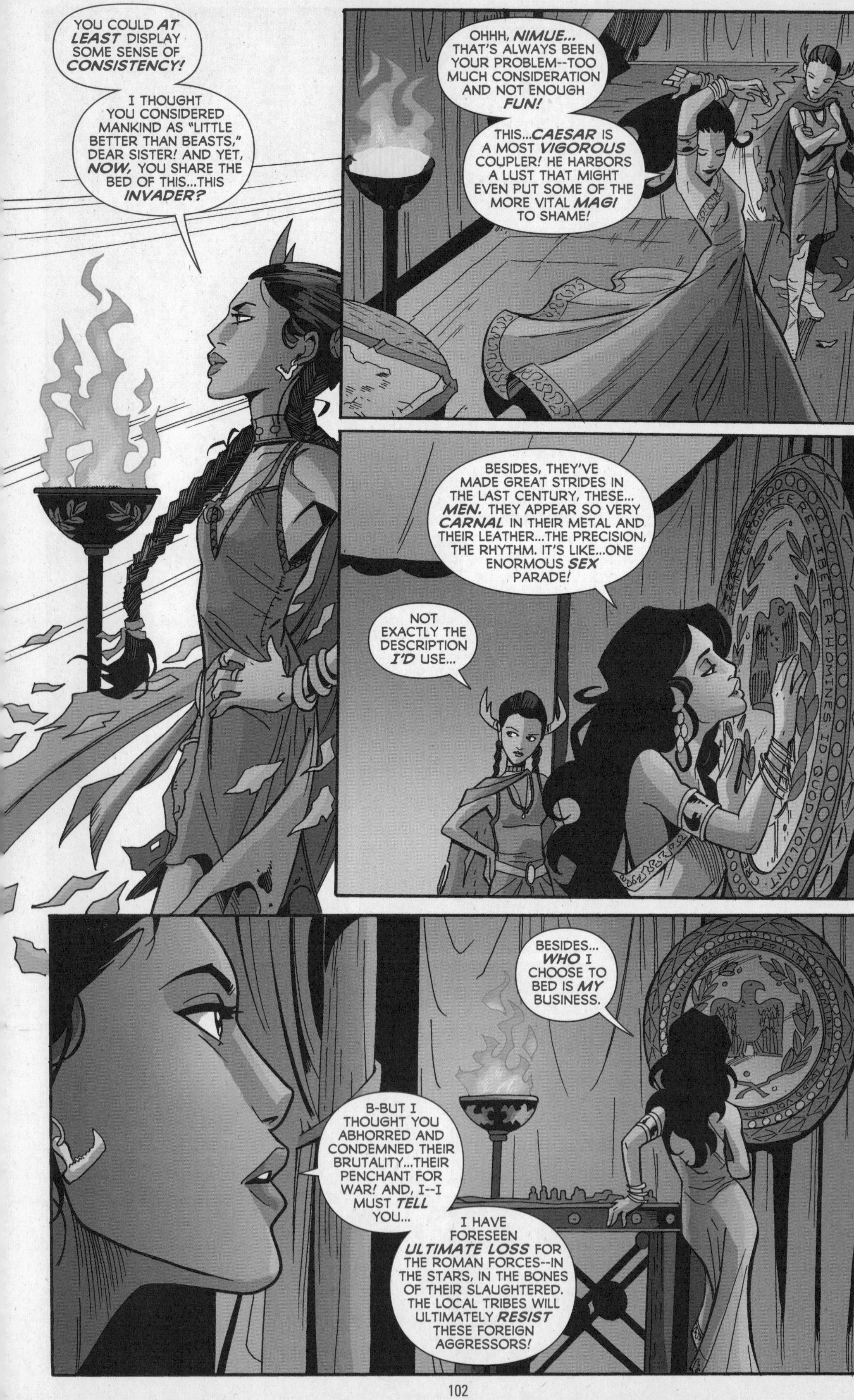

YOU COULD AT LEAST DISPLAY SOME SENSE OF CONSISTENCY!
I THOUGHT YOU CONSIDERED MANKIND AS "LITTLE BETTER THAN BEASTS," DEAR SISTER! AND YET, NOW, YOU SHARE THE BED OF THIS...THIS INVADER?
OHHH, NIMUE... THAT'S ALWAYS BEEN YOUR PROBLEM--TOO MUCH CONSIDERATION AND NOT ENOUGH FUN!
THIS...CAESAR IS A MOST VIGOROUS COUPLER! HE HARBORS A LUST THAT MIGHT EVEN PUT SOME OF THE MORE VITAL MAGI TO SHAME!
BESIDES, THEY'VE MADE GREAT STRIDES IN THE LAST CENTURY, THESE... MEN. THEY APPEAR SO VERY CARNAL IN THEIR METAL AND THEIR LEATHER...THE PRECISION, THE RHYTHM. IT'S LIKE...ONE ENORMOUS SEX PARADE!
NOT EXACTLY THE DESCRIPTION I'D USE...
BESIDES... WHO I CHOOSE TO BED IS MY BUSINESS.
B-BUT I THOUGHT YOU ABHORRED AND CONDEMNED THEIR BRUTALITY...THEIR PENCHANT FOR WAR! AND, I--I MUST TELL YOU...
I HAVE FORESEEN ULTIMATE LOSS FOR THE ROMAN FORCES--IN THE STARS, IN THE BONES OF THEIR SLAUGHTERED. THE LOCAL TRIBES WILL ULTIMATELY RESIST THESE FOREIGN AGGRESSORS!

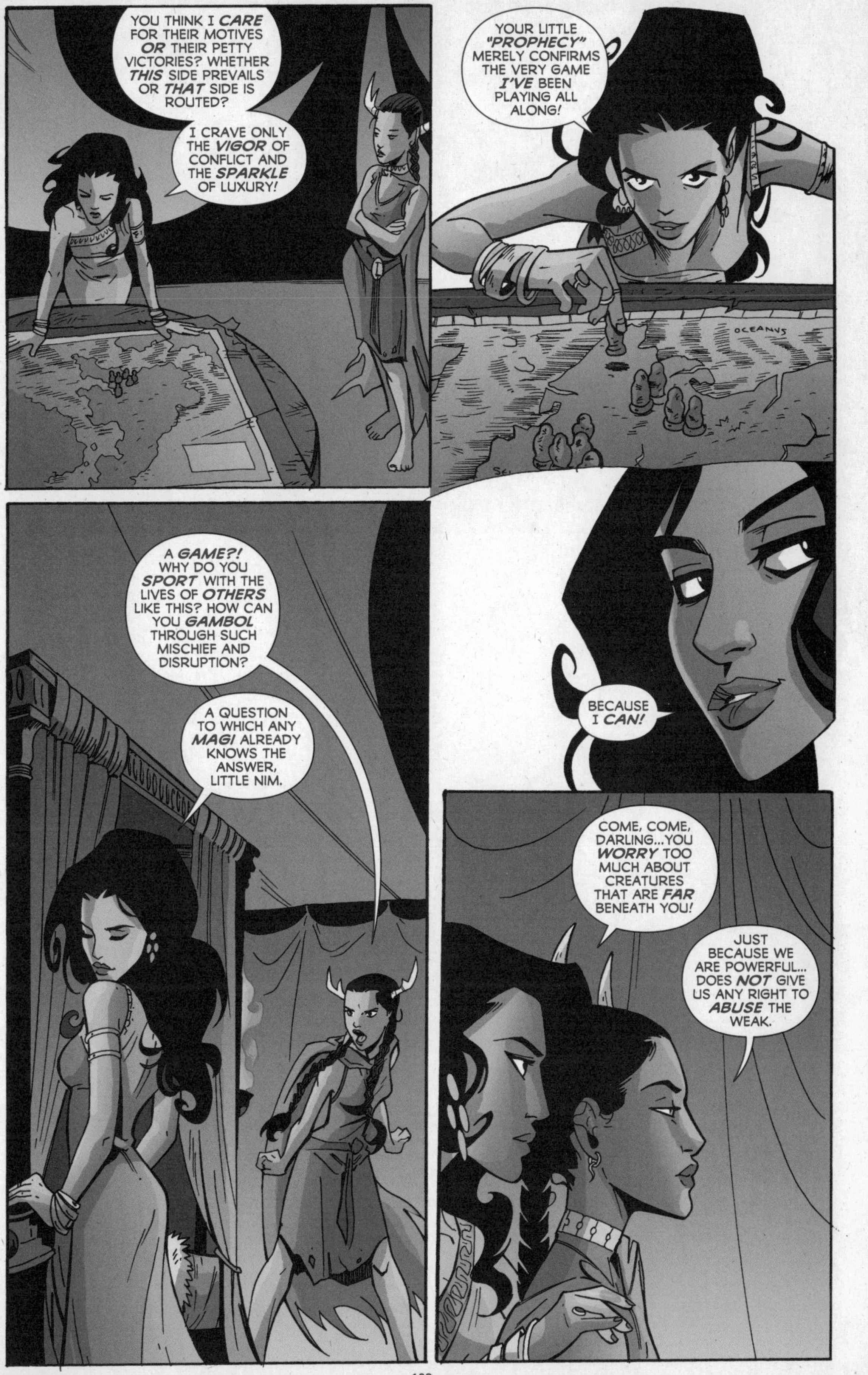
YOU THINK I CARE FOR THEIR MOTIVES OR THEIR PETTY VICTORIES? WHETHER THIS SIDE PREVAILS OR THAT SIDE IS ROUTED?
I CRAVE ONLY THE VIGOR OF CONFLICT AND THE SPARKLE OF LUXURY!
YOUR LITTLE "PROPHECY" MERELY CONFIRMS THE VERY GAME I'VE BEEN PLAYING ALL ALONG!
OCEANUS
A GAME?! WHY DO YOU SPORT WITH THE LIVES OF OTHERS LIKE THIS? HOW CAN YOU GAMBOL THROUGH SUCH MISCHIEF AND DISRUPTION?
A QUESTION TO WHICH ANY MAGI ALREADY KNOWS THE ANSWER, LITTLE NIM.
BECAUSE I CAN!
COME, COME, DARLING...YOU WORRY TOO MUCH ABOUT CREATURES THAT ARE FAR BENEATH YOU!
JUST BECAUSE WE ARE POWERFUL... DOES NOT GIVE US ANY RIGHT TO ABUSE THE WEAK.

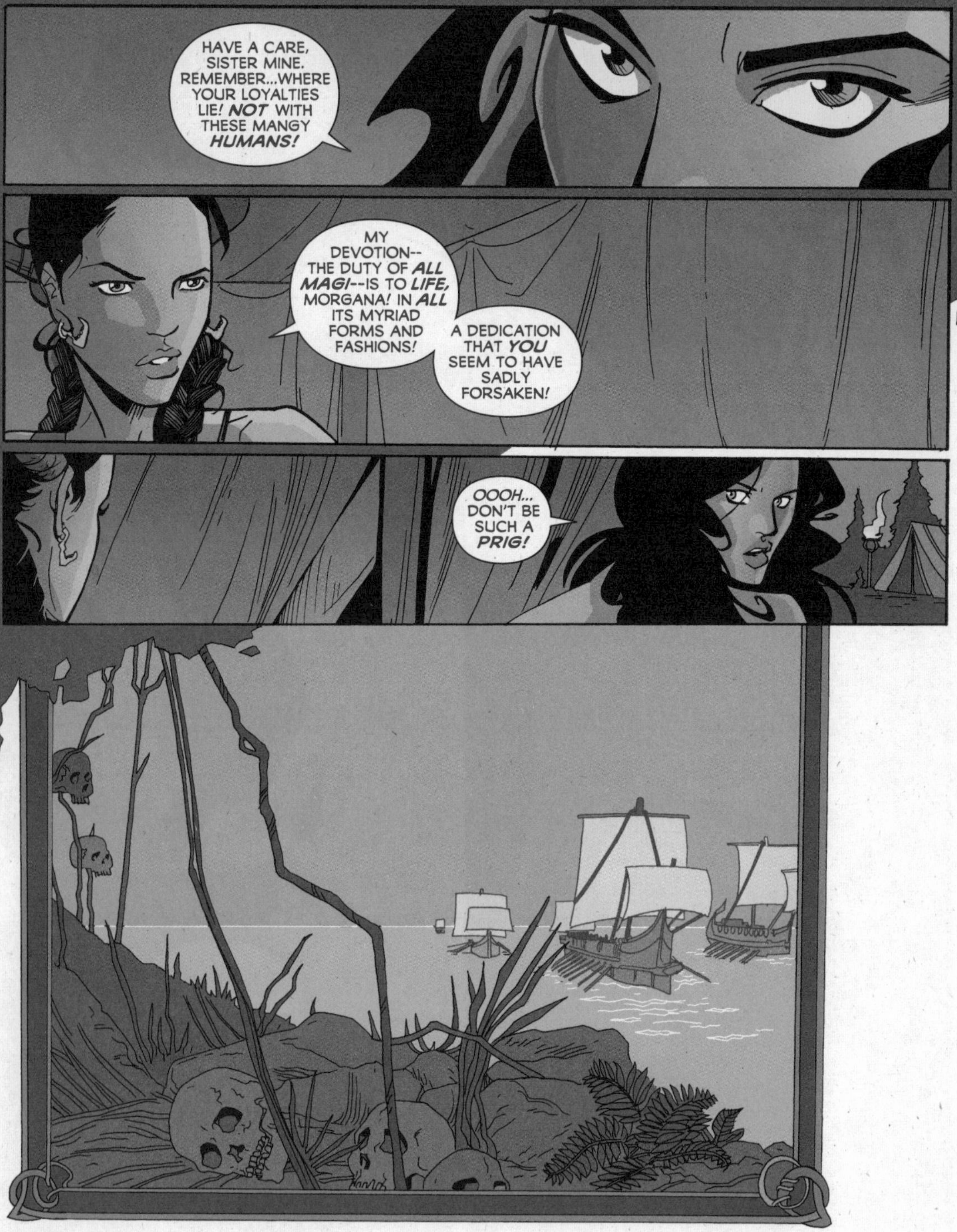
HAVE A CARE, SISTER MINE. REMEMBER...WHERE YOUR LOYALTIES LIE! *NOT* WITH THESE MANGY *HUMANS!*
MY DEVOTION-- THE DUTY OF *ALL MAGI*--IS TO *LIFE,* MORGANA! IN *ALL* ITS MYRIAD FORMS AND FASHIONS!
A DEDICATION THAT *YOU* SEEM TO HAVE SADLY FORSAKEN!
OOOH... DON'T BE SUCH A *PRIG!*

SO IT CAME TO PASS, THE RESISTANCE PROVED TOO FLINTY, THE SEASONS TOO DREAR. CAESAR'S BRISK INTEREST WANED AND THE ROMANS QUIT THE LAND, LEAVING DEATH IN THEIR WAKE, THE SOIL SEWN WITH BLOOD.

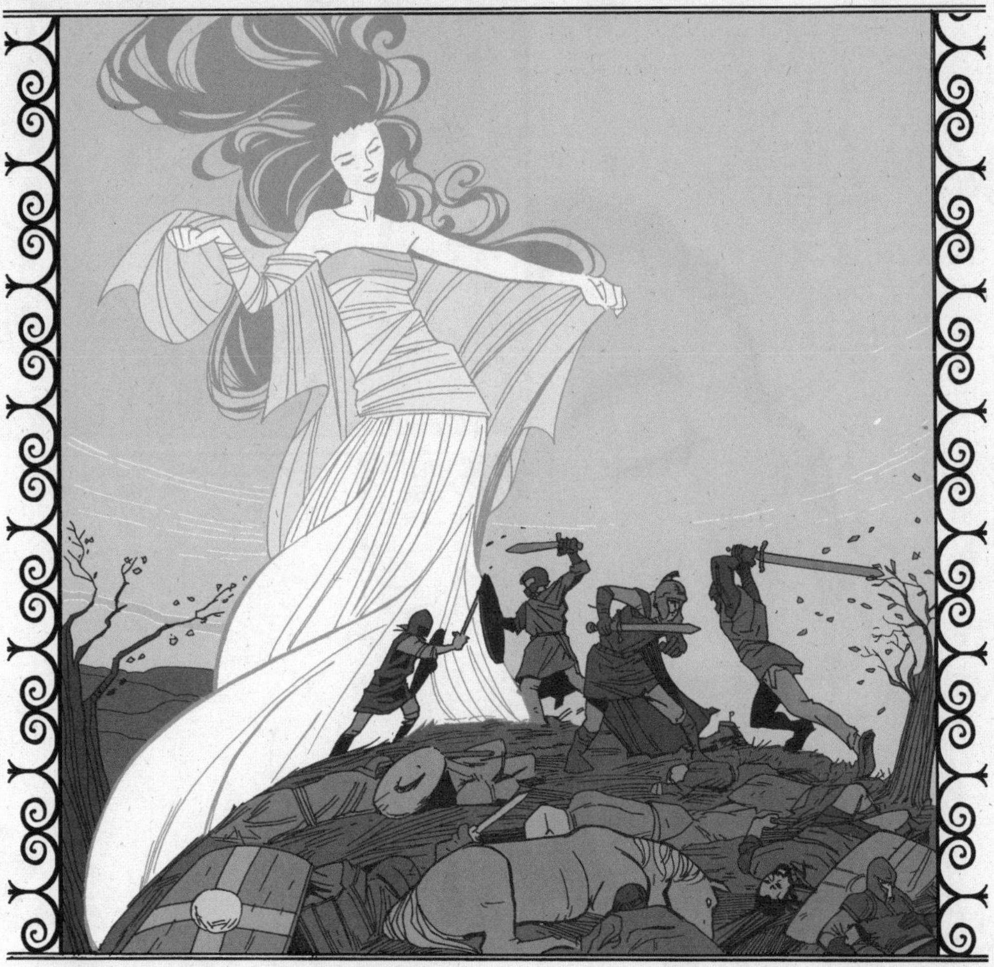

In the aftermath of the occupation, conflict fermented as chieftain and brother and liege, each swollen by the sting of Rome's rapacious model, hungered for power and supremecy. So battles clashed as generations fought, all in sport for the temptress, Morgana. Her sway, ever present, sowing the seeds of betrayal suspicion and doubt with her presence became fear seductive charms could like a wisp of morning de ere *the land* dreamed of sang of sorrow and dread unto this tearful tableau war, war, never-ending war bloody echoes of time

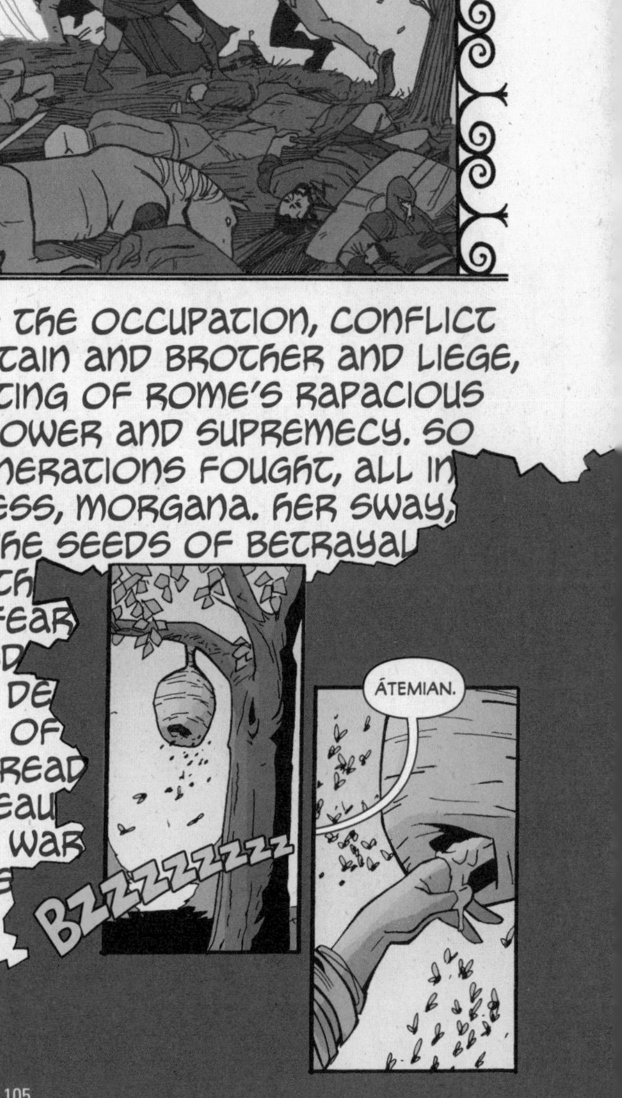

BZZZZZZZZZ
ÁTEMIAN.

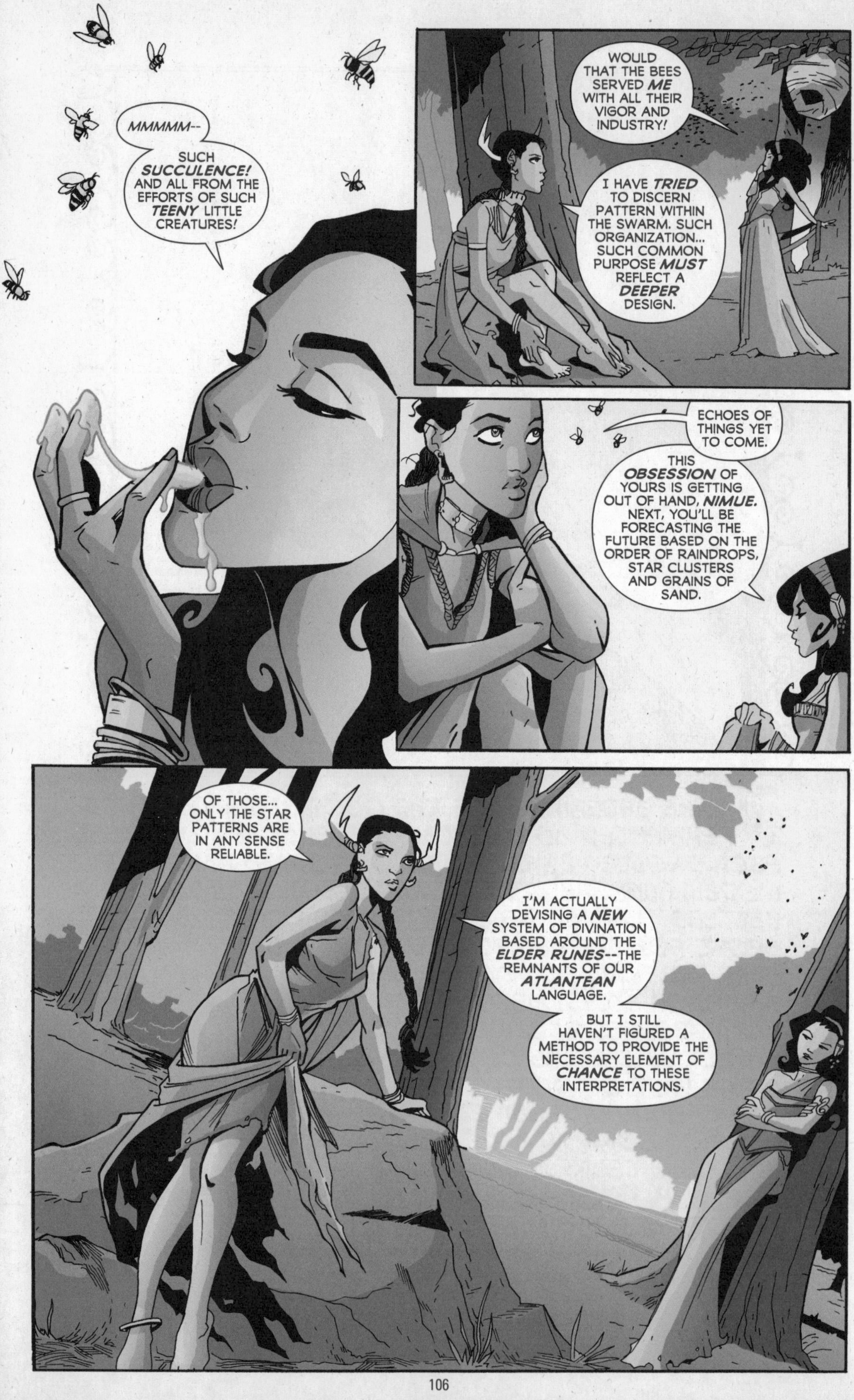

MMMMM--
SUCH SUCCULENCE! AND ALL FROM THE EFFORTS OF SUCH TEENY LITTLE CREATURES!
WOULD THAT THE BEES SERVED ME WITH ALL THEIR VIGOR AND INDUSTRY!
I HAVE TRIED TO DISCERN PATTERN WITHIN THE SWARM. SUCH ORGANIZATION... SUCH COMMON PURPOSE MUST REFLECT A DEEPER DESIGN.
ECHOES OF THINGS YET TO COME.
THIS OBSESSION OF YOURS IS GETTING OUT OF HAND, NIMUE. NEXT, YOU'LL BE FORECASTING THE FUTURE BASED ON THE ORDER OF RAINDROPS, STAR CLUSTERS AND GRAINS OF SAND.
OF THOSE... ONLY THE STAR PATTERNS ARE IN ANY SENSE RELIABLE.
I'M ACTUALLY DEVISING A NEW SYSTEM OF DIVINATION BASED AROUND THE ELDER RUNES--THE REMNANTS OF OUR ATLANTEAN LANGUAGE.
BUT I STILL HAVEN'T FIGURED A METHOD TO PROVIDE THE NECESSARY ELEMENT OF CHANCE TO THESE INTERPRETATIONS.

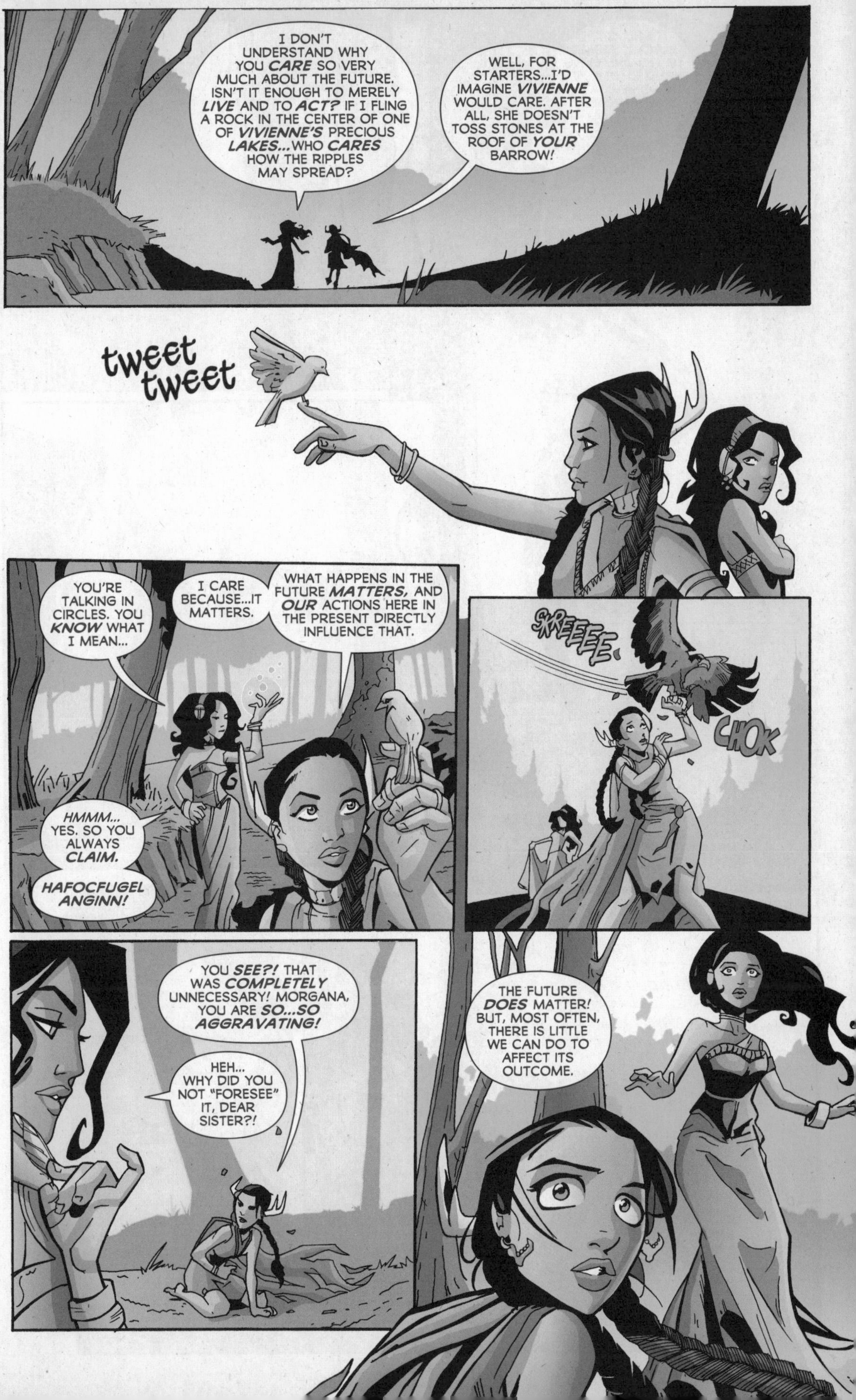
I DON'T UNDERSTAND WHY YOU CARE SO VERY MUCH ABOUT THE FUTURE. ISN'T IT ENOUGH TO MERELY LIVE AND TO ACT? IF I FLING A ROCK IN THE CENTER OF ONE OF VIVIENNE'S PRECIOUS LAKES...WHO CARES HOW THE RIPPLES MAY SPREAD?
WELL, FOR STARTERS...I'D IMAGINE VIVIENNE WOULD CARE. AFTER ALL, SHE DOESN'T TOSS STONES AT THE ROOF OF YOUR BARROW!
tweet tweet
YOU'RE TALKING IN CIRCLES. YOU KNOW WHAT I MEAN...
I CARE BECAUSE...IT MATTERS.
WHAT HAPPENS IN THE FUTURE MATTERS, AND OUR ACTIONS HERE IN THE PRESENT DIRECTLY INFLUENCE THAT.
HMMM... YES. SO YOU ALWAYS CLAIM.
HAFOCFUGEL ANGINN!
SKREEEEE
CHOK
YOU SEE?! THAT WAS COMPLETELY UNNECESSARY! MORGANA, YOU ARE SO...SO AGGRAVATING!
HEH... WHY DID YOU NOT "FORESEE" IT, DEAR SISTER?!
THE FUTURE DOES MATTER! BUT, MOST OFTEN, THERE IS LITTLE WE CAN DO TO AFFECT ITS OUTCOME.

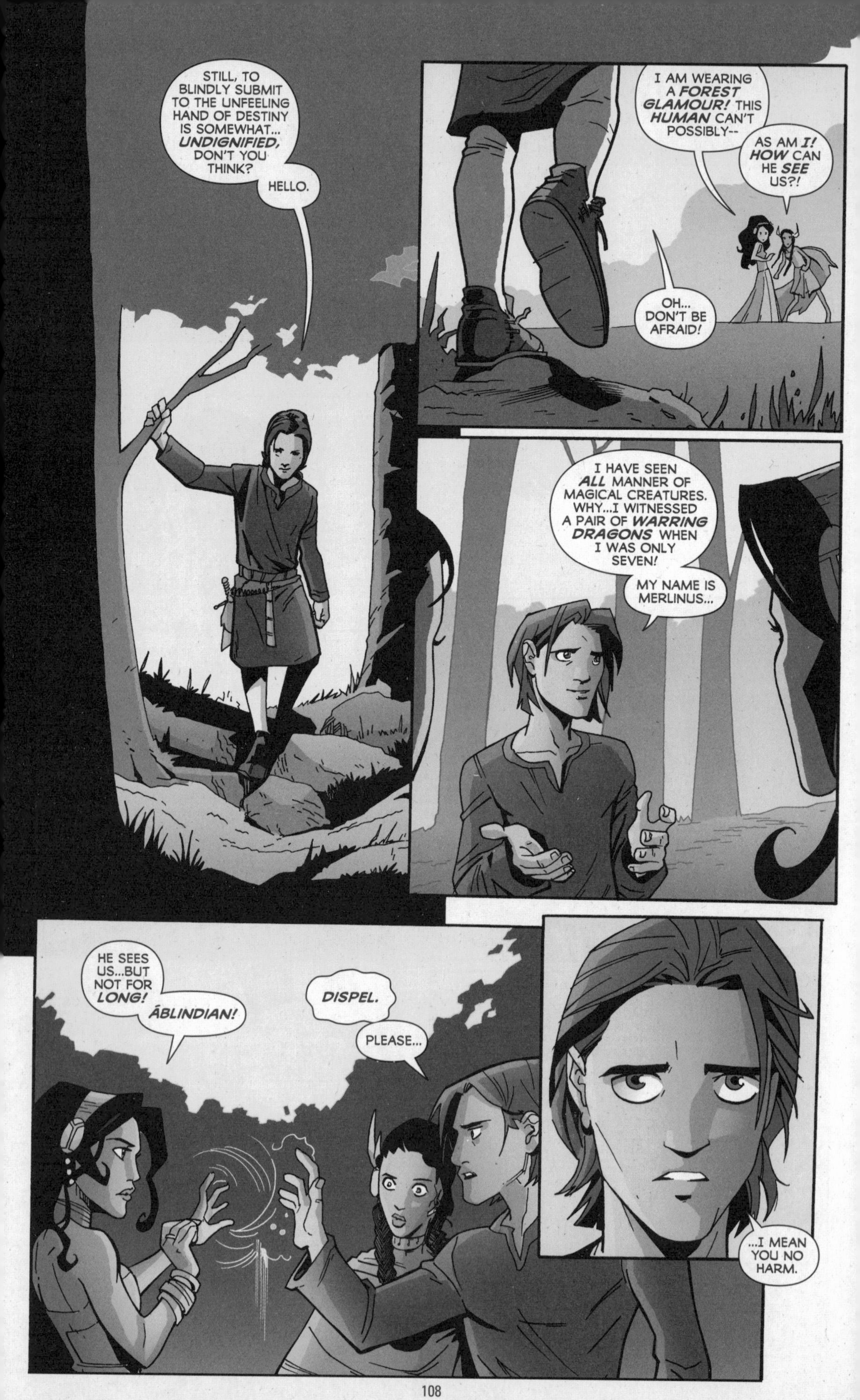
STILL, TO BLINDLY SUBMIT TO THE UNFEELING HAND OF DESTINY IS SOMEWHAT... UNDIGNIFIED, DON'T YOU THINK?
HELLO.
I AM WEARING A FOREST GLAMOUR! THIS HUMAN CAN'T POSSIBLY--
AS AM I! HOW CAN HE SEE US?!
OH... DON'T BE AFRAID!
I HAVE SEEN ALL MANNER OF MAGICAL CREATURES. WHY...I WITNESSED A PAIR OF WARRING DRAGONS WHEN I WAS ONLY SEVEN!
MY NAME IS MERLINUS...
HE SEES US...BUT NOT FOR LONG!
ÁBLINDIAN!
DISPEL.
PLEASE...
...I MEAN YOU NO HARM.

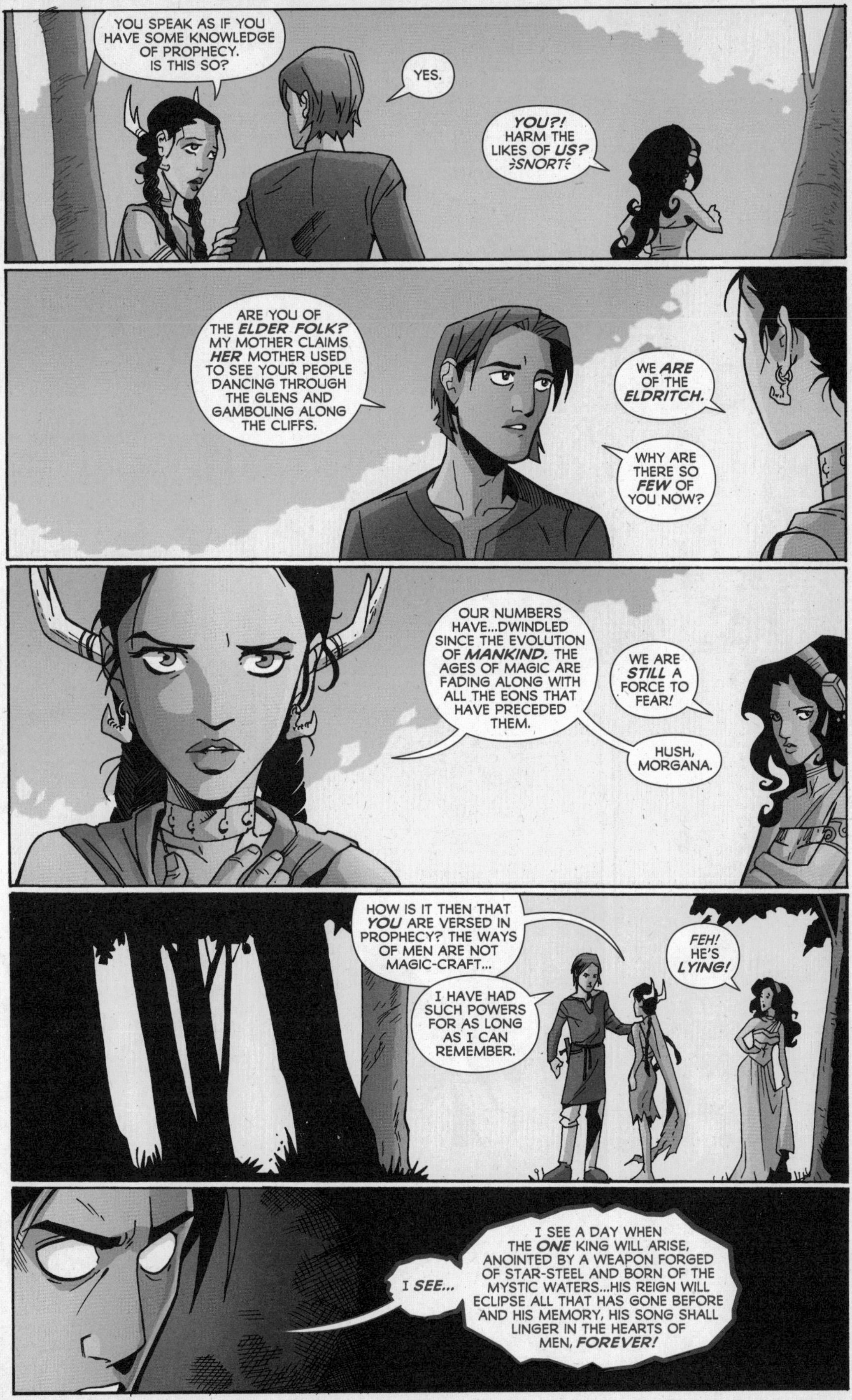
YOU SPEAK AS IF YOU HAVE SOME KNOWLEDGE OF PROPHECY. IS THIS SO?
YES.
YOU?! HARM THE LIKES OF US? *SNORT*
ARE YOU OF THE ELDER FOLK? MY MOTHER CLAIMS HER MOTHER USED TO SEE YOUR PEOPLE DANCING THROUGH THE GLENS AND GAMBOLING ALONG THE CLIFFS.
WE ARE OF THE ELDRITCH.
WHY ARE THERE SO FEW OF YOU NOW?
OUR NUMBERS HAVE...DWINDLED SINCE THE EVOLUTION OF MANKIND. THE AGES OF MAGIC ARE FADING ALONG WITH ALL THE EONS THAT HAVE PRECEDED THEM.
WE ARE STILL A FORCE TO FEAR!
HUSH, MORGANA.
HOW IS IT THEN THAT YOU ARE VERSED IN PROPHECY? THE WAYS OF MEN ARE NOT MAGIC-CRAFT...
I HAVE HAD SUCH POWERS FOR AS LONG AS I CAN REMEMBER.
FEH! HE'S LYING!
I SEE...
I SEE A DAY WHEN THE ONE KING WILL ARISE, ANOINTED BY A WEAPON FORGED OF STAR-STEEL AND BORN OF THE MYSTIC WATERS...HIS REIGN WILL ECLIPSE ALL THAT HAS GONE BEFORE AND HIS MEMORY, HIS SONG SHALL LINGER IN THE HEARTS OF MEN, FOREVER!

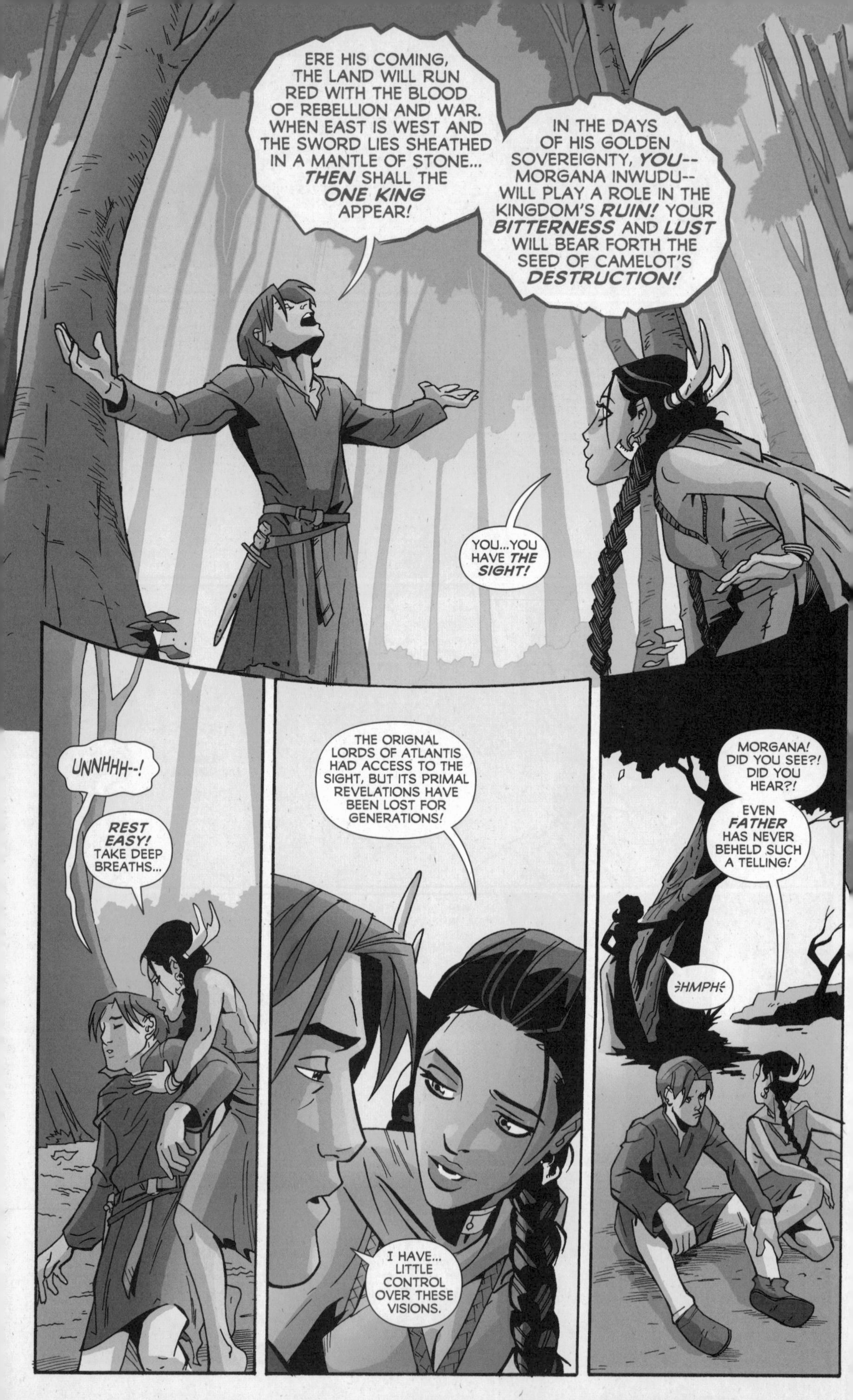
ERE HIS COMING, THE LAND WILL RUN RED WITH THE BLOOD OF REBELLION AND WAR. WHEN EAST IS WEST AND THE SWORD LIES SHEATHED IN A MANTLE OF STONE... THEN SHALL THE ONE KING APPEAR!
IN THE DAYS OF HIS GOLDEN SOVEREIGNTY, YOU-- MORGANA INWUDU-- WILL PLAY A ROLE IN THE KINGDOM'S RUIN! YOUR BITTERNESS AND LUST WILL BEAR FORTH THE SEED OF CAMELOT'S DESTRUCTION!
YOU...YOU HAVE THE SIGHT!
UNNHHH--!
REST EASY! TAKE DEEP BREATHS...
THE ORIGNAL LORDS OF ATLANTIS HAD ACCESS TO THE SIGHT, BUT ITS PRIMAL REVELATIONS HAVE BEEN LOST FOR GENERATIONS!
I HAVE... LITTLE CONTROL OVER THESE VISIONS.
MORGANA! DID YOU SEE?! DID YOU HEAR?!
EVEN FATHER HAS NEVER BEHELD SUCH A TELLING!
HMPH

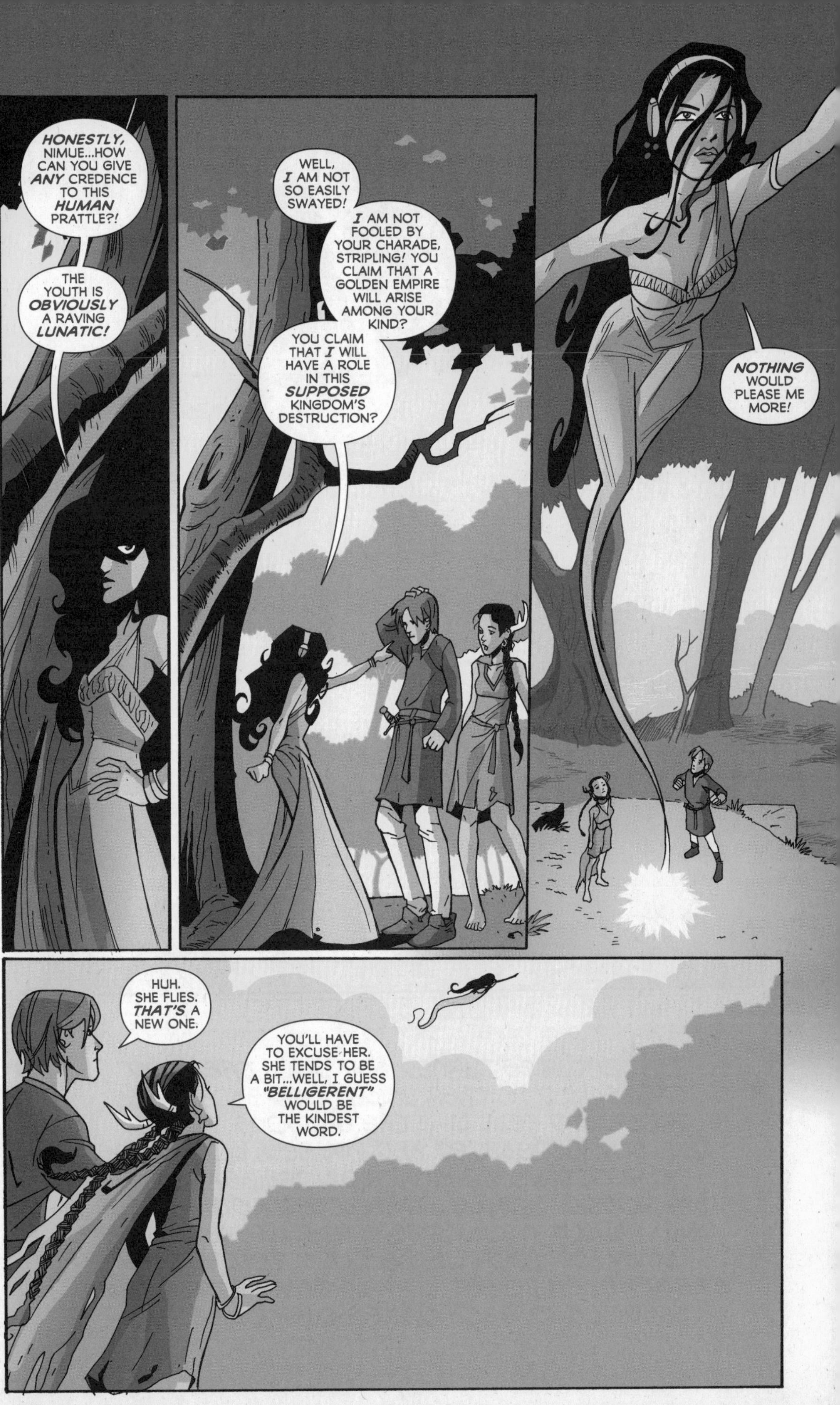
HONESTLY, NIMUE...HOW CAN YOU GIVE ANY CREDENCE TO THIS HUMAN PRATTLE?!
THE YOUTH IS OBVIOUSLY A RAVING LUNATIC!
WELL, I AM NOT SO EASILY SWAYED!
I AM NOT FOOLED BY YOUR CHARADE, STRIPLING! YOU CLAIM THAT A GOLDEN EMPIRE WILL ARISE AMONG YOUR KIND?
YOU CLAIM THAT I WILL HAVE A ROLE IN THIS SUPPOSED KINGDOM'S DESTRUCTION?
NOTHING WOULD PLEASE ME MORE!
HUH. SHE FLIES. THAT'S A NEW ONE.
YOU'LL HAVE TO EXCUSE HER. SHE TENDS TO BE A BIT...WELL, I GUESS "BELLIGERENT" WOULD BE THE KINDEST WORD.

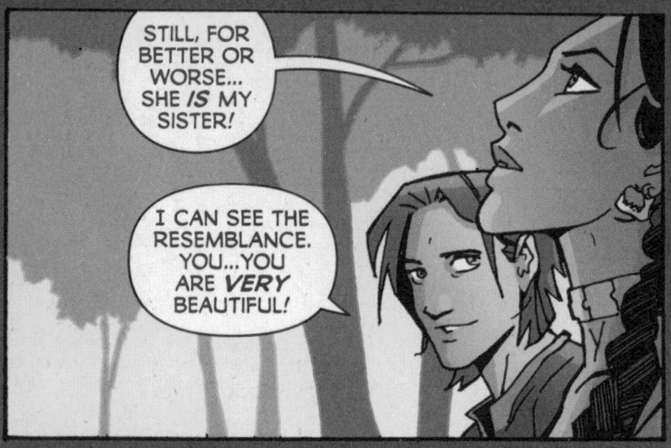
STILL, FOR BETTER OR WORSE... SHE *IS* MY SISTER!
I CAN SEE THE RESEMBLANCE. YOU...YOU ARE *VERY* BEAUTIFUL!

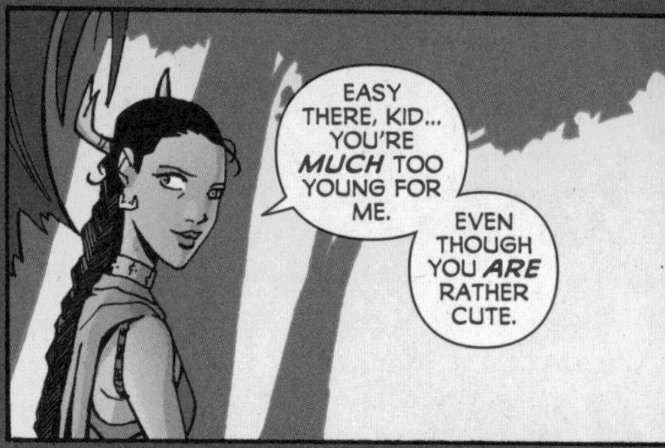
EASY THERE, KID... YOU'RE *MUCH* TOO YOUNG FOR ME.
EVEN THOUGH YOU *ARE* RATHER CUTE.

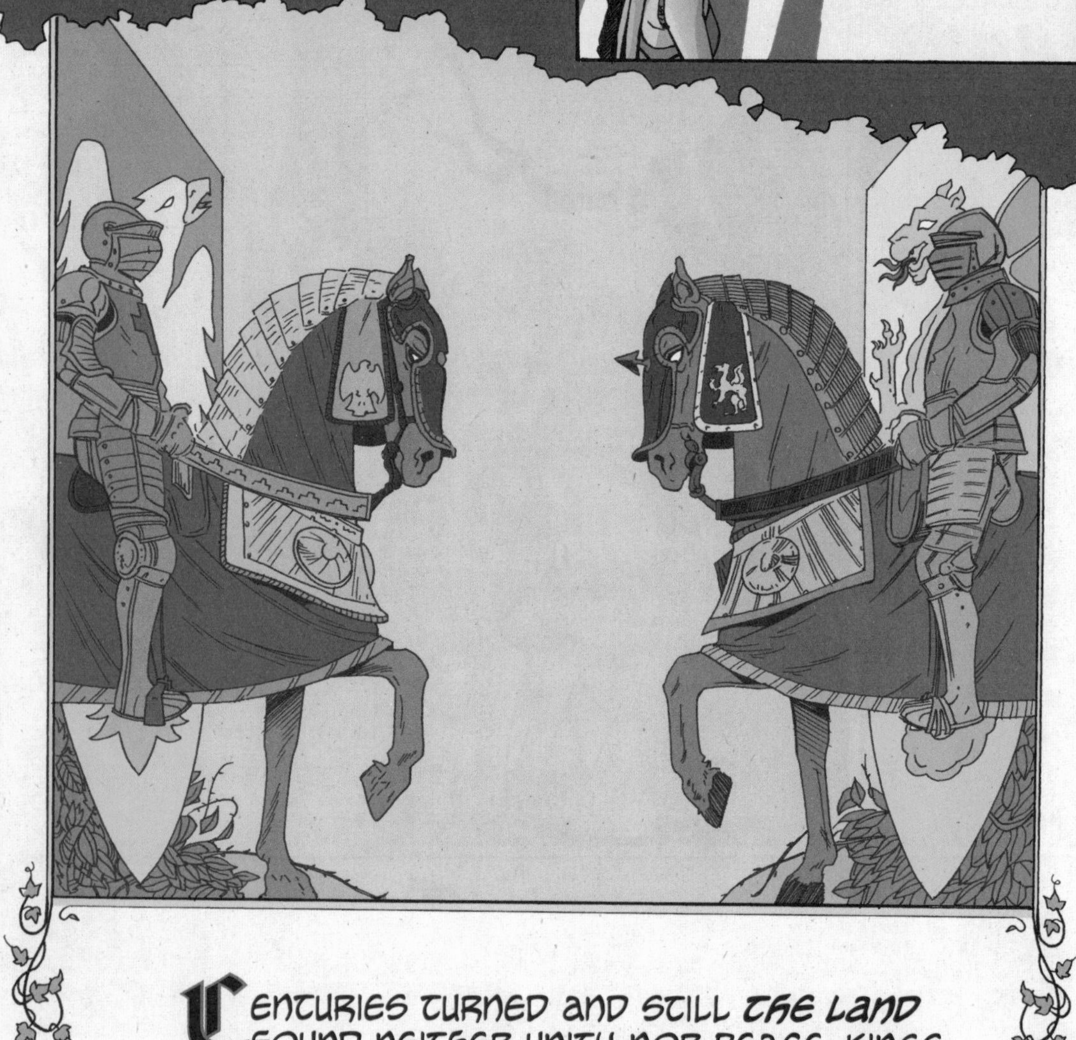

Centuries turned and still *the land* found neither unity nor peace. Kings rose and fell like the seasons; Danius, Idvallo, Beldgabred and Pir, Heli, Lud, Marius, and Octavius, even unto Vortigern and Ambrosius. Finally, long after *Rome* itself had fallen into strife, a pair of warlords emerged, each laying claim to the *one crown*, each poised to rain down either amity or discord, each on the cusp of legend.

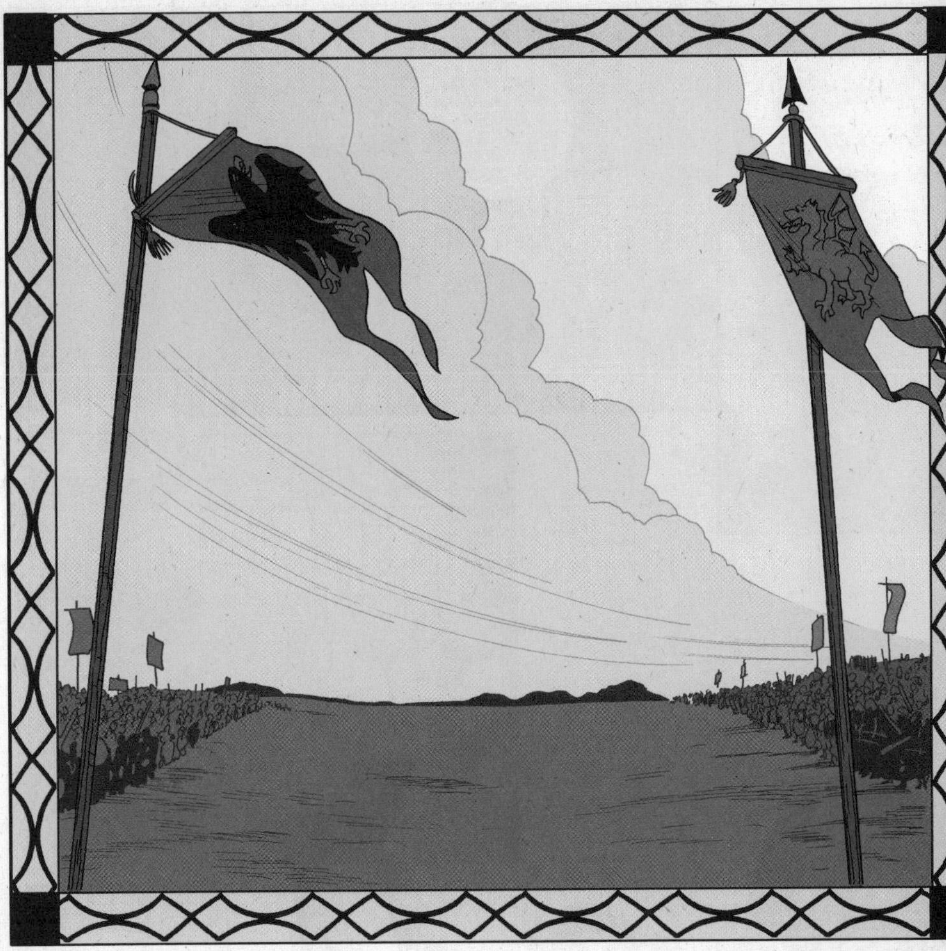

Again and again clashed the armies, east and west, neither gaining sway; ***Gorlois, the Red-beak***, Duke of Cornwall 'gainst bold ***Uther, the Pendragon***, Prince of Britannia. The lifeblood of sire and serf alike ran red o'er field
The Land ached for tranquility, until
called upon his enemy to concede the
meet in equity, there to discuss an ul
halt of transgressions and
establish a lingering peace
under mutual agreement, the
armies stilled, their weapons
a fragile armistice prevailed
unbroken by deed or thought
midst ***the land***.

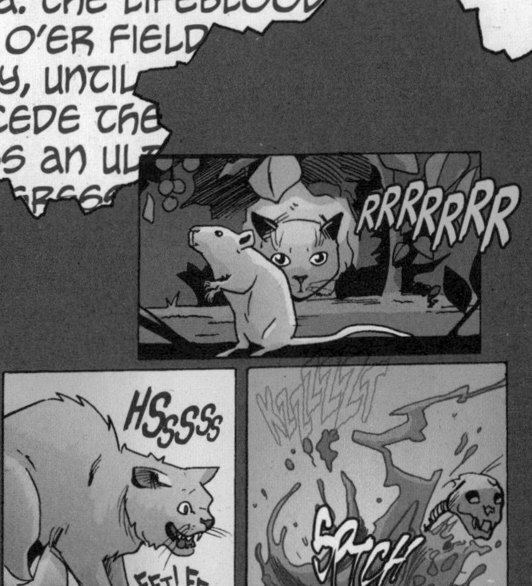
RRRRRRR
HSSSSS
FFT! FFT!
SPTCH

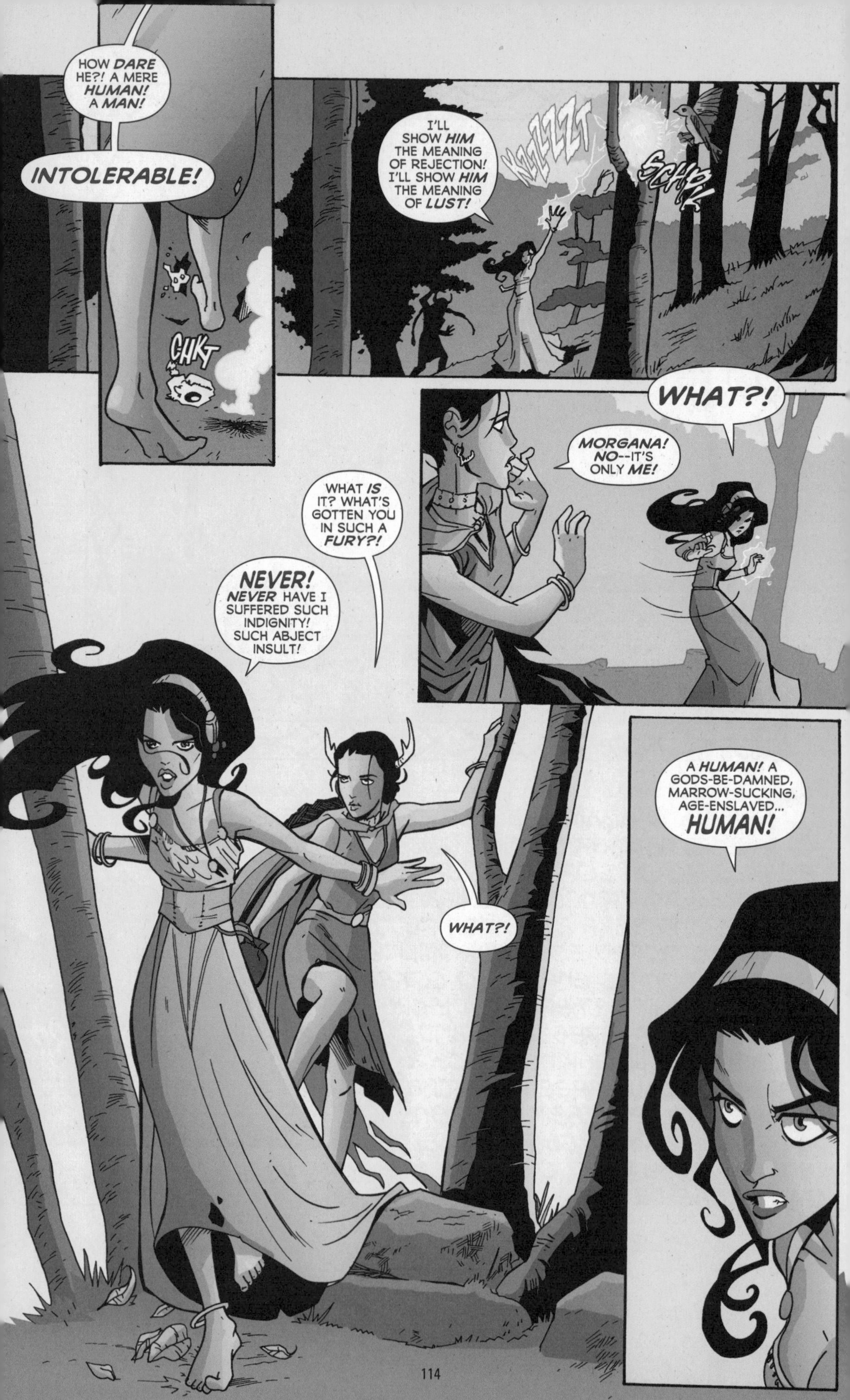

HOW DARE HE?! A MERE HUMAN! A MAN!
INTOLERABLE!
CHKT
I'LL SHOW HIM THE MEANING OF REJECTION! I'LL SHOW HIM THE MEANING OF LUST!
SCHOK
WHAT?!
MORGANA! NO--IT'S ONLY ME!
WHAT IS IT? WHAT'S GOTTEN YOU IN SUCH A FURY?!
NEVER! NEVER HAVE I SUFFERED SUCH INDIGNITY! SUCH ABJECT INSULT!
WHAT?!
A HUMAN! A GODS-BE-DAMNED, MARROW-SUCKING, AGE-ENSLAVED... HUMAN!

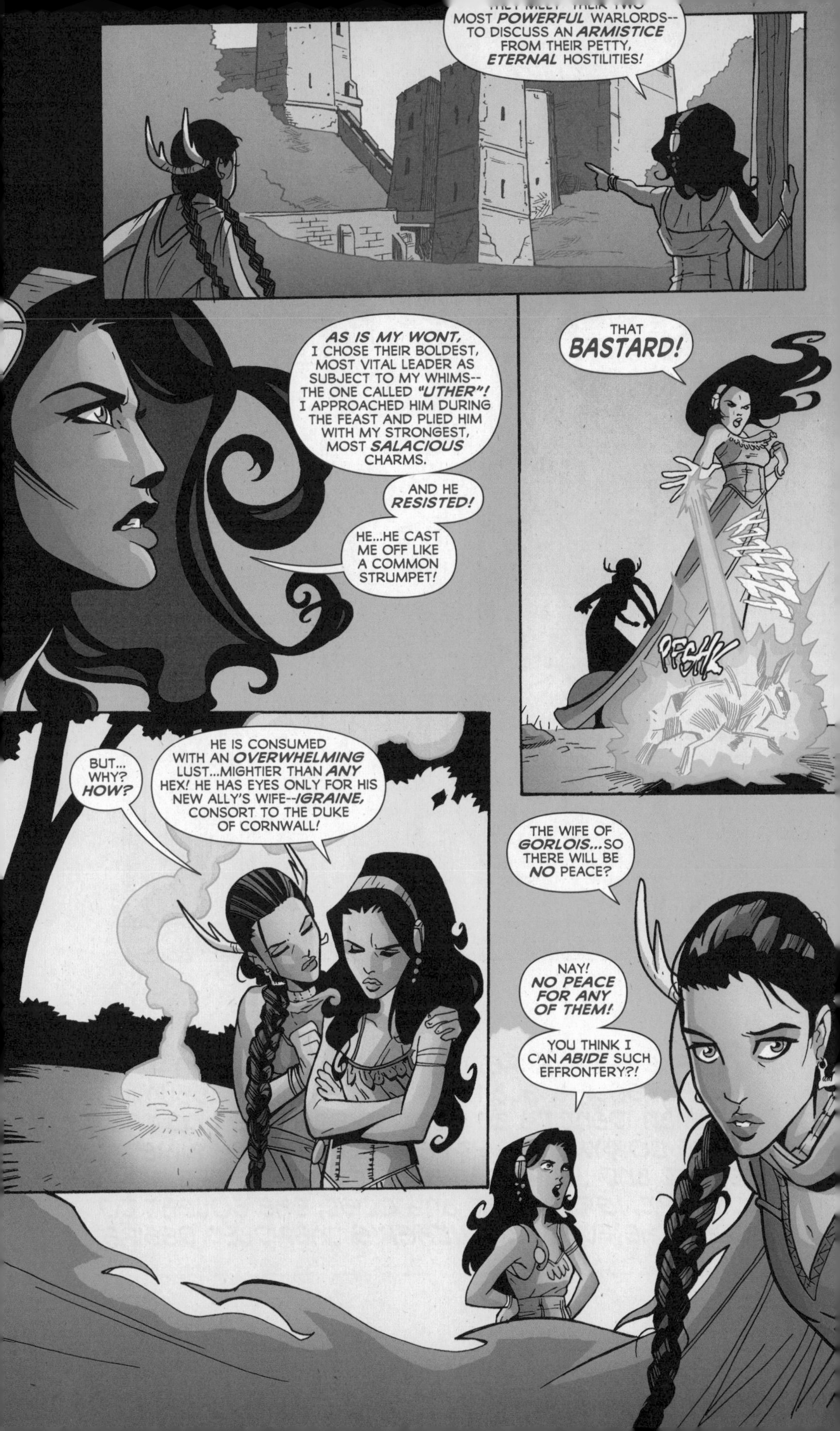
MOST POWERFUL WARLORDS--
TO DISCUSS AN ARMISTICE
FROM THEIR PETTY,
ETERNAL HOSTILITIES!
AS IS MY WONT, I CHOSE THEIR BOLDEST, MOST VITAL LEADER AS SUBJECT TO MY WHIMS-- THE ONE CALLED "UTHER"! I APPROACHED HIM DURING THE FEAST AND PLIED HIM WITH MY STRONGEST, MOST SALACIOUS CHARMS.
AND HE RESISTED!
HE...HE CAST ME OFF LIKE A COMMON STRUMPET!
THAT BASTARD!
PFSHK
BUT... WHY? HOW?
HE IS CONSUMED WITH AN OVERWHELMING LUST...MIGHTIER THAN ANY HEX! HE HAS EYES ONLY FOR HIS NEW ALLY'S WIFE--IGRAINE, CONSORT TO THE DUKE OF CORNWALL!
THE WIFE OF GORLOIS...SO THERE WILL BE NO PEACE?
NAY! NO PEACE FOR ANY OF THEM!
YOU THINK I CAN ABIDE SUCH EFFRONTERY?!

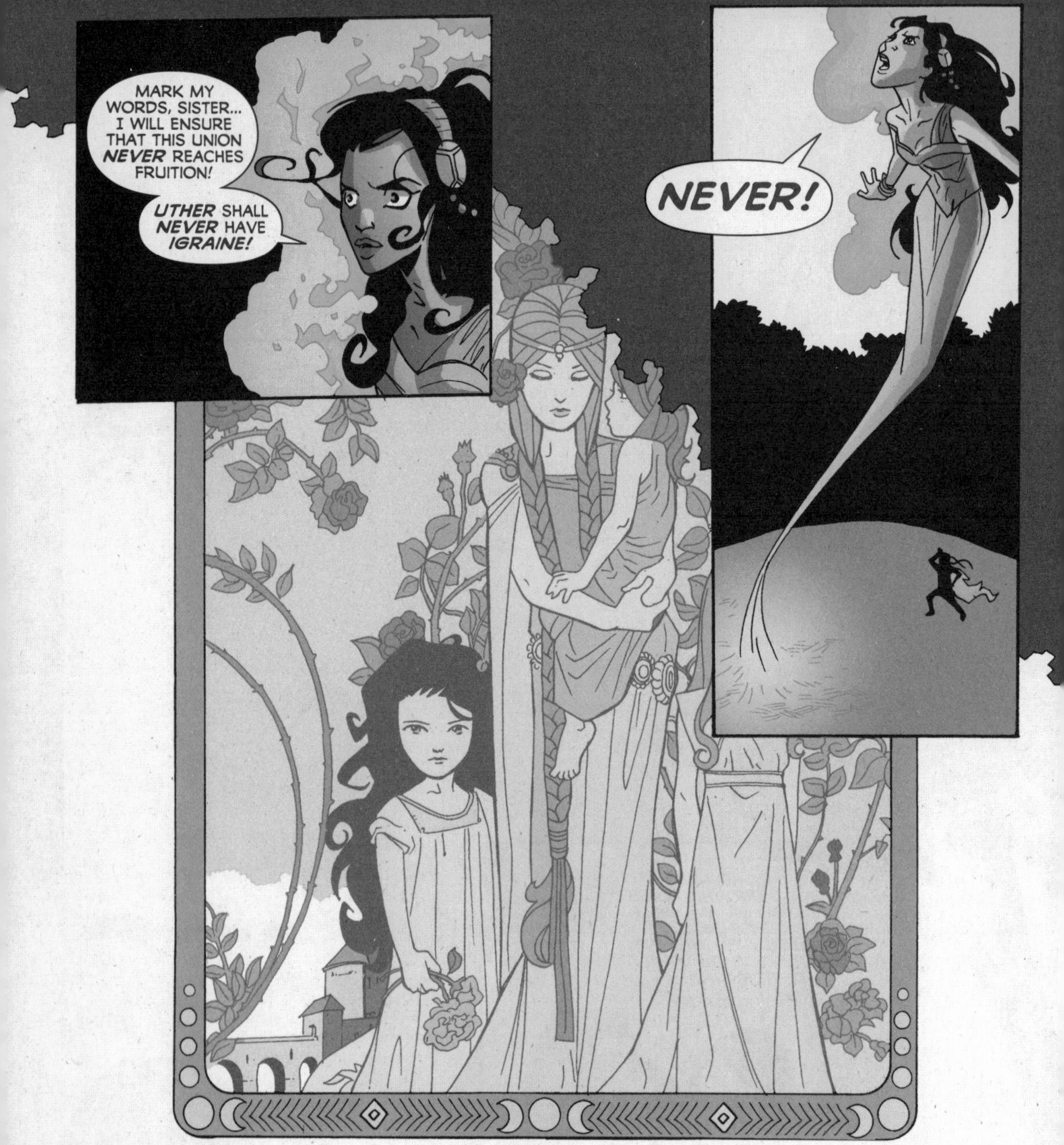
MARK MY WORDS, SISTER... I WILL ENSURE THAT THIS UNION NEVER REACHES FRUITION!
UTHER SHALL NEVER HAVE IGRAINE!
NEVER!

True to her ire, Morgana took upon herself a glamour of disguise, assuming a human identity as second daughter to the Duke of Cornwall. Her fell conspiracy aimed to distract and usurp the attentions of the royal consort, ***Igraine***; at any cost, she sought to douse the flame of ***Uther's*** unbridled desire.

FOR, DESPITE ANY ENTENTE WITH HIS RIVAL, THE LUSTY **PENDRAGON** FOUND HE COULD NOT CONTAIN HIS DESIRES. HE ACHED FOR EVEN THE SLIGHTEST TOUCH FROM THE FAIR **IGRAINE** AND FOUND NO EASE IN ANY OTHER'S EMBRACE. HIS VIGOR WAS UNQUENCHABLE AND, WORSE, IMPOSSIBLE TO CONCEAL. ANON, CORNWALL CAUGHT THE WIND OF BRITANNIA'S ARDOR, A RANK AND GARISH BETRAYAL OF THEIR TRUCE. FURIOUS, GORLOIS AGAIN TOOK UP ARMS AND DECLARED WAR ON THE WEST.

NOW ENTER THE WILES OF **PRINCE UTHER'S** ADVISOR-- DRAGON-SAGE, SHAPE-SHIFTER, SWORD-STEWARD, DEMON-SPAWN AND KINGMAKER--THE ARCHWIZARD **MERLIN**. FOR DECADES, HE HAD MOLDED AND MANIPULATED THE COURSE OF HUMAN AFFAIRS, ALIGNING BOTH PLAYERS AND EVENTS TO BEAR FRUIT TO HIS GREATEST PROPHECY; THE RISE OF **THE ONE KING** WHO WOULD UNITE ALL OF **THE LAND** AND REIGN O'ER A GOLDEN ERA OF PEACE.

THE MAGE SPELLED A GLAMOUR UPON **UTHER**, CASTING HIM IN THE IMAGE OF **CORNWALL**. THUS VEILED, THE PRINCE SLIPPED INTO HIS RIVAL'S CASTLE AND WAS AT LAST ABLE TO SLAKE HIS HEATED THIRST IN THE COOL, PALE LOINS OF FAIR **IGRAINE**.

THUS, A LEGEND WAS SEEDED: THUS, **ARTHUR** WAS BORN.

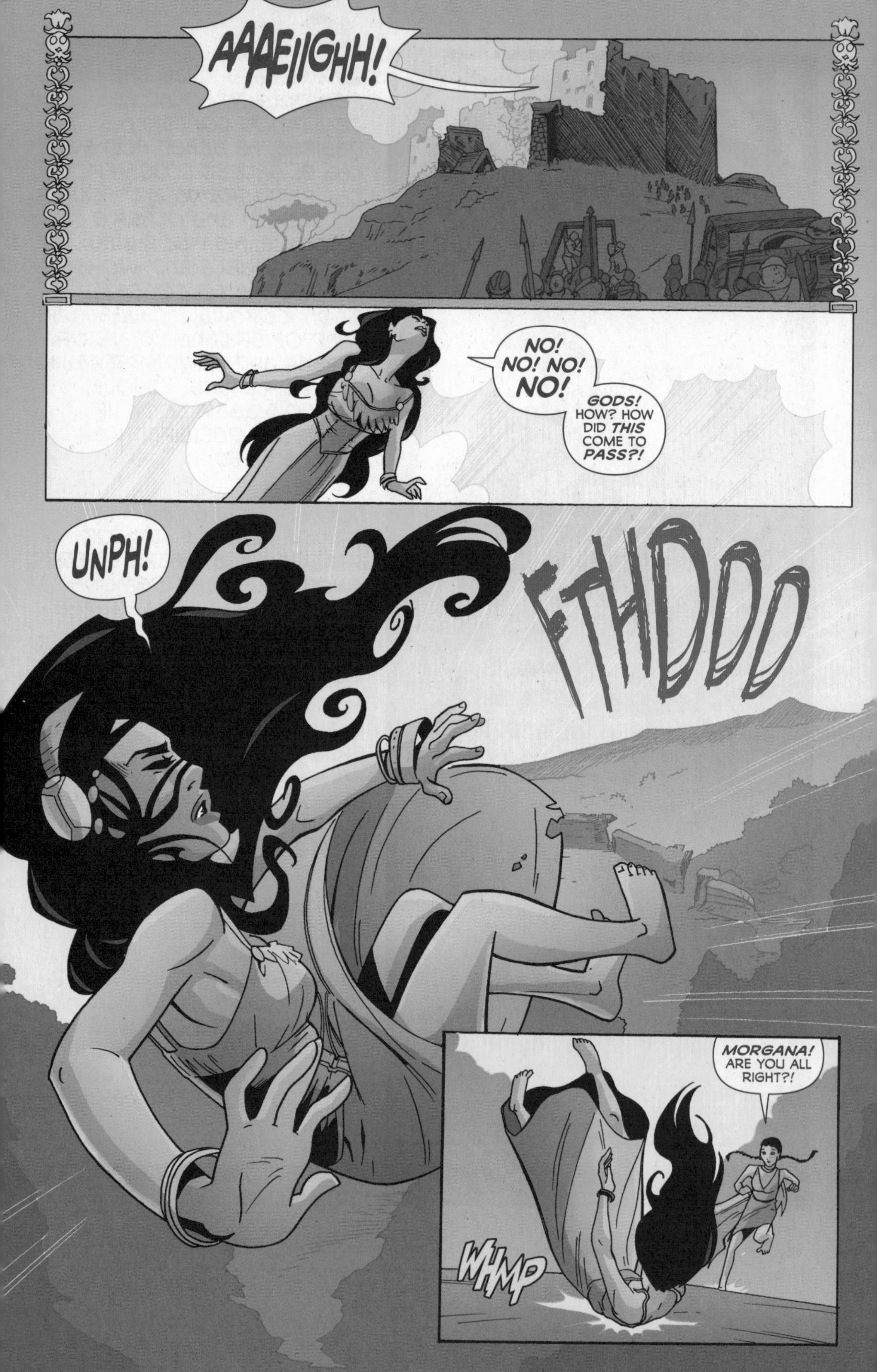
AAAEIIGHH!
NO! NO! NO! NO!
GODS! HOW? HOW DID THIS COME TO PASS?!
UNPH!
FTHDDD
MORGANA! ARE YOU ALL RIGHT?!
WHMP

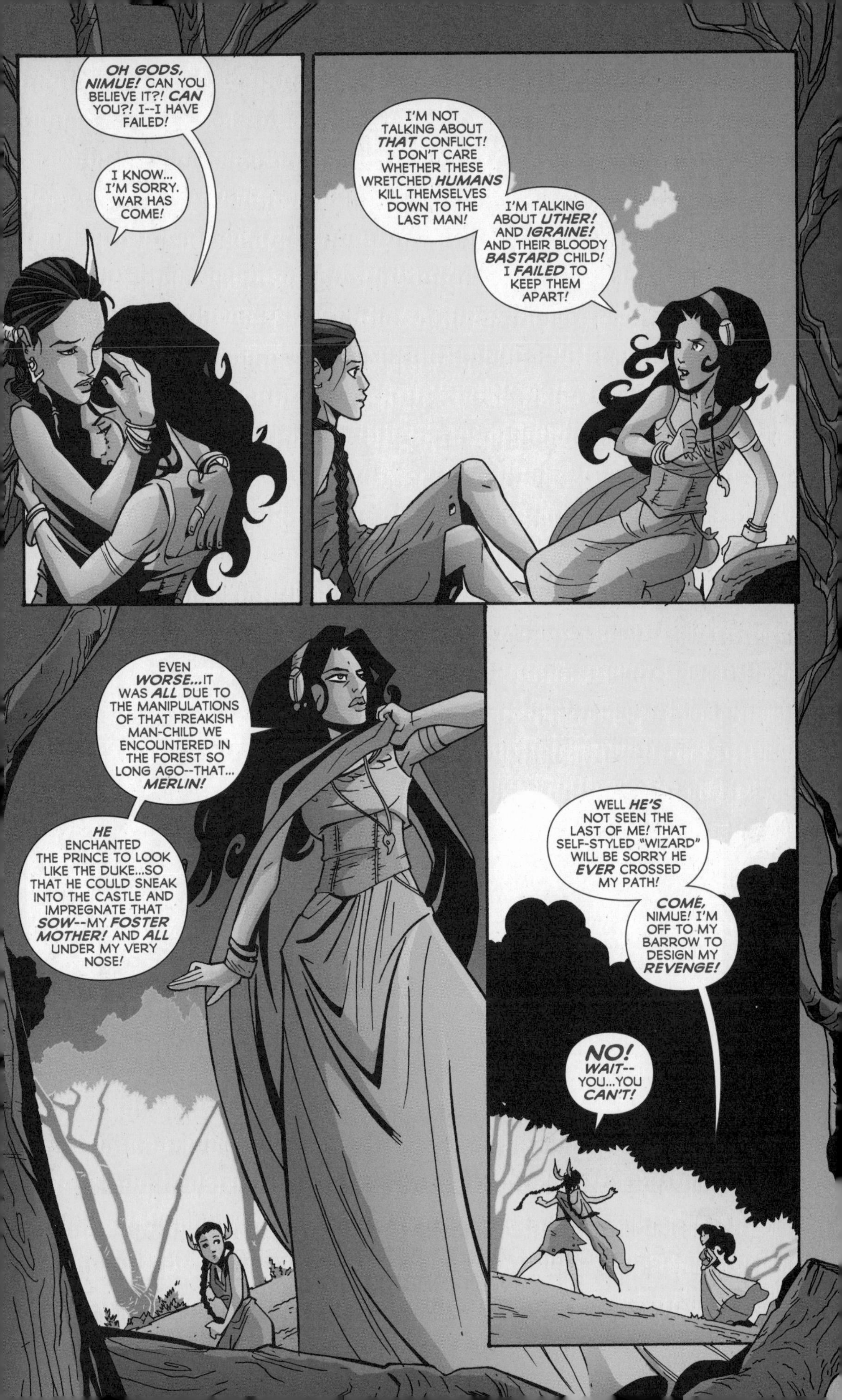
OH GODS, NIMUE! CAN YOU BELIEVE IT?! CAN YOU?! I--I HAVE FAILED!
I KNOW... I'M SORRY. WAR HAS COME!
I'M NOT TALKING ABOUT THAT CONFLICT! I DON'T CARE WHETHER THESE WRETCHED HUMANS KILL THEMSELVES DOWN TO THE LAST MAN!
I'M TALKING ABOUT UTHER! AND IGRAINE! AND THEIR BLOODY BASTARD CHILD! I FAILED TO KEEP THEM APART!
EVEN WORSE...IT WAS ALL DUE TO THE MANIPULATIONS OF THAT FREAKISH MAN-CHILD WE ENCOUNTERED IN THE FOREST SO LONG AGO--THAT... MERLIN!
HE ENCHANTED THE PRINCE TO LOOK LIKE THE DUKE...SO THAT HE COULD SNEAK INTO THE CASTLE AND IMPREGNATE THAT SOW--MY FOSTER MOTHER! AND ALL UNDER MY VERY NOSE!
WELL HE'S NOT SEEN THE LAST OF ME! THAT SELF-STYLED "WIZARD" WILL BE SORRY HE EVER CROSSED MY PATH!
COME, NIMUE! I'M OFF TO MY BARROW TO DESIGN MY REVENGE!
NO! WAIT-- YOU...YOU CAN'T!

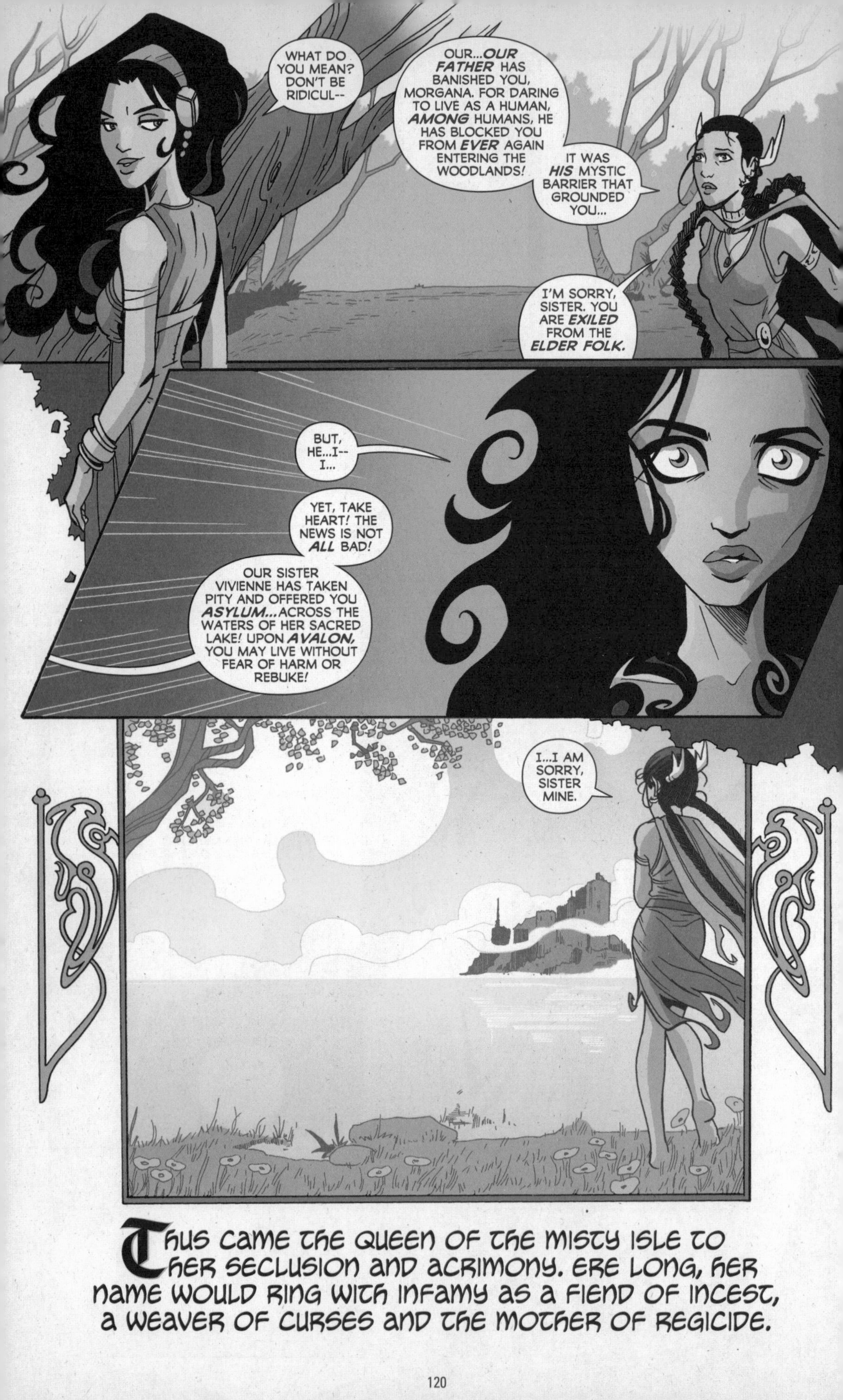
WHAT DO YOU MEAN? DON'T BE RIDICUL--
OUR...OUR FATHER HAS BANISHED YOU, MORGANA. FOR DARING TO LIVE AS A HUMAN, AMONG HUMANS, HE HAS BLOCKED YOU FROM EVER AGAIN ENTERING THE WOODLANDS!
IT WAS HIS MYSTIC BARRIER THAT GROUNDED YOU...
I'M SORRY, SISTER. YOU ARE EXILED FROM THE ELDER FOLK.
BUT, HE...I-- I...
YET, TAKE HEART! THE NEWS IS NOT ALL BAD!
OUR SISTER VIVIENNE HAS TAKEN PITY AND OFFERED YOU ASYLUM...ACROSS THE WATERS OF HER SACRED LAKE! UPON AVALON, YOU MAY LIVE WITHOUT FEAR OF HARM OR REBUKE!
I...I AM SORRY, SISTER MINE.
Thus came the queen of the misty isle to her seclusion and acrimony. Ere long, her name would ring with infamy as a fiend of incest, a weaver of curses and the mother of regicide.

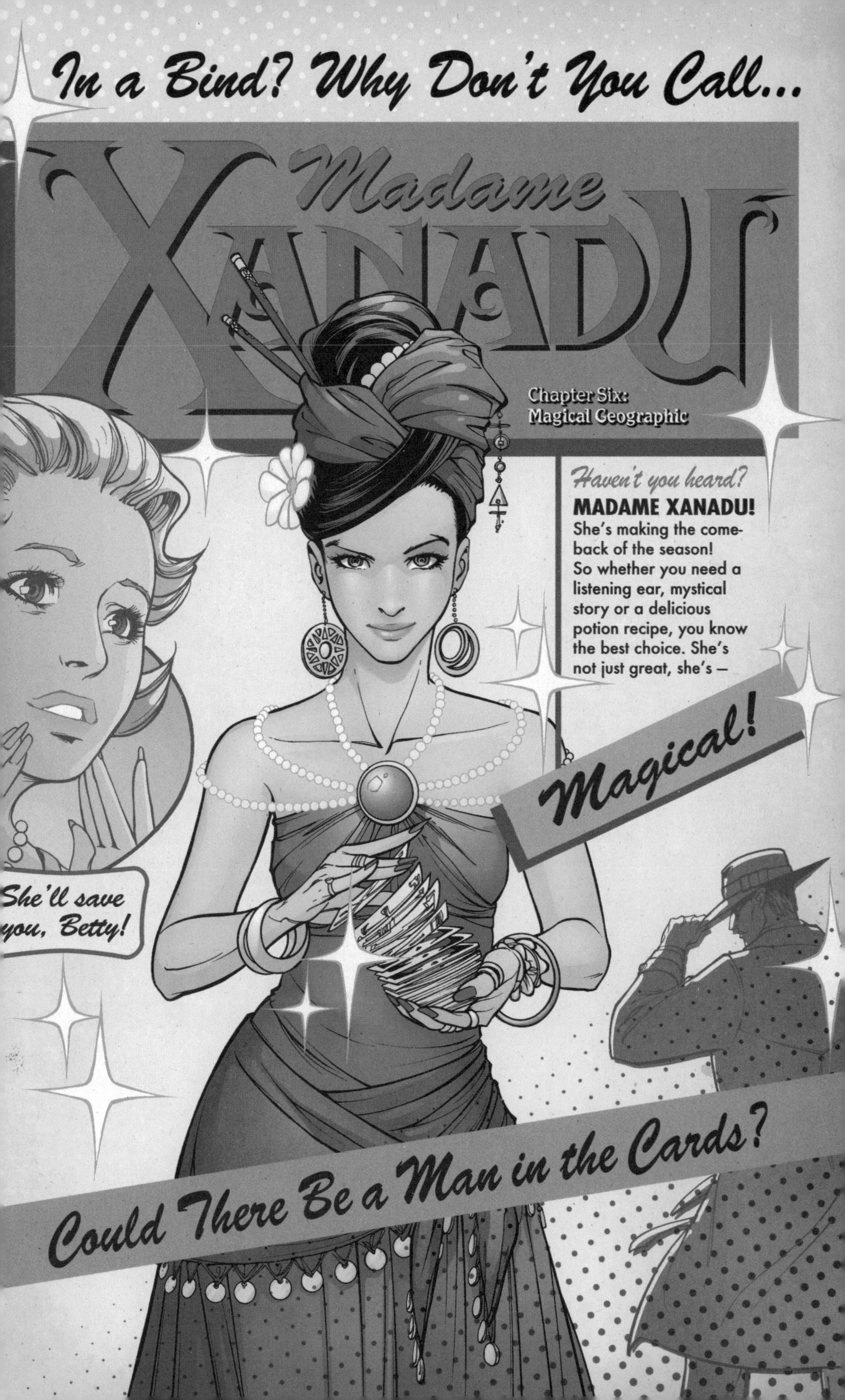
In a Bind? Why Don't You Call...
Madame
XANADU
Chapter Six:
Magical Geographic
Haven't you heard?
MADAME XANADU!
She's making the come-back of the season! So whether you need a listening ear, mystical story or a delicious potion recipe, you know the best choice. She's not just great, she's —
Magical!
She'll save you, Betty!
Could There Be a Man in the Cards?

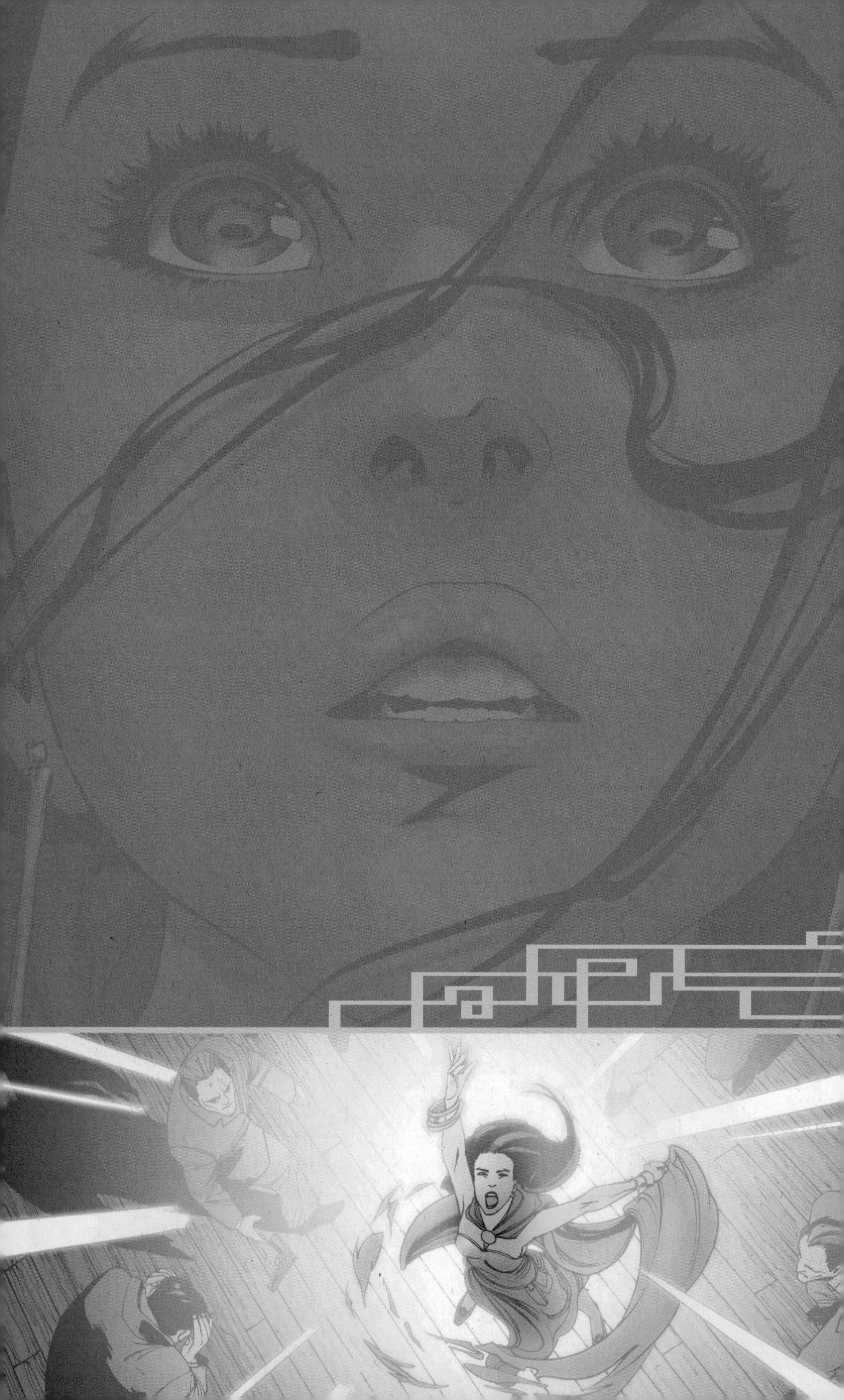

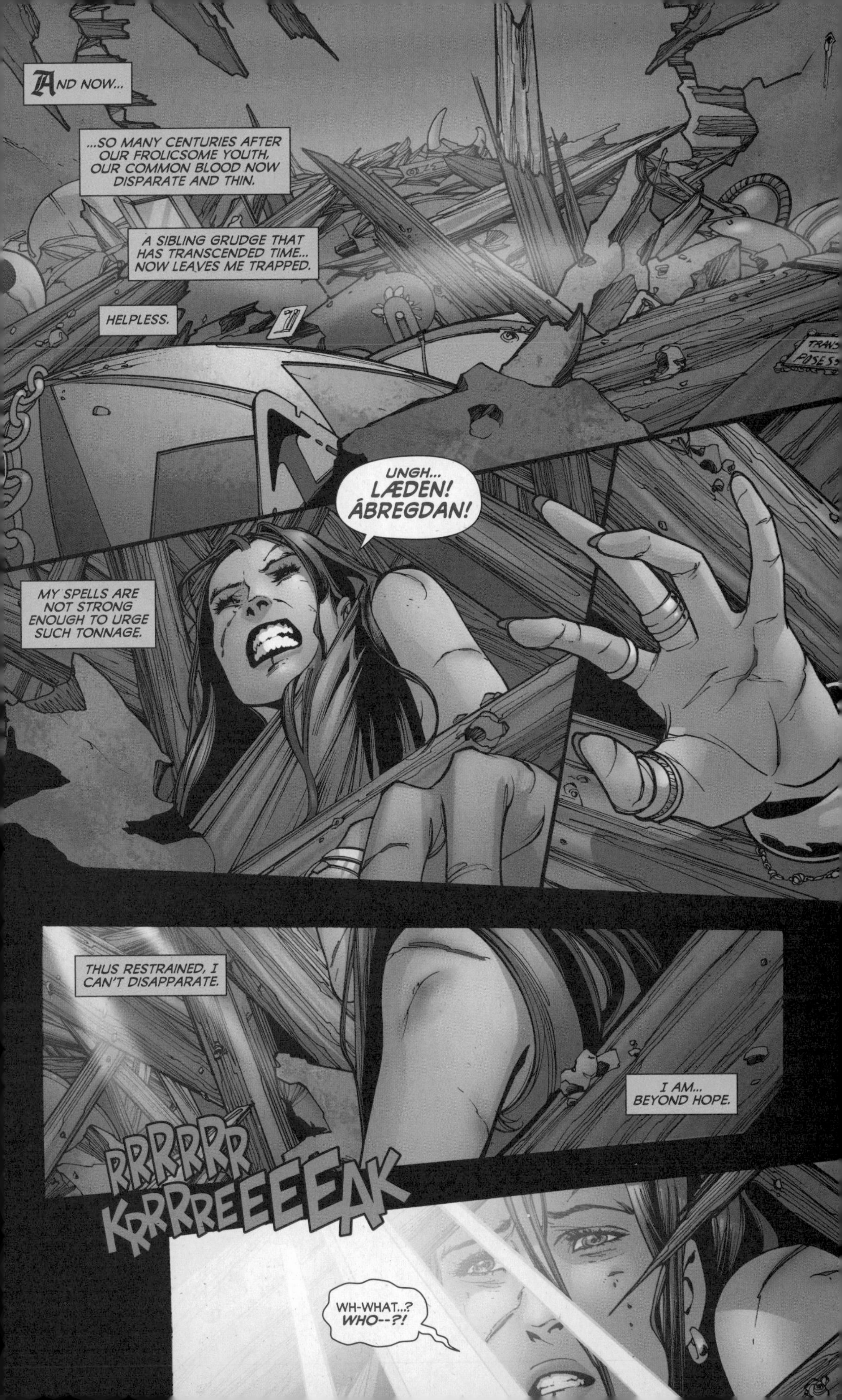
AND NOW...
...SO MANY CENTURIES AFTER OUR FROLICSOME YOUTH, OUR COMMON BLOOD NOW DISPARATE AND THIN.
A SIBLING GRUDGE THAT HAS TRANSCENDED TIME... NOW LEAVES ME TRAPPED.
HELPLESS.
UNGH... LÆDEN! ÁBREGDAN!
MY SPELLS ARE NOT STRONG ENOUGH TO URGE SUCH TONNAGE.
THUS RESTRAINED, I CAN'T DISAPPARATE.
I AM... BEYOND HOPE.
RRRRRR KRRRREEEEAK
WH-WHAT...? WHO--?!

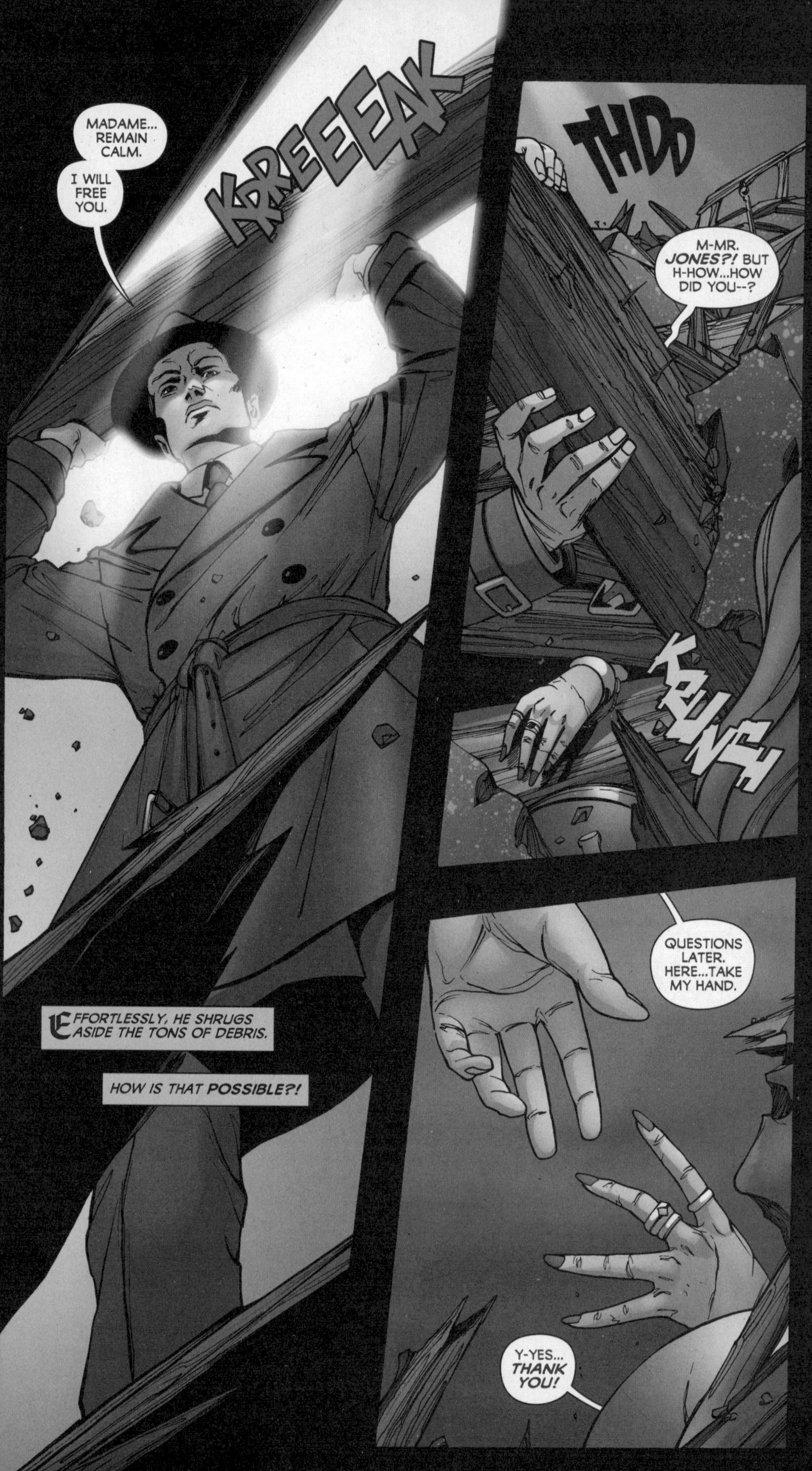
MADAME... REMAIN CALM.
I WILL FREE YOU.
KRREEEAK
EFFORTLESSLY, HE SHRUGS ASIDE THE TONS OF DEBRIS.
HOW IS THAT POSSIBLE?!
THDD
M-MR. JONES?! BUT H-HOW...HOW DID YOU--?
KRUNCH
QUESTIONS LATER. HERE...TAKE MY HAND.
Y-YES... THANK YOU!

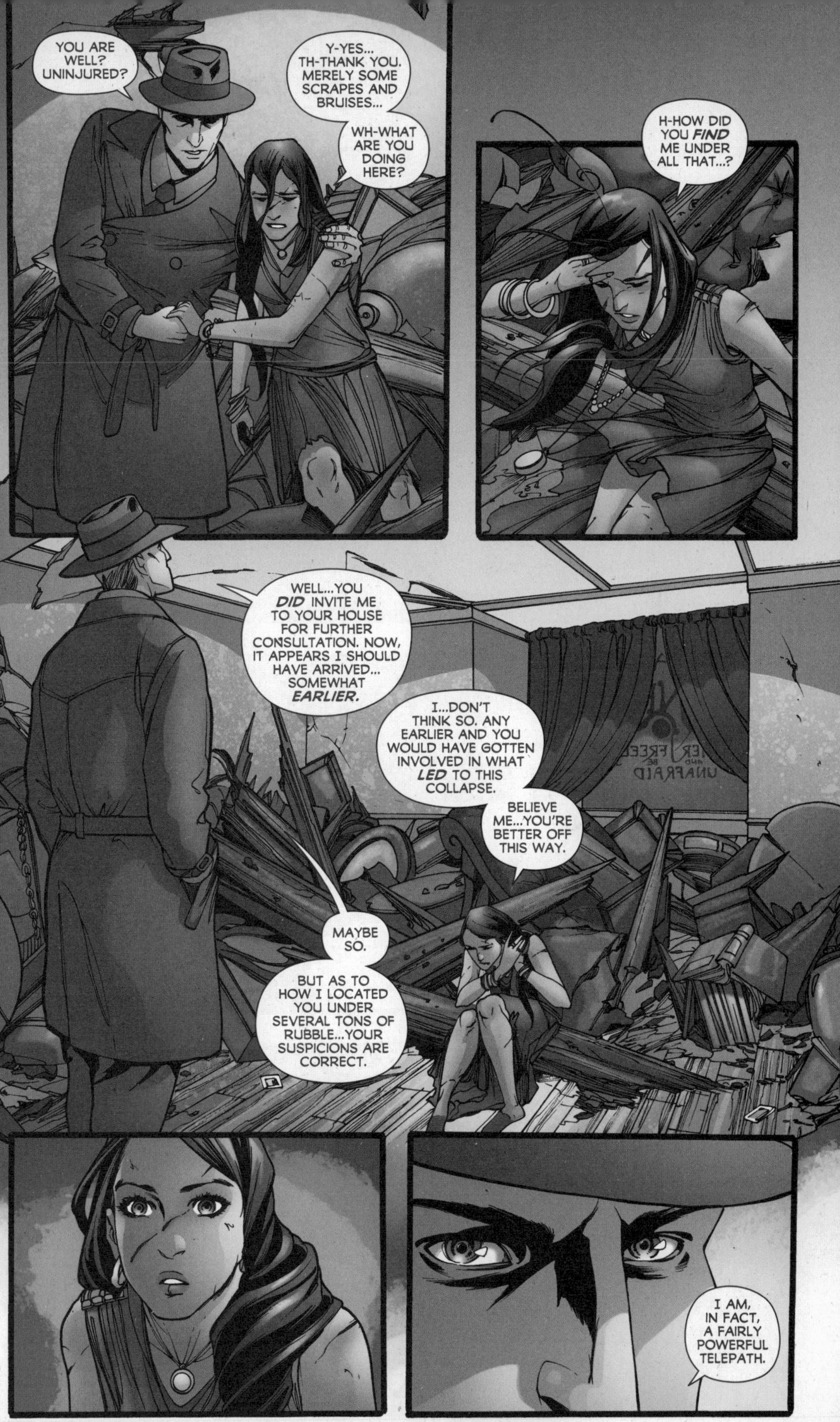
YOU ARE WELL? UNINJURED?
Y-YES... TH-THANK YOU. MERELY SOME SCRAPES AND BRUISES...
WH-WHAT ARE YOU DOING HERE?
H-HOW DID YOU *FIND* ME UNDER ALL THAT...?
WELL...YOU *DID* INVITE ME TO YOUR HOUSE FOR FURTHER CONSULTATION. NOW, IT APPEARS I SHOULD HAVE ARRIVED... SOMEWHAT *EARLIER.*
I...DON'T THINK SO. ANY EARLIER AND YOU WOULD HAVE GOTTEN INVOLVED IN WHAT *LED* TO THIS COLLAPSE.
BELIEVE ME...YOU'RE BETTER OFF THIS WAY.
MAYBE SO.
BUT AS TO HOW I LOCATED YOU UNDER SEVERAL TONS OF RUBBLE...YOUR SUSPICIONS ARE CORRECT.
I AM, IN FACT, A FAIRLY POWERFUL TELEPATH.

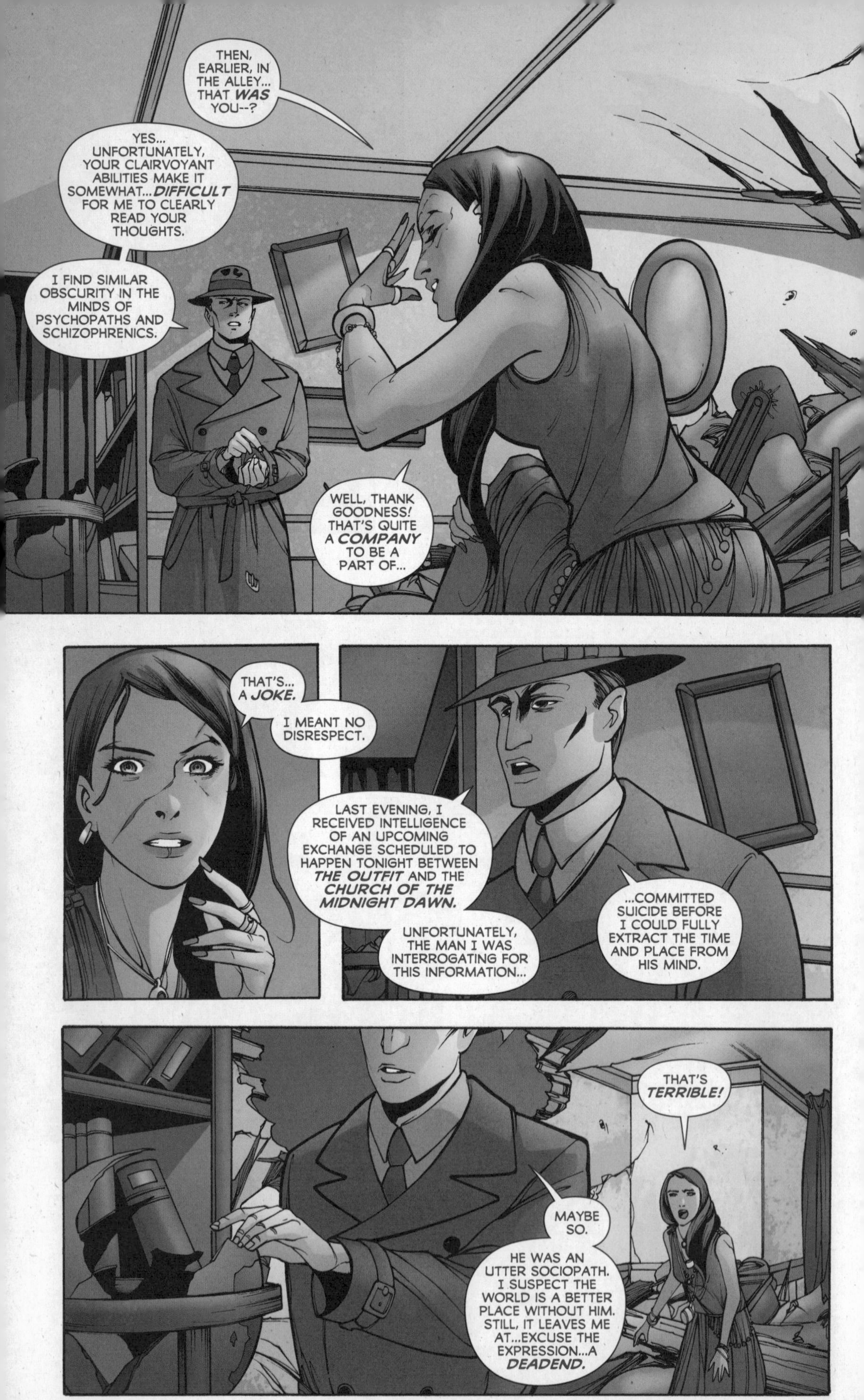
THEN, EARLIER, IN THE ALLEY... THAT WAS YOU--?
YES... UNFORTUNATELY, YOUR CLAIRVOYANT ABILITIES MAKE IT SOMEWHAT...DIFFICULT FOR ME TO CLEARLY READ YOUR THOUGHTS.
I FIND SIMILAR OBSCURITY IN THE MINDS OF PSYCHOPATHS AND SCHIZOPHRENICS.
WELL, THANK GOODNESS! THAT'S QUITE A COMPANY TO BE A PART OF...
THAT'S... A JOKE.
I MEANT NO DISRESPECT.
LAST EVENING, I RECEIVED INTELLIGENCE OF AN UPCOMING EXCHANGE SCHEDULED TO HAPPEN TONIGHT BETWEEN THE OUTFIT AND THE CHURCH OF THE MIDNIGHT DAWN.
UNFORTUNATELY, THE MAN I WAS INTERROGATING FOR THIS INFORMATION...
...COMMITTED SUICIDE BEFORE I COULD FULLY EXTRACT THE TIME AND PLACE FROM HIS MIND.
THAT'S TERRIBLE!
MAYBE SO.
HE WAS AN UTTER SOCIOPATH. I SUSPECT THE WORLD IS A BETTER PLACE WITHOUT HIM. STILL, IT LEAVES ME AT...EXCUSE THE EXPRESSION...A DEADEND.

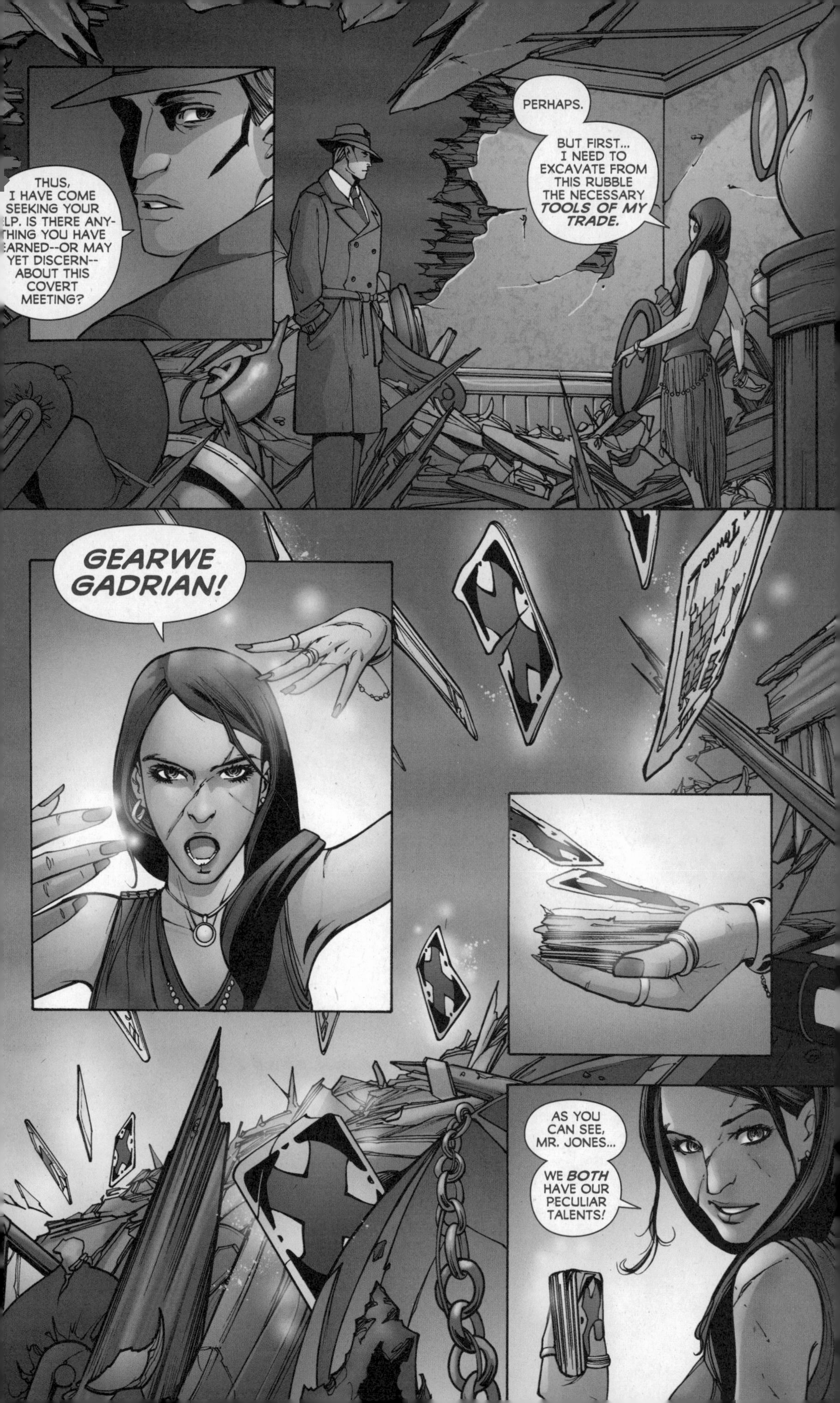

THUS, I HAVE COME SEEKING YOUR ELP. IS THERE ANYTHING YOU HAVE EARNED--OR MAY YET DISCERN--ABOUT THIS COVERT MEETING?
PERHAPS.
BUT FIRST... I NEED TO EXCAVATE FROM THIS RUBBLE THE NECESSARY TOOLS OF MY TRADE.
GEARWE GADRIAN!
AS YOU CAN SEE, MR. JONES...
WE BOTH HAVE OUR PECULIAR TALENTS!

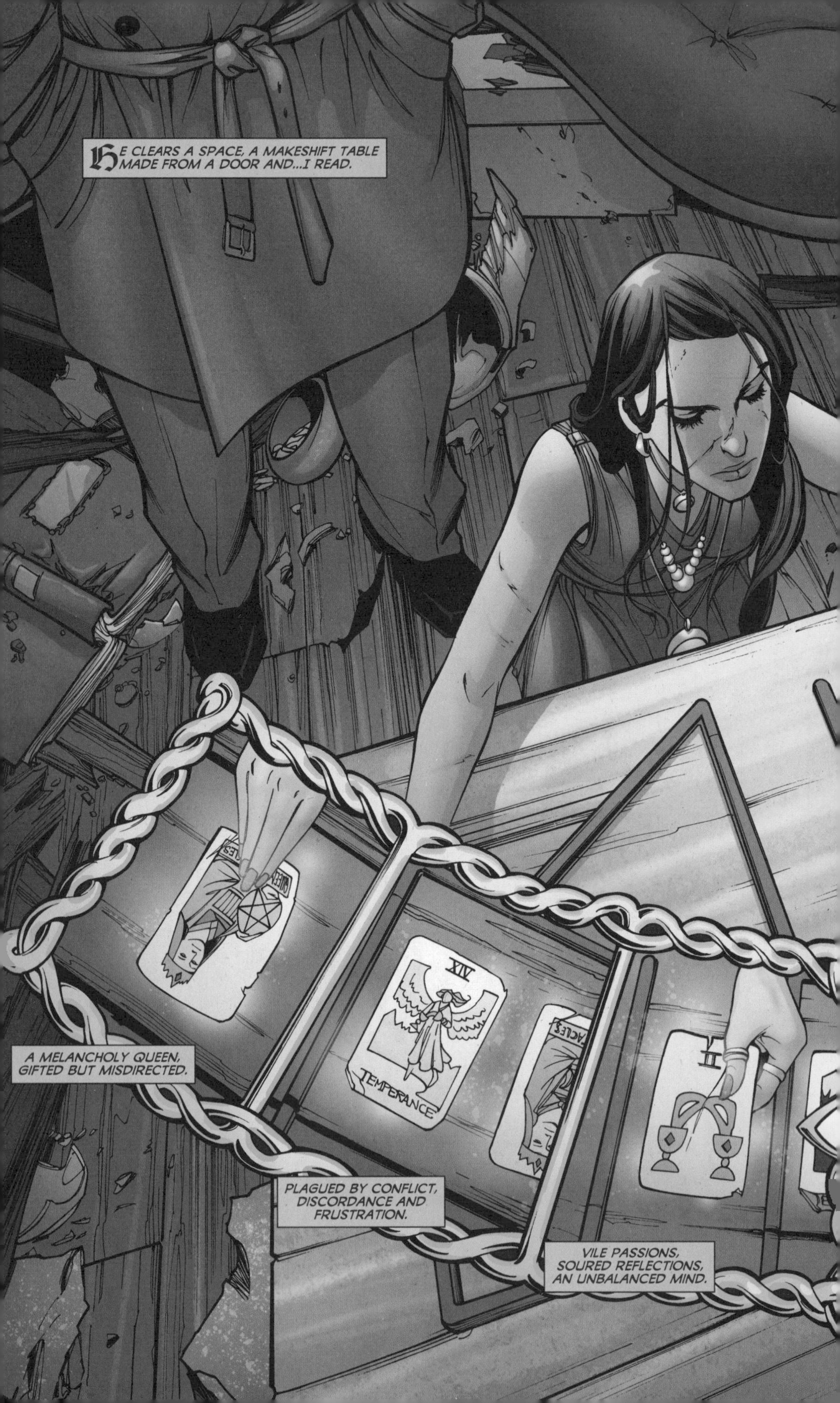
HE CLEARS A SPACE, A MAKESHIFT TABLE MADE FROM A DOOR AND...I READ.
A MELANCHOLY QUEEN, GIFTED BUT MISDIRECTED.
PLAGUED BY CONFLICT, DISCORDANCE AND FRUSTRATION.
VILE PASSIONS, SOURED REFLECTIONS, AN UNBALANCED MIND.
XIV
TEMPERANCE

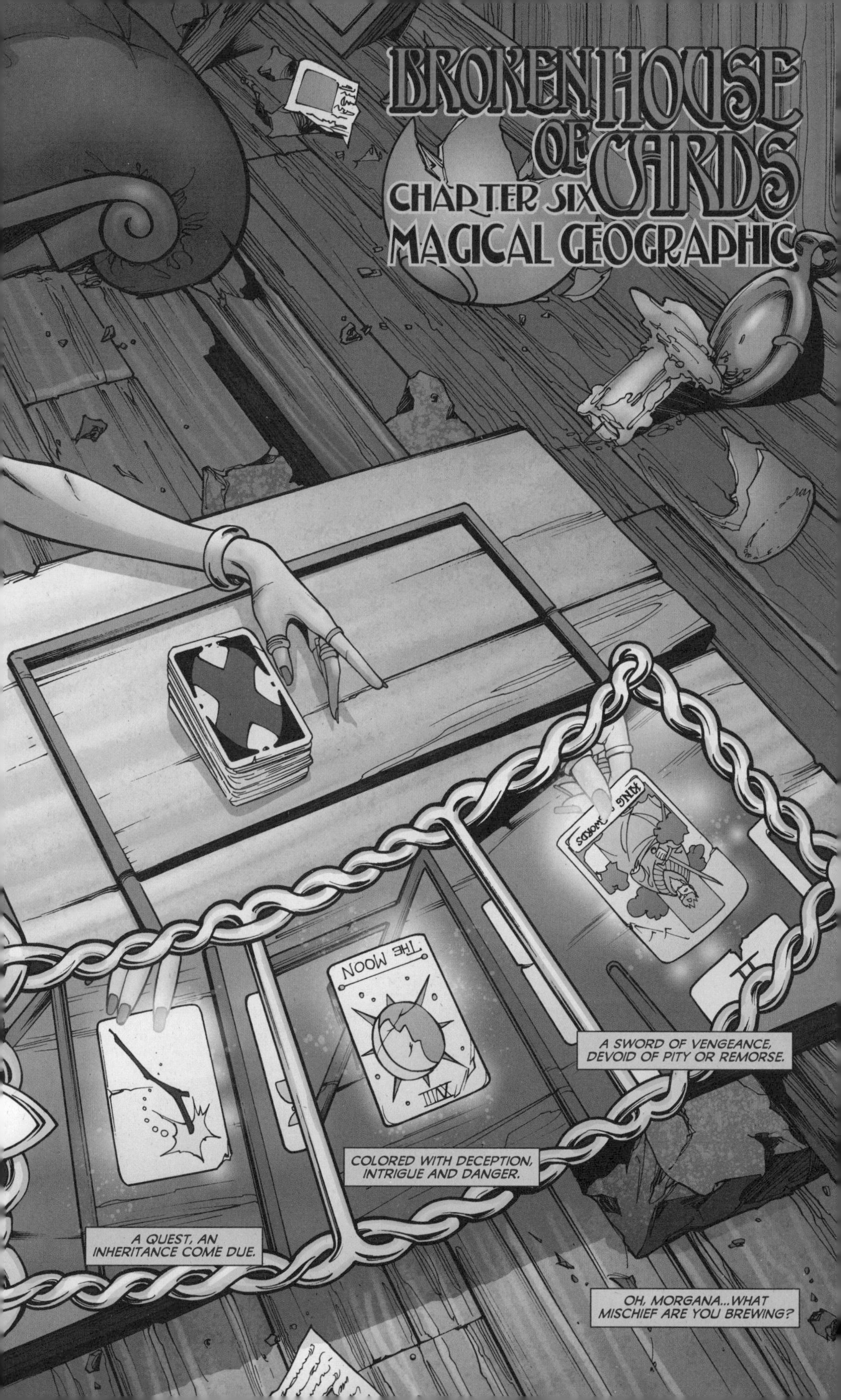
BROKEN HOUSE OF CARDS
CHAPTER SIX
MAGICAL GEOGRAPHIC
KING SWORDS
THE MOON
A SWORD OF VENGEANCE, DEVOID OF PITY OR REMORSE.
COLORED WITH DECEPTION, INTRIGUE AND DANGER.
A QUEST, AN INHERITANCE COME DUE.
OH, MORGANA...WHAT MISCHIEF ARE YOU BREWING?

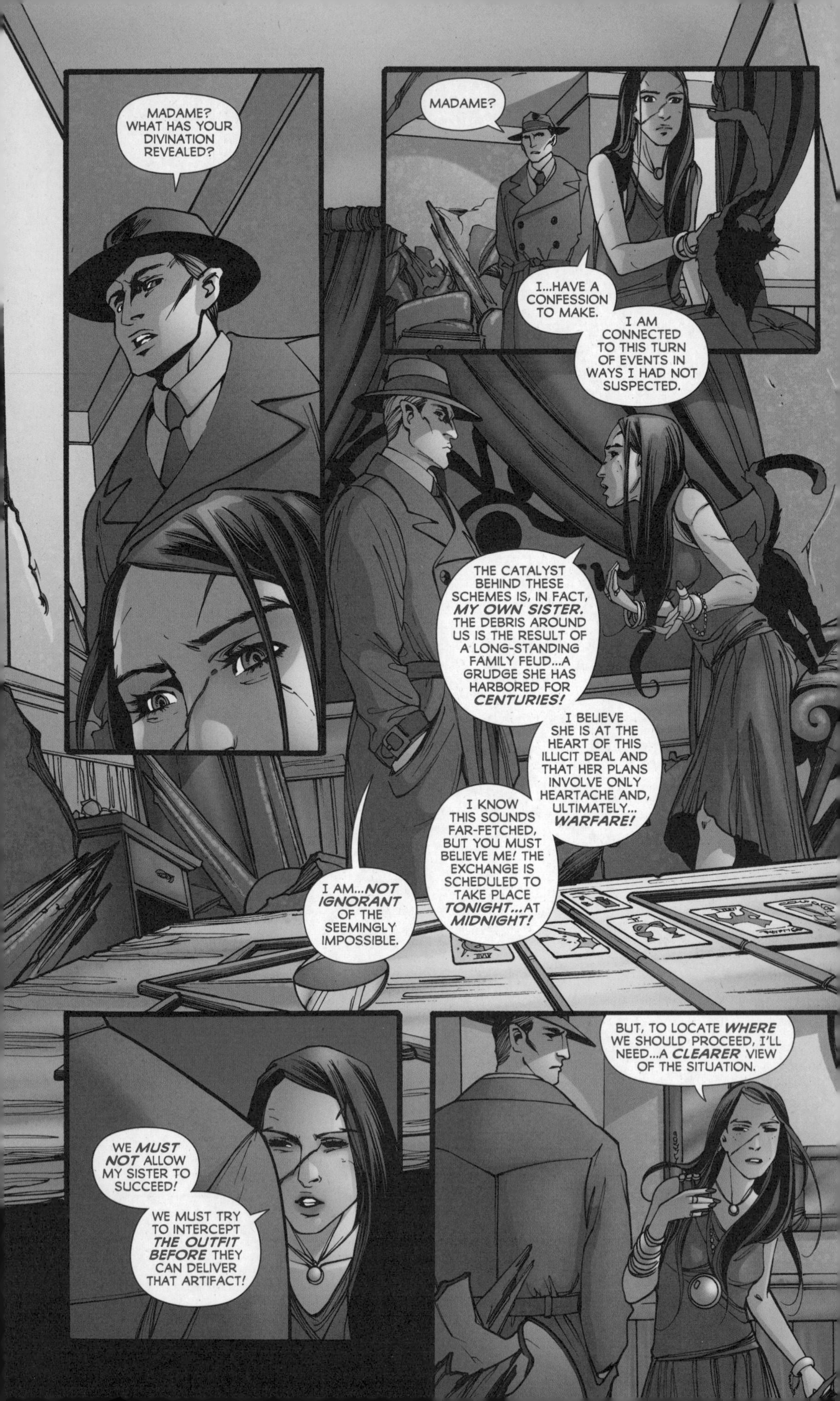
MADAME? WHAT HAS YOUR DIVINATION REVEALED?
MADAME?
I...HAVE A CONFESSION TO MAKE.
I AM CONNECTED TO THIS TURN OF EVENTS IN WAYS I HAD NOT SUSPECTED.
THE CATALYST BEHIND THESE SCHEMES IS, IN FACT, MY OWN SISTER. THE DEBRIS AROUND US IS THE RESULT OF A LONG-STANDING FAMILY FEUD...A GRUDGE SHE HAS HARBORED FOR CENTURIES!
I BELIEVE SHE IS AT THE HEART OF THIS ILLICIT DEAL AND THAT HER PLANS INVOLVE ONLY HEARTACHE AND, ULTIMATELY... WARFARE!
I KNOW THIS SOUNDS FAR-FETCHED, BUT YOU MUST BELIEVE ME! THE EXCHANGE IS SCHEDULED TO TAKE PLACE TONIGHT...AT MIDNIGHT!
I AM...NOT IGNORANT OF THE SEEMINGLY IMPOSSIBLE.
WE MUST NOT ALLOW MY SISTER TO SUCCEED!
WE MUST TRY TO INTERCEPT THE OUTFIT BEFORE THEY CAN DELIVER THAT ARTIFACT!
BUT, TO LOCATE WHERE WE SHOULD PROCEED, I'LL NEED...A CLEARER VIEW OF THE SITUATION.

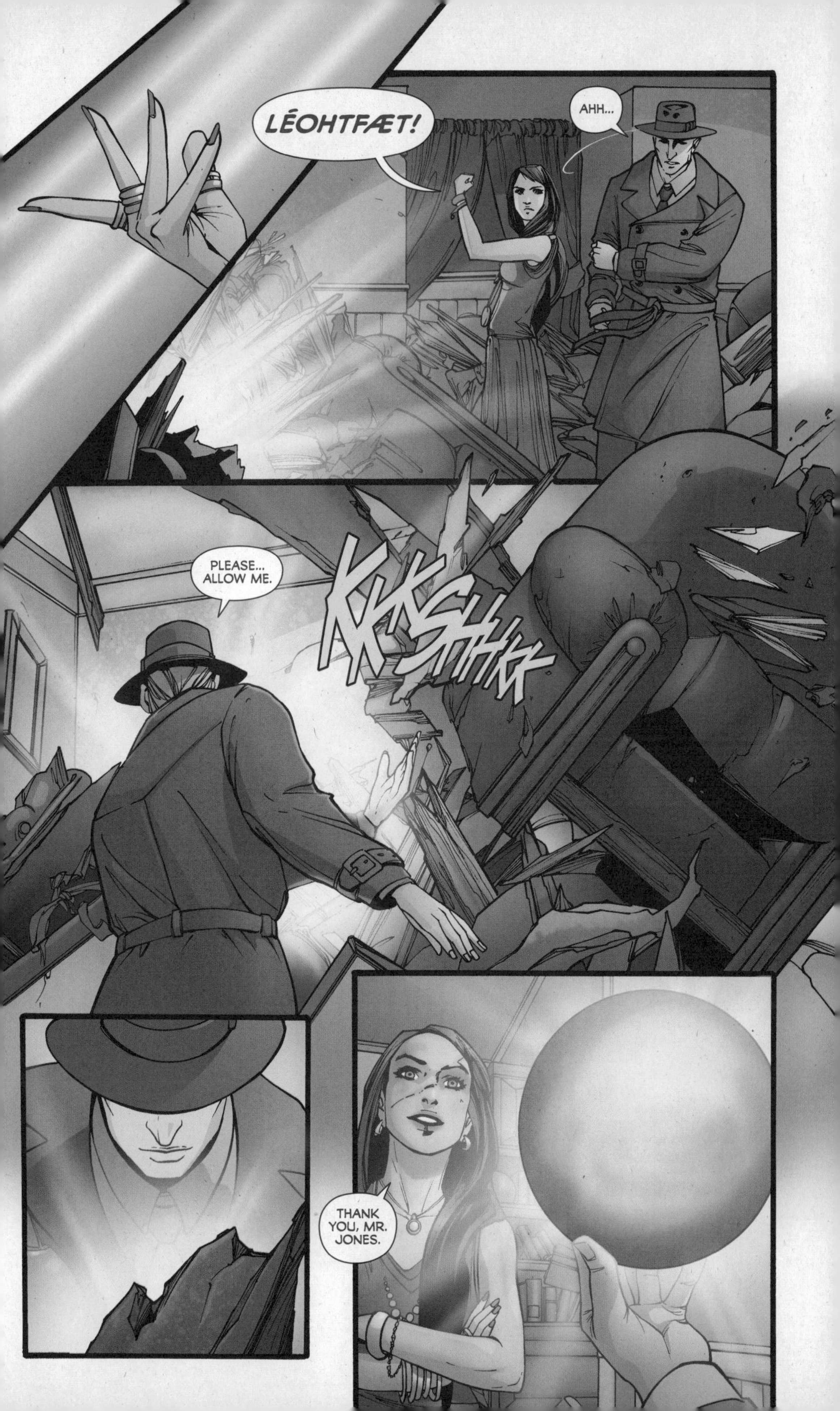
LÉOHTFÆT!
AHH...
PLEASE... ALLOW ME.
KKKSHHKK
THANK YOU, MR. JONES.

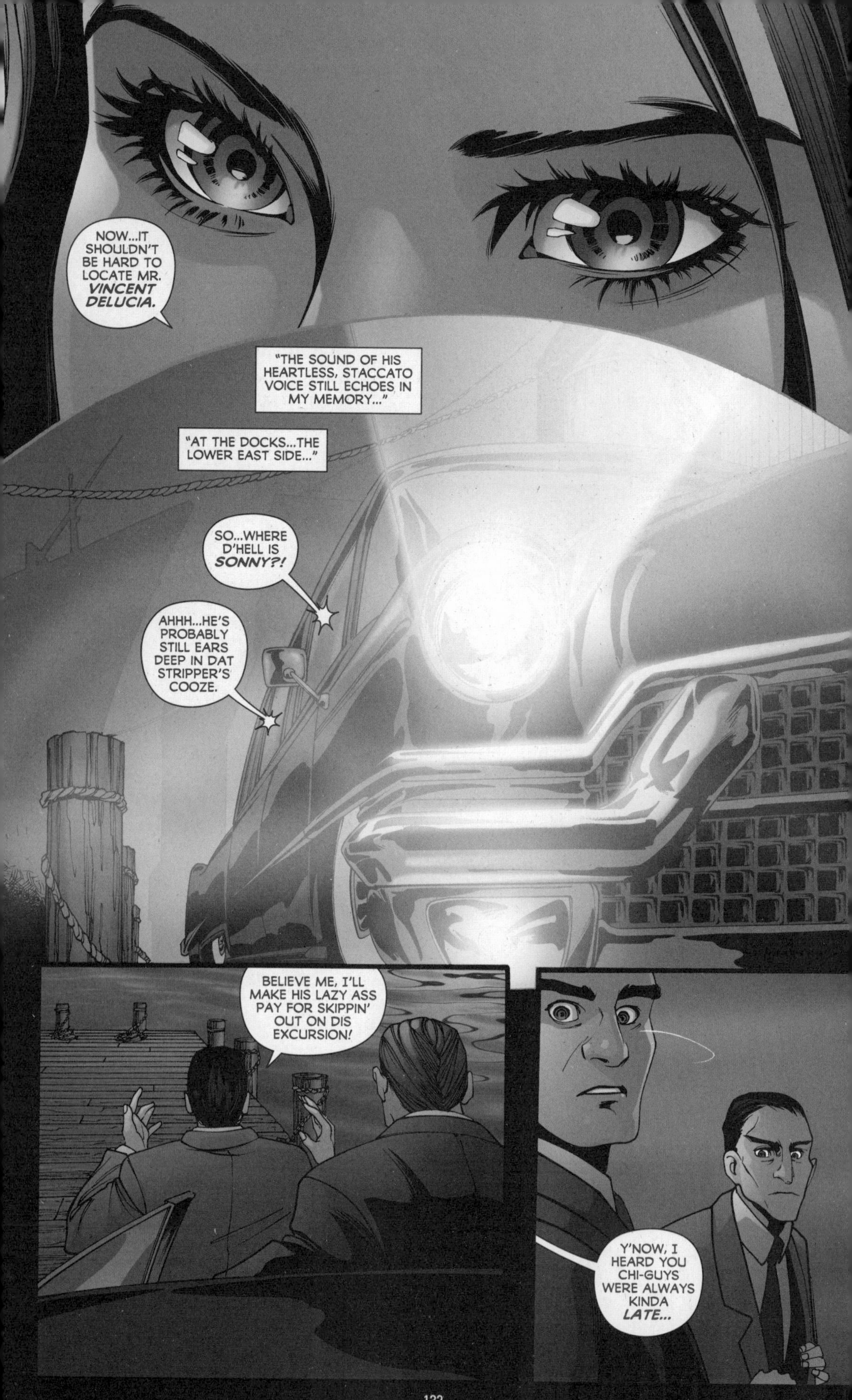

NOW...IT SHOULDN'T BE HARD TO LOCATE MR. **VINCENT DELUCIA.**
"THE SOUND OF HIS HEARTLESS, STACCATO VOICE STILL ECHOES IN MY MEMORY..."
"AT THE DOCKS...THE LOWER EAST SIDE..."
SO...WHERE D'HELL IS **SONNY?!**
AHHH...HE'S PROBABLY STILL EARS DEEP IN DAT STRIPPER'S COOZE.
BELIEVE ME, I'LL MAKE HIS LAZY ASS PAY FOR SKIPPIN' OUT ON DIS EXCURSION!
Y'NOW, I HEARD YOU CHI-GUYS WERE ALWAYS KINDA **LATE...**

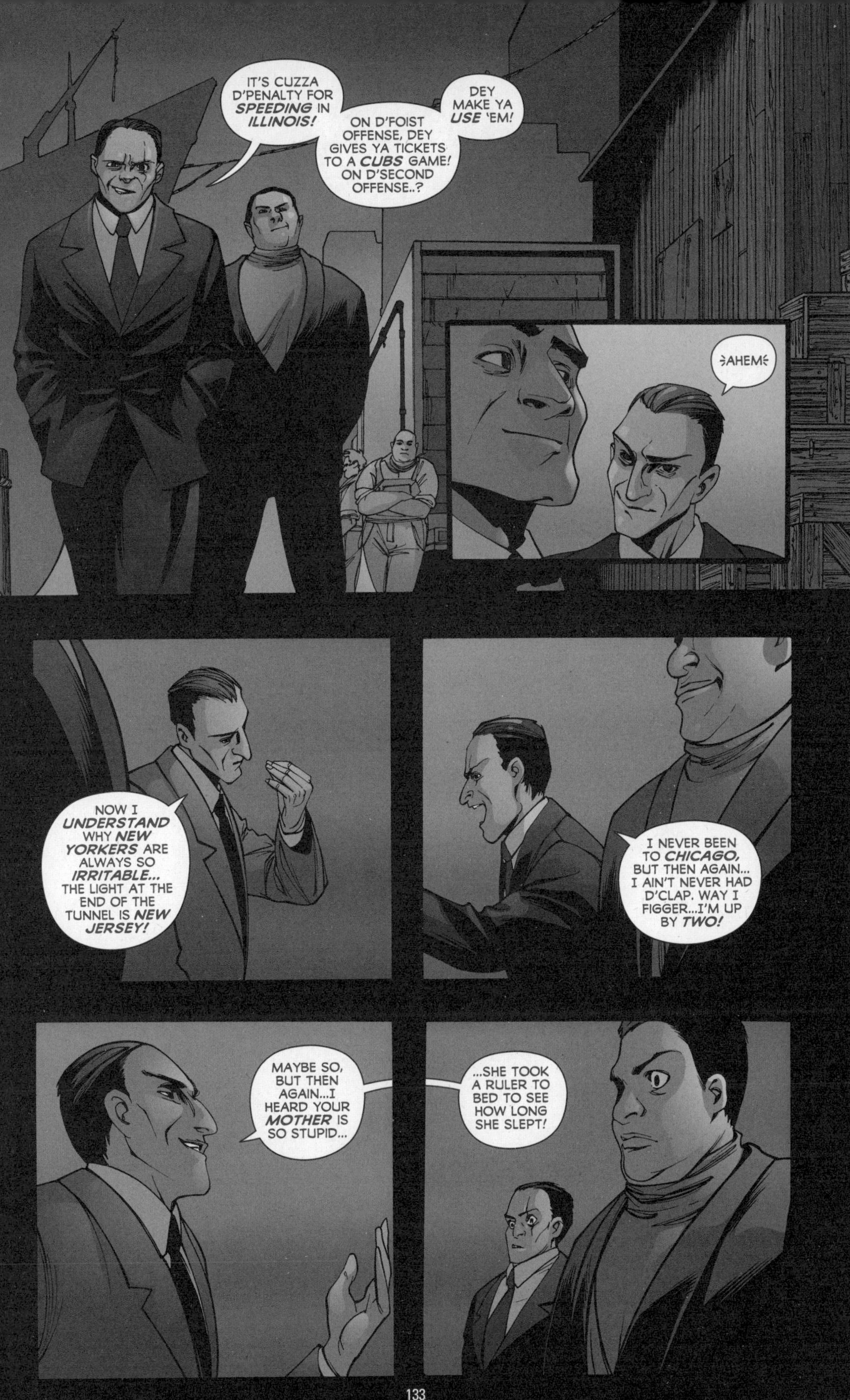
IT'S CUZZA D'PENALTY FOR SPEEDING IN ILLINOIS!
ON D'FOIST OFFENSE, DEY GIVES YA TICKETS TO A CUBS GAME! ON D'SECOND OFFENSE..?
DEY MAKE YA USE 'EM!
AHEM
NOW I UNDERSTAND WHY NEW YORKERS ARE ALWAYS SO IRRITABLE... THE LIGHT AT THE END OF THE TUNNEL IS NEW JERSEY!
I NEVER BEEN TO CHICAGO, BUT THEN AGAIN... I AIN'T NEVER HAD D'CLAP. WAY I FIGGER...I'M UP BY TWO!
MAYBE SO, BUT THEN AGAIN...I HEARD YOUR MOTHER IS SO STUPID...
...SHE TOOK A RULER TO BED TO SEE HOW LONG SHE SLEPT!

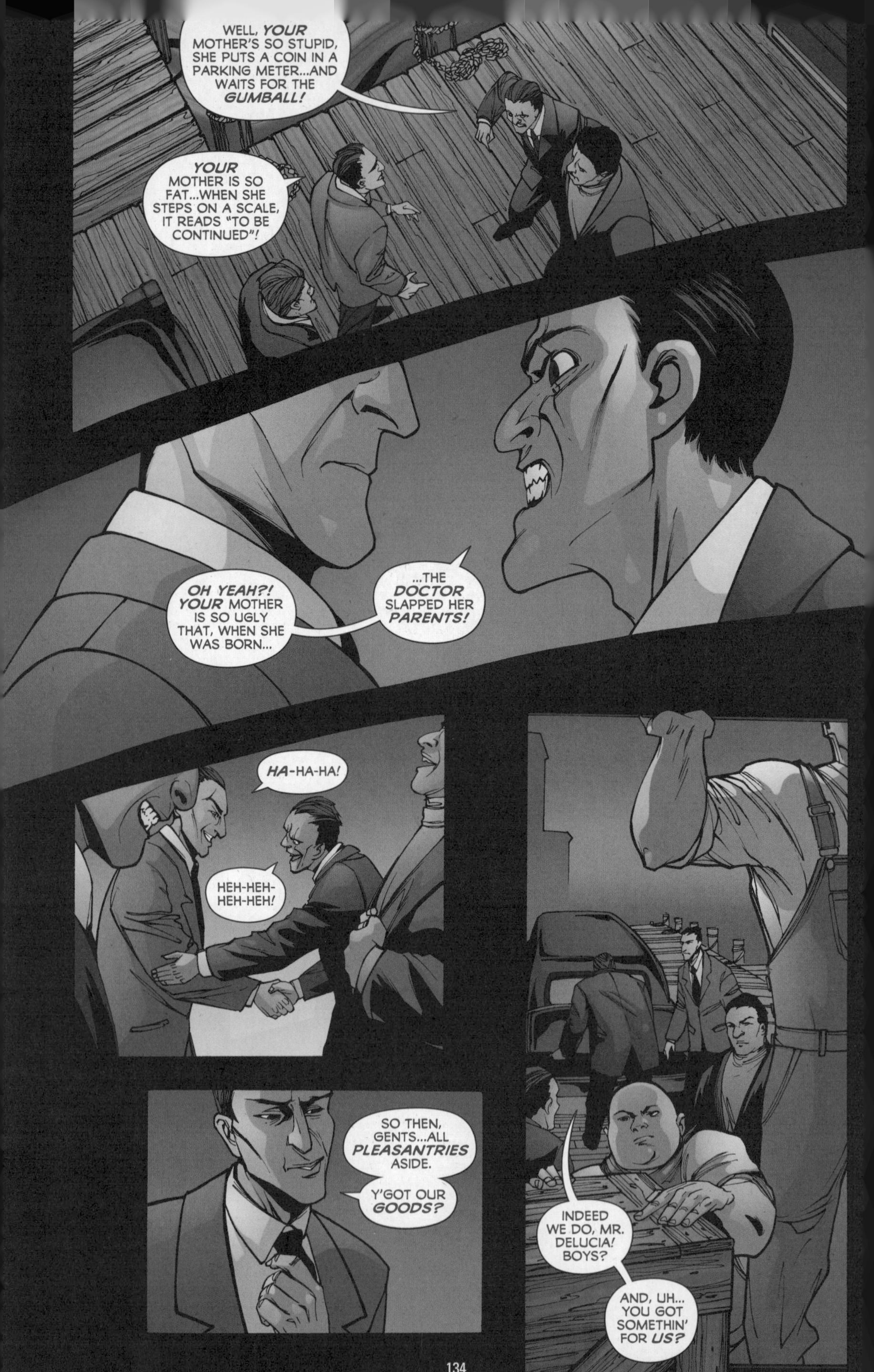
WELL, YOUR MOTHER'S SO STUPID, SHE PUTS A COIN IN A PARKING METER...AND WAITS FOR THE GUMBALL!
YOUR MOTHER IS SO FAT...WHEN SHE STEPS ON A SCALE, IT READS "TO BE CONTINUED"!
OH YEAH?! YOUR MOTHER IS SO UGLY THAT, WHEN SHE WAS BORN...
...THE DOCTOR SLAPPED HER PARENTS!
HA-HA-HA!
HEH-HEH-HEH-HEH!
SO THEN, GENTS...ALL PLEASANTRIES ASIDE.
Y'GOT OUR GOODS?
INDEED WE DO, MR. DELUCIA! BOYS?
AND, UH... YOU GOT SOMETHIN' FOR US?

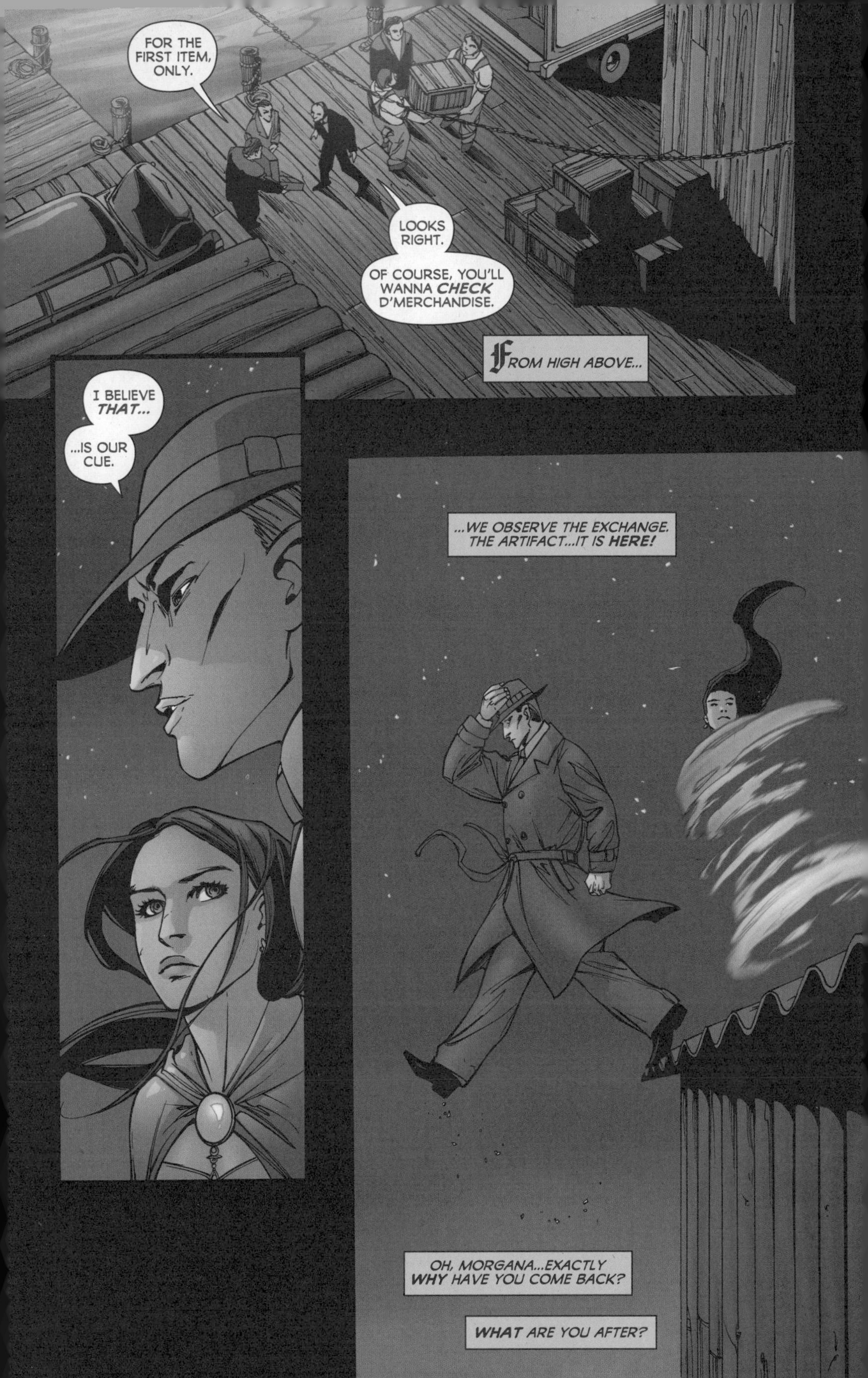

FOR THE FIRST ITEM, ONLY.
LOOKS RIGHT.
OF COURSE, YOU'LL WANNA CHECK D'MERCHANDISE.
FROM HIGH ABOVE...
I BELIEVE THAT...
...IS OUR CUE.
...WE OBSERVE THE EXCHANGE. THE ARTIFACT...IT IS HERE!
OH, MORGANA...EXACTLY WHY HAVE YOU COME BACK?
WHAT ARE YOU AFTER?

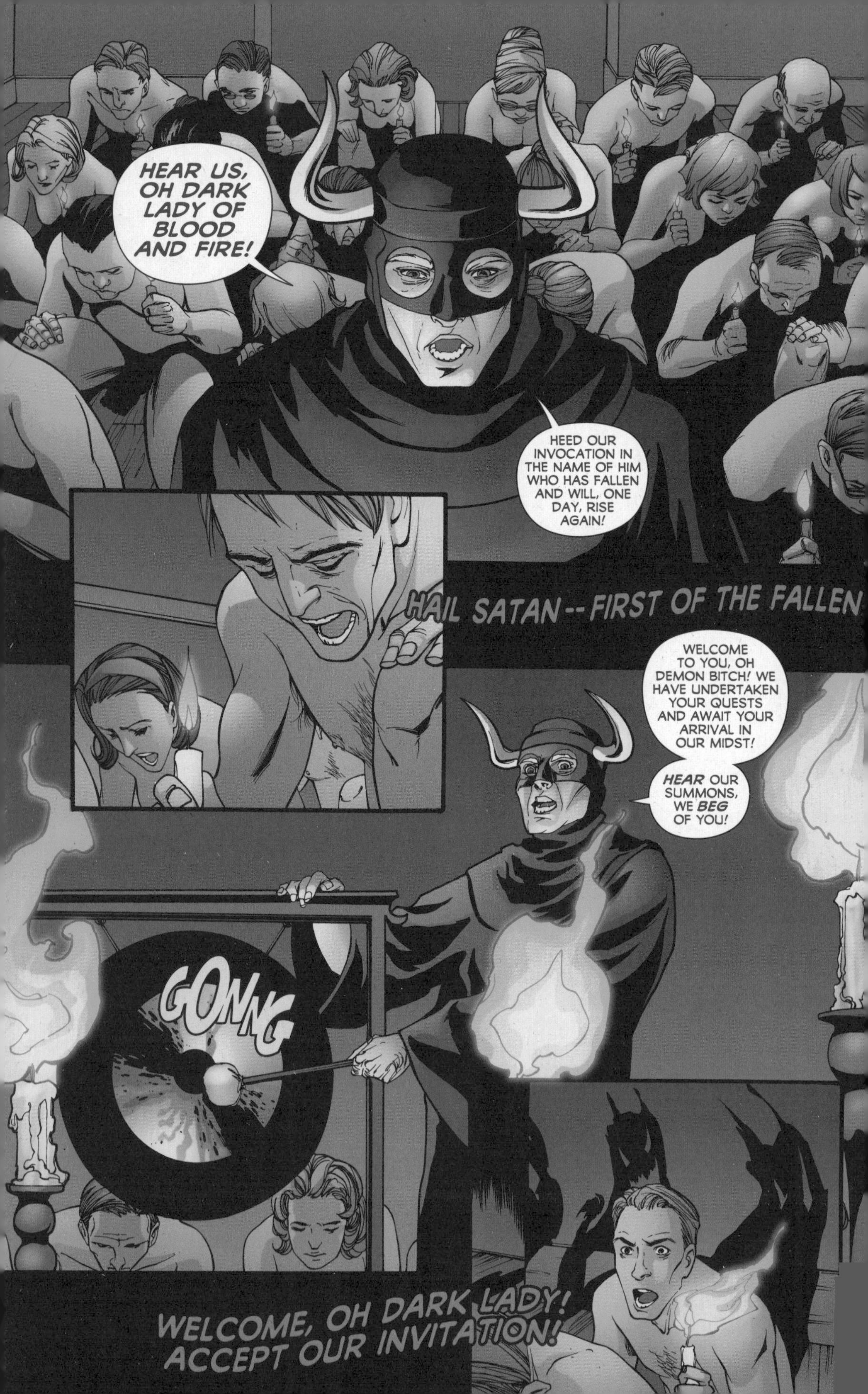

HEAR US, OH DARK LADY OF BLOOD AND FIRE!
HEED OUR INVOCATION IN THE NAME OF HIM WHO HAS FALLEN AND WILL, ONE DAY, RISE AGAIN!
HAIL SATAN -- FIRST OF THE FALLEN
WELCOME TO YOU, OH DEMON BITCH! WE HAVE UNDERTAKEN YOUR QUESTS AND AWAIT YOUR ARRIVAL IN OUR MIDST!
HEAR OUR SUMMONS, WE BEG OF YOU!
GONNG
WELCOME, OH DARK LADY! ACCEPT OUR INVITATION!

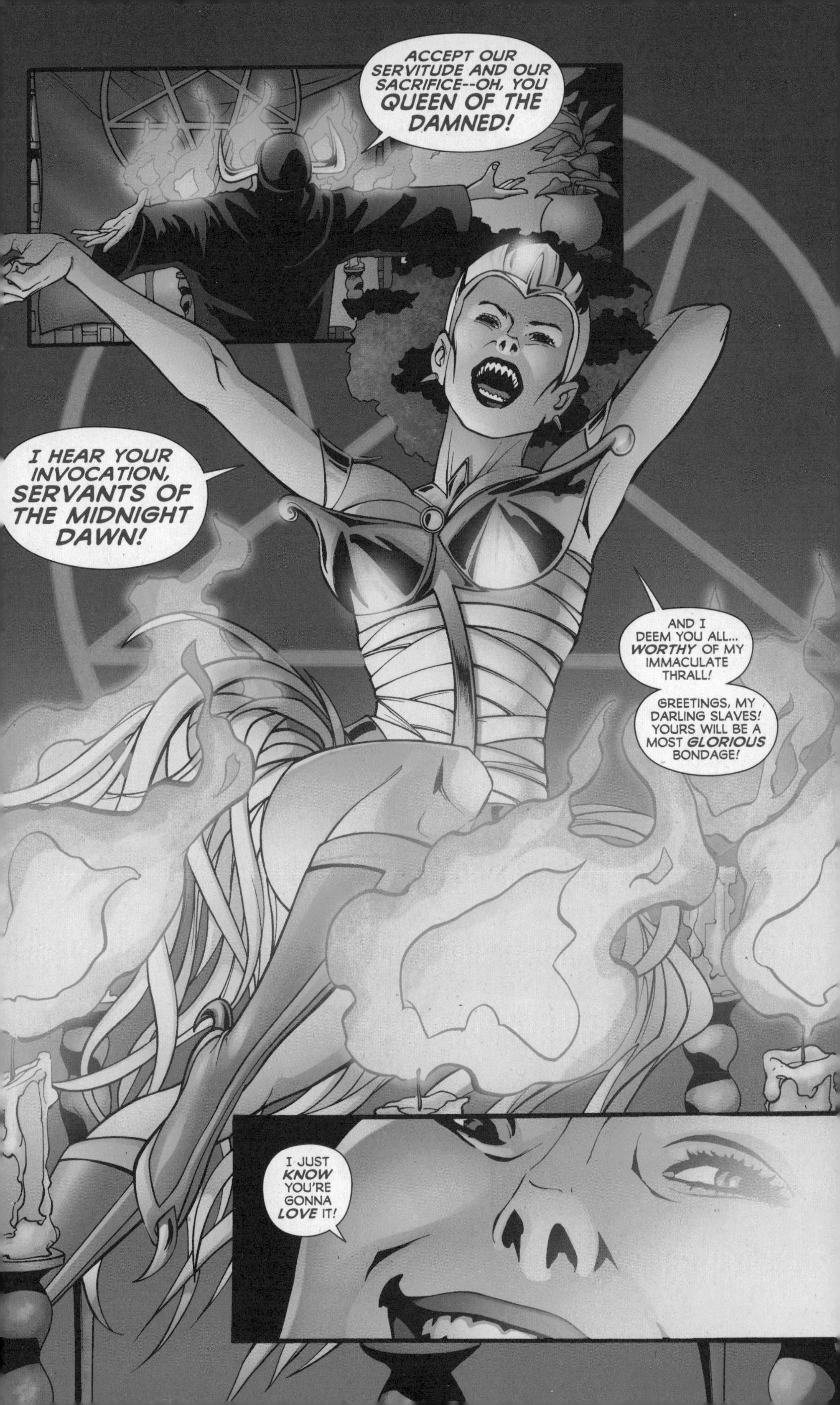
ACCEPT OUR SERVITUDE AND OUR SACRIFICE--OH, YOU QUEEN OF THE DAMNED!
I HEAR YOUR INVOCATION, SERVANTS OF THE MIDNIGHT DAWN!
AND I DEEM YOU ALL... WORTHY OF MY IMMACULATE THRALL!
GREETINGS, MY DARLING SLAVES! YOURS WILL BE A MOST GLORIOUS BONDAGE!
I JUST KNOW YOU'RE GONNA LOVE IT!

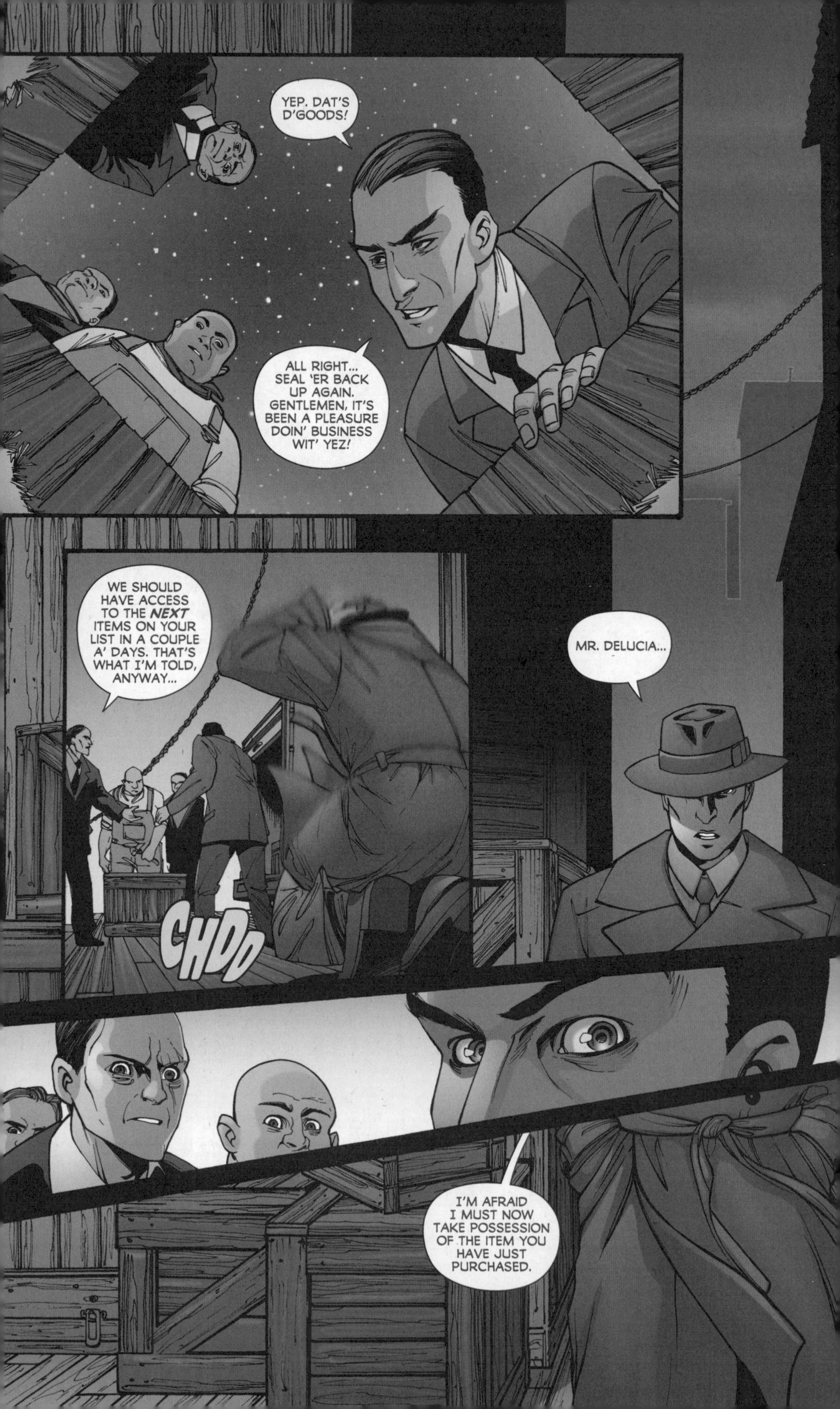
YEP. DAT'S D'GOODS!
ALL RIGHT... SEAL 'ER BACK UP AGAIN. GENTLEMEN, IT'S BEEN A PLEASURE DOIN' BUSINESS WIT' YEZ!
WE SHOULD HAVE ACCESS TO THE *NEXT* ITEMS ON YOUR LIST IN A COUPLE A' DAYS. THAT'S WHAT I'M TOLD, ANYWAY...
CHDD
MR. DELUCIA...
I'M AFRAID I MUST NOW TAKE POSSESSION OF THE ITEM YOU HAVE JUST PURCHASED.

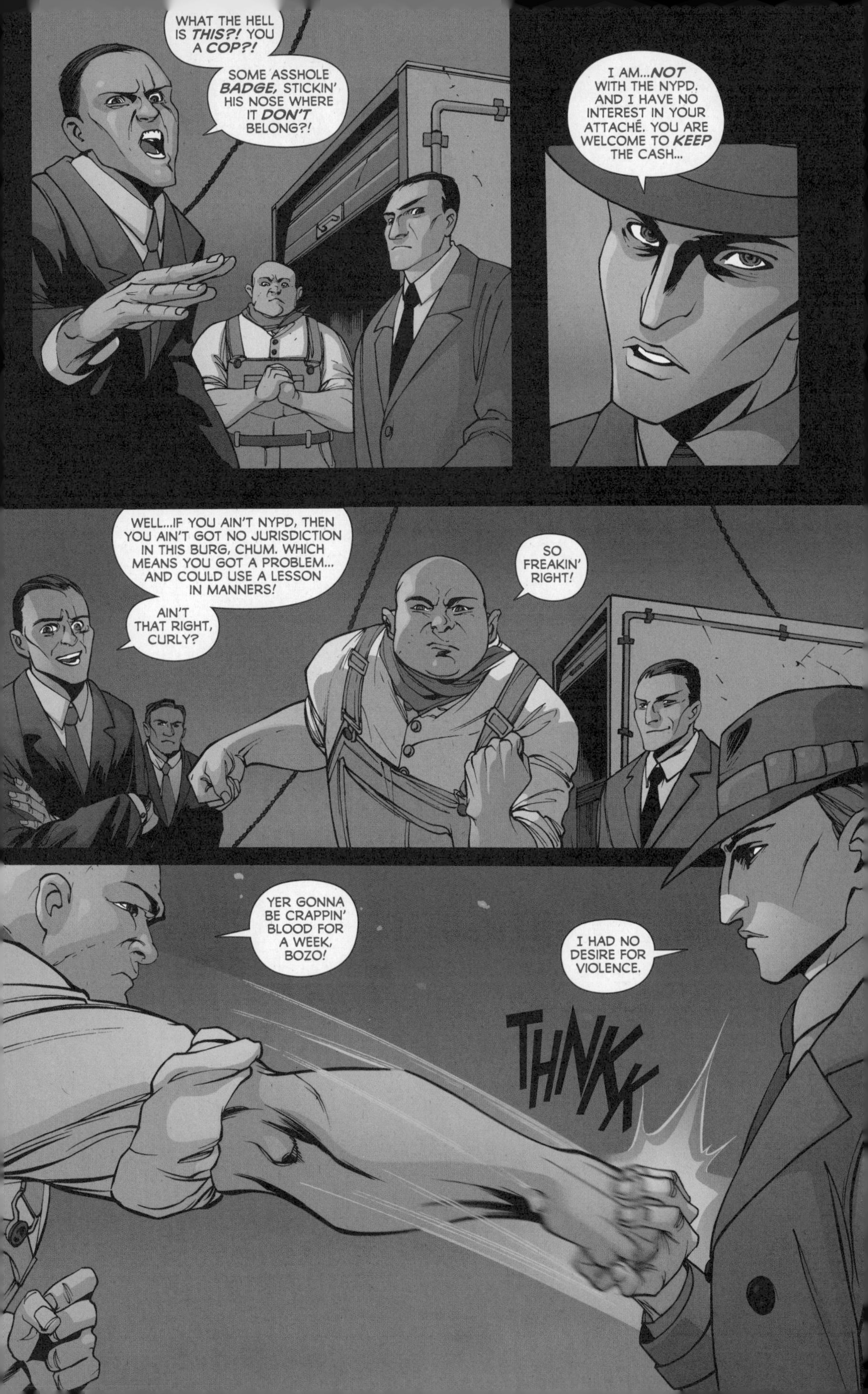
WHAT THE HELL IS THIS?! YOU A COP?!
SOME ASSHOLE BADGE, STICKIN' HIS NOSE WHERE IT DON'T BELONG?!
I AM...NOT WITH THE NYPD. AND I HAVE NO INTEREST IN YOUR ATTACHÉ. YOU ARE WELCOME TO KEEP THE CASH...
WELL...IF YOU AIN'T NYPD, THEN YOU AIN'T GOT NO JURISDICTION IN THIS BURG, CHUM. WHICH MEANS YOU GOT A PROBLEM... AND COULD USE A LESSON IN MANNERS!
AIN'T THAT RIGHT, CURLY?
SO FREAKIN' RIGHT!
YER GONNA BE CRAPPIN' BLOOD FOR A WEEK, BOZO!
I HAD NO DESIRE FOR VIOLENCE.
THNKK

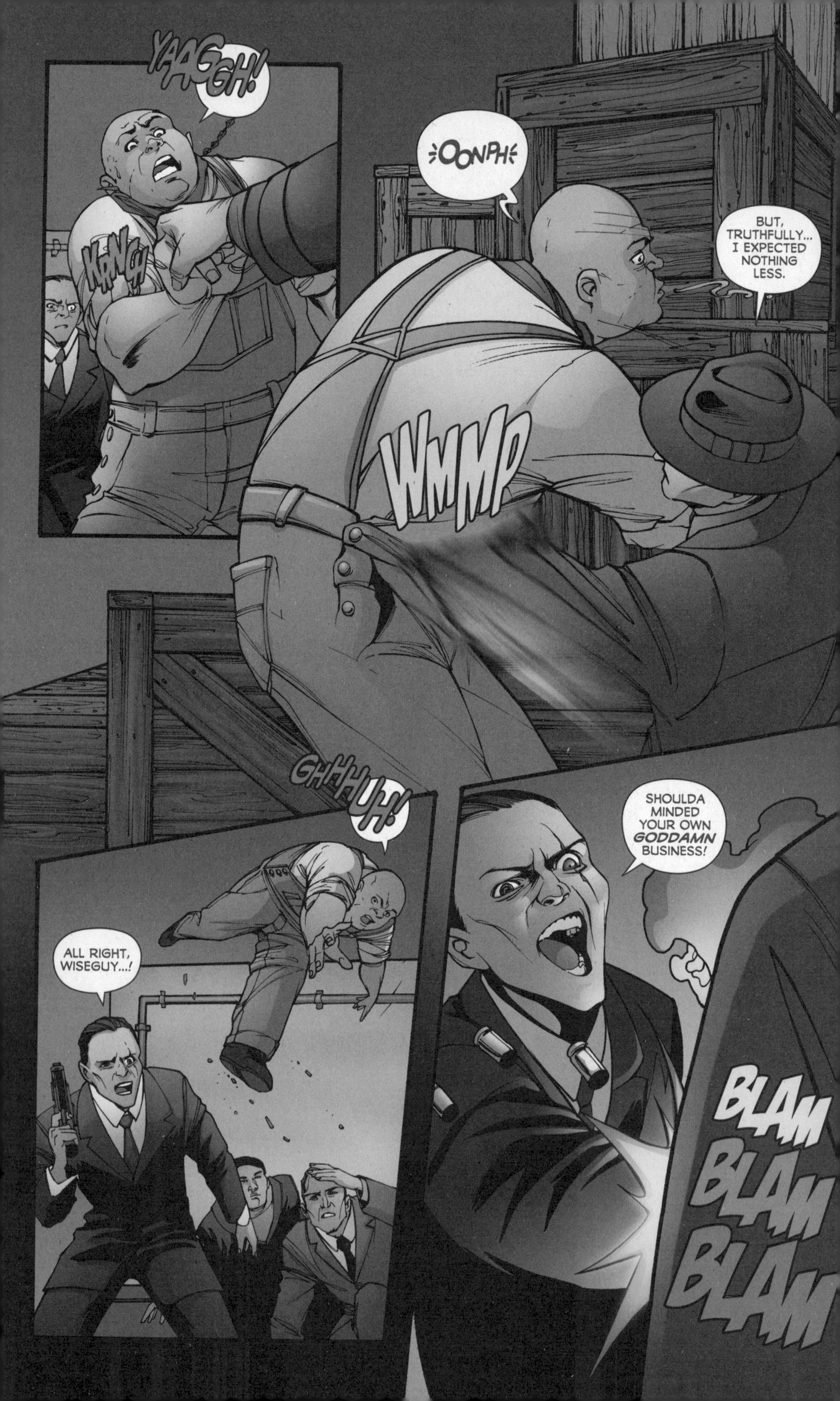
YAAGGH!
KRNCH
OONPH
BUT, TRUTHFULLY... I EXPECTED NOTHING LESS.
WMMP
GHHHUH!
ALL RIGHT, WISEGUY...!
SHOULDA MINDED YOUR OWN *GODDAMN* BUSINESS!
BLAM
BLAM
BLAM

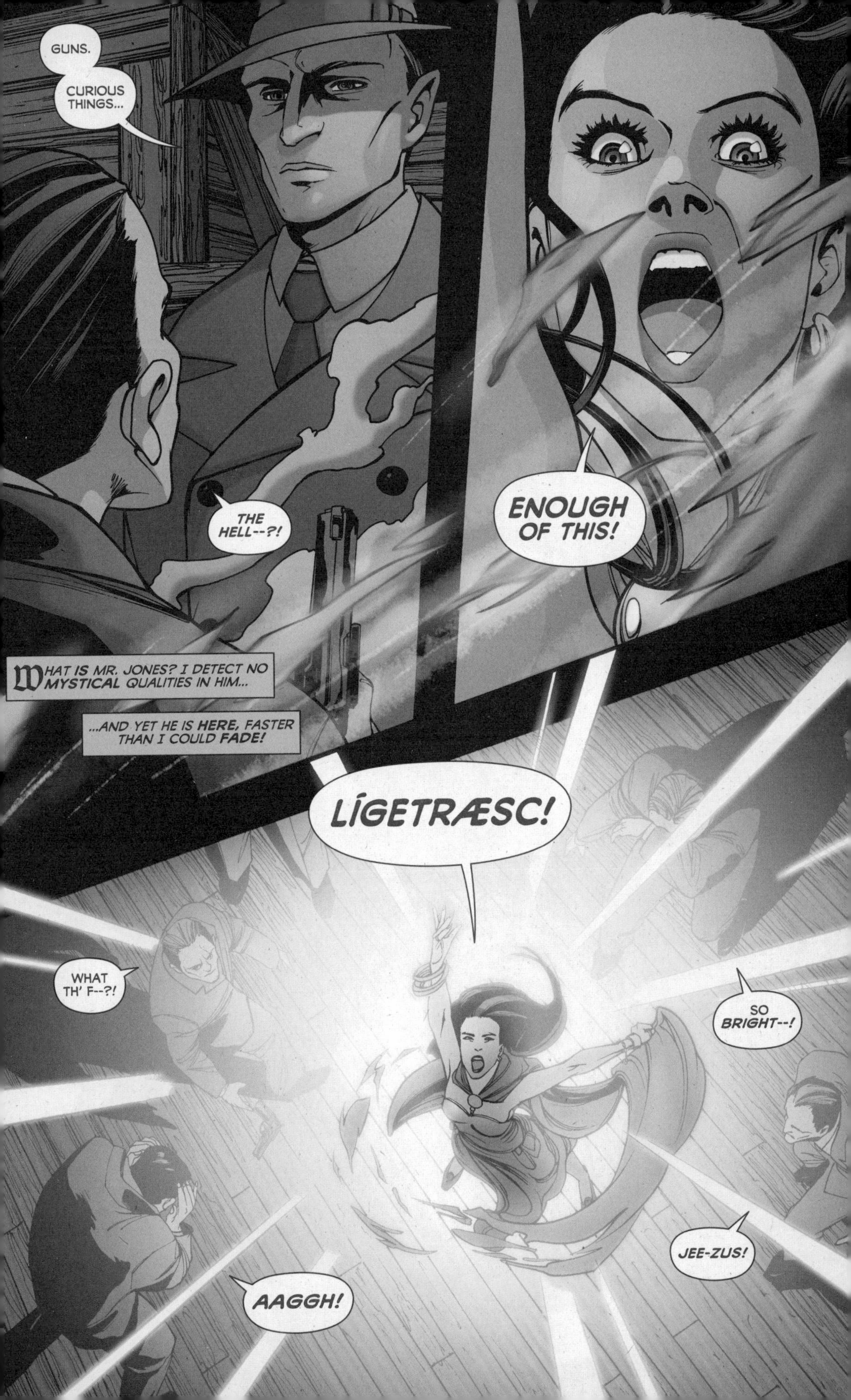
GUNS.
CURIOUS THINGS...
THE HELL--?!
ENOUGH OF THIS!
WHAT IS MR. JONES? I DETECT NO MYSTICAL QUALITIES IN HIM...
...AND YET HE IS HERE, FASTER THAN I COULD FADE!
LÍGETRÆSC!
WHAT TH' F--?!
SO BRIGHT--!
JEE-ZUS!
AAGGH!

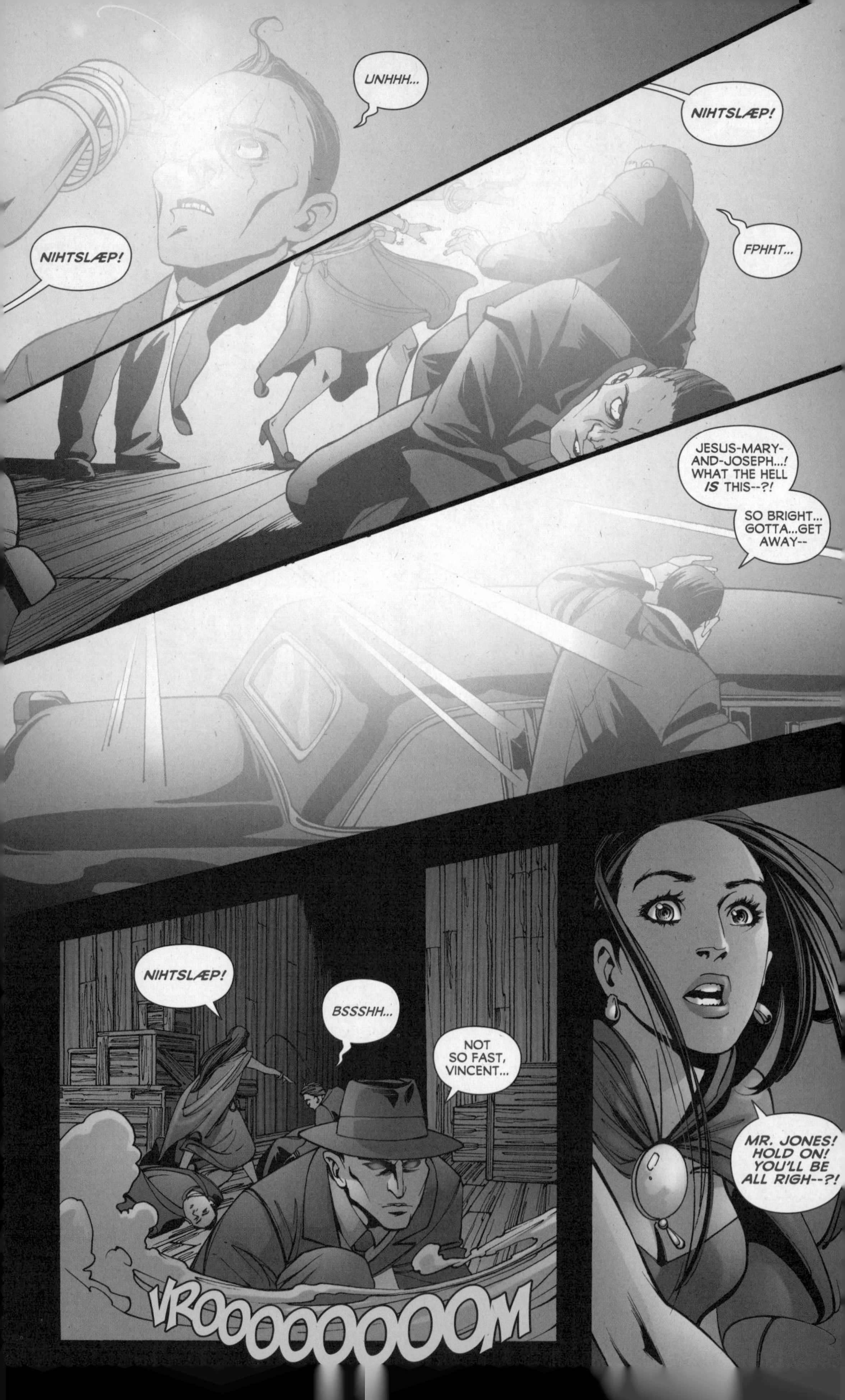
UNHHH...
NIHTSLÆP!
NIHTSLÆP!
FPHHT...
JESUS-MARY-AND-JOSEPH...! WHAT THE HELL IS THIS--?!
SO BRIGHT... GOTTA...GET AWAY--
NIHTSLÆP!
BSSSHH...
NOT SO FAST, VINCENT...
MR. JONES! HOLD ON! YOU'LL BE ALL RIGH--?!
VROOOOOOOOOM

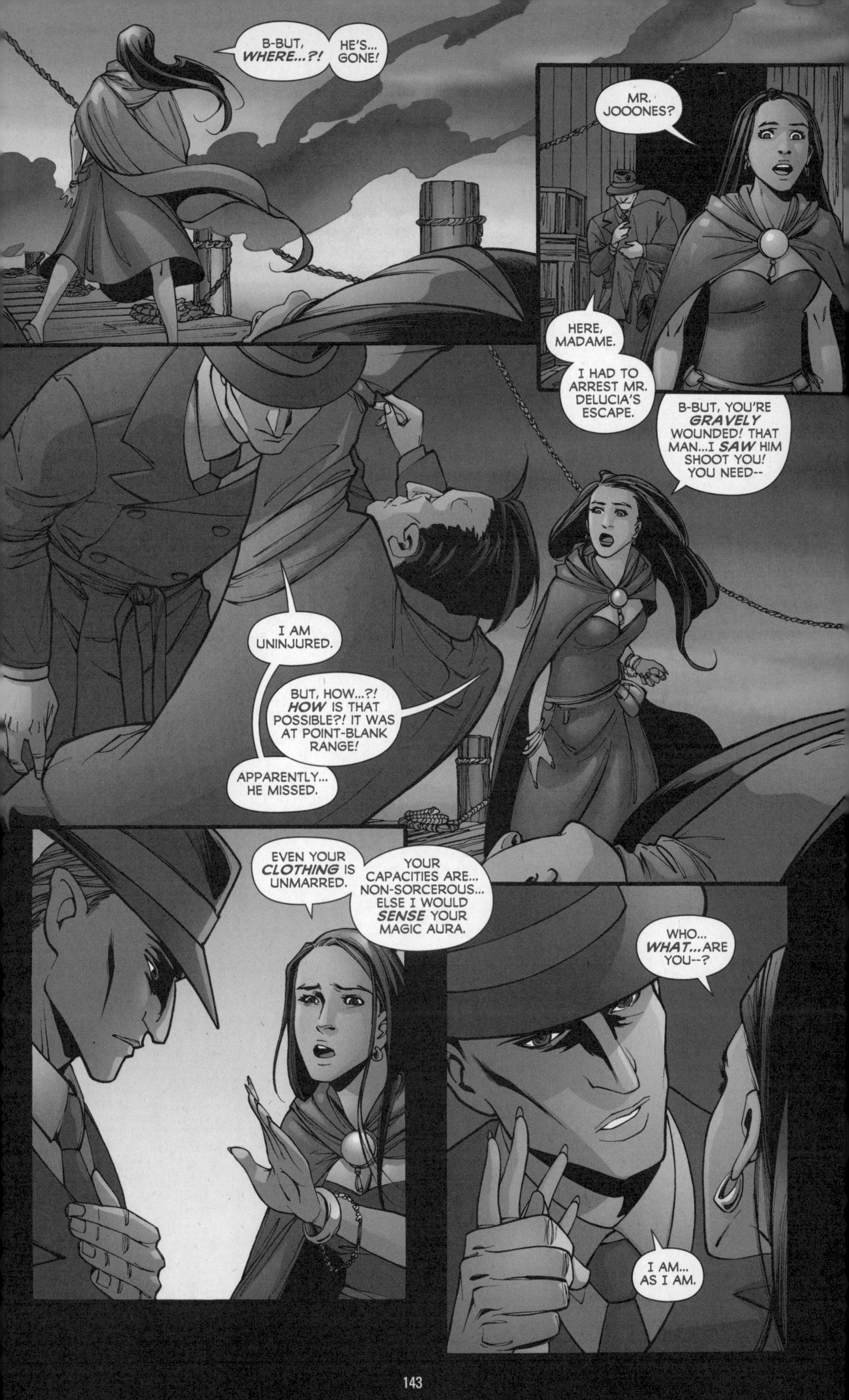
B-BUT, WHERE...?!
HE'S... GONE!
MR. JOOONES?
HERE, MADAME.
I HAD TO ARREST MR. DELUCIA'S ESCAPE.
B-BUT, YOU'RE GRAVELY WOUNDED! THAT MAN...I SAW HIM SHOOT YOU! YOU NEED--
I AM UNINJURED.
BUT, HOW...?! HOW IS THAT POSSIBLE?! IT WAS AT POINT-BLANK RANGE!
APPARENTLY... HE MISSED.
EVEN YOUR CLOTHING IS UNMARRED.
YOUR CAPACITIES ARE... NON-SORCEROUS... ELSE I WOULD SENSE YOUR MAGIC AURA.
WHO... WHAT...ARE YOU--?
I AM... AS I AM.

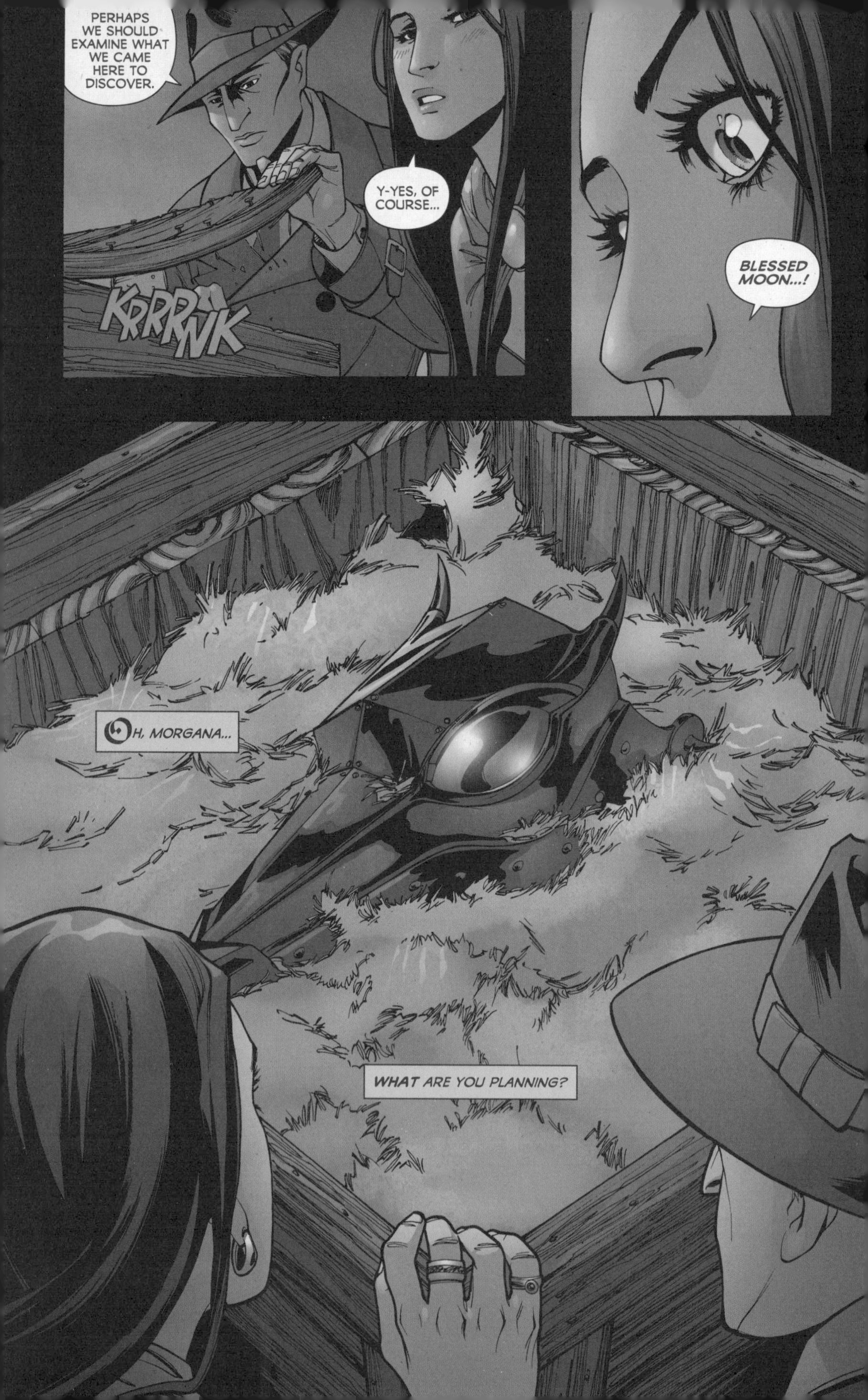
PERHAPS WE SHOULD EXAMINE WHAT WE CAME HERE TO DISCOVER.
Y-YES, OF COURSE...
KRRRNK
BLESSED MOON...!
OH, MORGANA...
WHAT ARE YOU PLANNING?

Chapter Seven: Harkens Bizarre

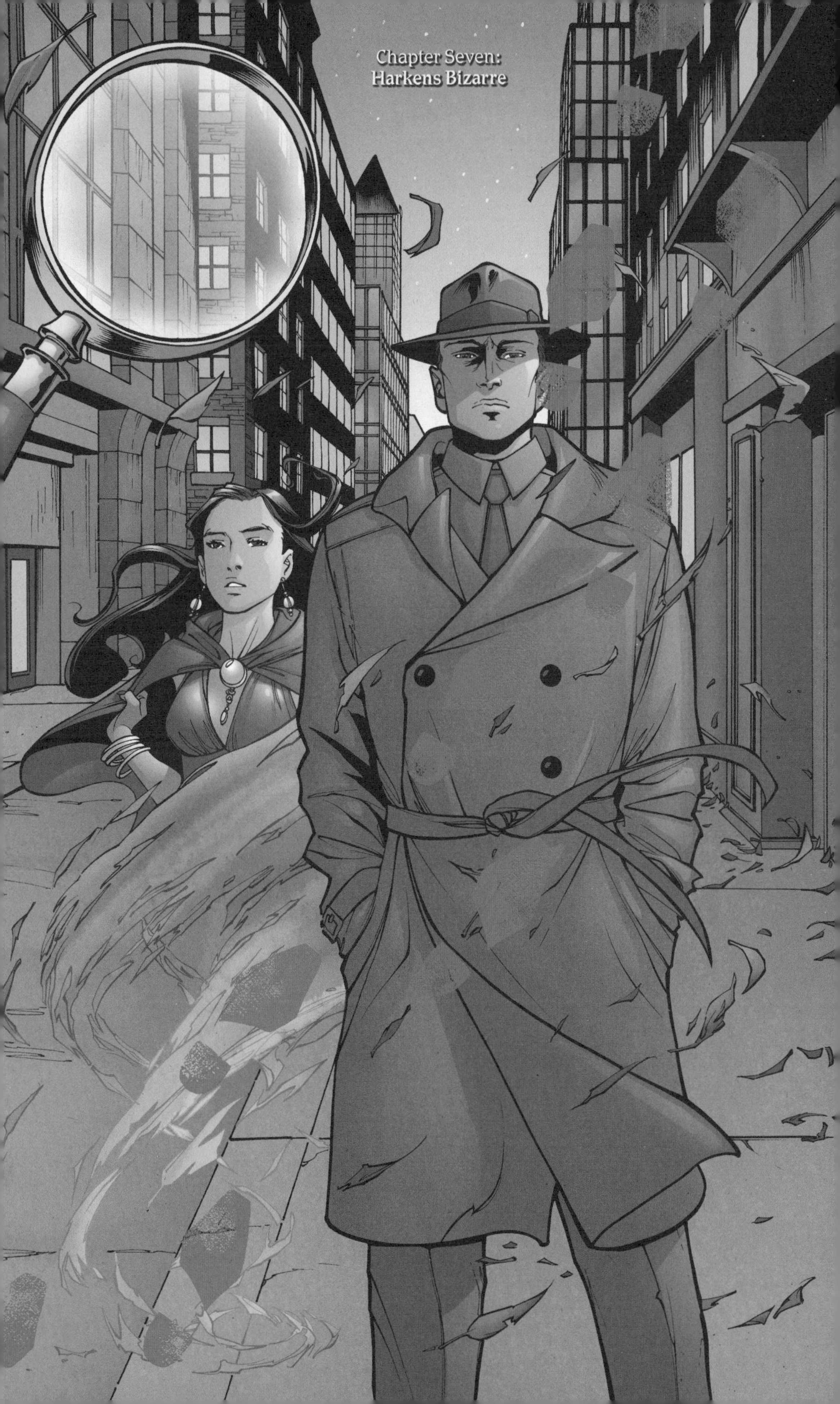

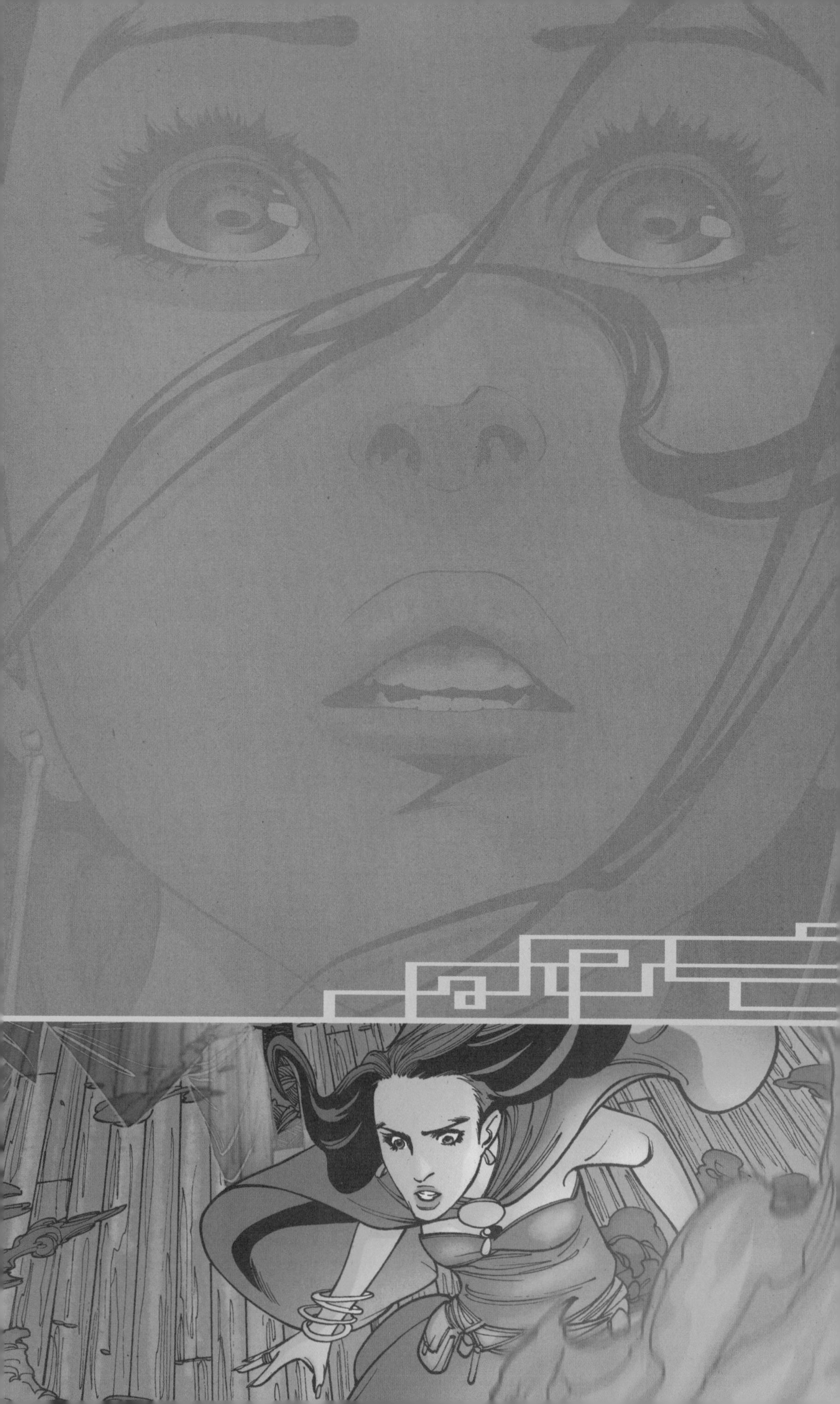

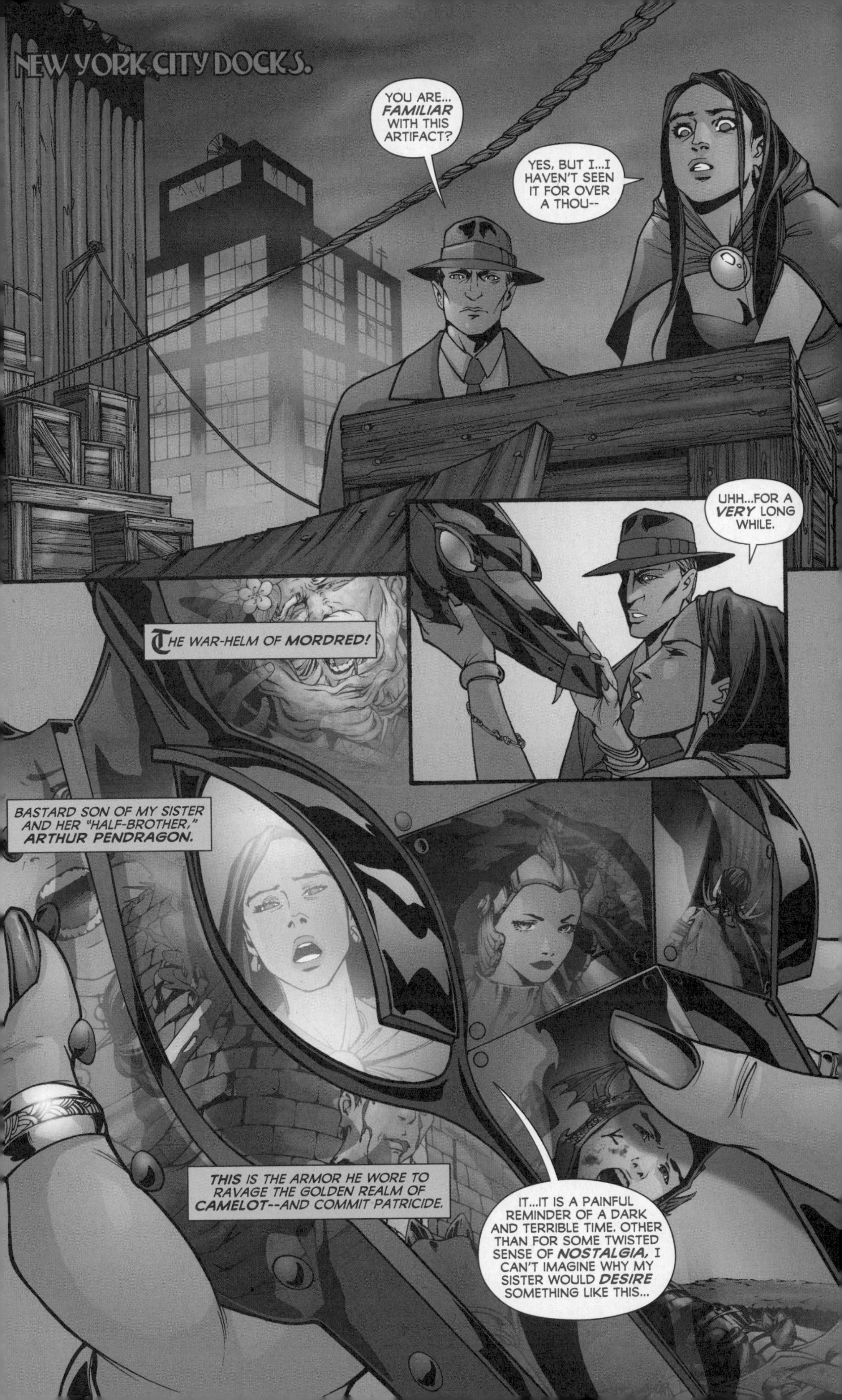
NEW YORK CITY DOCKS.
YOU ARE... FAMILIAR WITH THIS ARTIFACT?
YES, BUT I...I HAVEN'T SEEN IT FOR OVER A THOU--
UHH...FOR A VERY LONG WHILE.
THE WAR-HELM OF MORDRED!
BASTARD SON OF MY SISTER AND HER "HALF-BROTHER," ARTHUR PENDRAGON.
THIS IS THE ARMOR HE WORE TO RAVAGE THE GOLDEN REALM OF CAMELOT--AND COMMIT PATRICIDE.
IT...IT IS A PAINFUL REMINDER OF A DARK AND TERRIBLE TIME. OTHER THAN FOR SOME TWISTED SENSE OF NOSTALGIA, I CAN'T IMAGINE WHY MY SISTER WOULD DESIRE SOMETHING LIKE THIS...

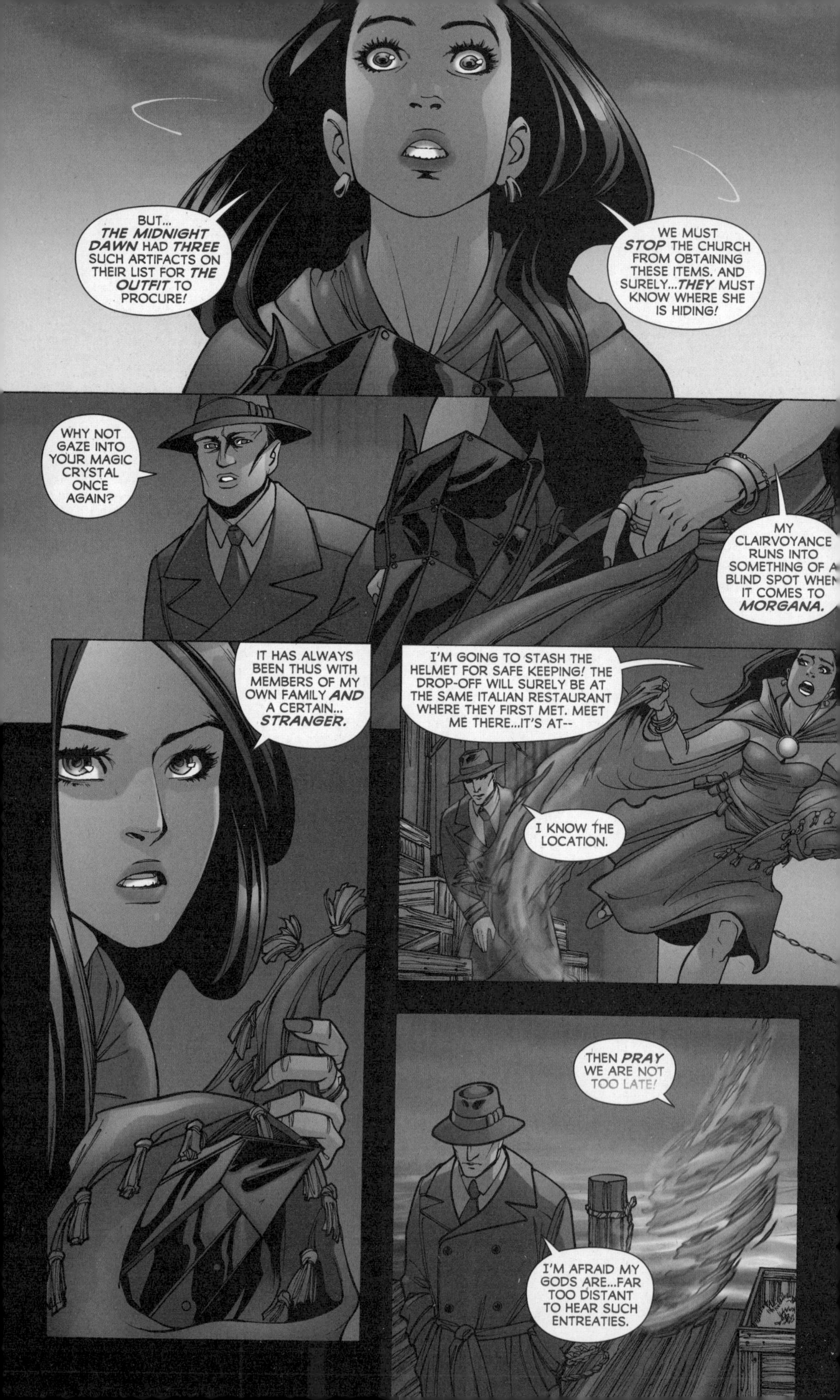
BUT... THE MIDNIGHT DAWN HAD THREE SUCH ARTIFACTS ON THEIR LIST FOR THE OUTFIT TO PROCURE!
WE MUST STOP THE CHURCH FROM OBTAINING THESE ITEMS. AND SURELY...THEY MUST KNOW WHERE SHE IS HIDING!
WHY NOT GAZE INTO YOUR MAGIC CRYSTAL ONCE AGAIN?
MY CLAIRVOYANCE RUNS INTO SOMETHING OF A BLIND SPOT WHEN IT COMES TO MORGANA.
IT HAS ALWAYS BEEN THUS WITH MEMBERS OF MY OWN FAMILY AND A CERTAIN... STRANGER.
I'M GOING TO STASH THE HELMET FOR SAFE KEEPING! THE DROP-OFF WILL SURELY BE AT THE SAME ITALIAN RESTAURANT WHERE THEY FIRST MET. MEET ME THERE...IT'S AT--
I KNOW THE LOCATION.
THEN PRAY WE ARE NOT TOO LATE!
I'M AFRAID MY GODS ARE...FAR TOO DISTANT TO HEAR SUCH ENTREATIES.

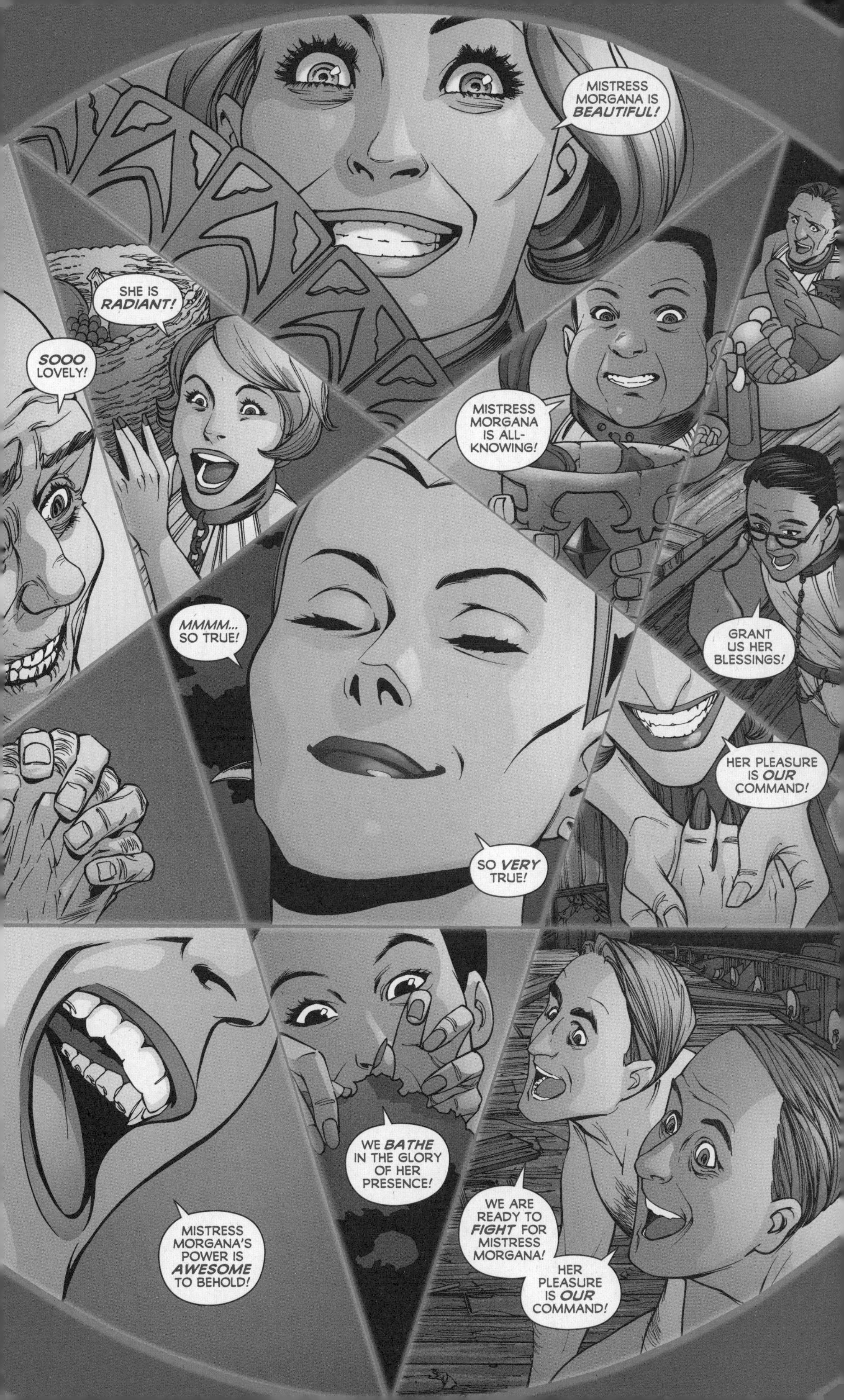
MISTRESS MORGANA IS BEAUTIFUL!
SHE IS RADIANT!
SOOO LOVELY!
MISTRESS MORGANA IS ALL-KNOWING!
GRANT US HER BLESSINGS!
MMMM... SO TRUE!
HER PLEASURE IS OUR COMMAND!
SO VERY TRUE!
WE BATHE IN THE GLORY OF HER PRESENCE!
MISTRESS MORGANA'S POWER IS AWESOME TO BEHOLD!
WE ARE READY TO FIGHT FOR MISTRESS MORGANA!
HER PLEASURE IS OUR COMMAND!

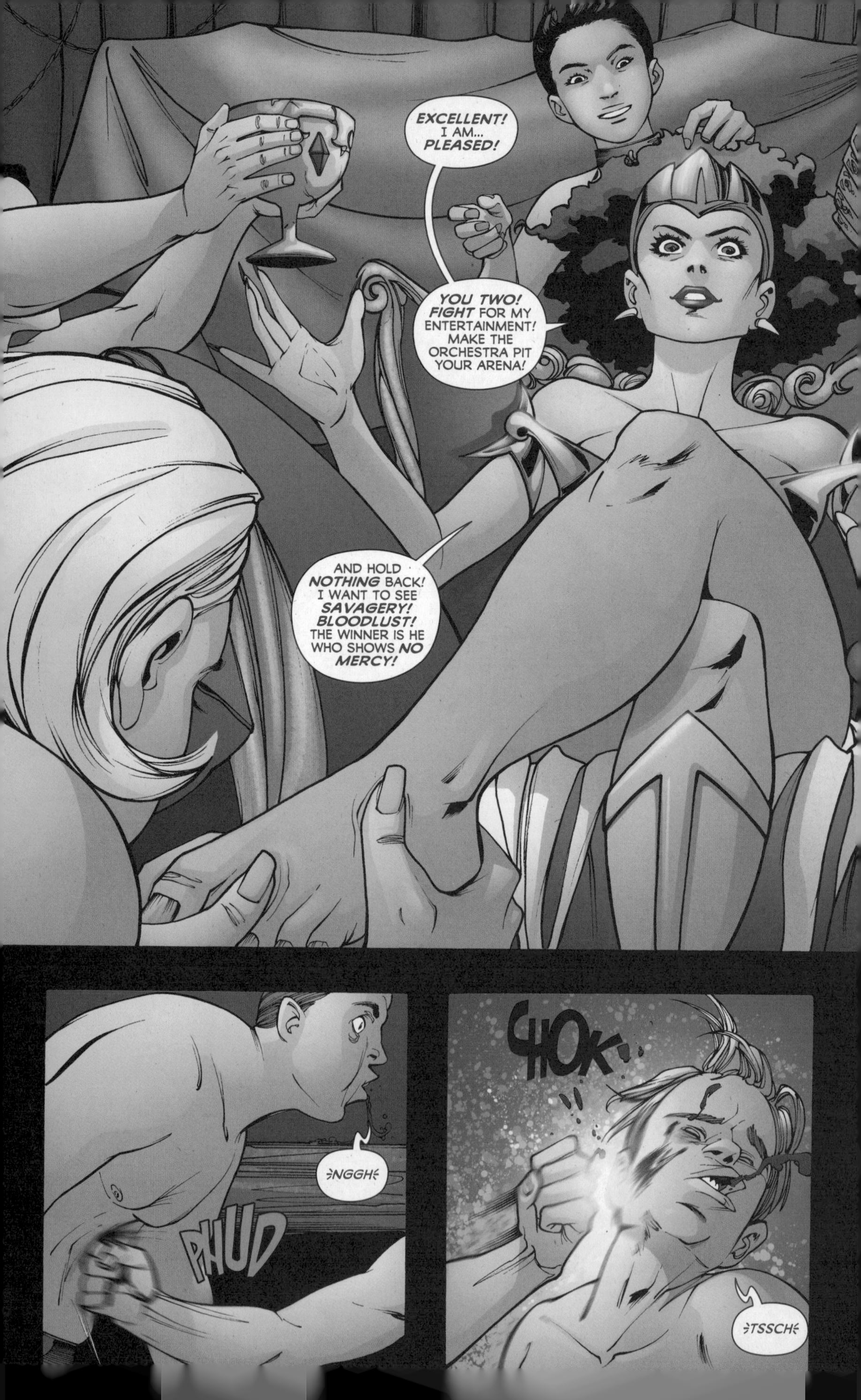
EXCELLENT! I AM... PLEASED!
YOU TWO! FIGHT FOR MY ENTERTAINMENT! MAKE THE ORCHESTRA PIT YOUR ARENA!
AND HOLD NOTHING BACK! I WANT TO SEE SAVAGERY! BLOODLUST! THE WINNER IS HE WHO SHOWS NO MERCY!
NGGH
PHUD
CHOK
TSSCH

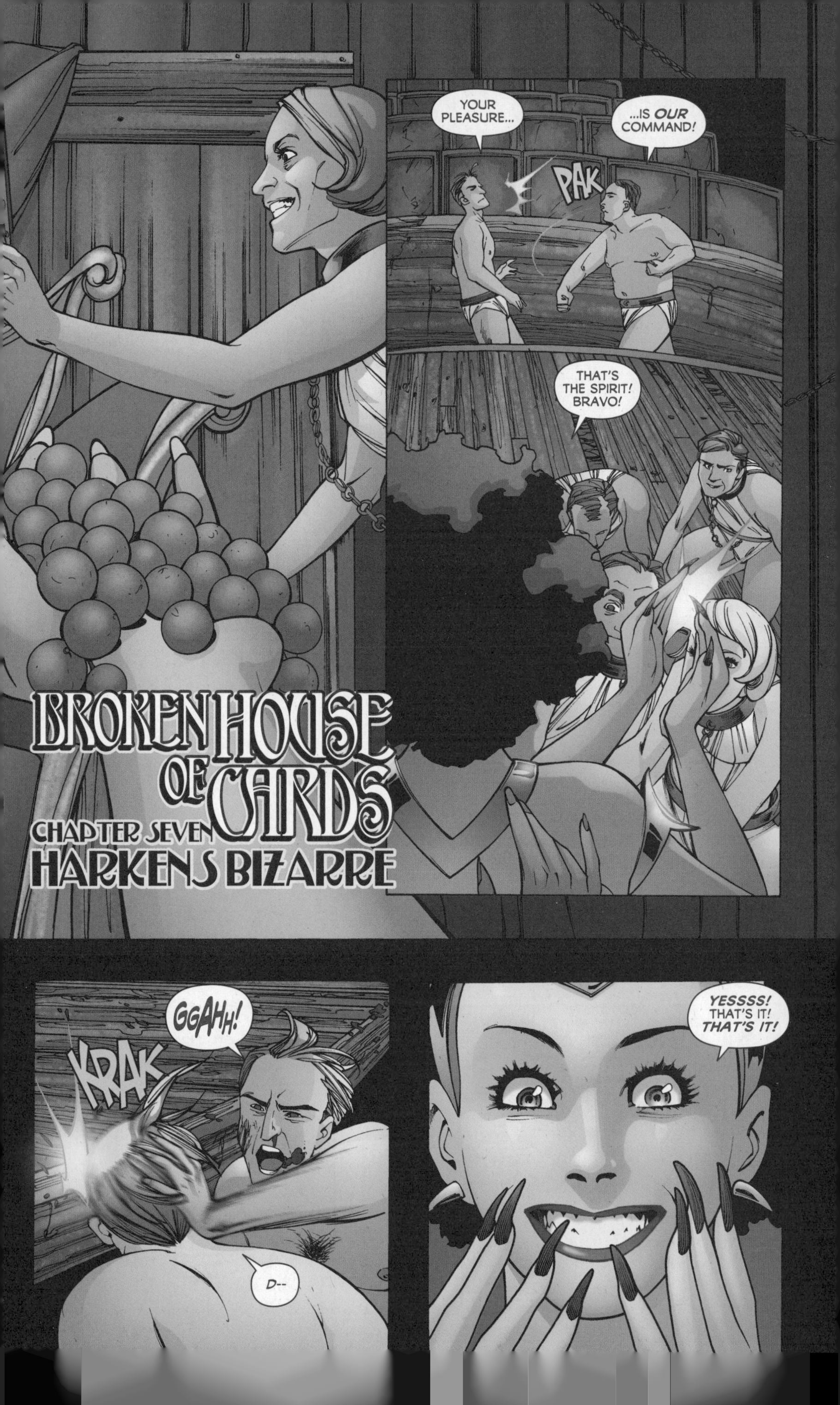

YOUR PLEASURE...
...IS OUR COMMAND!
PAK
THAT'S THE SPIRIT! BRAVO!
BROKEN HOUSE OF CARDS
CHAPTER SEVEN
HARKENS BIZARRE
KRAK
GGAHH!
D--
YESSSS! THAT'S IT! THAT'S IT!

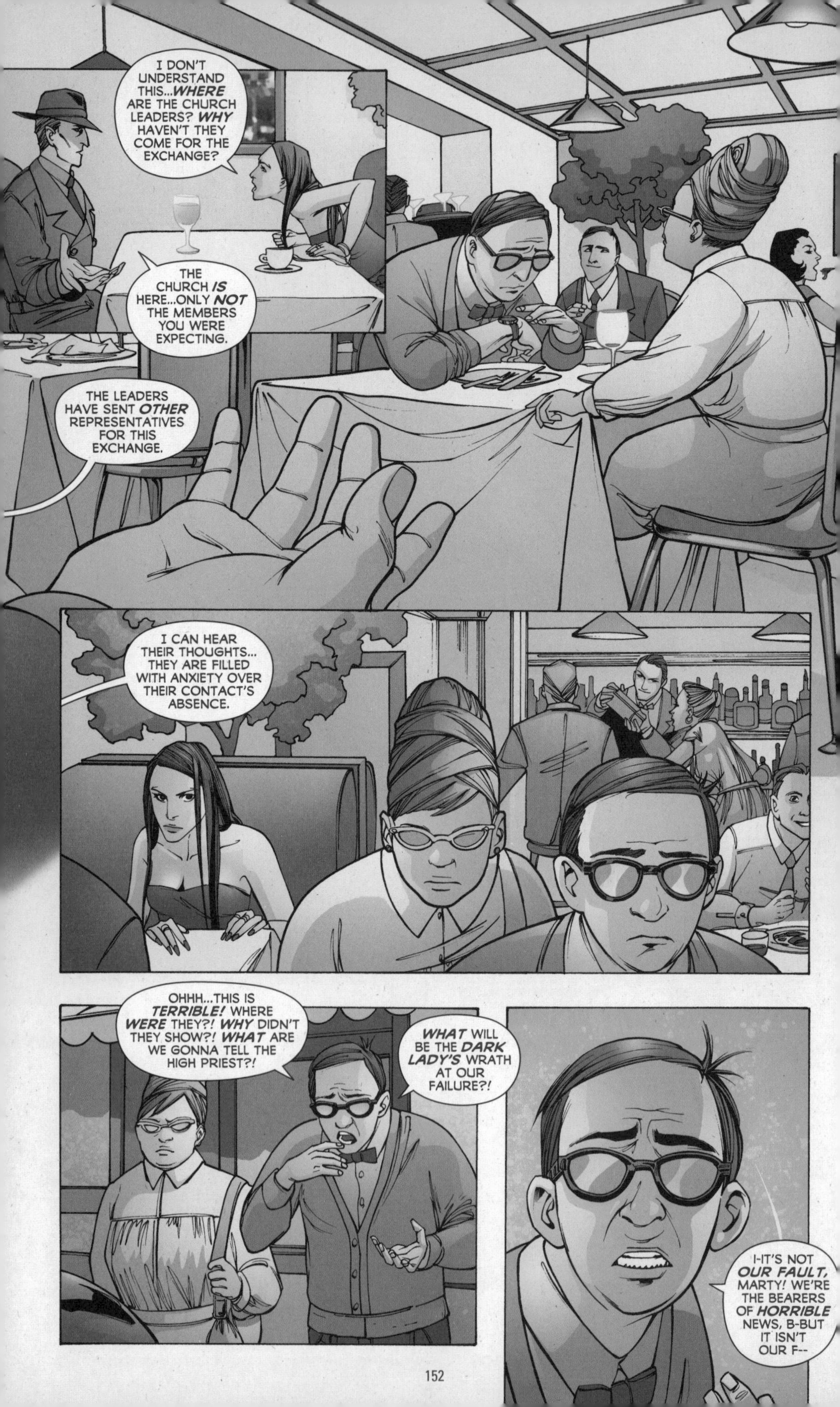
I DON'T UNDERSTAND THIS...WHERE ARE THE CHURCH LEADERS? WHY HAVEN'T THEY COME FOR THE EXCHANGE?
THE CHURCH IS HERE...ONLY NOT THE MEMBERS YOU WERE EXPECTING.
THE LEADERS HAVE SENT OTHER REPRESENTATIVES FOR THIS EXCHANGE.
I CAN HEAR THEIR THOUGHTS... THEY ARE FILLED WITH ANXIETY OVER THEIR CONTACT'S ABSENCE.
OHHH...THIS IS TERRIBLE! WHERE WERE THEY?! WHY DIDN'T THEY SHOW?! WHAT ARE WE GONNA TELL THE HIGH PRIEST?!
WHAT WILL BE THE DARK LADY'S WRATH AT OUR FAILURE?!
I-IT'S NOT OUR FAULT, MARTY! WE'RE THE BEARERS OF HORRIBLE NEWS, B-BUT IT ISN'T OUR F--

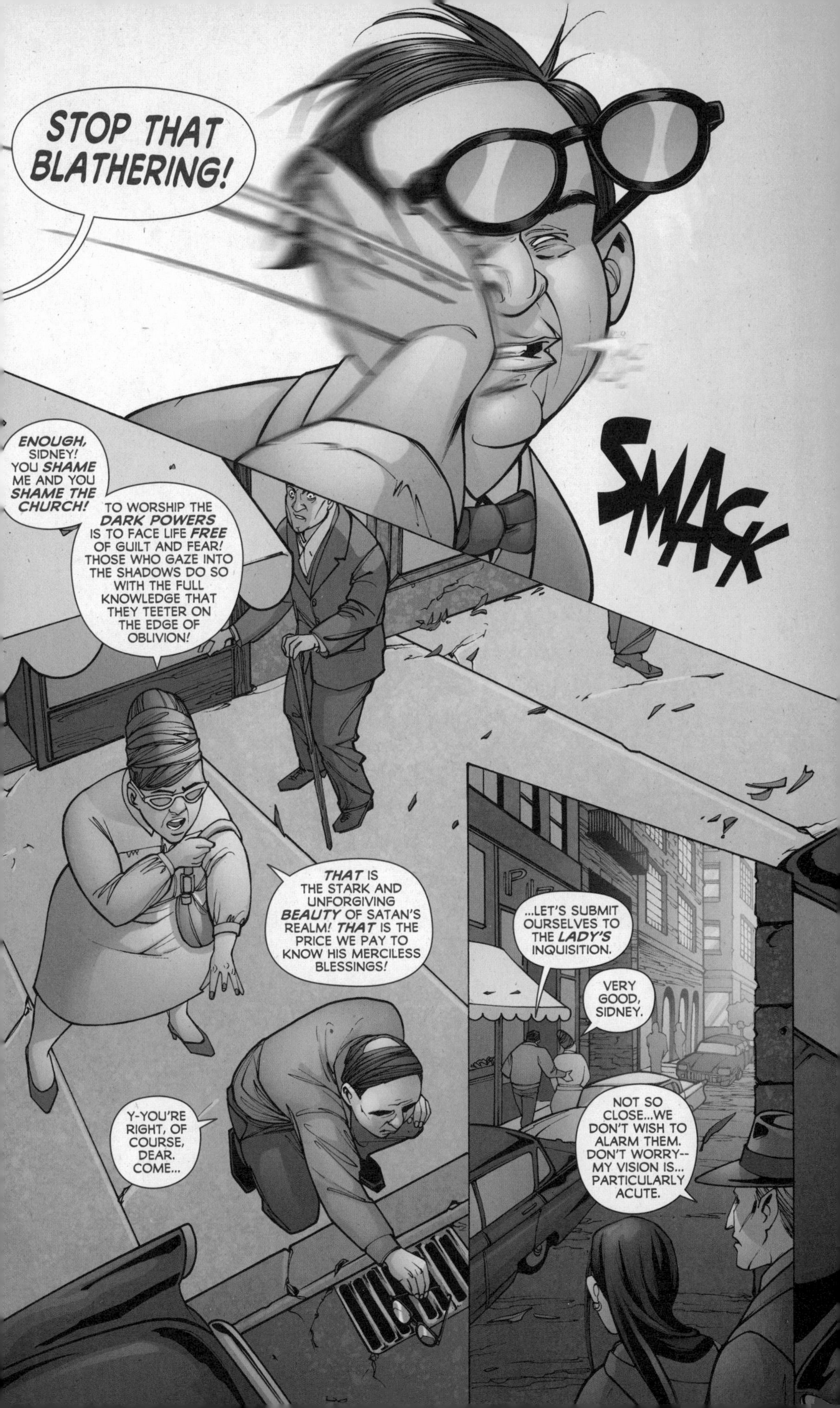
STOP THAT BLATHERING!
SMACK
ENOUGH, SIDNEY! YOU SHAME ME AND YOU SHAME THE CHURCH!
TO WORSHIP THE DARK POWERS IS TO FACE LIFE FREE OF GUILT AND FEAR! THOSE WHO GAZE INTO THE SHADOWS DO SO WITH THE FULL KNOWLEDGE THAT THEY TEETER ON THE EDGE OF OBLIVION!
THAT IS THE STARK AND UNFORGIVING BEAUTY OF SATAN'S REALM! THAT IS THE PRICE WE PAY TO KNOW HIS MERCILESS BLESSINGS!
Y-YOU'RE RIGHT, OF COURSE, DEAR. COME...
...LET'S SUBMIT OURSELVES TO THE LADY'S INQUISITION.
VERY GOOD, SIDNEY.
NOT SO CLOSE...WE DON'T WISH TO ALARM THEM. DON'T WORRY-- MY VISION IS... PARTICULARLY ACUTE.

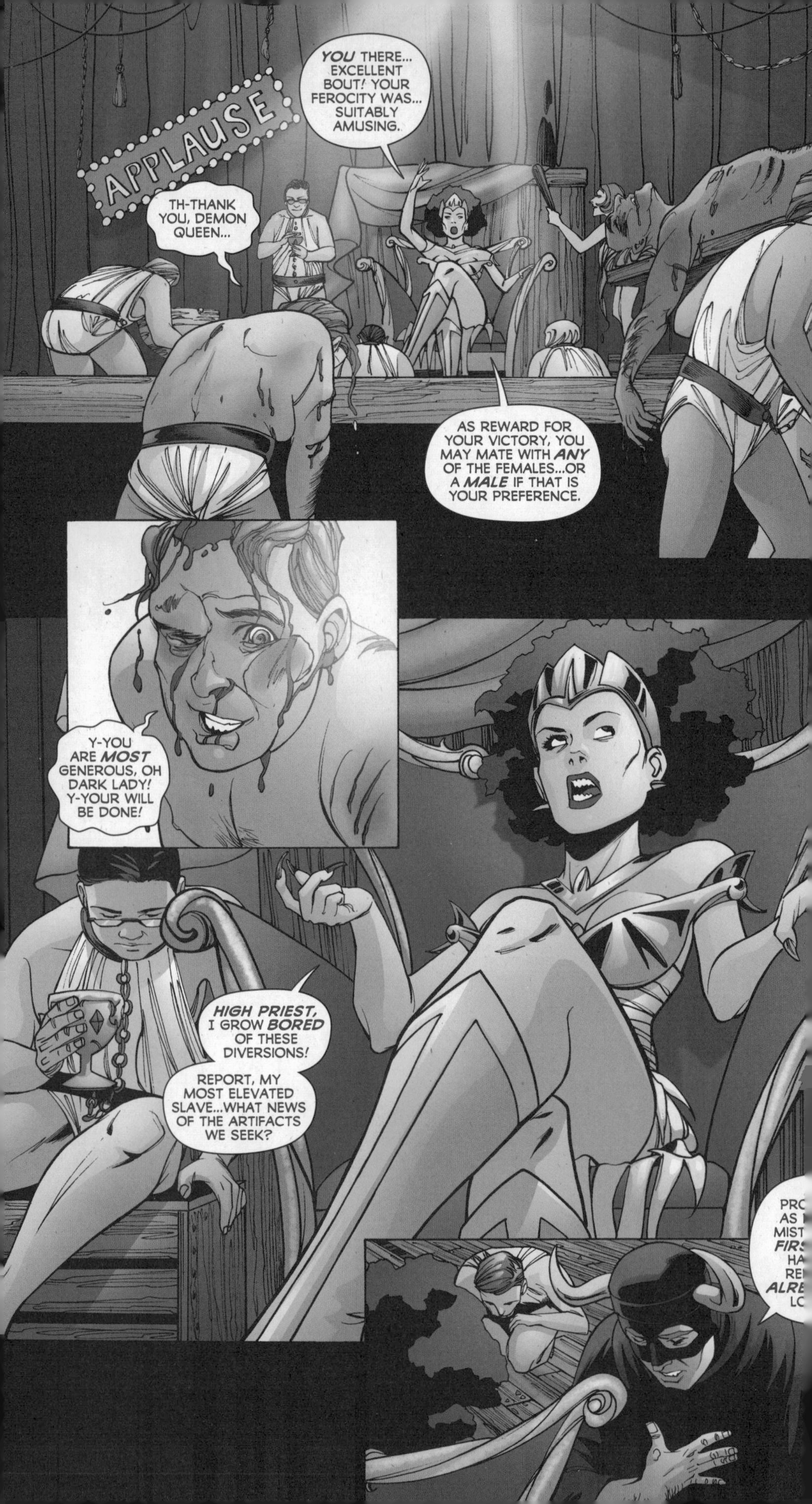
APPLAUSE
YOU THERE... EXCELLENT BOUT! YOUR FEROCITY WAS... SUITABLY AMUSING.
TH-THANK YOU, DEMON QUEEN...
AS REWARD FOR YOUR VICTORY, YOU MAY MATE WITH ANY OF THE FEMALES...OR A MALE IF THAT IS YOUR PREFERENCE.
Y-YOU ARE MOST GENEROUS, OH DARK LADY! Y-YOUR WILL BE DONE!
HIGH PRIEST, I GROW BORED OF THESE DIVERSIONS!
REPORT, MY MOST ELEVATED SLAVE...WHAT NEWS OF THE ARTIFACTS WE SEEK?

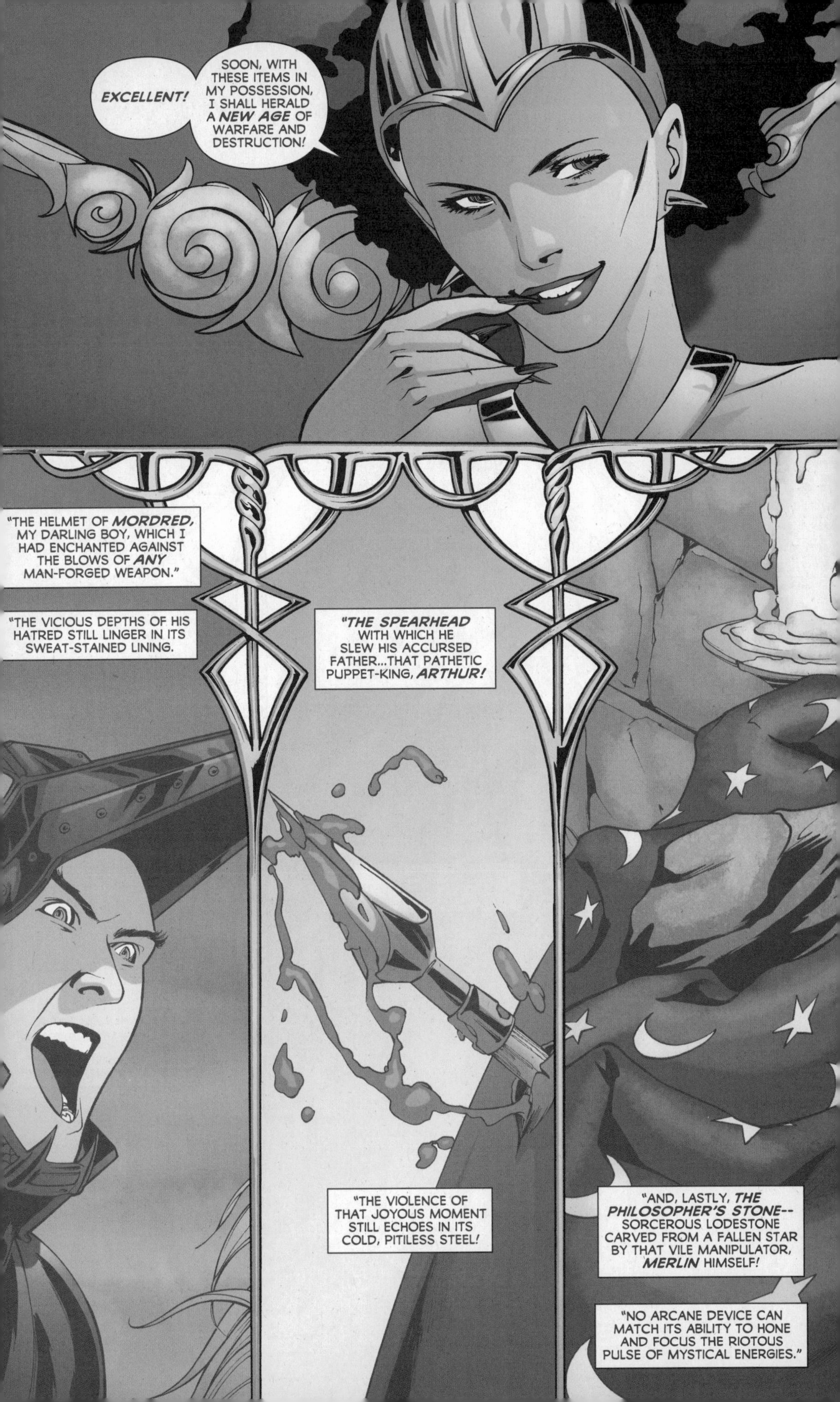
EXCELLENT!
SOON, WITH THESE ITEMS IN MY POSSESSION, I SHALL HERALD A NEW AGE OF WARFARE AND DESTRUCTION!
"THE HELMET OF MORDRED, MY DARLING BOY, WHICH I HAD ENCHANTED AGAINST THE BLOWS OF ANY MAN-FORGED WEAPON."
"THE VICIOUS DEPTHS OF HIS HATRED STILL LINGER IN ITS SWEAT-STAINED LINING.
"THE SPEARHEAD WITH WHICH HE SLEW HIS ACCURSED FATHER...THAT PATHETIC PUPPET-KING, ARTHUR!
"THE VIOLENCE OF THAT JOYOUS MOMENT STILL ECHOES IN ITS COLD, PITILESS STEEL!
"AND, LASTLY, THE PHILOSOPHER'S STONE-- SORCEROUS LODESTONE CARVED FROM A FALLEN STAR BY THAT VILE MANIPULATOR, MERLIN HIMSELF!
"NO ARCANE DEVICE CAN MATCH ITS ABILITY TO HONE AND FOCUS THE RIOTOUS PULSE OF MYSTICAL ENERGIES."

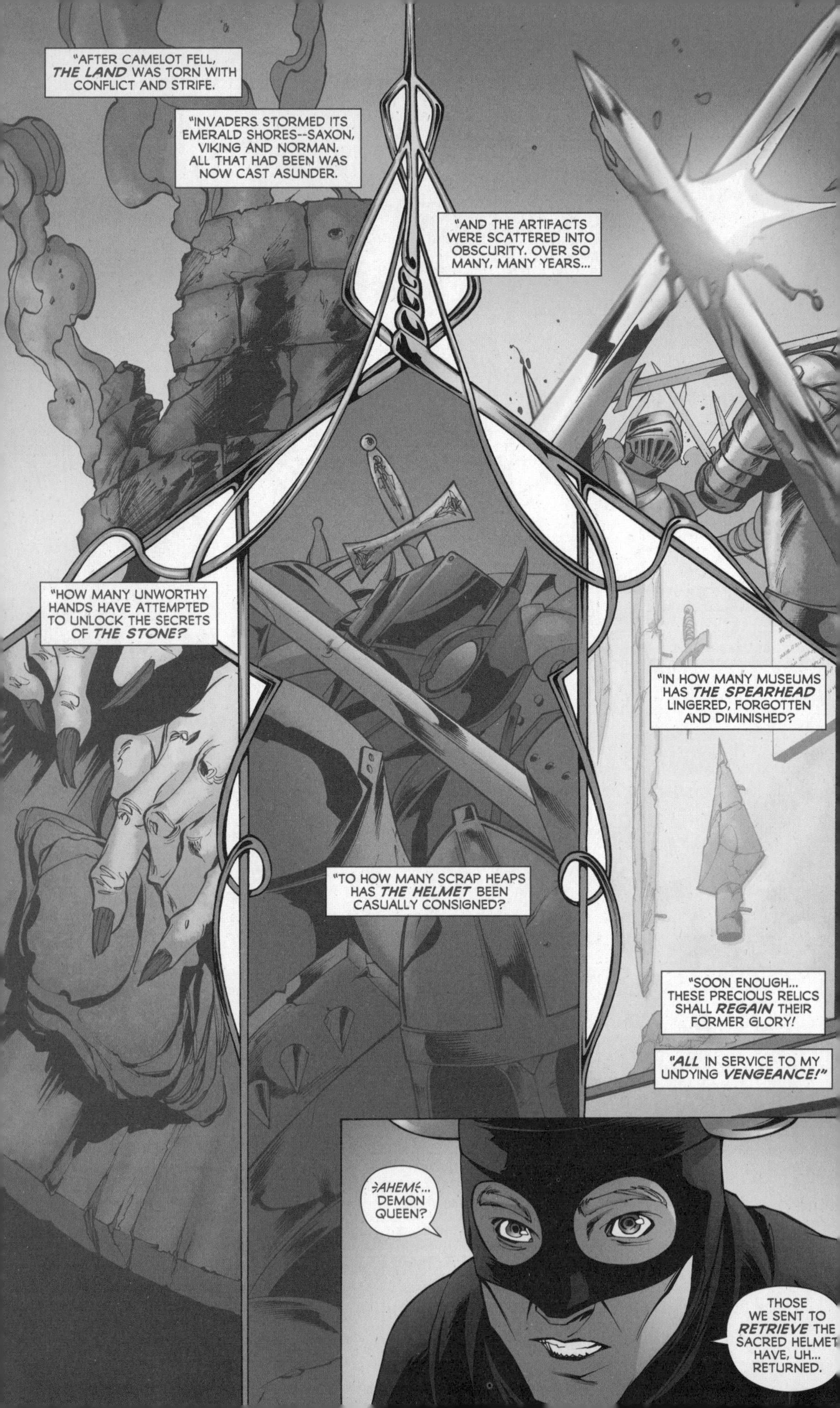
"AFTER CAMELOT FELL, THE LAND WAS TORN WITH CONFLICT AND STRIFE.
"INVADERS STORMED ITS EMERALD SHORES--SAXON, VIKING AND NORMAN. ALL THAT HAD BEEN WAS NOW CAST ASUNDER.
"AND THE ARTIFACTS WERE SCATTERED INTO OBSCURITY. OVER SO MANY, MANY YEARS...
"HOW MANY UNWORTHY HANDS HAVE ATTEMPTED TO UNLOCK THE SECRETS OF THE STONE?
"TO HOW MANY SCRAP HEAPS HAS THE HELMET BEEN CASUALLY CONSIGNED?
"IN HOW MANY MUSEUMS HAS THE SPEARHEAD LINGERED, FORGOTTEN AND DIMINISHED?
"SOON ENOUGH... THESE PRECIOUS RELICS SHALL REGAIN THEIR FORMER GLORY!
"ALL IN SERVICE TO MY UNDYING VENGEANCE!"
≥AHEM≤... DEMON QUEEN?
THOSE WE SENT TO RETRIEVE THE SACRED HELMET HAVE, UH... RETURNED.

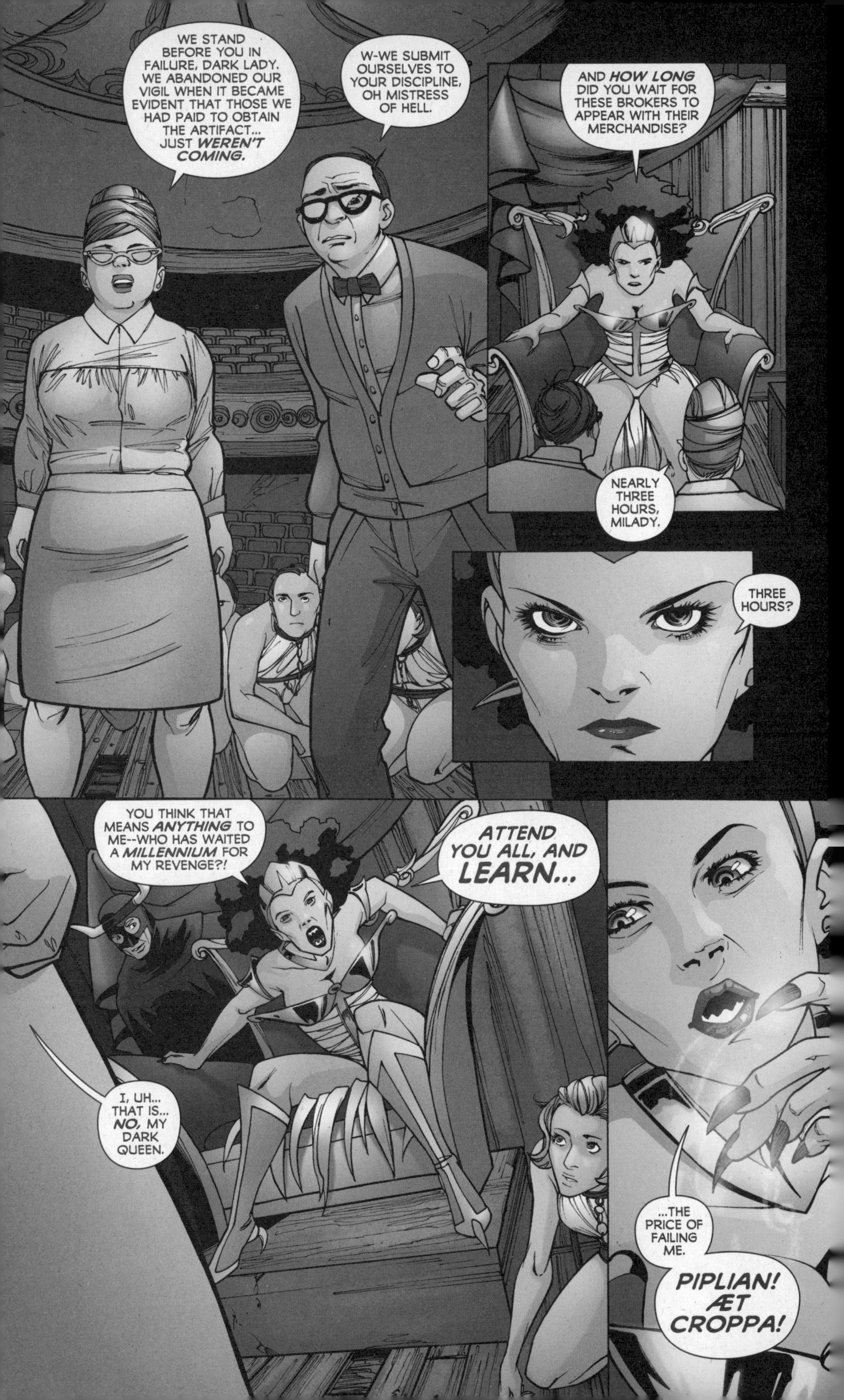
WE STAND BEFORE YOU IN FAILURE, DARK LADY. WE ABANDONED OUR VIGIL WHEN IT BECAME EVIDENT THAT THOSE WE HAD PAID TO OBTAIN THE ARTIFACT... JUST *WEREN'T COMING.*
W-WE SUBMIT OURSELVES TO YOUR DISCIPLINE, OH MISTRESS OF HELL.
AND *HOW LONG* DID YOU WAIT FOR THESE BROKERS TO APPEAR WITH THEIR MERCHANDISE?
NEARLY THREE HOURS, MILADY.
THREE HOURS?
YOU THINK THAT MEANS *ANYTHING* TO ME--WHO HAS WAITED A *MILLENNIUM* FOR MY REVENGE?!
I, UH... THAT IS... *NO,* MY DARK QUEEN.
ATTEND YOU ALL, AND LEARN...
...THE PRICE OF FAILING ME.
PIPLIAN! ÆT CROPPA!

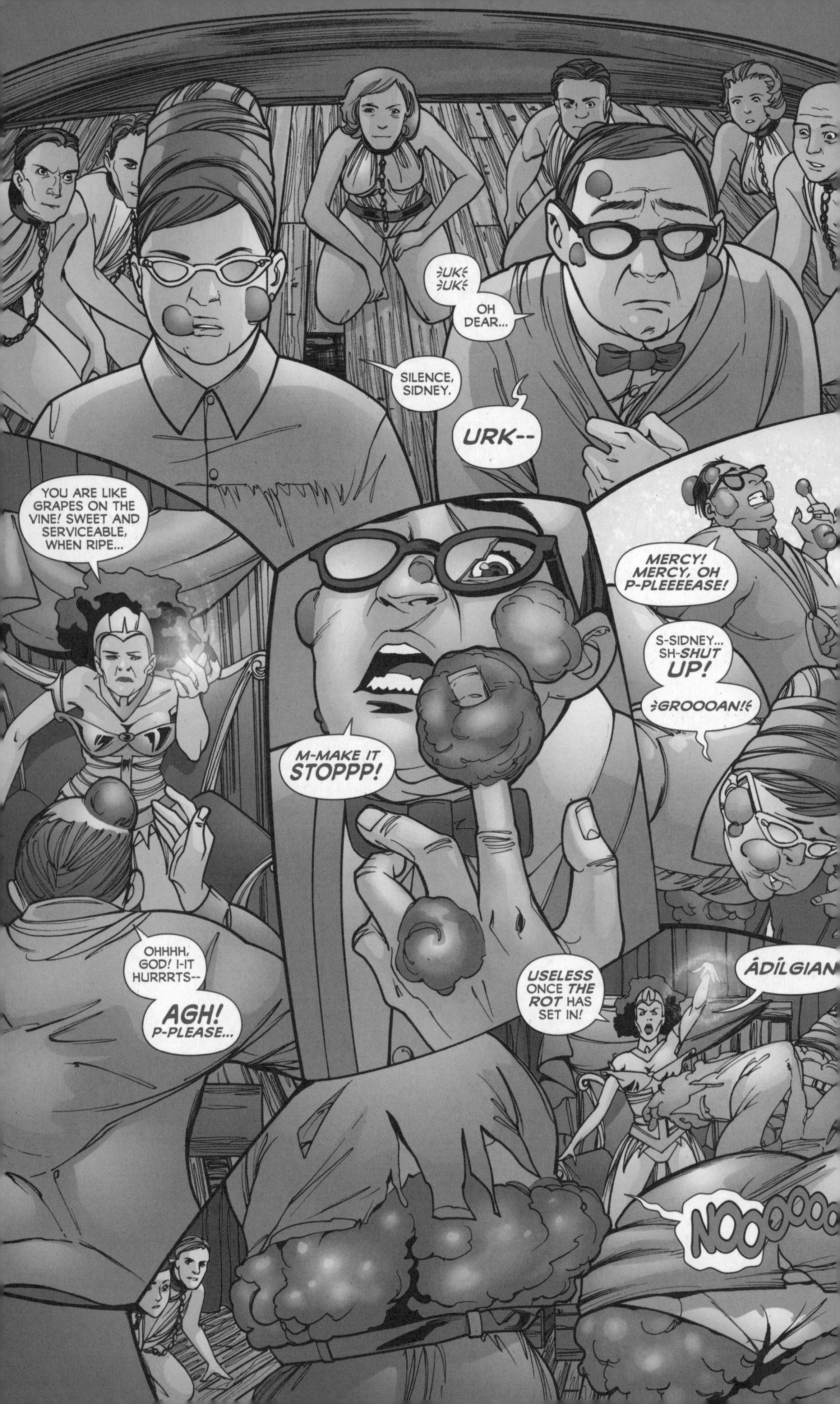
UK UK
OH DEAR...
SILENCE, SIDNEY.
URK--
YOU ARE LIKE GRAPES ON THE VINE! SWEET AND SERVICEABLE, WHEN RIPE...
M-MAKE IT STOPPP!
MERCY! MERCY, OH P-PLEEEEEASE!
S-SIDNEY... SH-SHUT UP!
GROOOAN!
OHHHH, GOD! I-IT HURRRTS--
AGH! P-PLEASE...
USELESS ONCE THE ROT HAS SET IN!
ÁDÍLGIAN
NOOOOOO

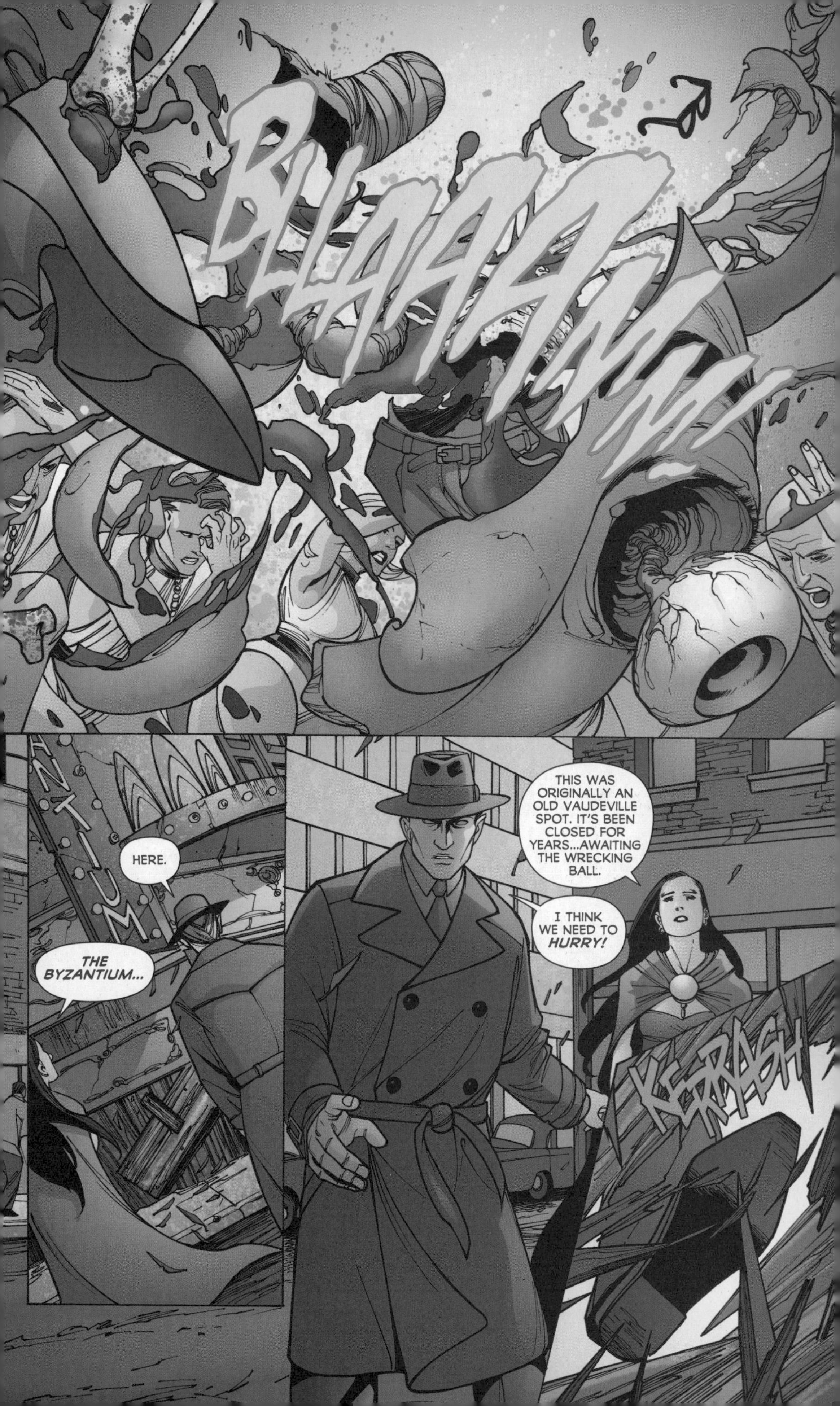
BLAAAAMMM!
HERE.
THE BYZANTIUM...
THIS WAS ORIGINALLY AN OLD VAUDEVILLE SPOT. IT'S BEEN CLOSED FOR YEARS...AWAITING THE WRECKING BALL.
I THINK WE NEED TO HURRY!
KERASH

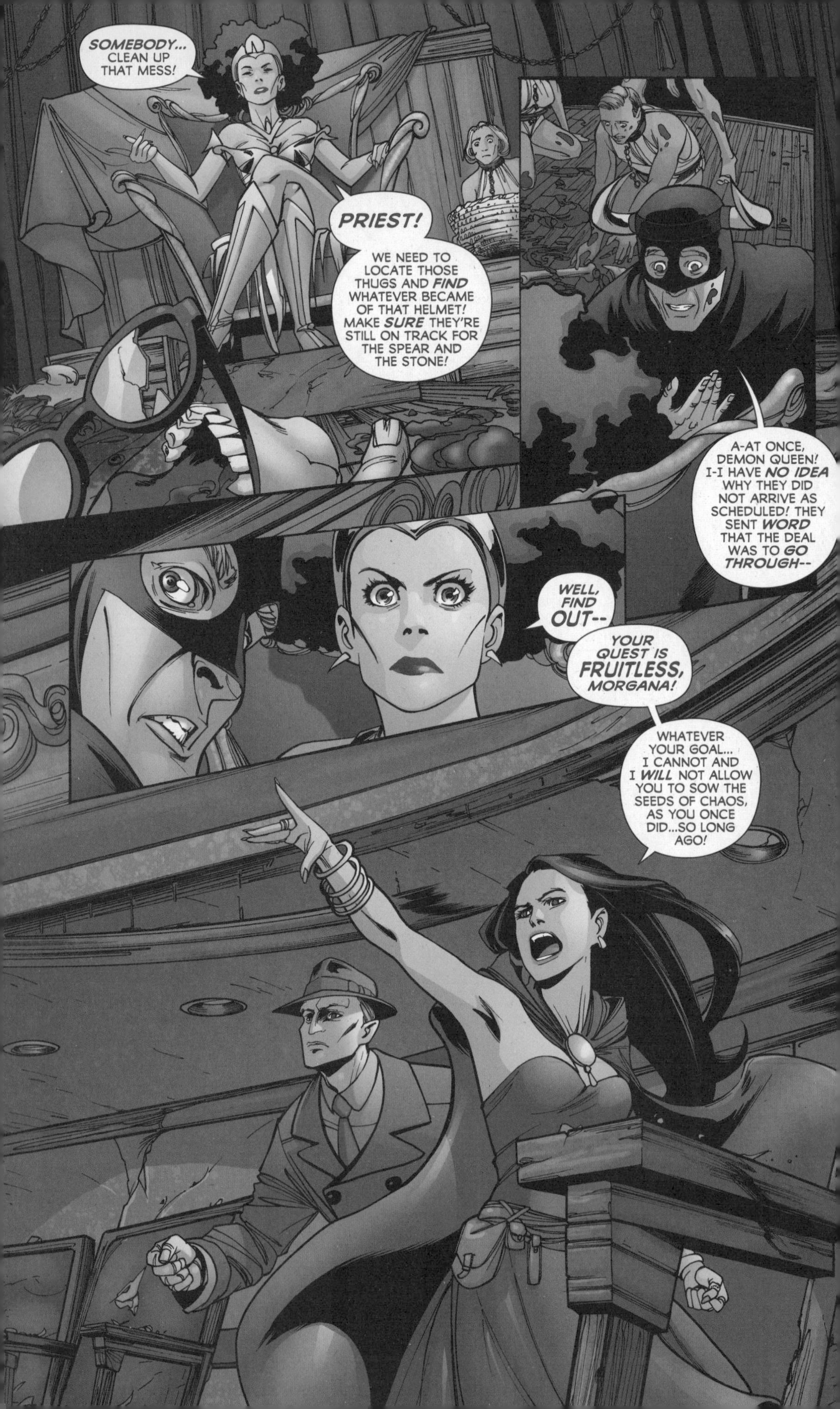
SOMEBODY... CLEAN UP THAT MESS!
PRIEST!
WE NEED TO LOCATE THOSE THUGS AND FIND WHATEVER BECAME OF THAT HELMET! MAKE SURE THEY'RE STILL ON TRACK FOR THE SPEAR AND THE STONE!
A-AT ONCE, DEMON QUEEN! I-I HAVE NO IDEA WHY THEY DID NOT ARRIVE AS SCHEDULED! THEY SENT WORD THAT THE DEAL WAS TO GO THROUGH--
WELL, FIND OUT--
YOUR QUEST IS FRUITLESS, MORGANA!
WHATEVER YOUR GOAL... I CANNOT AND I WILL NOT ALLOW YOU TO SOW THE SEEDS OF CHAOS, AS YOU ONCE DID...SO LONG AGO!

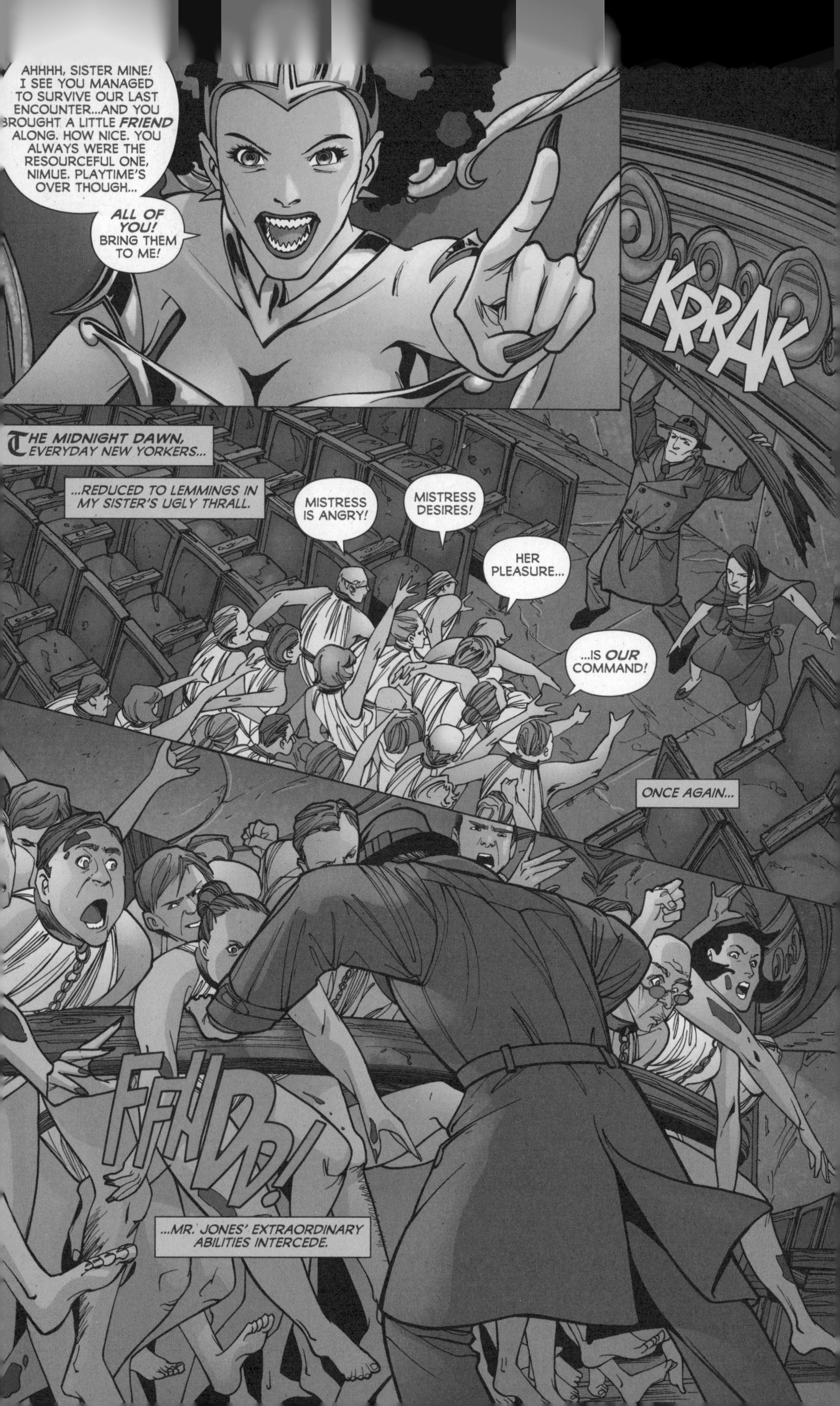
AHHHH, SISTER MINE! I SEE YOU MANAGED TO SURVIVE OUR LAST ENCOUNTER...AND YOU BROUGHT A LITTLE FRIEND ALONG. HOW NICE. YOU ALWAYS WERE THE RESOURCEFUL ONE, NIMUE. PLAYTIME'S OVER THOUGH...
ALL OF YOU! BRING THEM TO ME!
KRRAK
THE MIDNIGHT DAWN, EVERYDAY NEW YORKERS...
...REDUCED TO LEMMINGS IN MY SISTER'S UGLY THRALL.
MISTRESS IS ANGRY!
MISTRESS DESIRES!
HER PLEASURE...
...IS OUR COMMAND!
ONCE AGAIN...
FFHUBI
...MR. JONES' EXTRAORDINARY ABILITIES INTERCEDE.

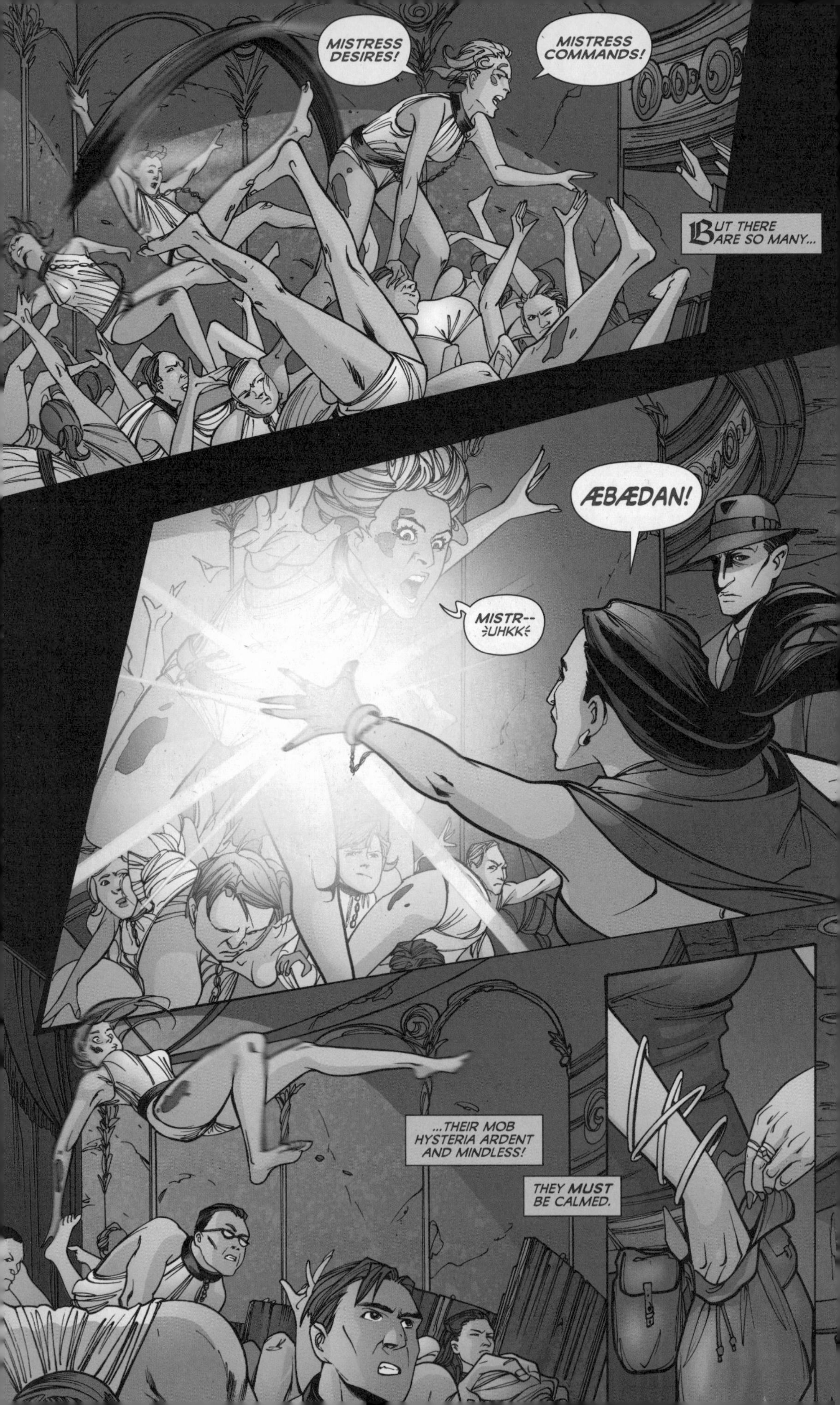

MISTRESS DESIRES!
MISTRESS COMMANDS!
BUT THERE ARE SO MANY...
ÆBÆDAN!
MISTR-- UHKK
...THEIR MOB HYSTERIA ARDENT AND MINDLESS!
THEY MUST BE CALMED.

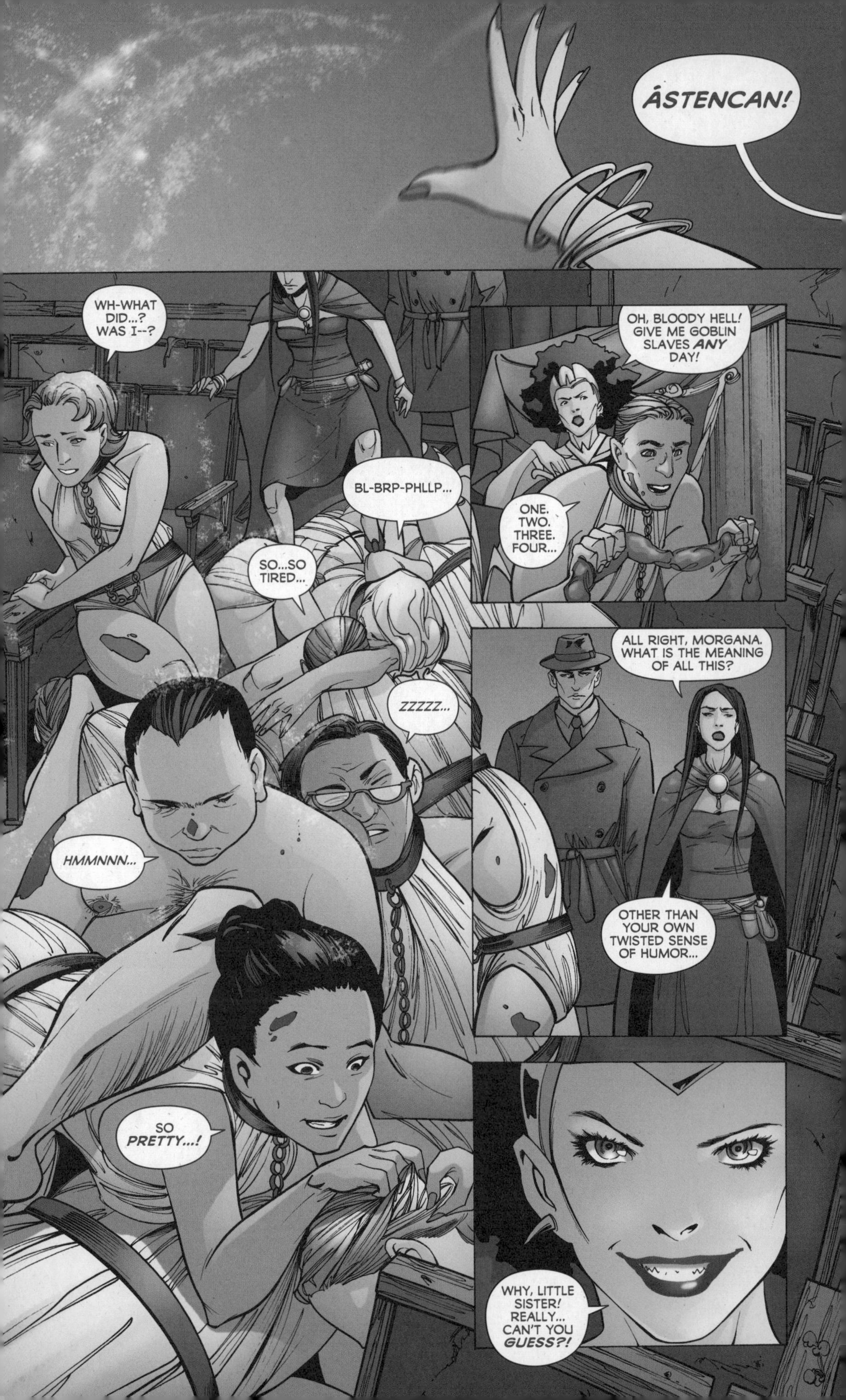
ÅSTENCAN!
WH-WHAT DID...? WAS I--?
BL-BRP-PHLLP...
SO...SO TIRED...
ZZZZZ...
HMMNNN...
SO PRETTY...!
OH, BLOODY HELL! GIVE ME GOBLIN SLAVES ANY DAY!
ONE. TWO. THREE. FOUR...
ALL RIGHT, MORGANA. WHAT IS THE MEANING OF ALL THIS?
OTHER THAN YOUR OWN TWISTED SENSE OF HUMOR...
WHY, LITTLE SISTER! REALLY... CAN'T YOU GUESS?!

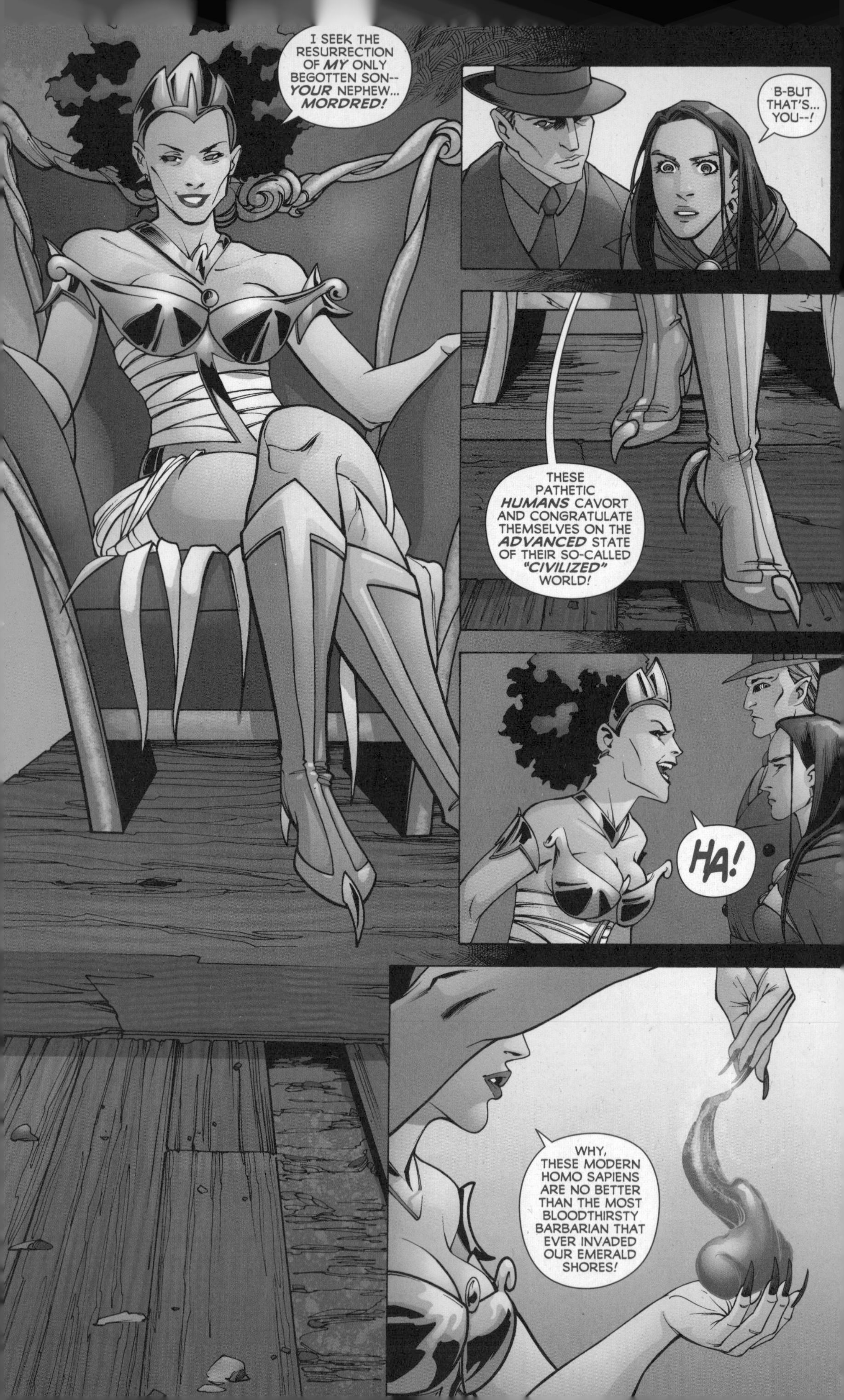
I SEEK THE RESURRECTION OF MY ONLY BEGOTTEN SON-- YOUR NEPHEW... MORDRED!
B-BUT THAT'S... YOU--!
THESE PATHETIC HUMANS CAVORT AND CONGRATULATE THEMSELVES ON THE ADVANCED STATE OF THEIR SO-CALLED "CIVILIZED" WORLD!
HA!
WHY, THESE MODERN HOMO SAPIENS ARE NO BETTER THAN THE MOST BLOODTHIRSTY BARBARIAN THAT EVER INVADED OUR EMERALD SHORES!

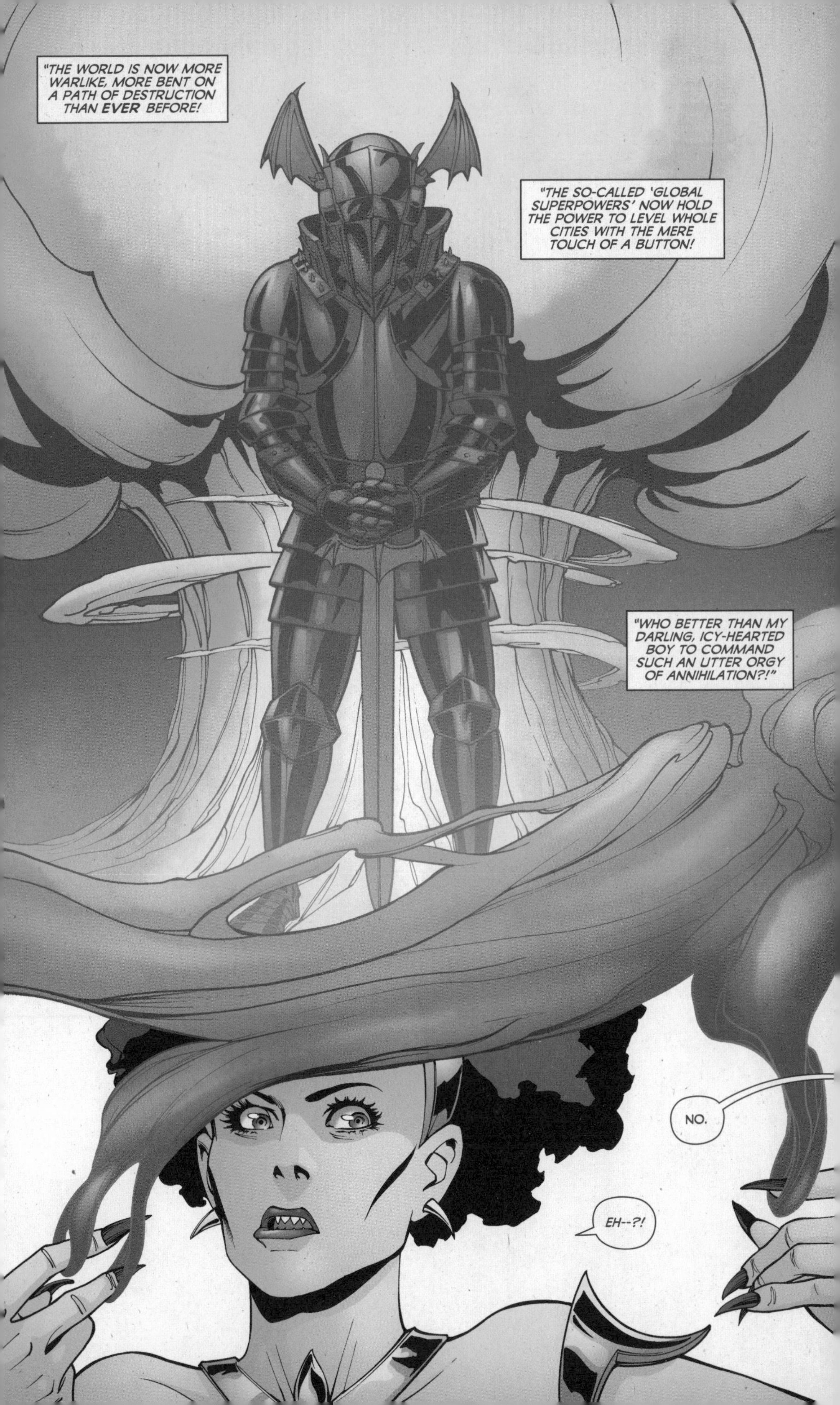
"THE WORLD IS NOW MORE WARLIKE, MORE BENT ON A PATH OF DESTRUCTION THAN **EVER** BEFORE!
"THE SO-CALLED 'GLOBAL SUPERPOWERS' NOW HOLD THE POWER TO LEVEL WHOLE CITIES WITH THE MERE TOUCH OF A BUTTON!
"WHO BETTER THAN MY DARLING, ICY-HEARTED BOY TO COMMAND SUCH AN UTTER ORGY OF ANNIHILATION?!"
NO.
EH--?!

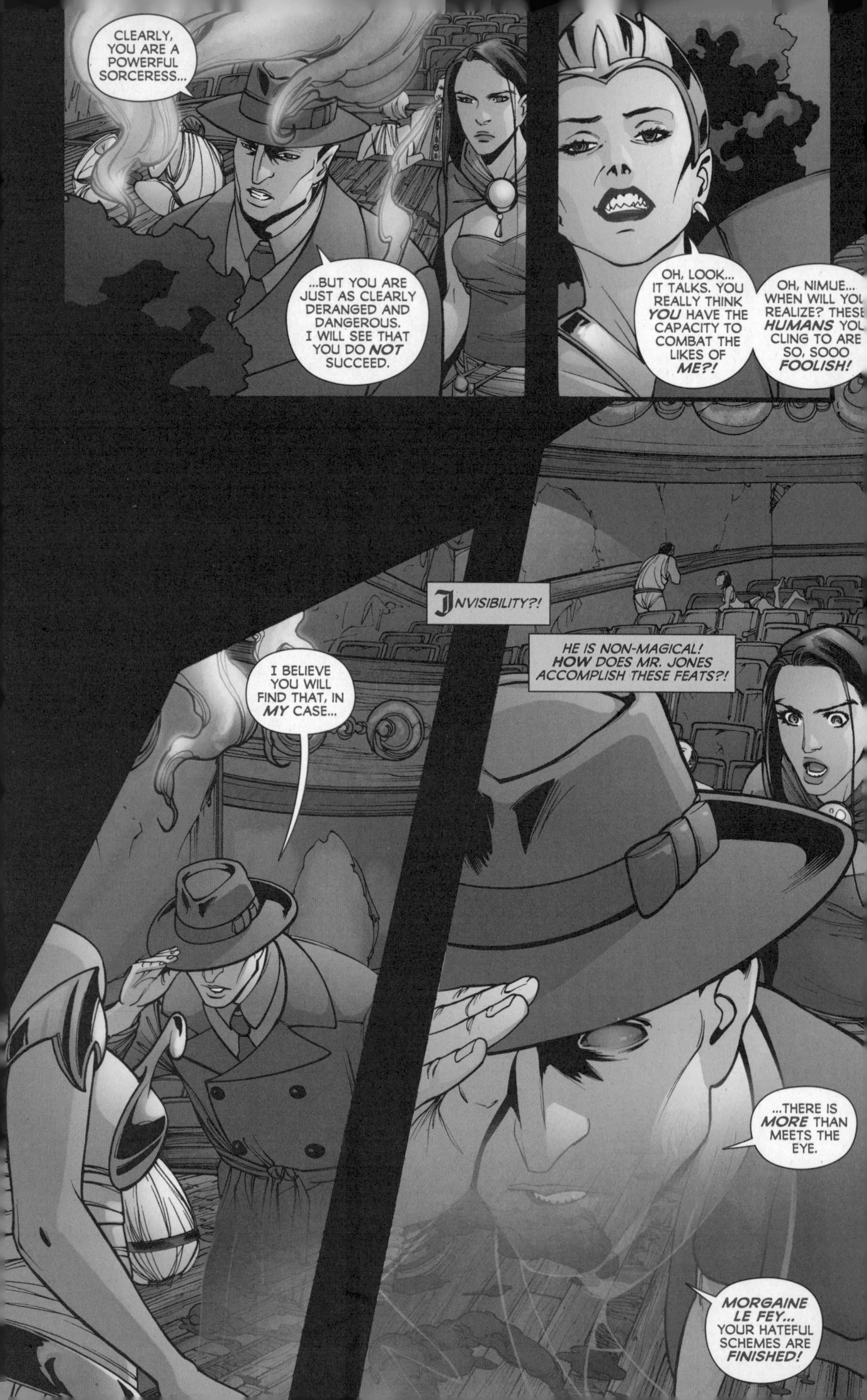

CLEARLY, YOU ARE A POWERFUL SORCERESS...
...BUT YOU ARE JUST AS CLEARLY DERANGED AND DANGEROUS. I WILL SEE THAT YOU DO NOT SUCCEED.
OH, LOOK... IT TALKS. YOU REALLY THINK YOU HAVE THE CAPACITY TO COMBAT THE LIKES OF ME?!
OH, NIMUE... WHEN WILL YOU REALIZE? THESE HUMANS YOU CLING TO ARE SO, SOOO FOOLISH!
INVISIBILITY?!
HE IS NON-MAGICAL! HOW DOES MR. JONES ACCOMPLISH THESE FEATS?!
I BELIEVE YOU WILL FIND THAT, IN MY CASE...
...THERE IS MORE THAN MEETS THE EYE.
MORGAINE LE FEY... YOUR HATEFUL SCHEMES ARE FINISHED!

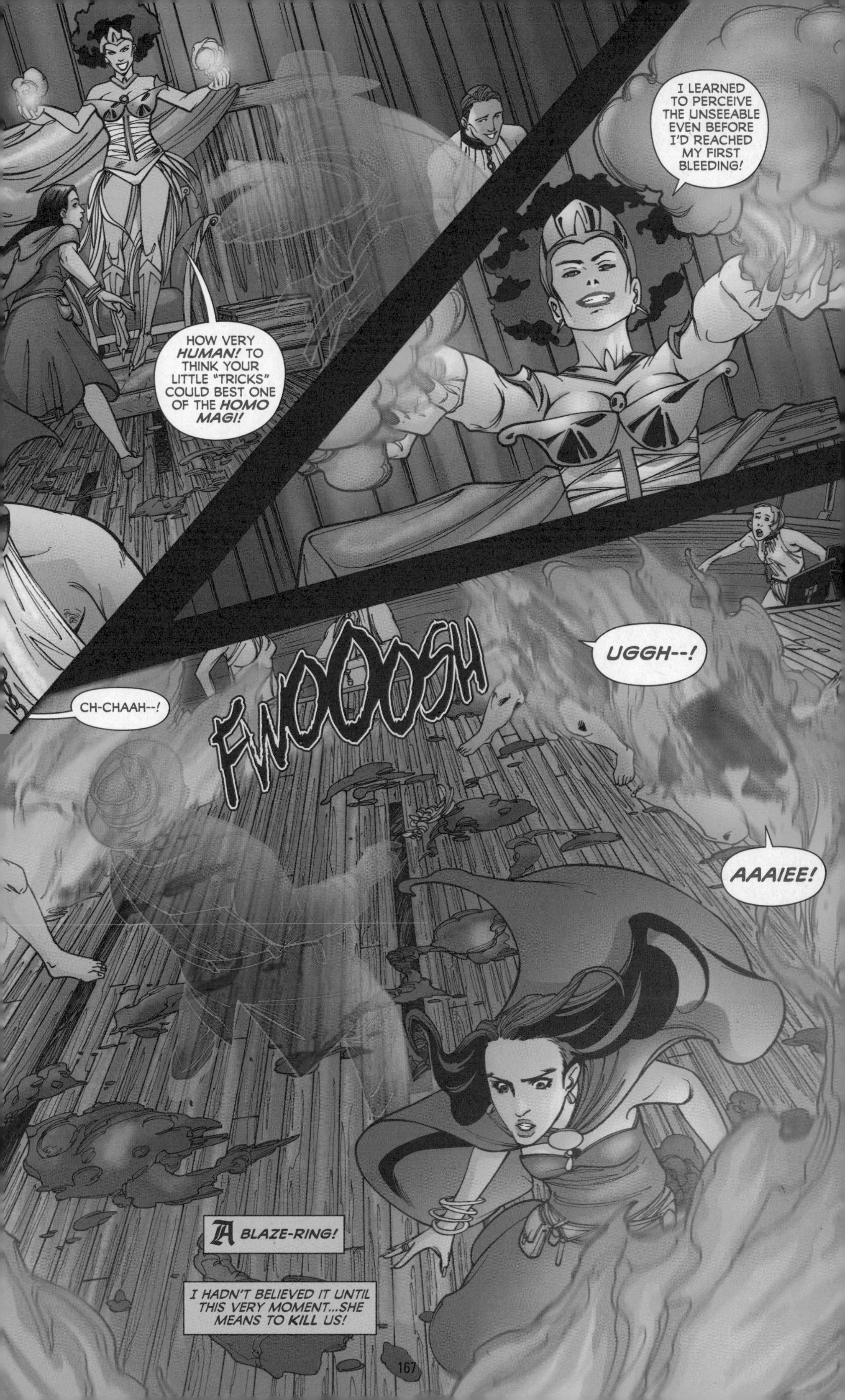
HOW VERY HUMAN! TO THINK YOUR LITTLE "TRICKS" COULD BEST ONE OF THE HOMO MAGI!
I LEARNED TO PERCEIVE THE UNSEEABLE EVEN BEFORE I'D REACHED MY FIRST BLEEDING!
CH-CHAAH--!
FWOOOSH
UGGH--!
AAAIEE!
A BLAZE-RING!
I HADN'T BELIEVED IT UNTIL THIS VERY MOMENT...SHE MEANS TO KILL US!

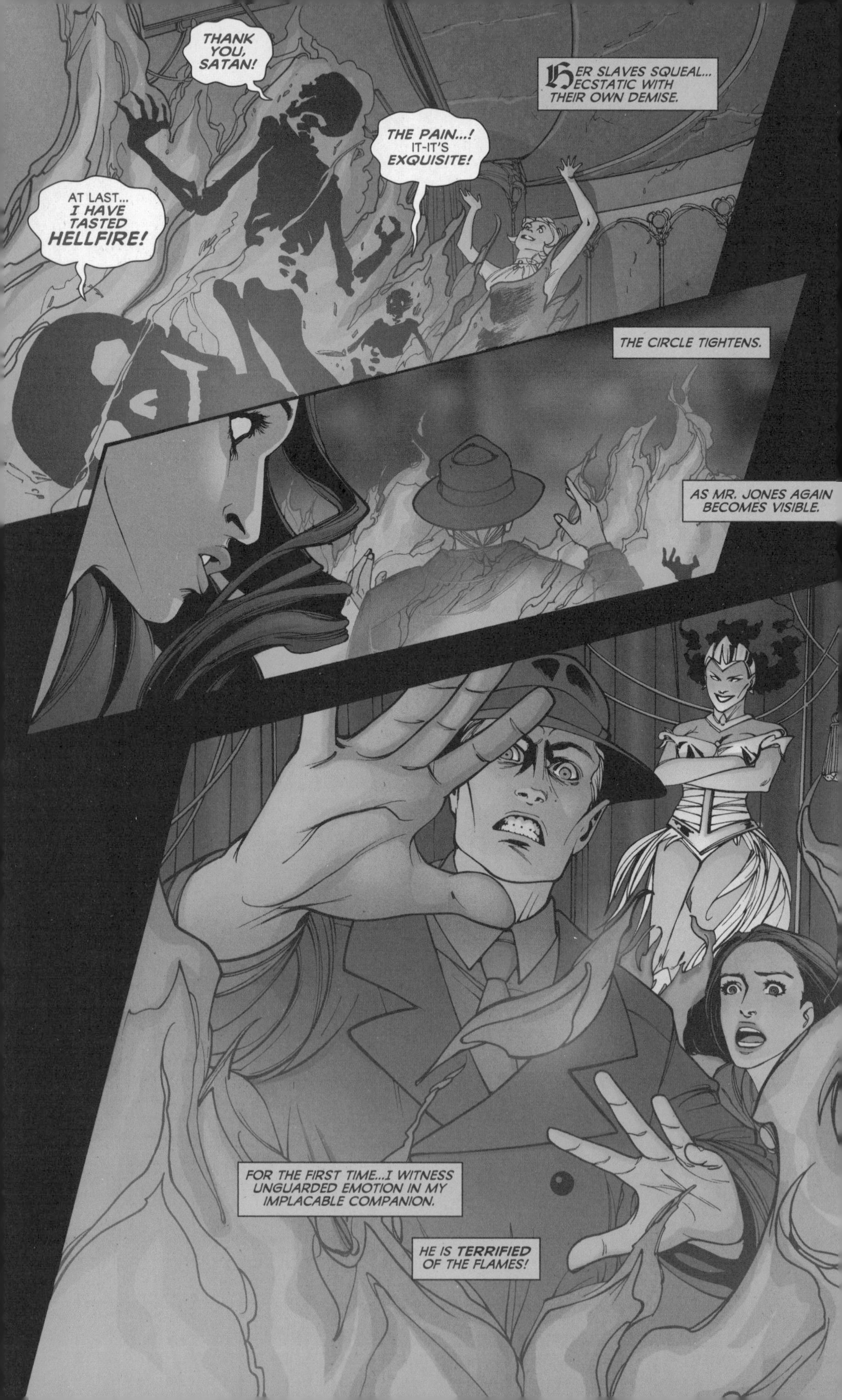
THANK YOU, SATAN!
HER SLAVES SQUEAL... ECSTATIC WITH THEIR OWN DEMISE.
THE PAIN...! IT-IT'S EXQUISITE!
AT LAST... I HAVE TASTED HELLFIRE!
THE CIRCLE TIGHTENS.
AS MR. JONES AGAIN BECOMES VISIBLE.
FOR THE FIRST TIME...I WITNESS UNGUARDED EMOTION IN MY IMPLACABLE COMPANION.
HE IS TERRIFIED OF THE FLAMES!

Chapter Eight: Yield & Scream

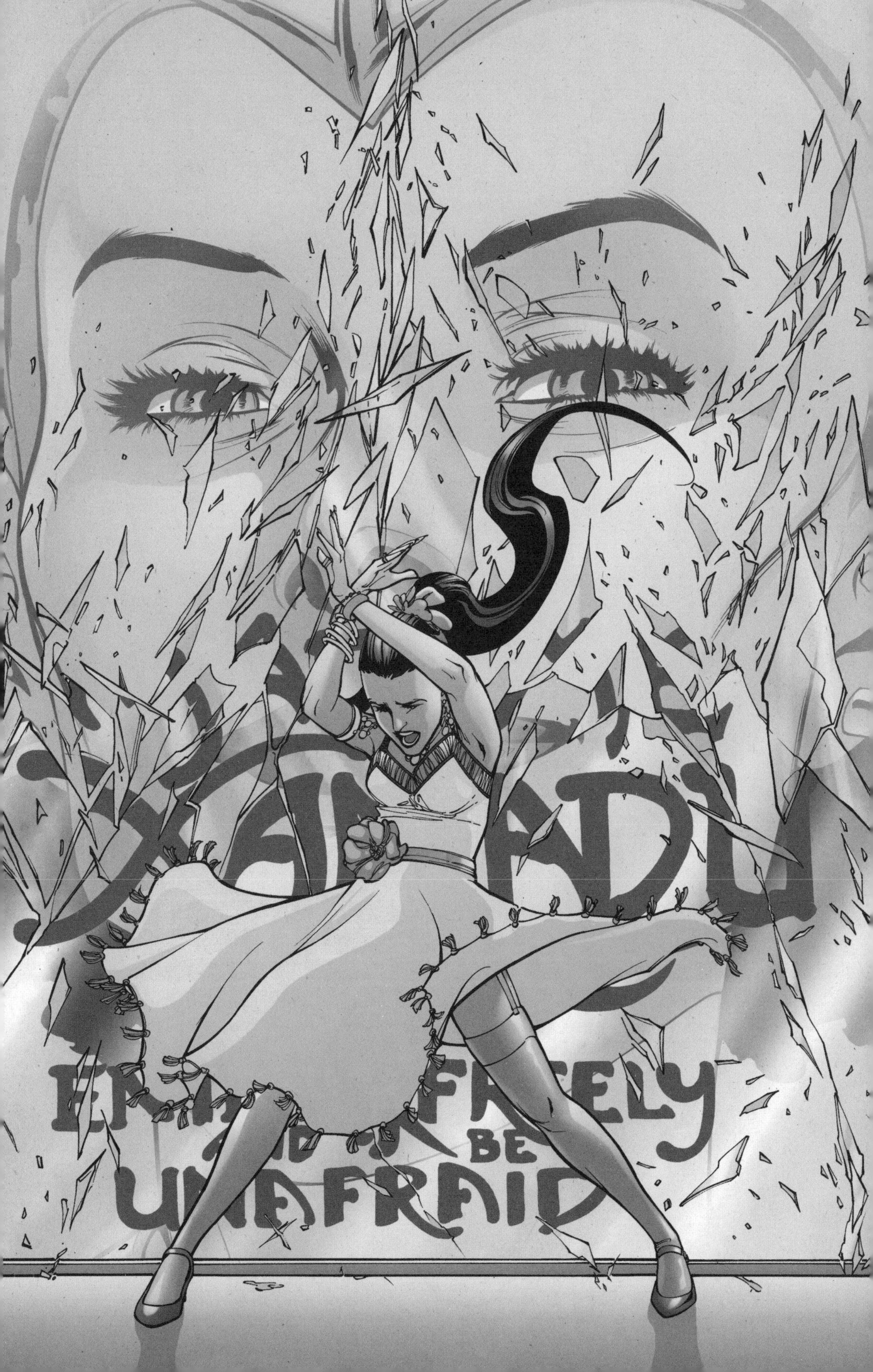
BE

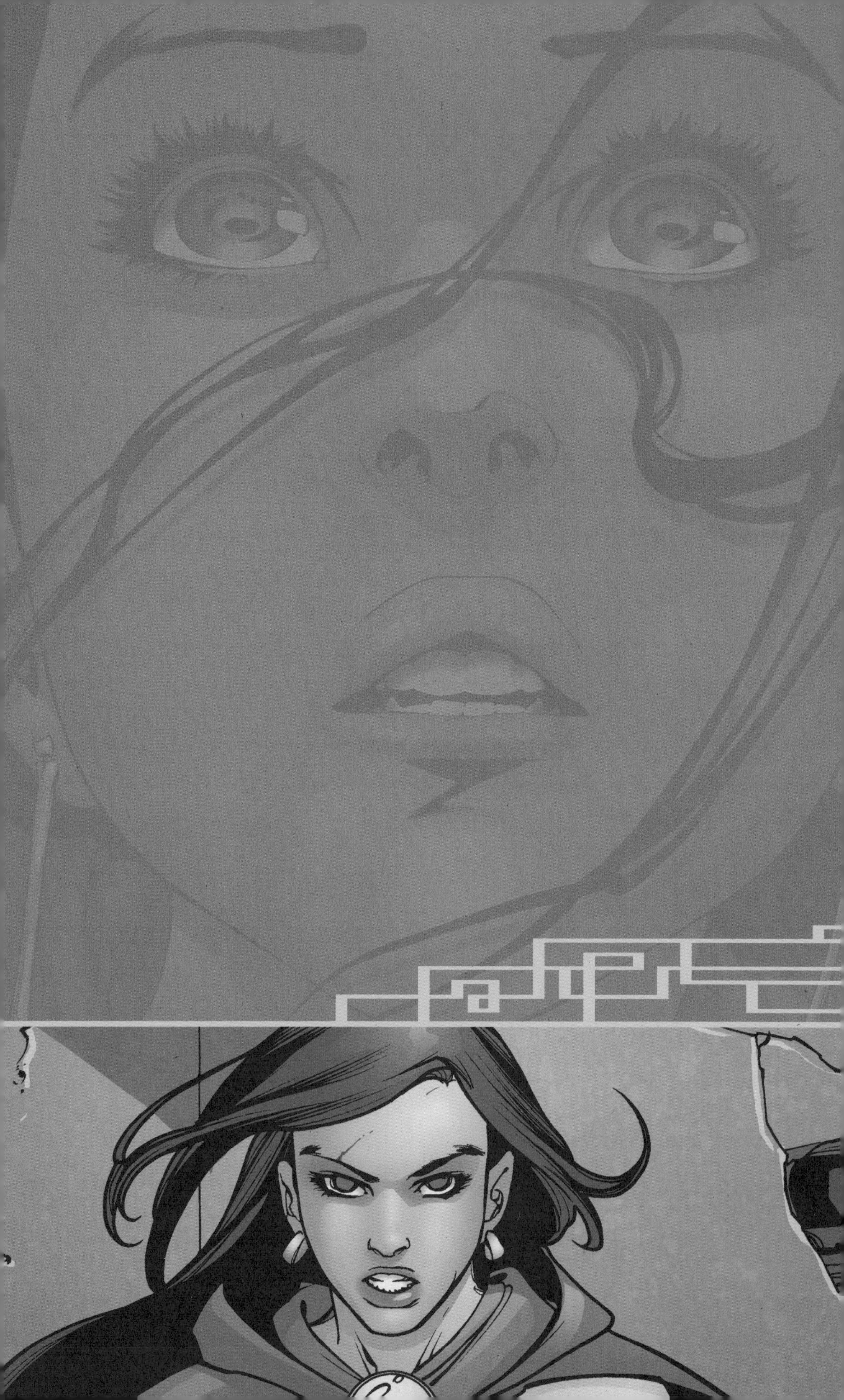

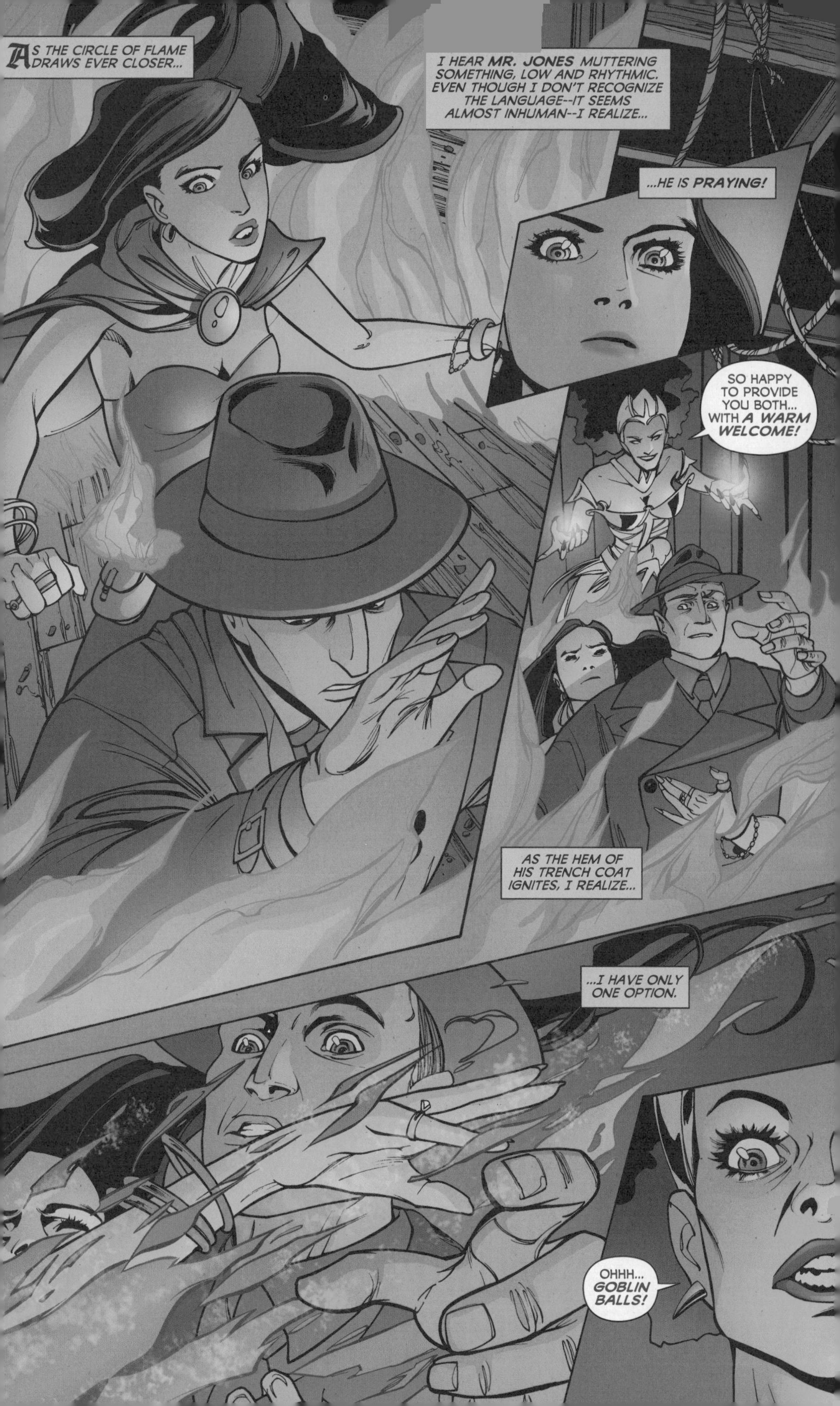
AS THE CIRCLE OF FLAME DRAWS EVER CLOSER...
I HEAR MR. JONES MUTTERING SOMETHING, LOW AND RHYTHMIC. EVEN THOUGH I DON'T RECOGNIZE THE LANGUAGE--IT SEEMS ALMOST INHUMAN--I REALIZE...
...HE IS PRAYING!
SO HAPPY TO PROVIDE YOU BOTH... WITH A WARM WELCOME!
AS THE HEM OF HIS TRENCH COAT IGNITES, I REALIZE...
...I HAVE ONLY ONE OPTION.
OHHH... GOBLIN BALLS!

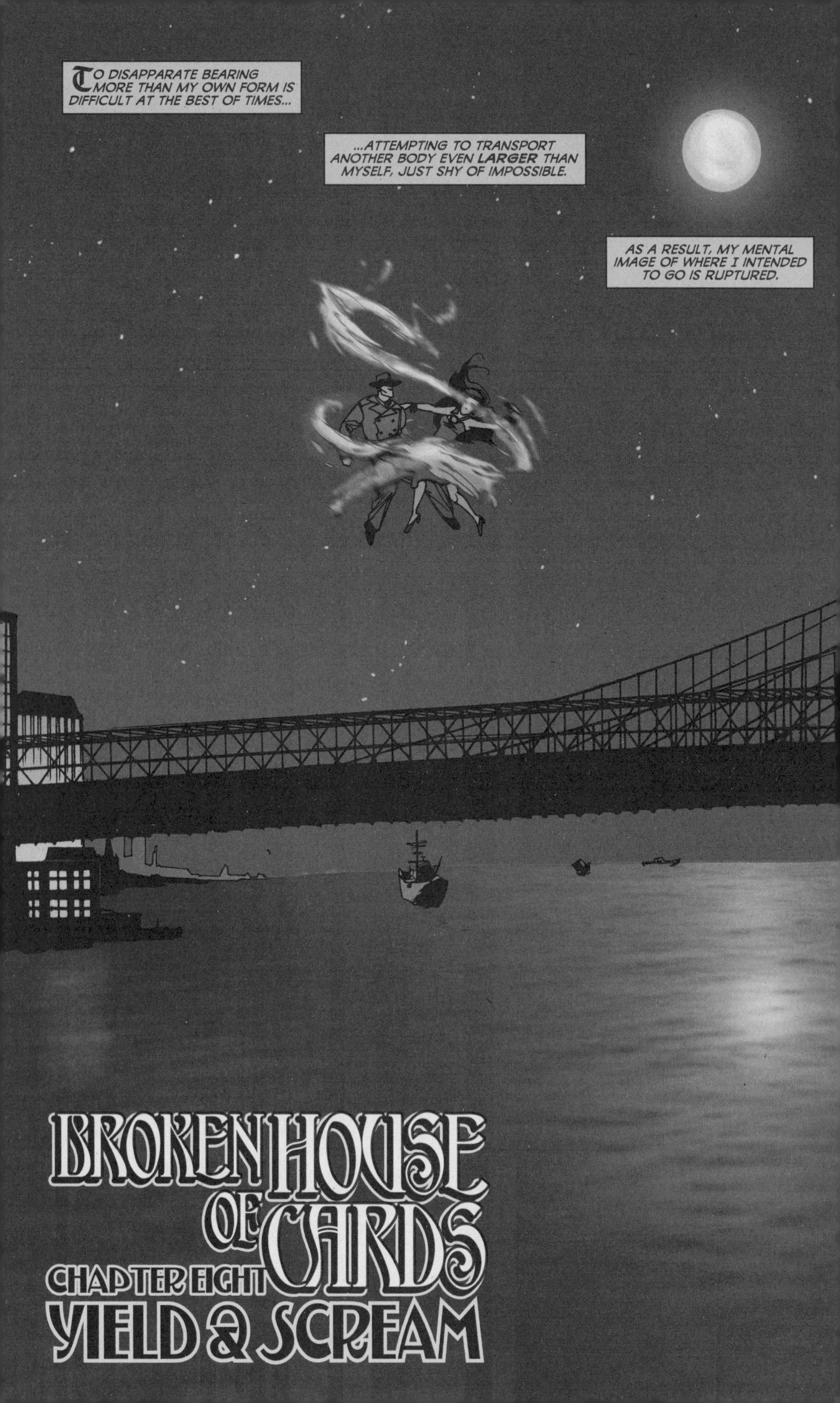
TO DISAPPARATE BEARING MORE THAN MY OWN FORM IS DIFFICULT AT THE BEST OF TIMES...
...ATTEMPTING TO TRANSPORT ANOTHER BODY EVEN LARGER THAN MYSELF, JUST SHY OF IMPOSSIBLE.
AS A RESULT, MY MENTAL IMAGE OF WHERE I INTENDED TO GO IS RUPTURED.
BROKEN HOUSE OF CARDS
CHAPTER EIGHT
YIELD & SCREAM

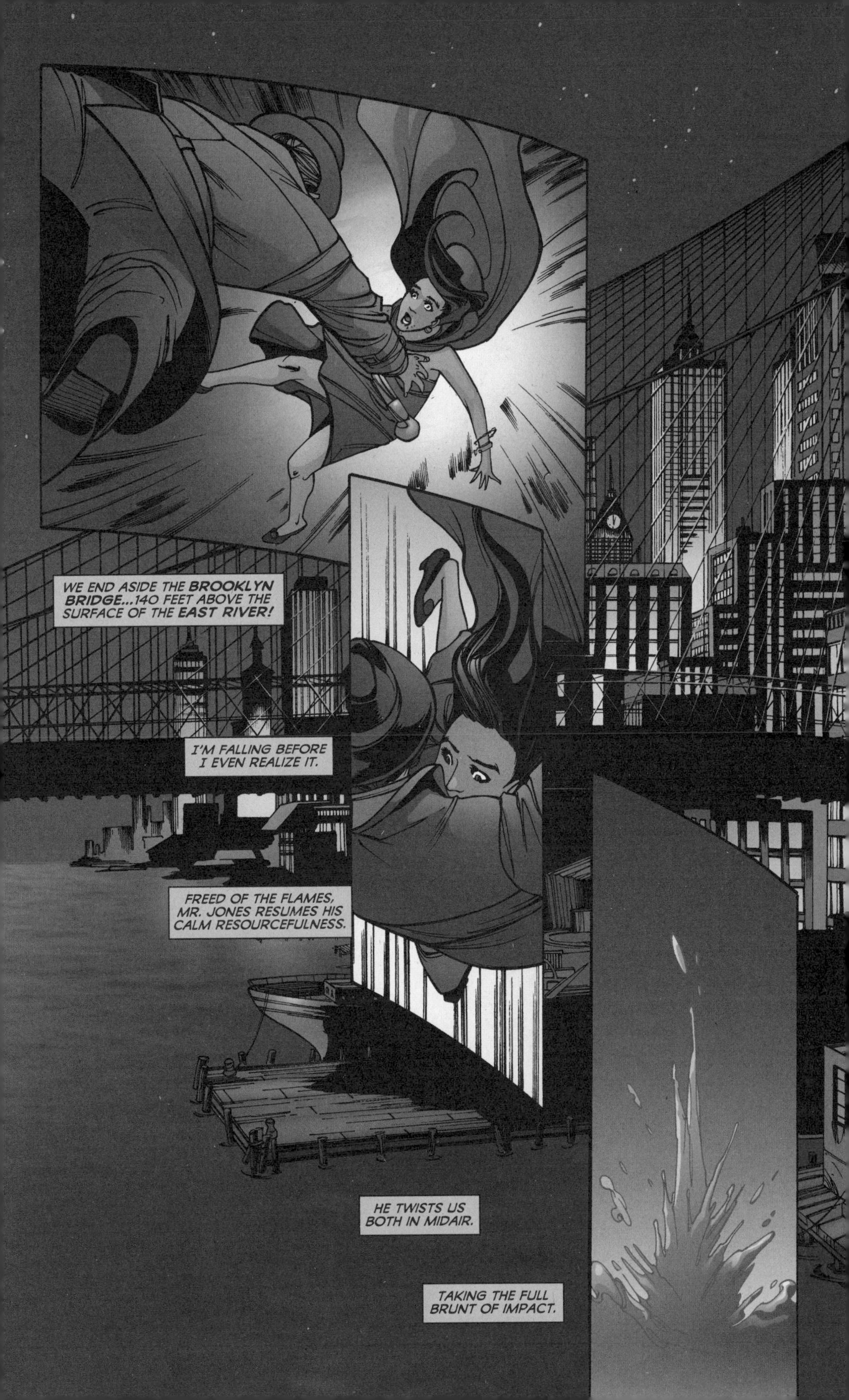
WE END ASIDE THE BROOKLYN BRIDGE...140 FEET ABOVE THE SURFACE OF THE EAST RIVER!
I'M FALLING BEFORE I EVEN REALIZE IT.
FREED OF THE FLAMES, MR. JONES RESUMES HIS CALM RESOURCEFULNESS.
HE TWISTS US BOTH IN MIDAIR.
TAKING THE FULL BRUNT OF IMPACT.

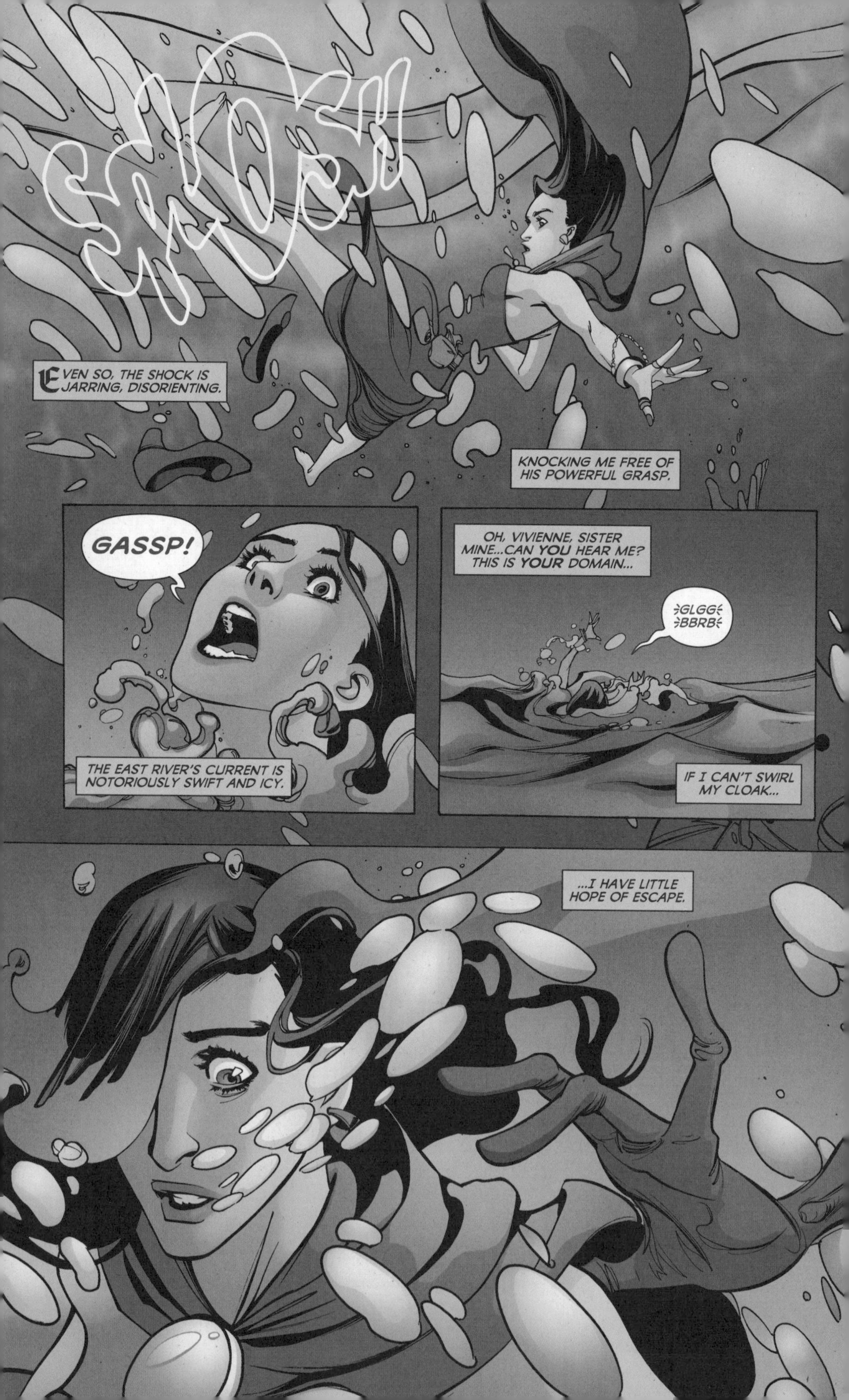
SHLOOSH
EVEN SO, THE SHOCK IS JARRING, DISORIENTING.
KNOCKING ME FREE OF HIS POWERFUL GRASP.
GASSP!
THE EAST RIVER'S CURRENT IS NOTORIOUSLY SWIFT AND ICY.
OH, VIVIENNE, SISTER MINE...CAN YOU HEAR ME? THIS IS YOUR DOMAIN...
GLGG BBRB
IF I CAN'T SWIRL MY CLOAK...
...I HAVE LITTLE HOPE OF ESCAPE.

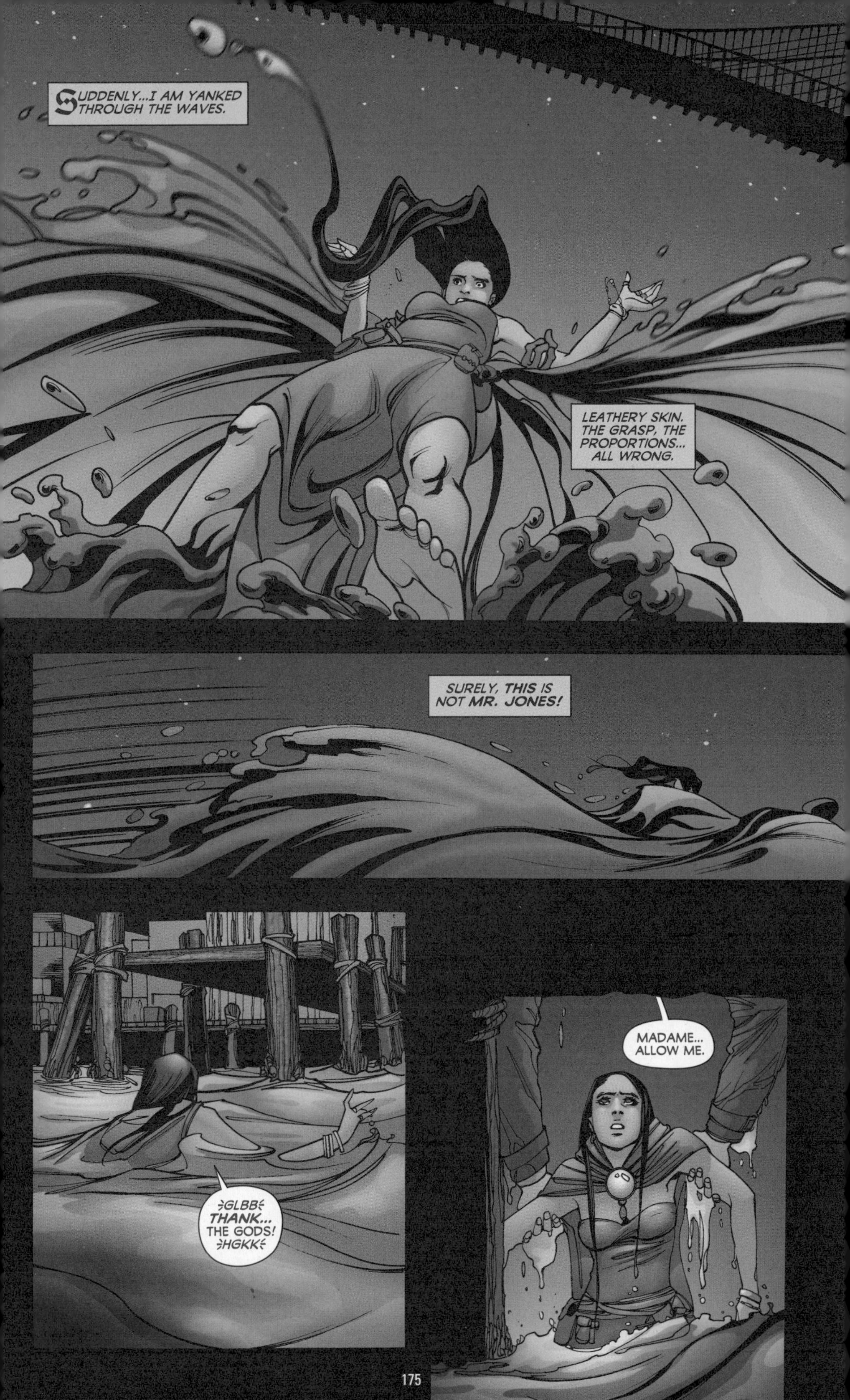
SUDDENLY...I AM YANKED THROUGH THE WAVES.
LEATHERY SKIN. THE GRASP, THE PROPORTIONS... ALL WRONG.
SURELY, THIS IS NOT MR. JONES!
GLBB THANK... THE GODS! HGKK
MADAME... ALLOW ME.

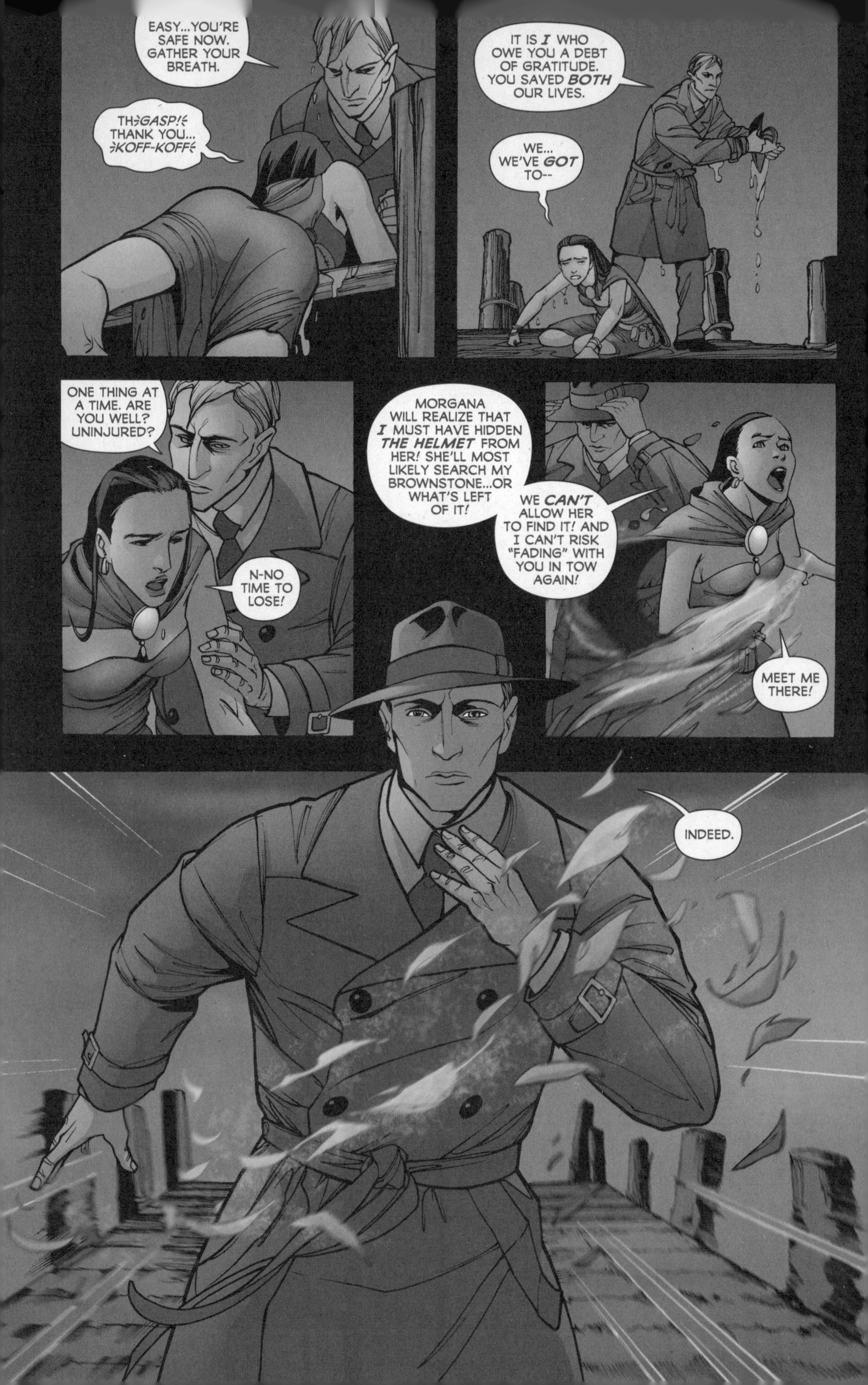
EASY...YOU'RE SAFE NOW. GATHER YOUR BREATH.
TH-GASP!- THANK YOU... -KOFF-KOFF-
IT IS I WHO OWE YOU A DEBT OF GRATITUDE. YOU SAVED BOTH OUR LIVES.
WE... WE'VE GOT TO--
ONE THING AT A TIME. ARE YOU WELL? UNINJURED?
N-NO TIME TO LOSE!
MORGANA WILL REALIZE THAT I MUST HAVE HIDDEN THE HELMET FROM HER! SHE'LL MOST LIKELY SEARCH MY BROWNSTONE...OR WHAT'S LEFT OF IT!
WE CAN'T ALLOW HER TO FIND IT! AND I CAN'T RISK "FADING" WITH YOU IN TOW AGAIN!
MEET ME THERE!
INDEED.

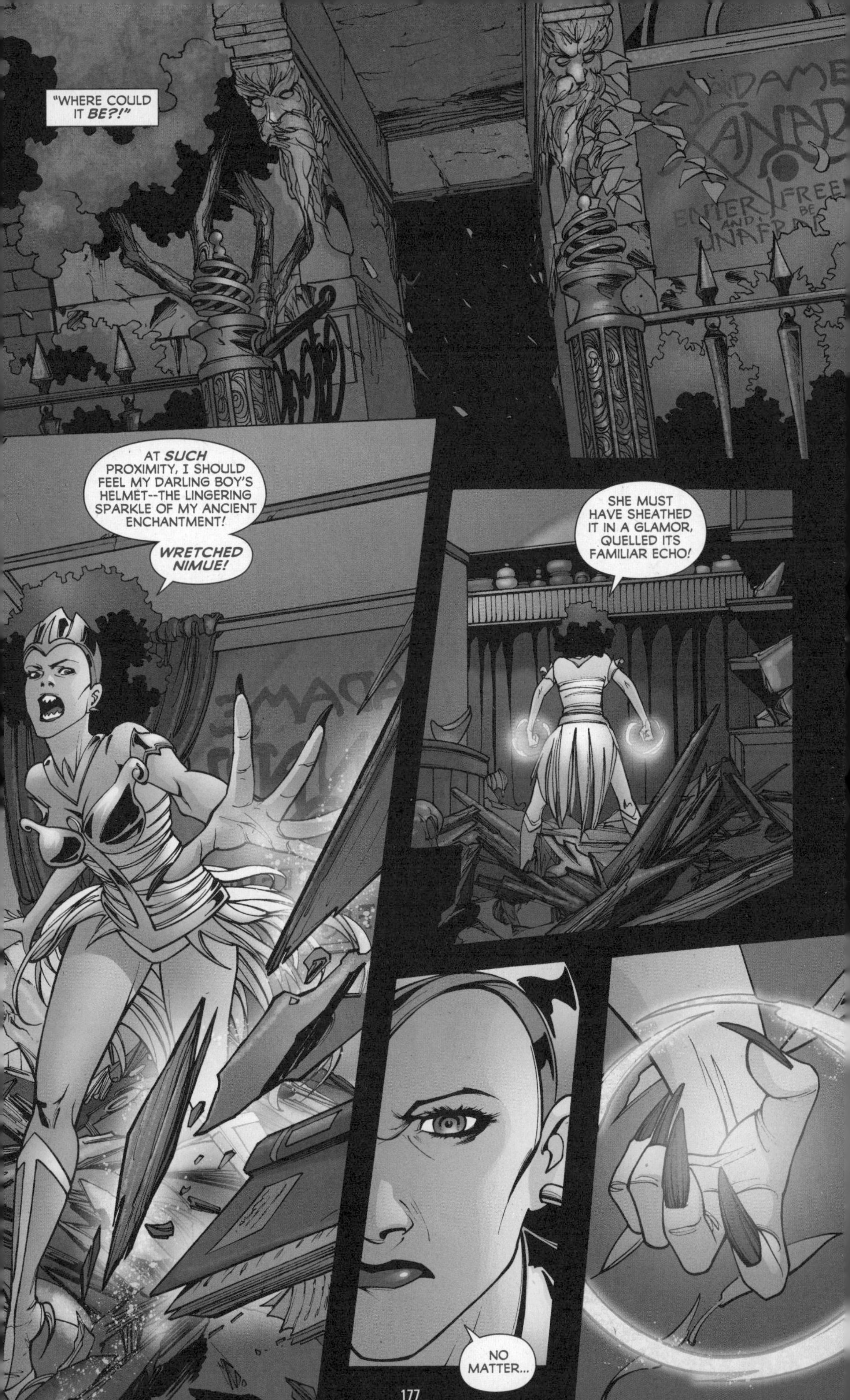
"WHERE COULD IT BE?!"
MADAME XANADU ENTER FREE AND BE UNAFRAID
AT SUCH PROXIMITY, I SHOULD FEEL MY DARLING BOY'S HELMET--THE LINGERING SPARKLE OF MY ANCIENT ENCHANTMENT!
WRETCHED NIMUE!
SHE MUST HAVE SHEATHED IT IN A GLAMOR, QUELLED ITS FAMILIAR ECHO!
NO MATTER...

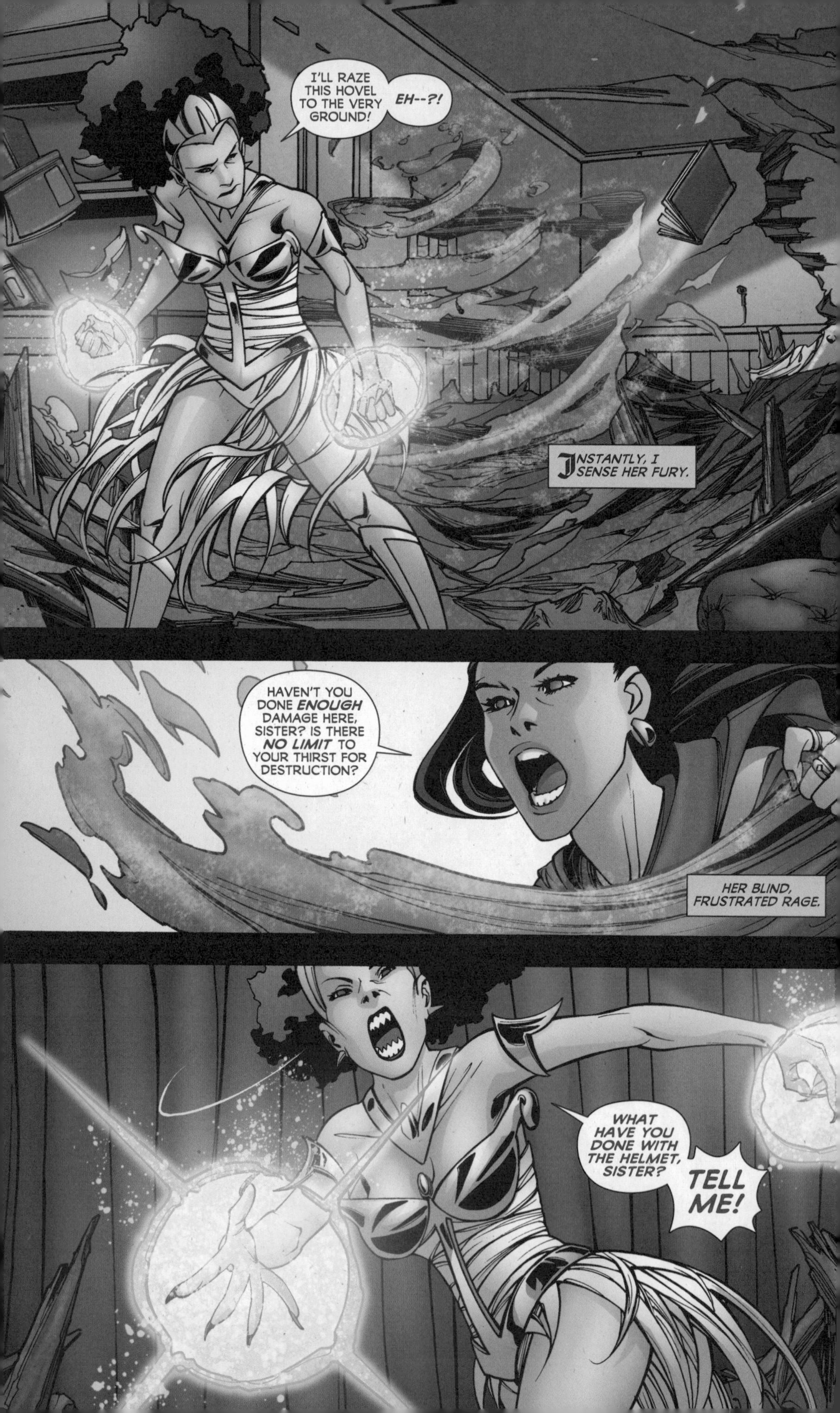
I'LL RAZE THIS HOVEL TO THE VERY GROUND!
EH--?!
INSTANTLY, I SENSE HER FURY.
HAVEN'T YOU DONE ENOUGH DAMAGE HERE, SISTER? IS THERE NO LIMIT TO YOUR THIRST FOR DESTRUCTION?
HER BLIND, FRUSTRATED RAGE.
WHAT HAVE YOU DONE WITH THE HELMET, SISTER?
TELL ME!

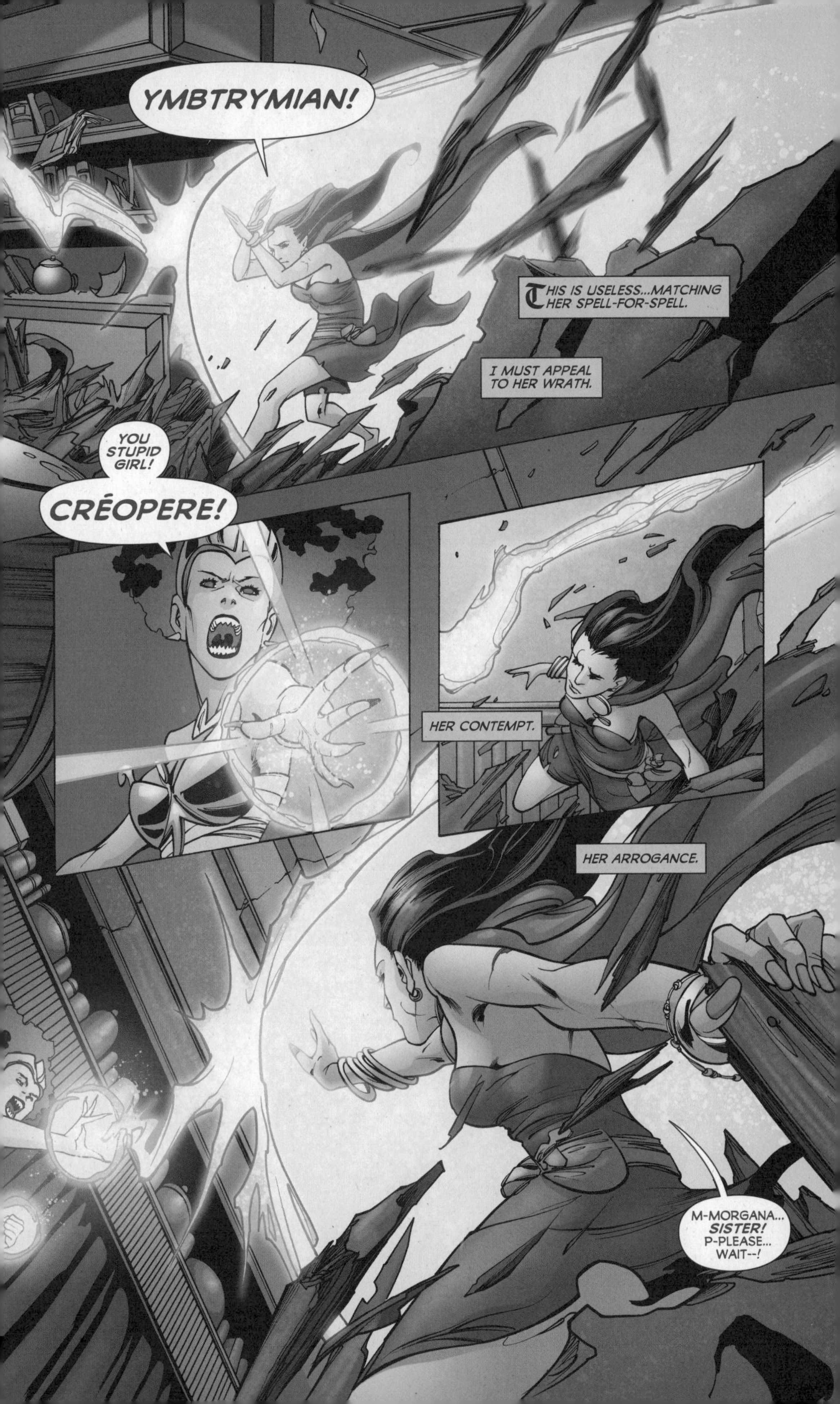
YMBTRYMIAN!
THIS IS USELESS...MATCHING HER SPELL-FOR-SPELL.
I MUST APPEAL TO HER WRATH.
YOU STUPID GIRL!
CRÉOPERE!
HER CONTEMPT.
HER ARROGANCE.
M-MORGANA... SISTER! P-PLEASE... WAIT--!

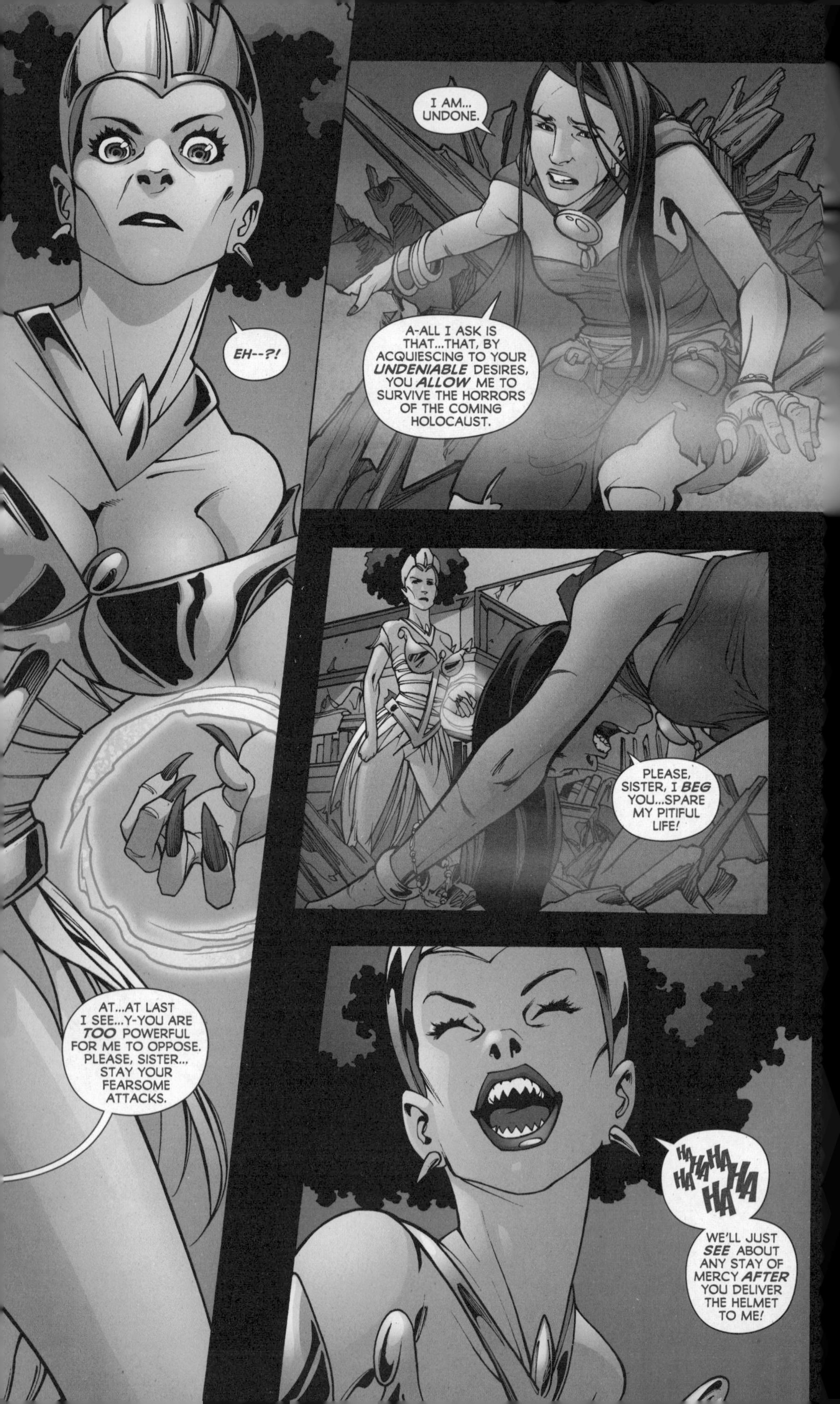
EH--?!
I AM... UNDONE.
A-ALL I ASK IS THAT...THAT, BY ACQUIESCING TO YOUR UNDENIABLE DESIRES, YOU ALLOW ME TO SURVIVE THE HORRORS OF THE COMING HOLOCAUST.
PLEASE, SISTER, I BEG YOU...SPARE MY PITIFUL LIFE!
AT...AT LAST I SEE...Y-YOU ARE TOO POWERFUL FOR ME TO OPPOSE. PLEASE, SISTER... STAY YOUR FEARSOME ATTACKS.
HAHAHAHAHAHAHA
WE'LL JUST SEE ABOUT ANY STAY OF MERCY AFTER YOU DELIVER THE HELMET TO ME!

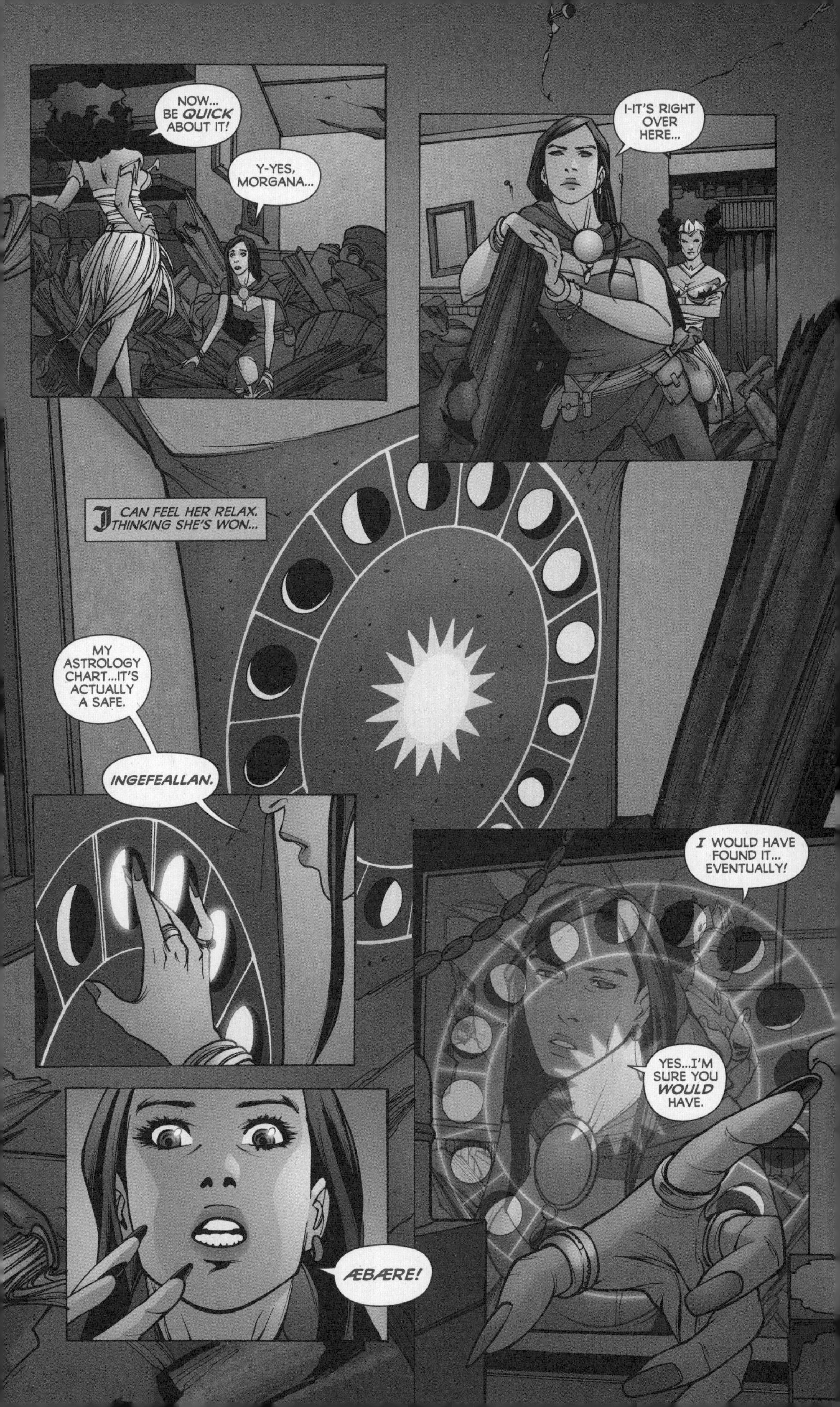

NOW... BE QUICK ABOUT IT!
Y-YES, MORGANA...
I-IT'S RIGHT OVER HERE...
I CAN FEEL HER RELAX. THINKING SHE'S WON...
MY ASTROLOGY CHART...IT'S ACTUALLY A SAFE.
INGEFEALLAN.
I WOULD HAVE FOUND IT... EVENTUALLY!
YES...I'M SURE YOU WOULD HAVE.
ÆBÆRE!

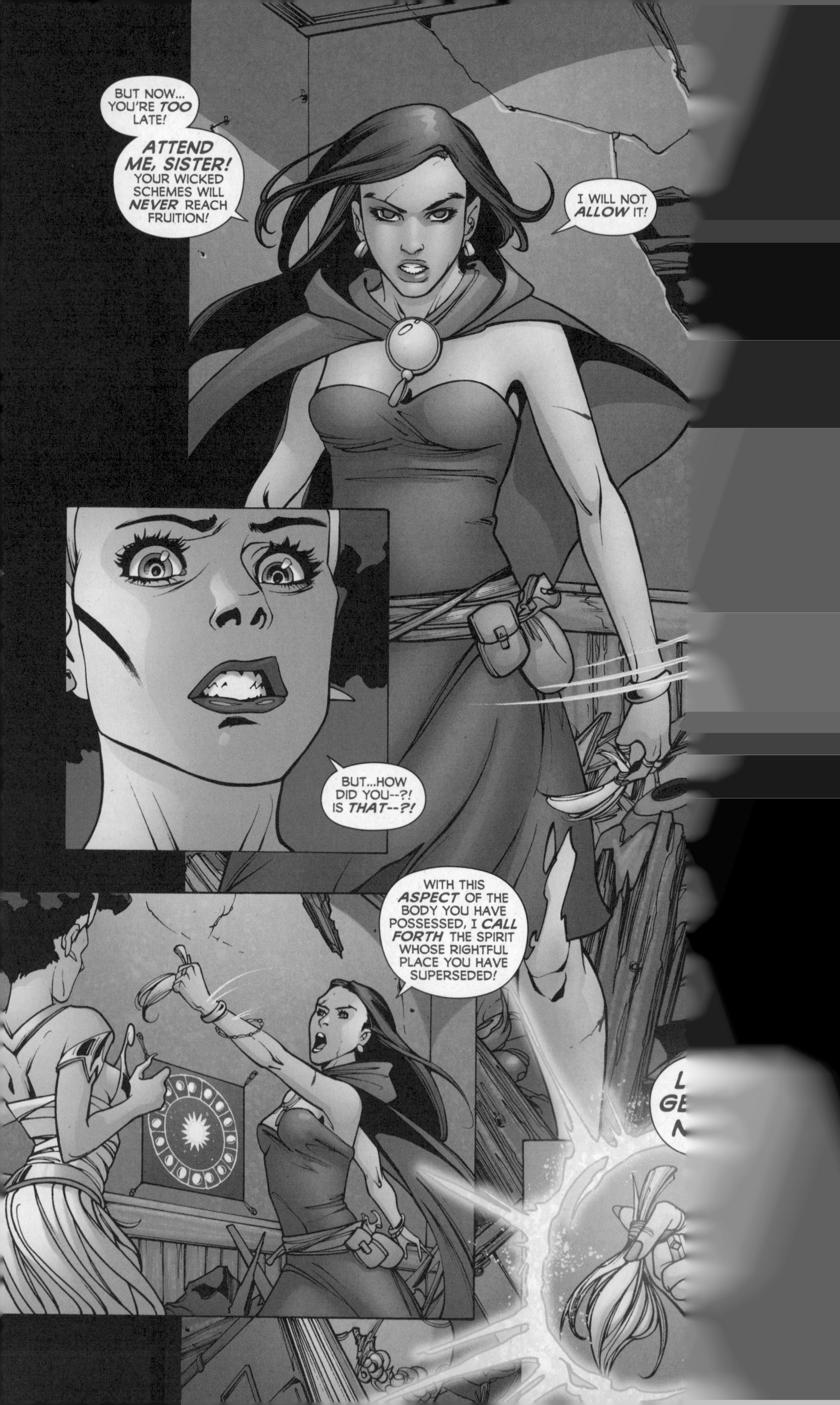
BUT NOW... YOU'RE TOO LATE!
ATTEND ME, SISTER! YOUR WICKED SCHEMES WILL NEVER REACH FRUITION!
I WILL NOT ALLOW IT!
BUT...HOW DID YOU--?! IS THAT--?!
WITH THIS ASPECT OF THE BODY YOU HAVE POSSESSED, I CALL FORTH THE SPIRIT WHOSE RIGHTFUL PLACE YOU HAVE SUPERSEDED!

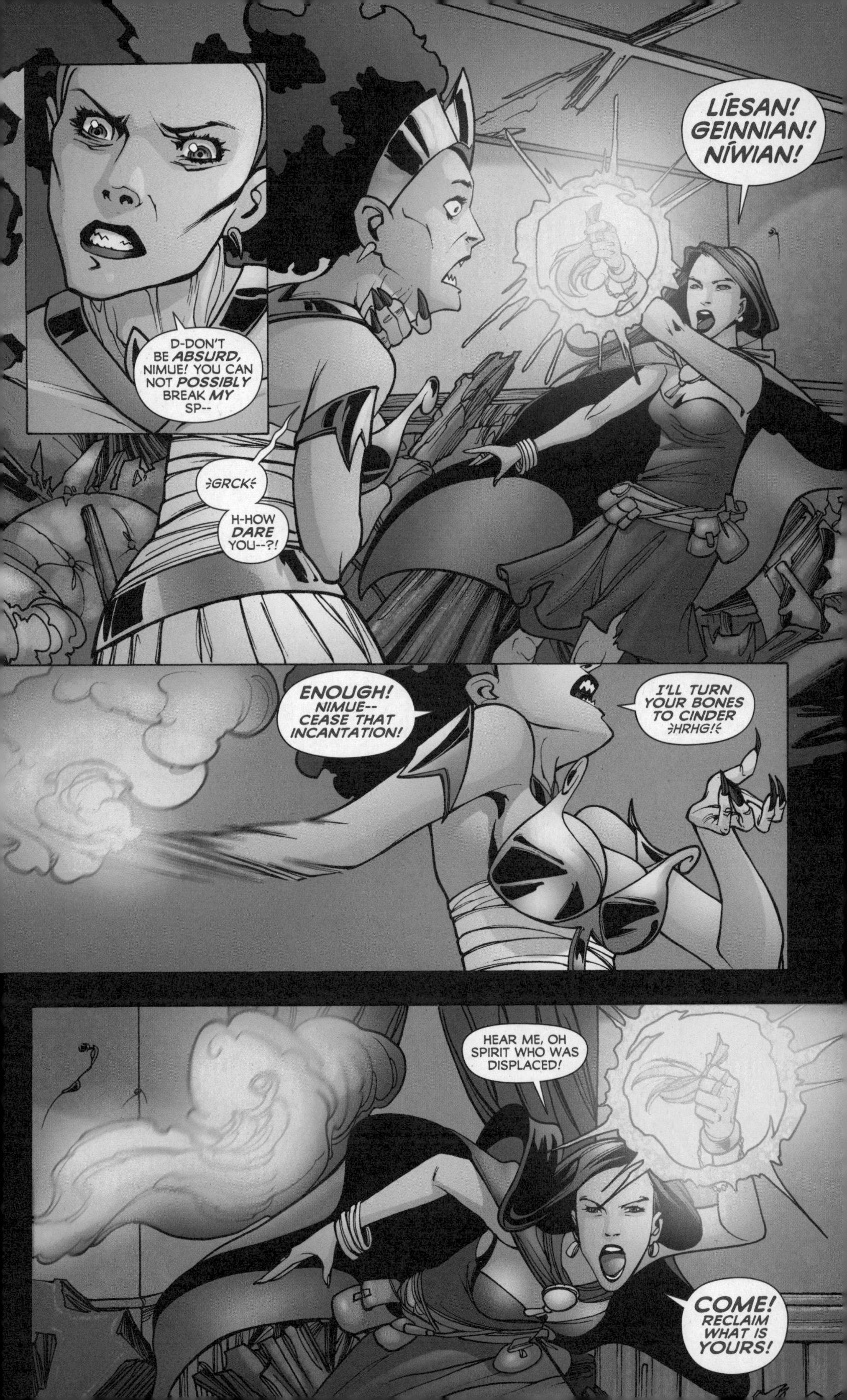
LÍESAN! GEINNIAN! NÍWIAN!
D-DON'T BE ABSURD, NIMUE! YOU CAN NOT POSSIBLY BREAK MY SP--
GRCK
H-HOW DARE YOU--?!
ENOUGH! NIMUE-- CEASE THAT INCANTATION!
I'LL TURN YOUR BONES TO CINDER
HRHG!
HEAR ME, OH SPIRIT WHO WAS DISPLACED!
COME! RECLAIM WHAT IS YOURS!

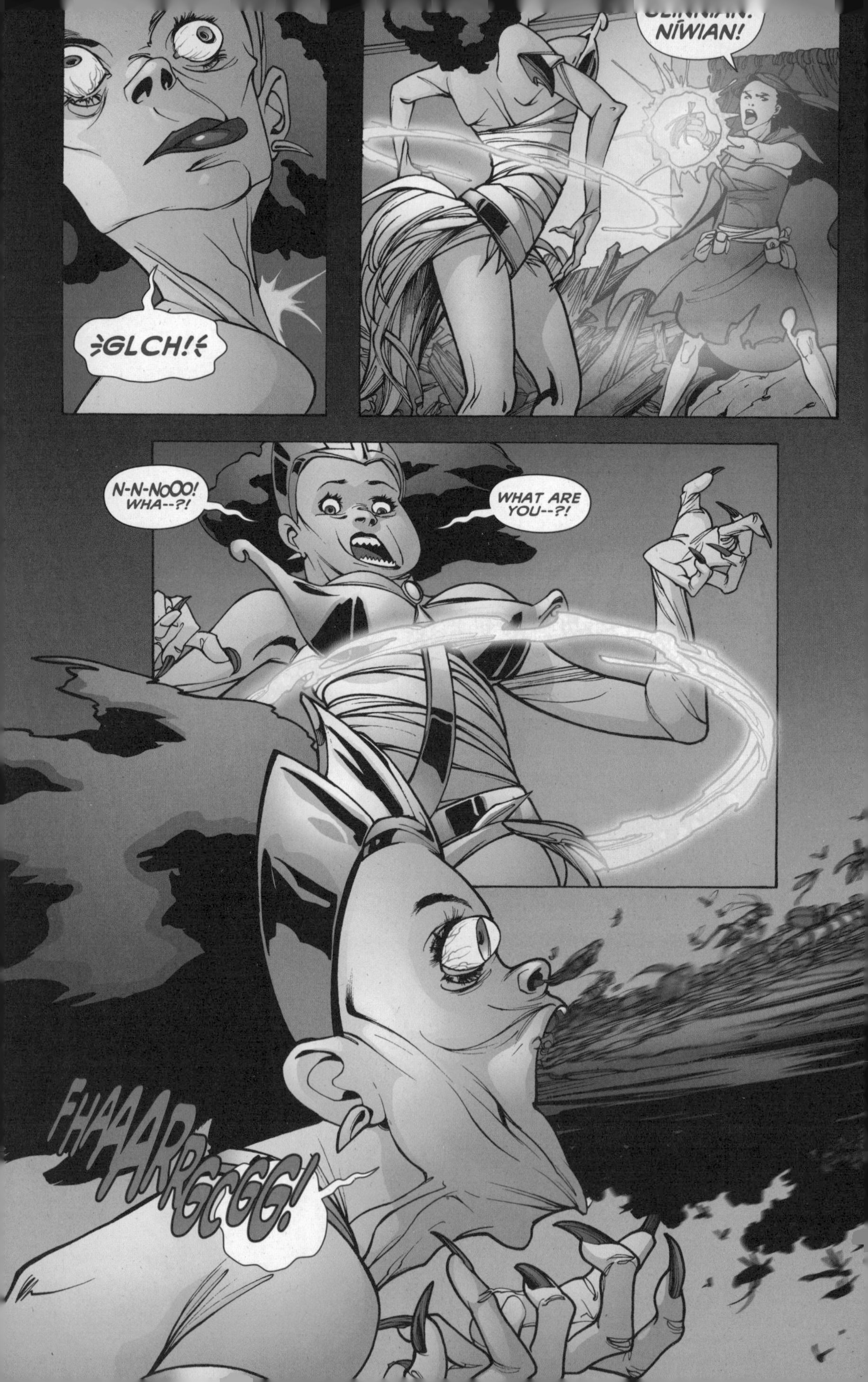

GLCH!
NÍWIAN!
N-N-NOOO! WHA--?!
WHAT ARE YOU--?!
FHAAARRGGGG!

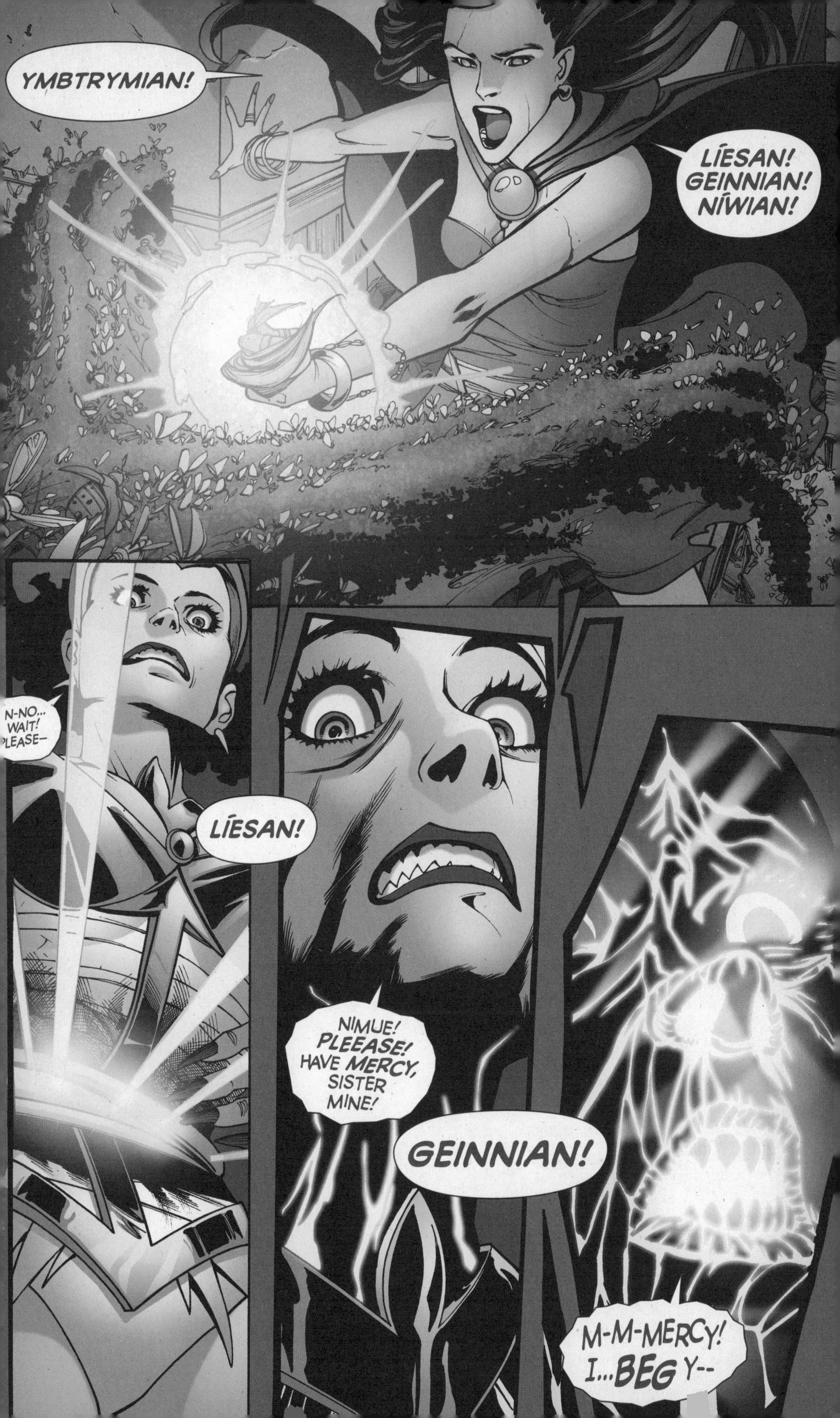
YMBTRYMIAN!
LÍESAN! GEINNIAN! NÍWIAN!
N-NO... WAIT! PLEASE--
LÍESAN!
NIMUE! PLEEASE! HAVE MERCY, SISTER MINE!
GEINNIAN!
M-M-MERCY! I...BEG Y--

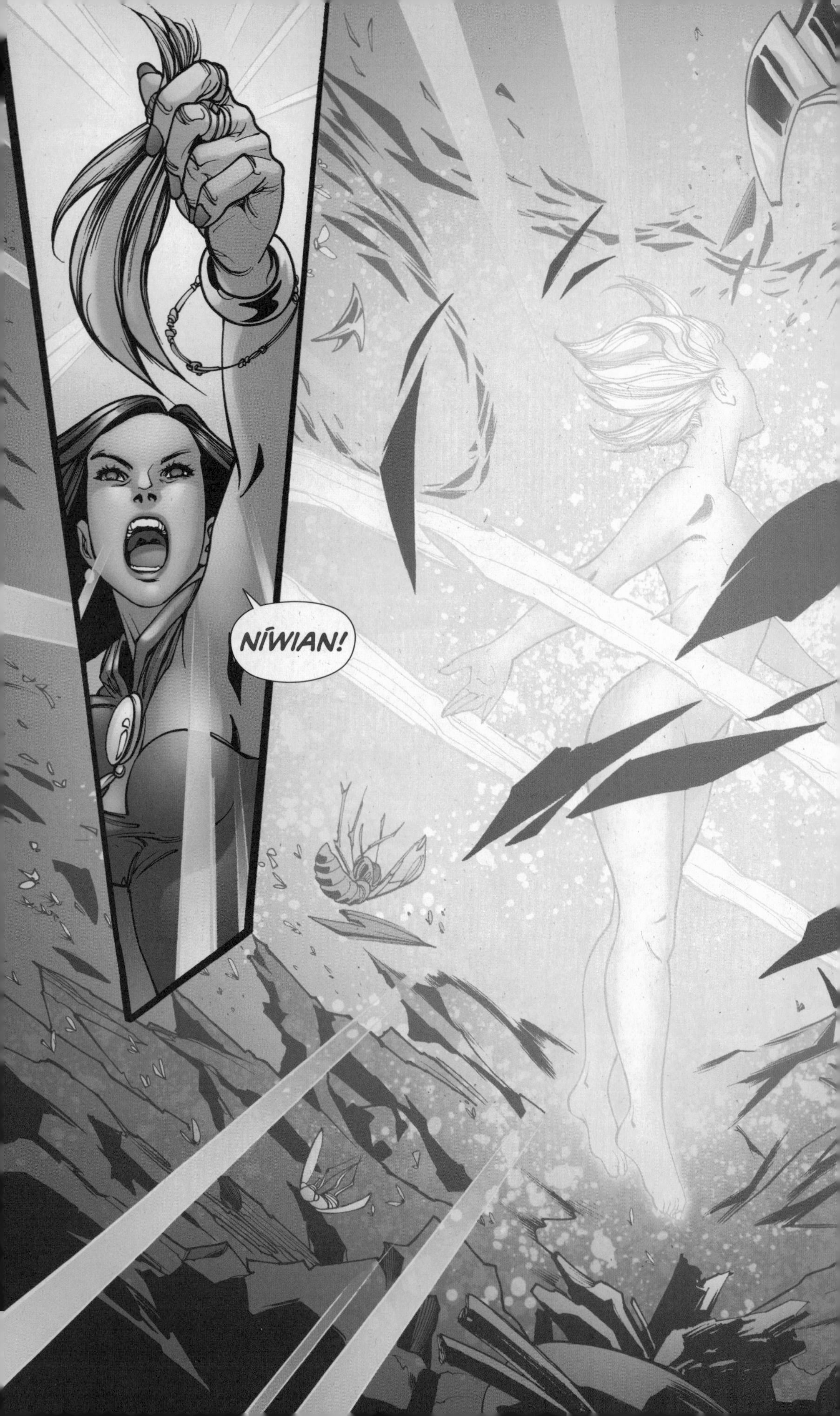
NÍWIAN!

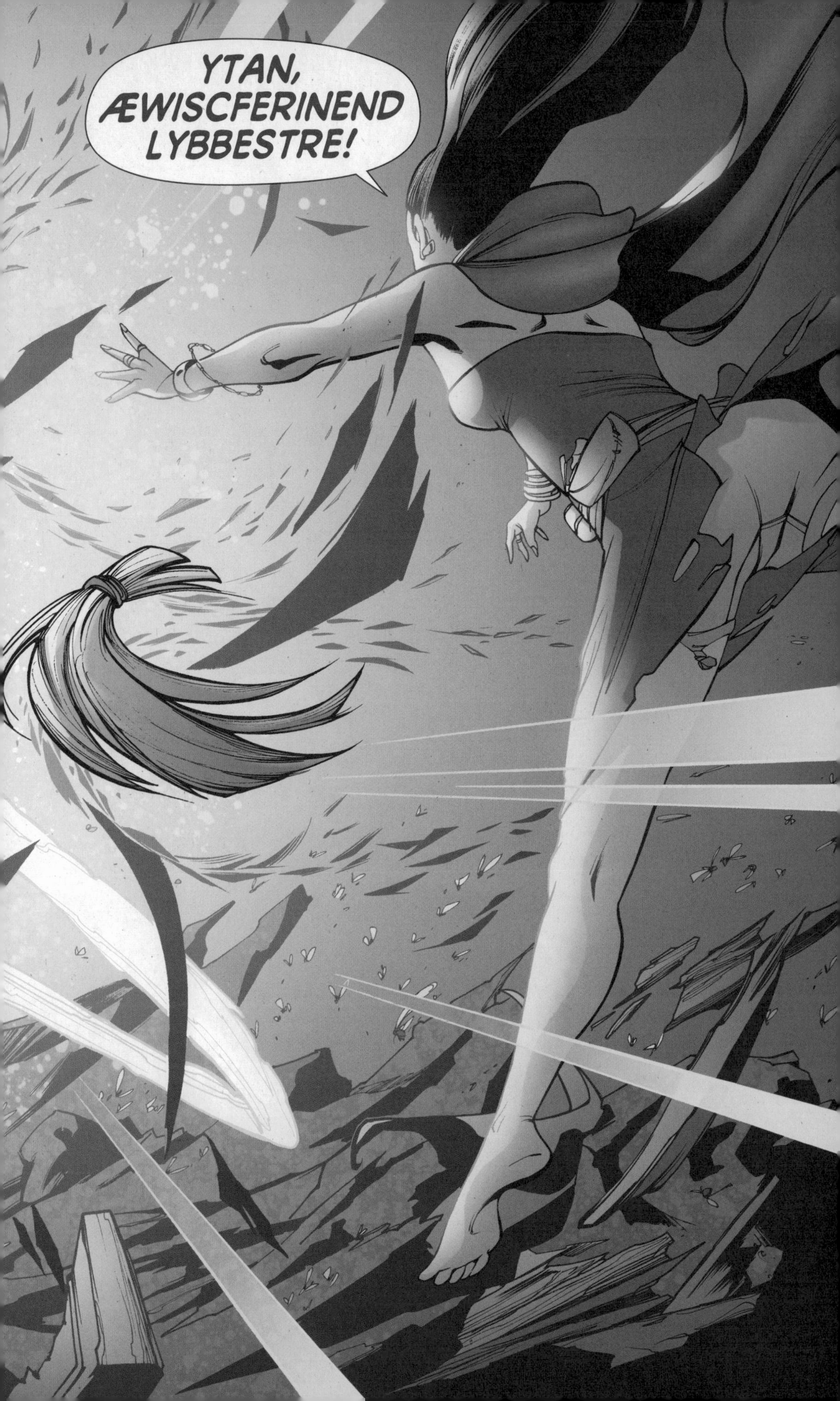
YTAN, ÆWISCFERINEND LYBBESTRE!

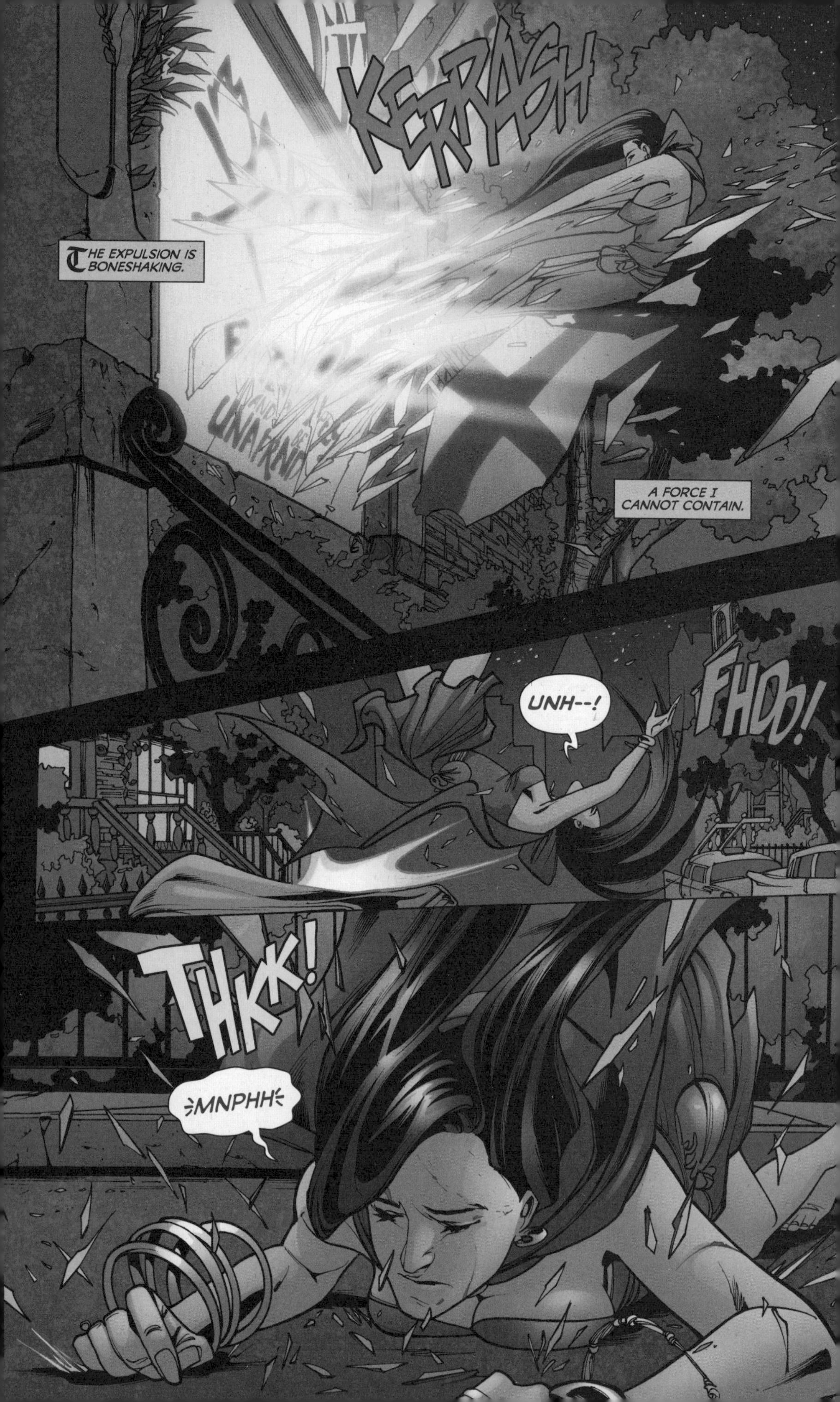
KERASH
THE EXPULSION IS BONESHAKING.
A FORCE I CANNOT CONTAIN.
UNH--!
FHOOD!
THKK!
MNPHH

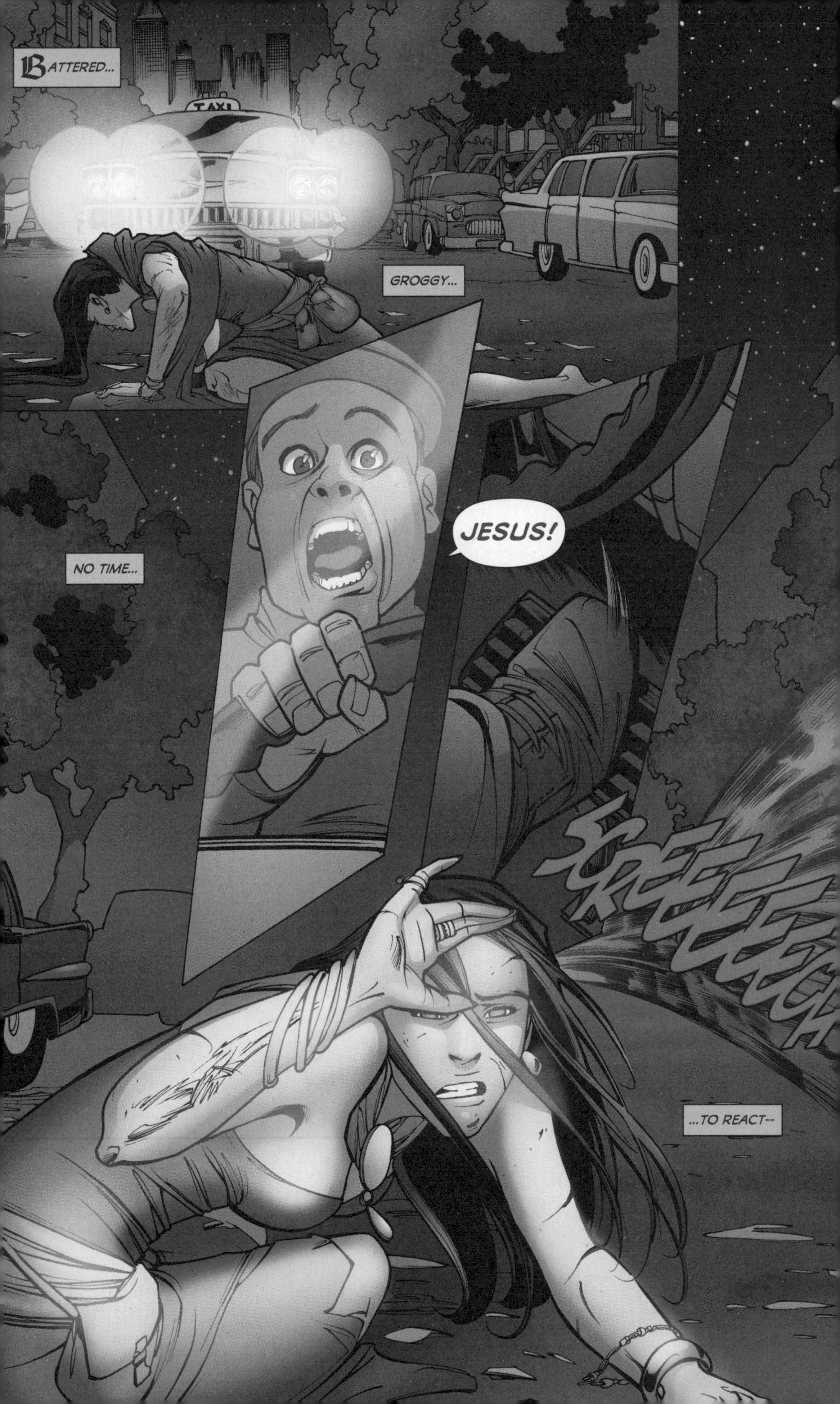
BATTERED...
TAXI
GROGGY...
JESUS!
NO TIME...
SCREEEEECH
...TO REACT--

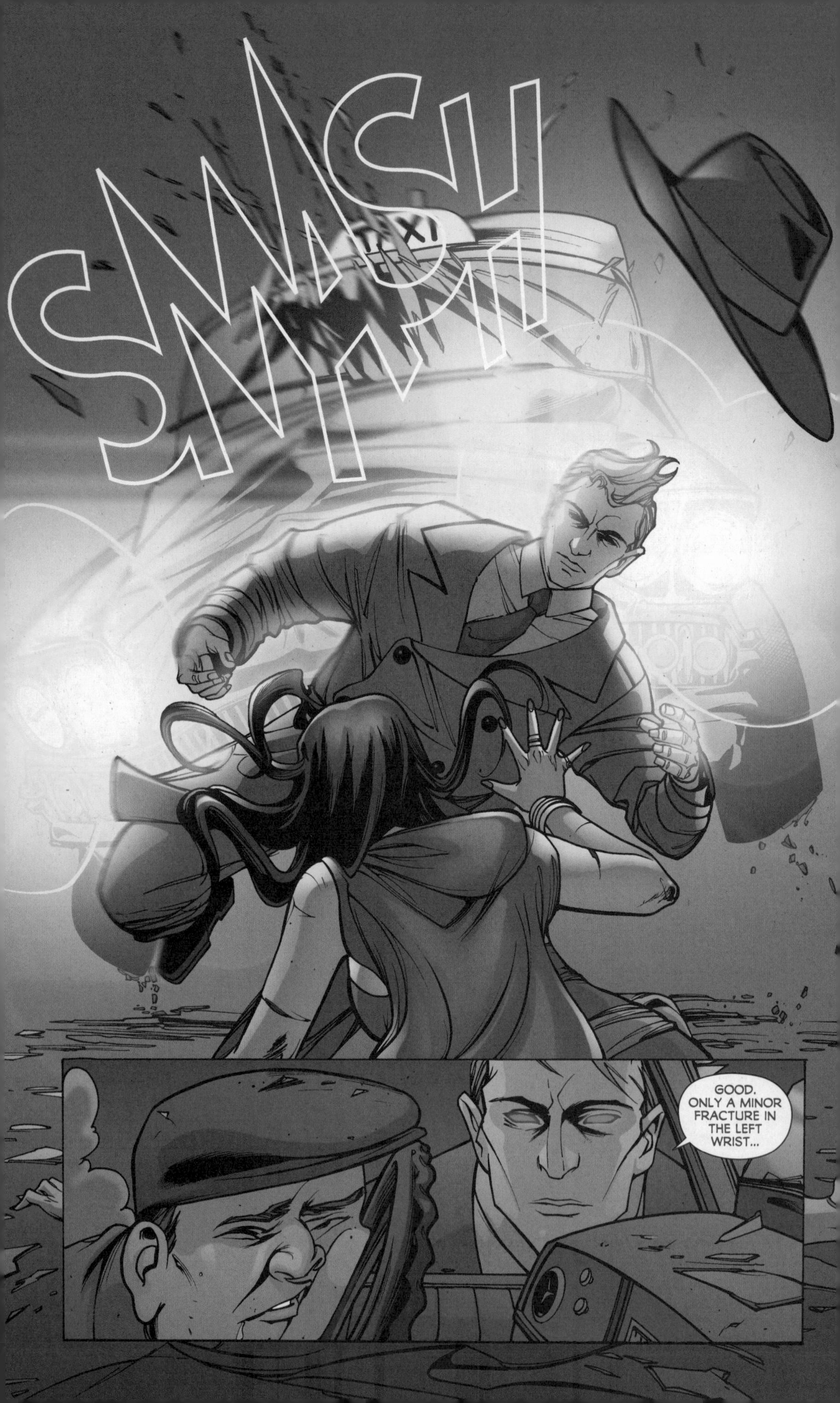
SMASH
TAXI
GOOD. ONLY A MINOR FRACTURE IN THE LEFT WRIST...

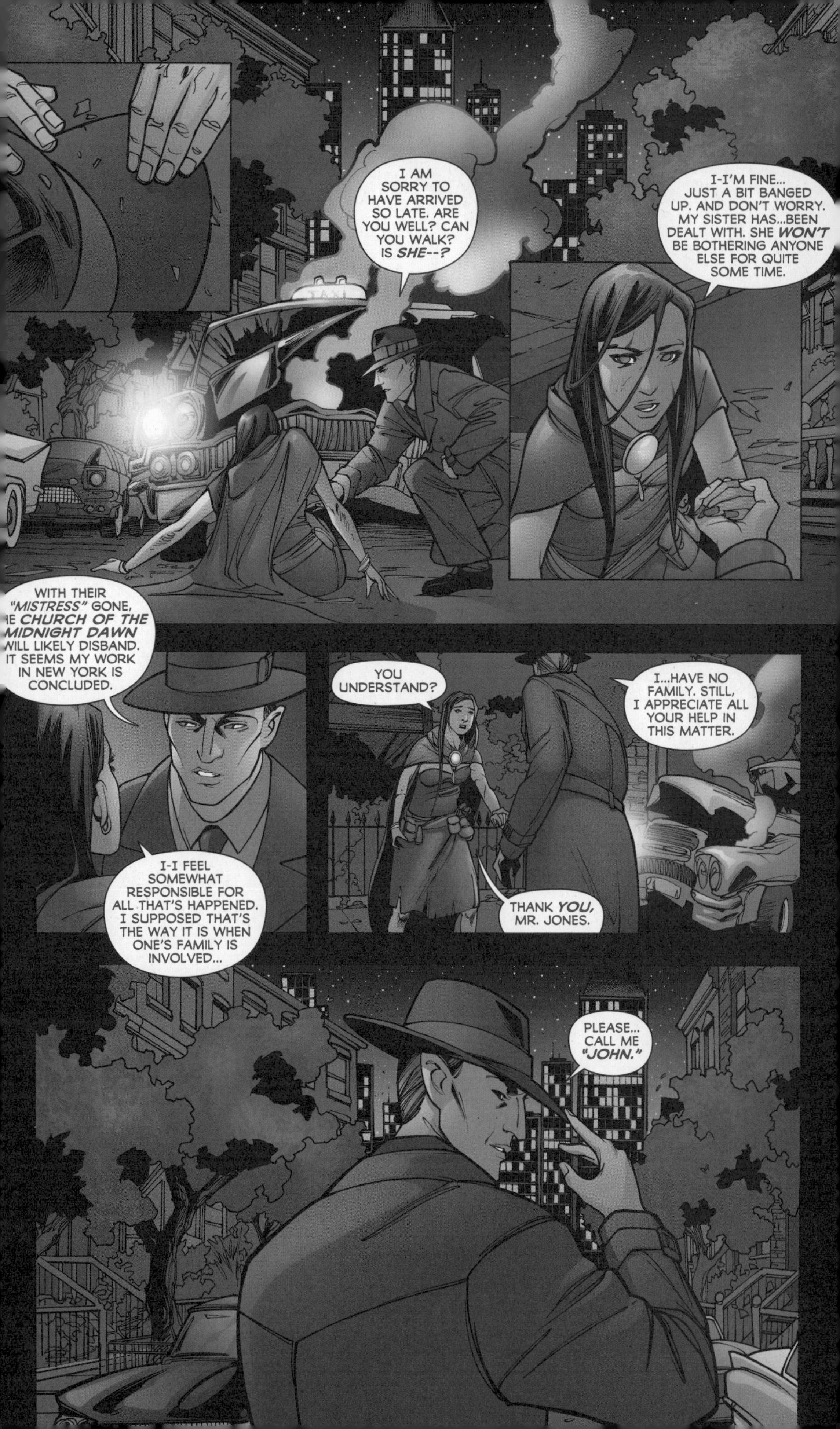
I AM SORRY TO HAVE ARRIVED SO LATE. ARE YOU WELL? CAN YOU WALK? IS *SHE--?*
I-I'M FINE... JUST A BIT BANGED UP. AND DON'T WORRY. MY SISTER HAS...BEEN DEALT WITH. SHE *WON'T* BE BOTHERING ANYONE ELSE FOR QUITE SOME TIME.
WITH THEIR *"MISTRESS"* GONE, HE *CHURCH OF THE MIDNIGHT DAWN* WILL LIKELY DISBAND. IT SEEMS MY WORK IN NEW YORK IS CONCLUDED.
I-I FEEL SOMEWHAT RESPONSIBLE FOR ALL THAT'S HAPPENED. I SUPPOSED THAT'S THE WAY IT IS WHEN ONE'S FAMILY IS INVOLVED...
YOU UNDERSTAND?
I...HAVE NO FAMILY. STILL, I APPRECIATE ALL YOUR HELP IN THIS MATTER.
THANK *YOU,* MR. JONES.
PLEASE... CALL ME *"JOHN."*

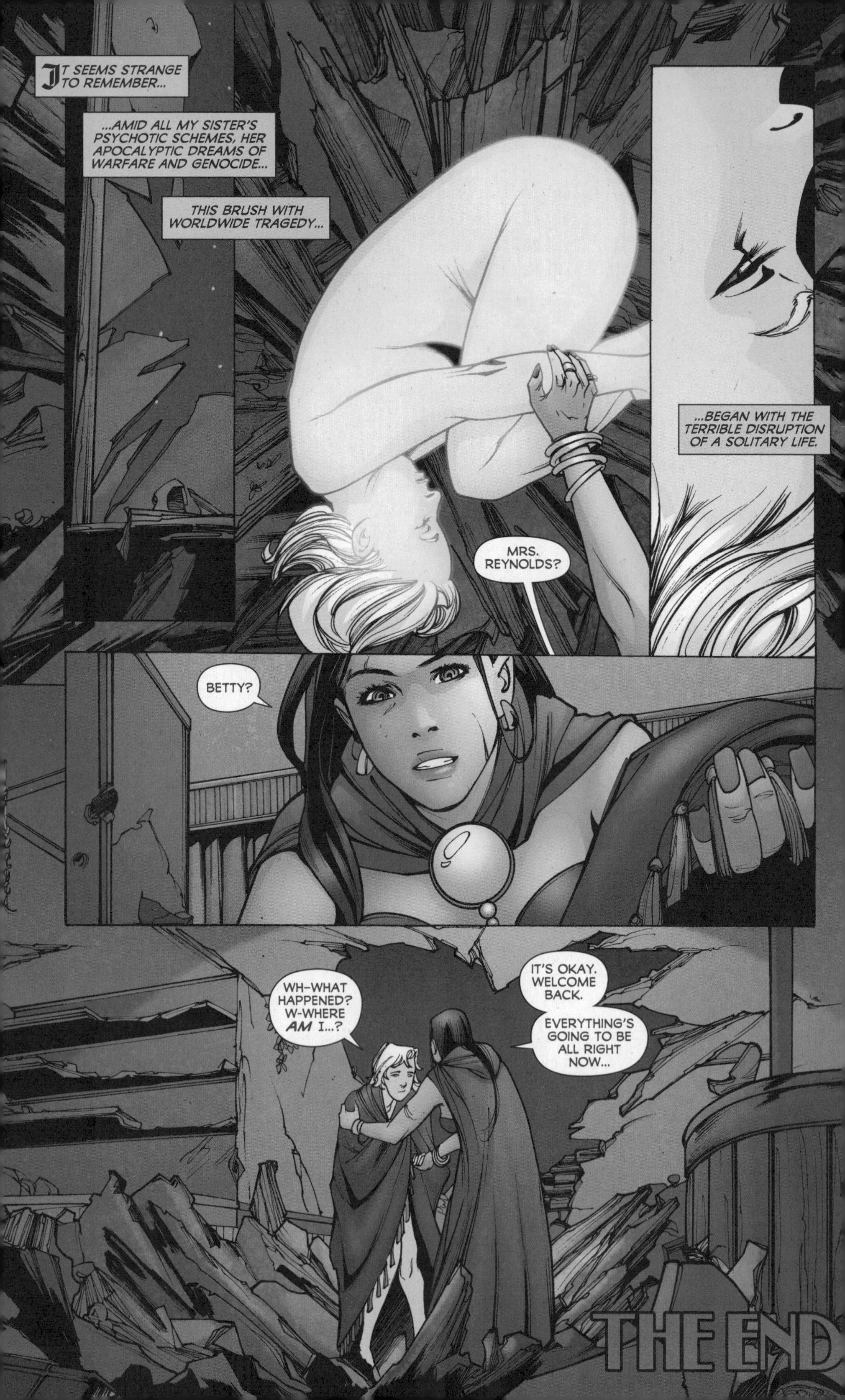
IT SEEMS STRANGE TO REMEMBER...
...AMID ALL MY SISTER'S PSYCHOTIC SCHEMES, HER APOCALYPTIC DREAMS OF WARFARE AND GENOCIDE...
THIS BRUSH WITH WORLDWIDE TRAGEDY...
...BEGAN WITH THE TERRIBLE DISRUPTION OF A SOLITARY LIFE.
MRS. REYNOLDS?
BETTY?
WH-WHAT HAPPENED? W-WHERE AM I...?
IT'S OKAY. WELCOME BACK.
EVERYTHING'S GOING TO BE ALL RIGHT NOW...
THE END

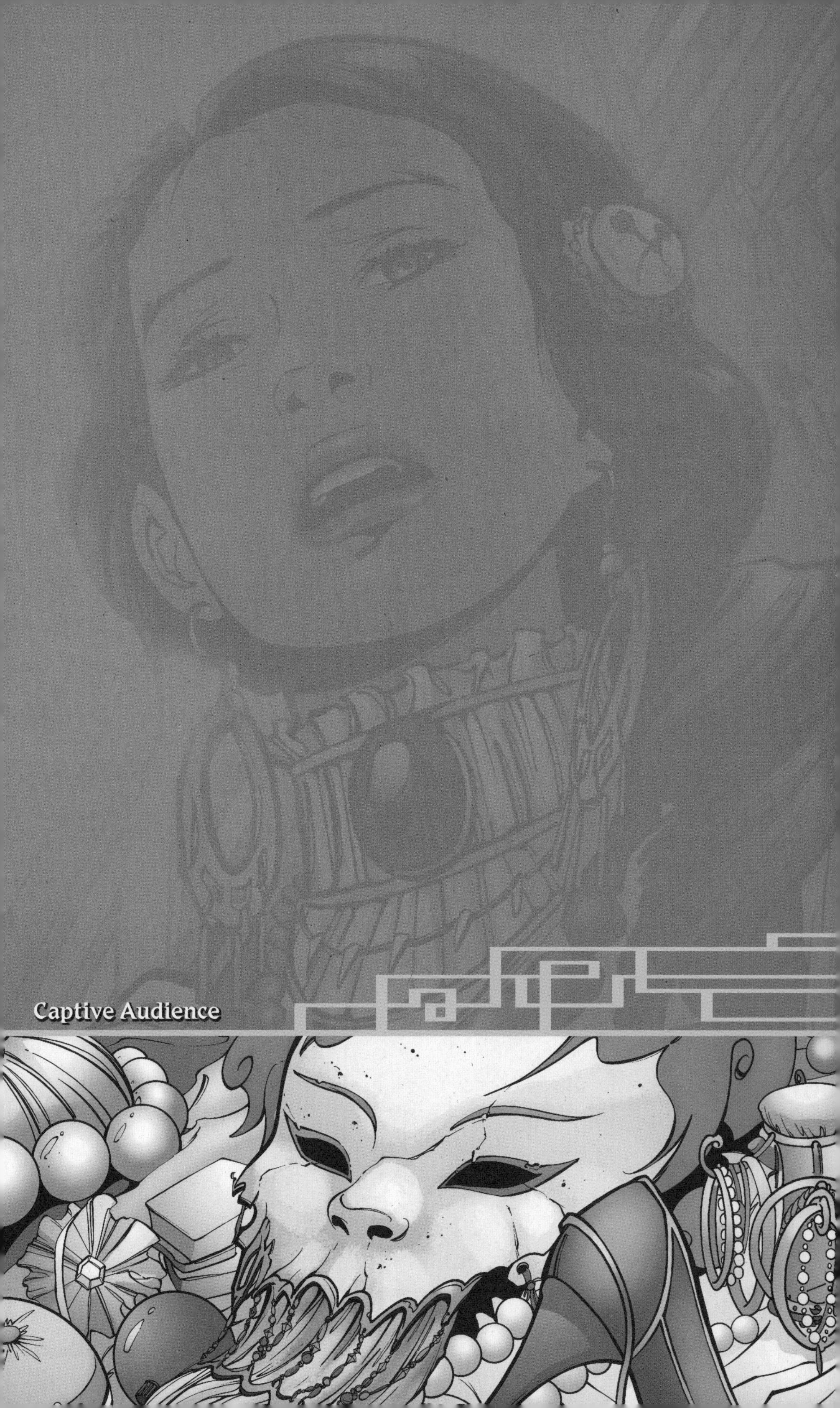
Captive Audience

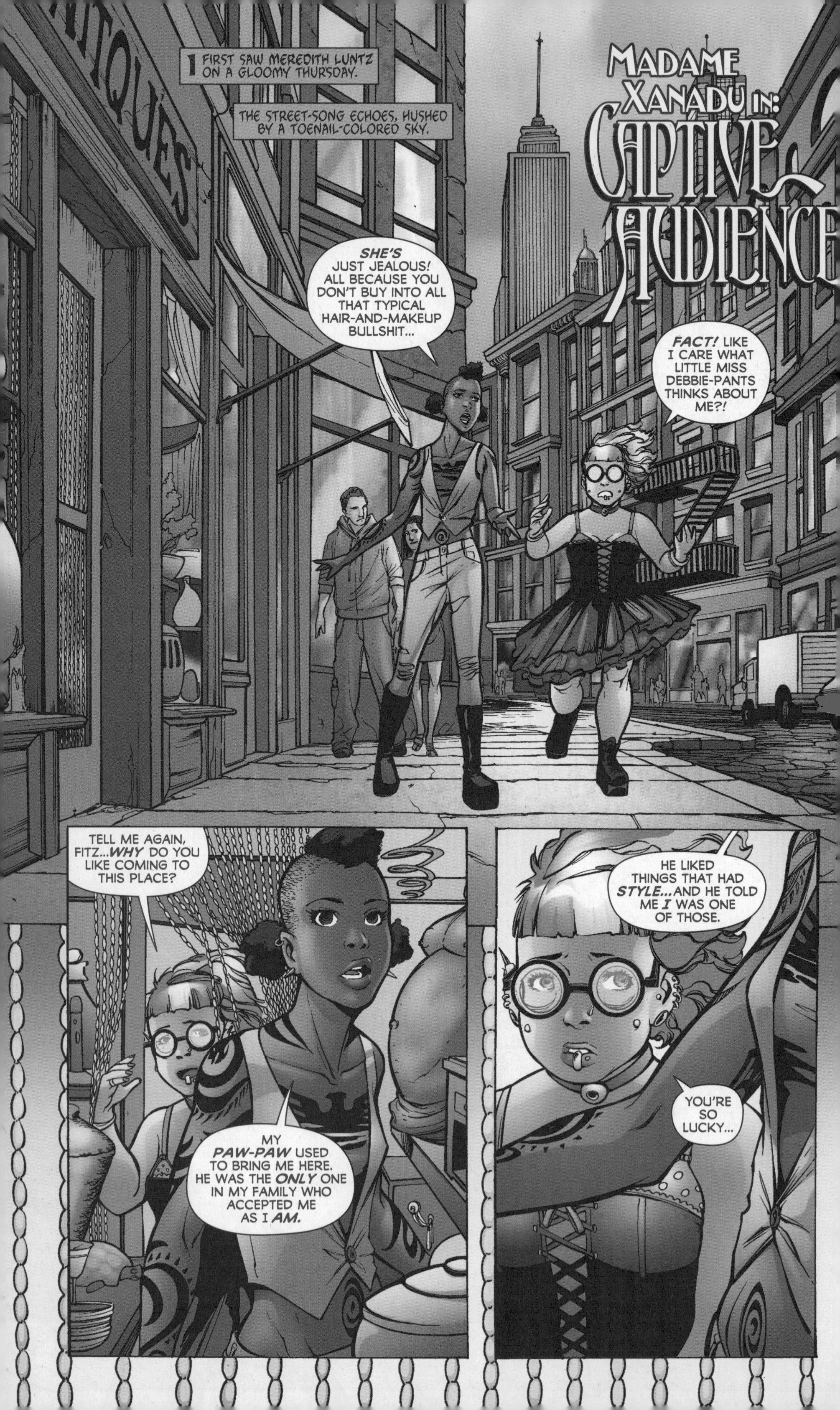
I FIRST SAW MEREDITH LUNTZ ON A GLOOMY THURSDAY.
THE STREET-SONG ECHOES, HUSHED BY A TOENAIL-COLORED SKY.
MADAME XANADU IN: CAPTIVE AUDIENCE
SHE'S JUST JEALOUS! ALL BECAUSE YOU DON'T BUY INTO ALL THAT TYPICAL HAIR-AND-MAKEUP BULLSHIT...
FACT! LIKE I CARE WHAT LITTLE MISS DEBBIE-PANTS THINKS ABOUT ME?!
TELL ME AGAIN, FITZ...WHY DO YOU LIKE COMING TO THIS PLACE?
MY PAW-PAW USED TO BRING ME HERE. HE WAS THE ONLY ONE IN MY FAMILY WHO ACCEPTED ME AS I AM.
HE LIKED THINGS THAT HAD STYLE...AND HE TOLD ME I WAS ONE OF THOSE.
YOU'RE SO LUCKY...

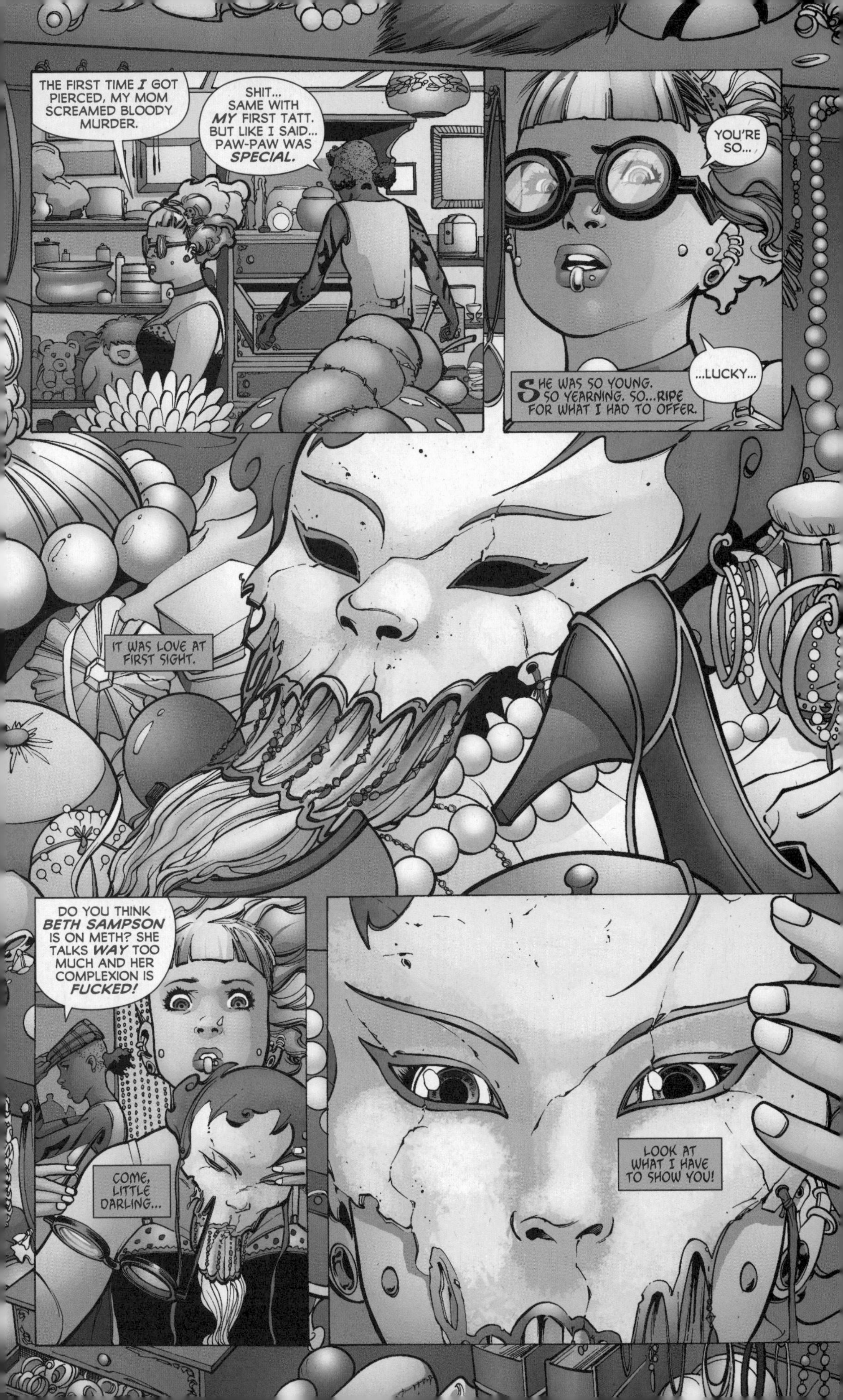
THE FIRST TIME *I* GOT PIERCED, MY MOM SCREAMED BLOODY MURDER.
SHIT... SAME WITH *MY* FIRST TATT. BUT LIKE I SAID... PAW-PAW WAS *SPECIAL.*
YOU'RE SO...
...LUCKY...
SHE WAS SO YOUNG. SO YEARNING. SO...RIPE FOR WHAT I HAD TO OFFER.
IT WAS LOVE AT FIRST SIGHT.
DO YOU THINK *BETH SAMPSON* IS ON METH? SHE TALKS *WAY* TOO MUCH AND HER COMPLEXION IS *FUCKED!*
COME, LITTLE DARLING...
LOOK AT WHAT I HAVE TO SHOW YOU!

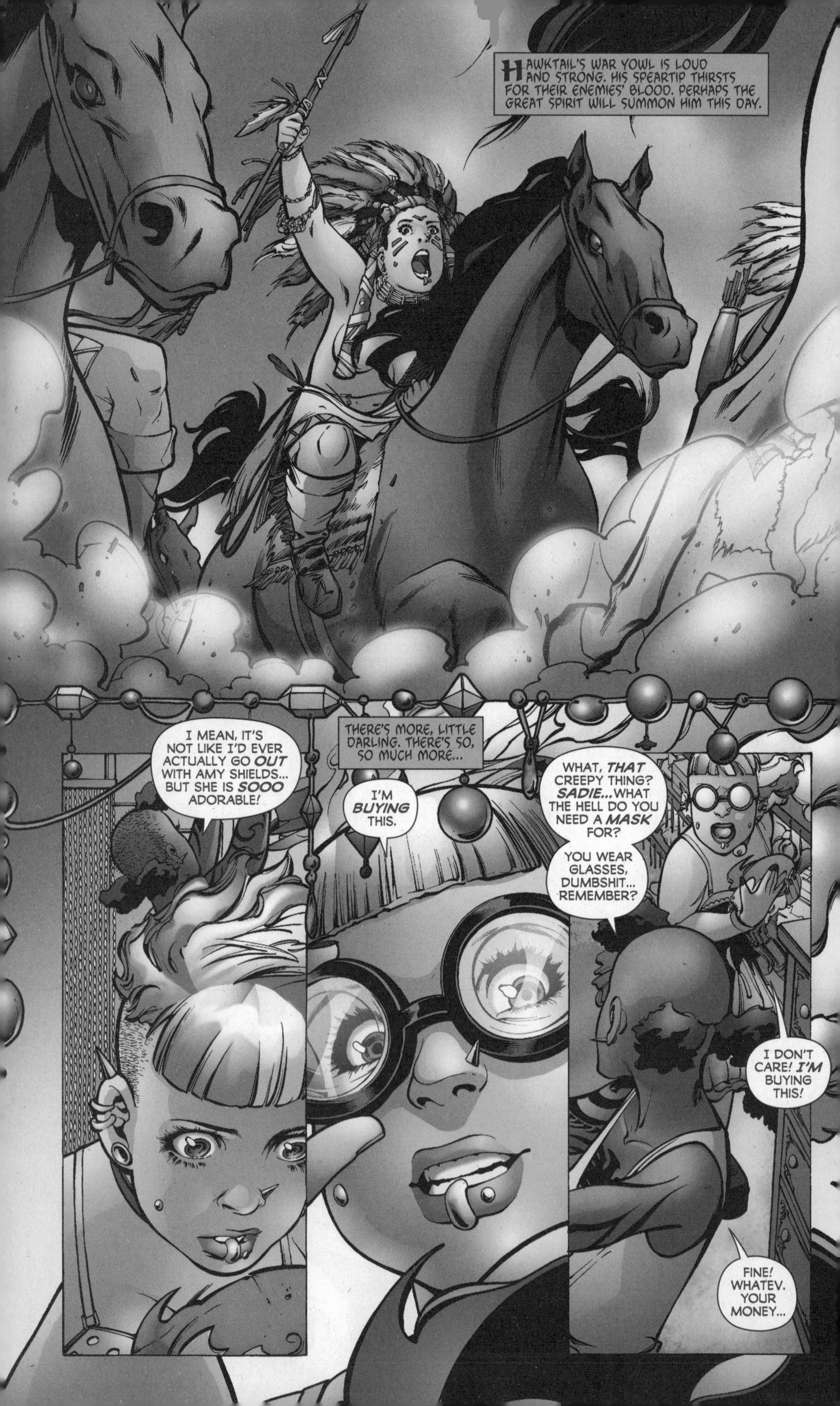
HAWKTAIL'S WAR YOWL IS LOUD AND STRONG. HIS SPEARTIP THIRSTS FOR THEIR ENEMIES' BLOOD. PERHAPS THE GREAT SPIRIT WILL SUMMON HIM THIS DAY.
I MEAN, IT'S NOT LIKE I'D EVER ACTUALLY GO OUT WITH AMY SHIELDS... BUT SHE IS SOOO ADORABLE!
THERE'S MORE, LITTLE DARLING. THERE'S SO, SO MUCH MORE...
I'M BUYING THIS.
WHAT, THAT CREEPY THING? SADIE...WHAT THE HELL DO YOU NEED A MASK FOR?
YOU WEAR GLASSES, DUMBSHIT... REMEMBER?
I DON'T CARE! I'M BUYING THIS!
FINE! WHATEV. YOUR MONEY...

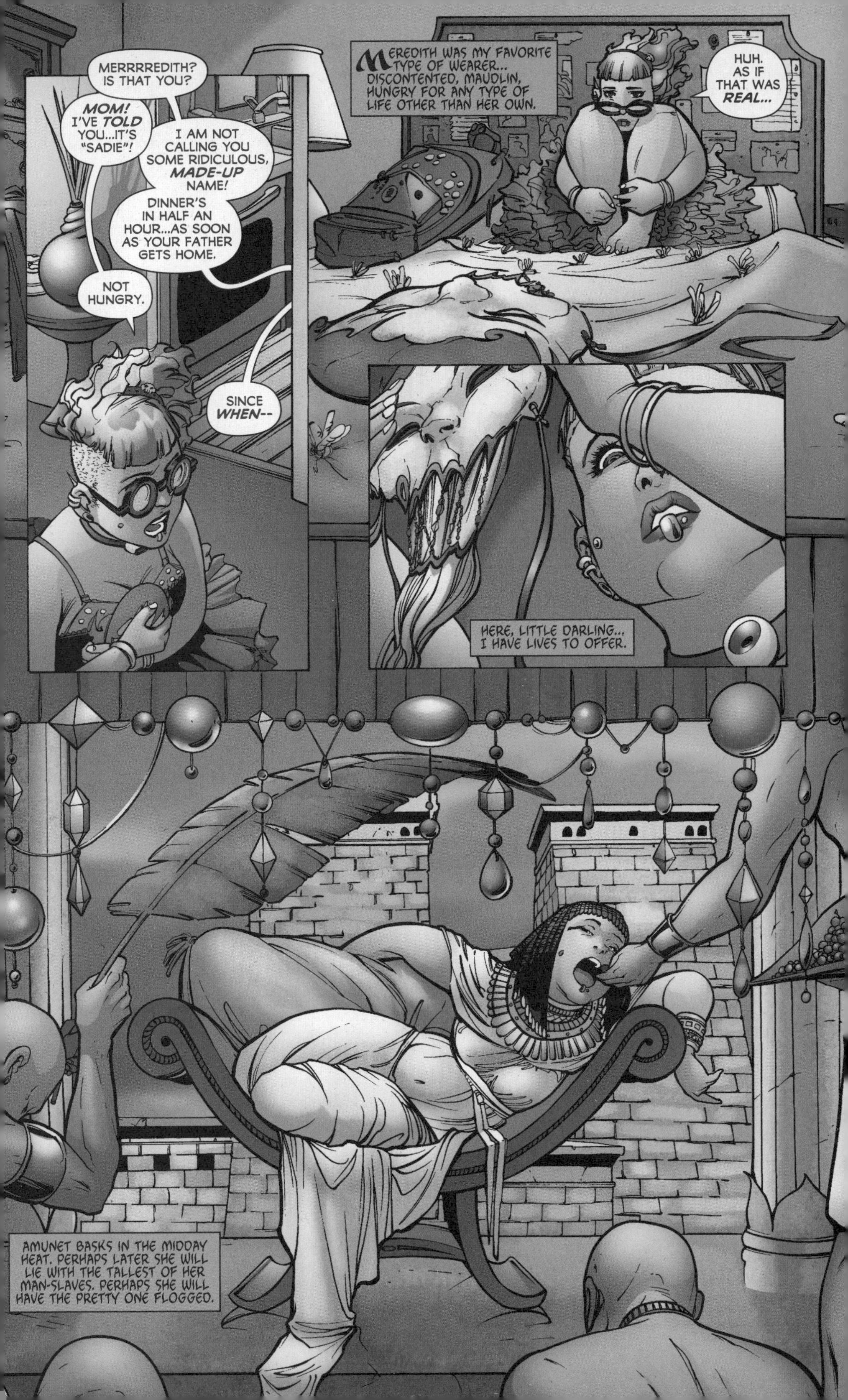
MERRRREDITH? IS THAT YOU?
MOM! I'VE TOLD YOU...IT'S "SADIE"!
I AM NOT CALLING YOU SOME RIDICULOUS, MADE-UP NAME!
DINNER'S IN HALF AN HOUR...AS SOON AS YOUR FATHER GETS HOME.
NOT HUNGRY.
SINCE WHEN--
MEREDITH WAS MY FAVORITE TYPE OF WEARER... DISCONTENTED, MAUDLIN, HUNGRY FOR ANY TYPE OF LIFE OTHER THAN HER OWN.
HUH. AS IF THAT WAS REAL...
HERE, LITTLE DARLING... I HAVE LIVES TO OFFER.
AMUNET BASKS IN THE MIDDAY HEAT. PERHAPS LATER SHE WILL LIE WITH THE TALLEST OF HER MAN-SLAVES. PERHAPS SHE WILL HAVE THE PRETTY ONE FLOGGED.

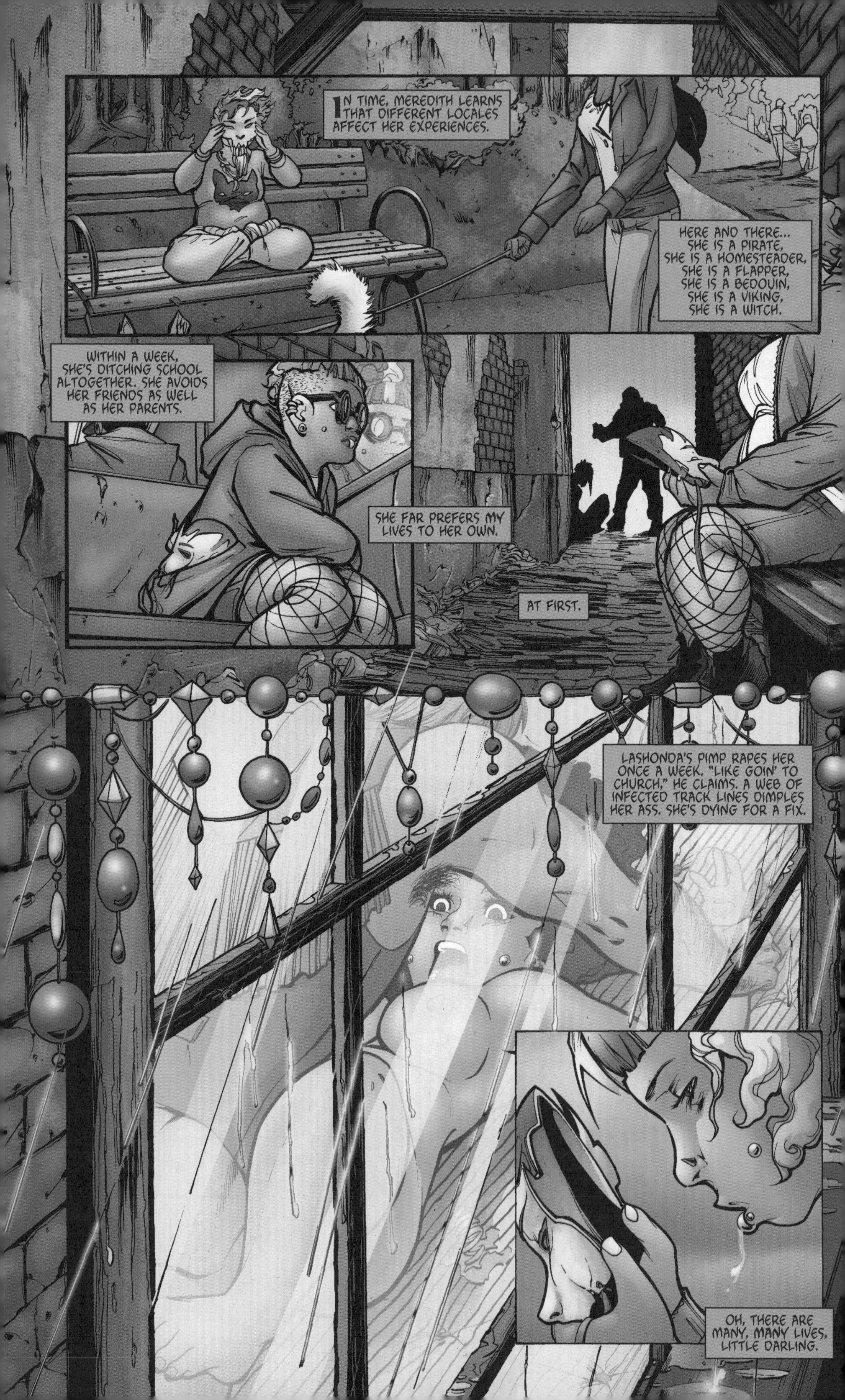
IN TIME, MEREDITH LEARNS THAT DIFFERENT LOCALES AFFECT HER EXPERIENCES.
HERE AND THERE... SHE IS A PIRATE, SHE IS A HOMESTEADER, SHE IS A FLAPPER, SHE IS A BEDOUIN, SHE IS A VIKING, SHE IS A WITCH.
WITHIN A WEEK, SHE'S DITCHING SCHOOL ALTOGETHER. SHE AVOIDS HER FRIENDS AS WELL AS HER PARENTS.
SHE FAR PREFERS MY LIVES TO HER OWN.
AT FIRST.
LASHONDA'S PIMP RAPES HER ONCE A WEEK. "LIKE GOIN' TO CHURCH," HE CLAIMS. A WEB OF INFECTED TRACK LINES DIMPLES HER ASS. SHE'S DYING FOR A FIX.
OH, THERE ARE MANY, MANY LIVES, LITTLE DARLING.

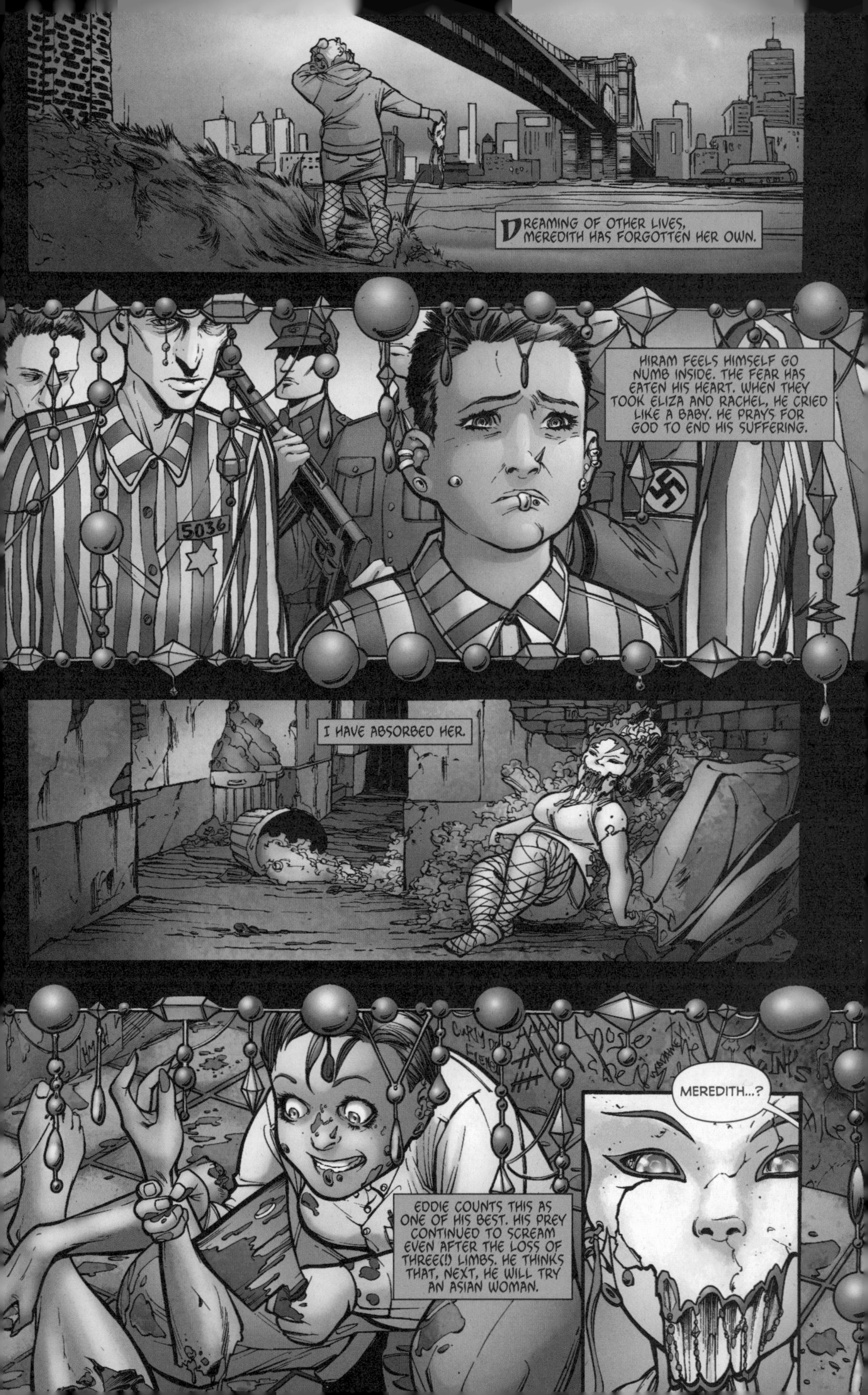
DREAMING OF OTHER LIVES, MEREDITH HAS FORGOTTEN HER OWN.
5036
HIRAM FEELS HIMSELF GO NUMB INSIDE. THE FEAR HAS EATEN HIS HEART. WHEN THEY TOOK ELIZA AND RACHEL, HE CRIED LIKE A BABY. HE PRAYS FOR GOD TO END HIS SUFFERING.
I HAVE ABSORBED HER.
EDDIE COUNTS THIS AS ONE OF HIS BEST. HIS PREY CONTINUED TO SCREAM EVEN AFTER THE LOSS OF THREE(!) LIMBS. HE THINKS THAT, NEXT, HE WILL TRY AN ASIAN WOMAN.
MEREDITH...?

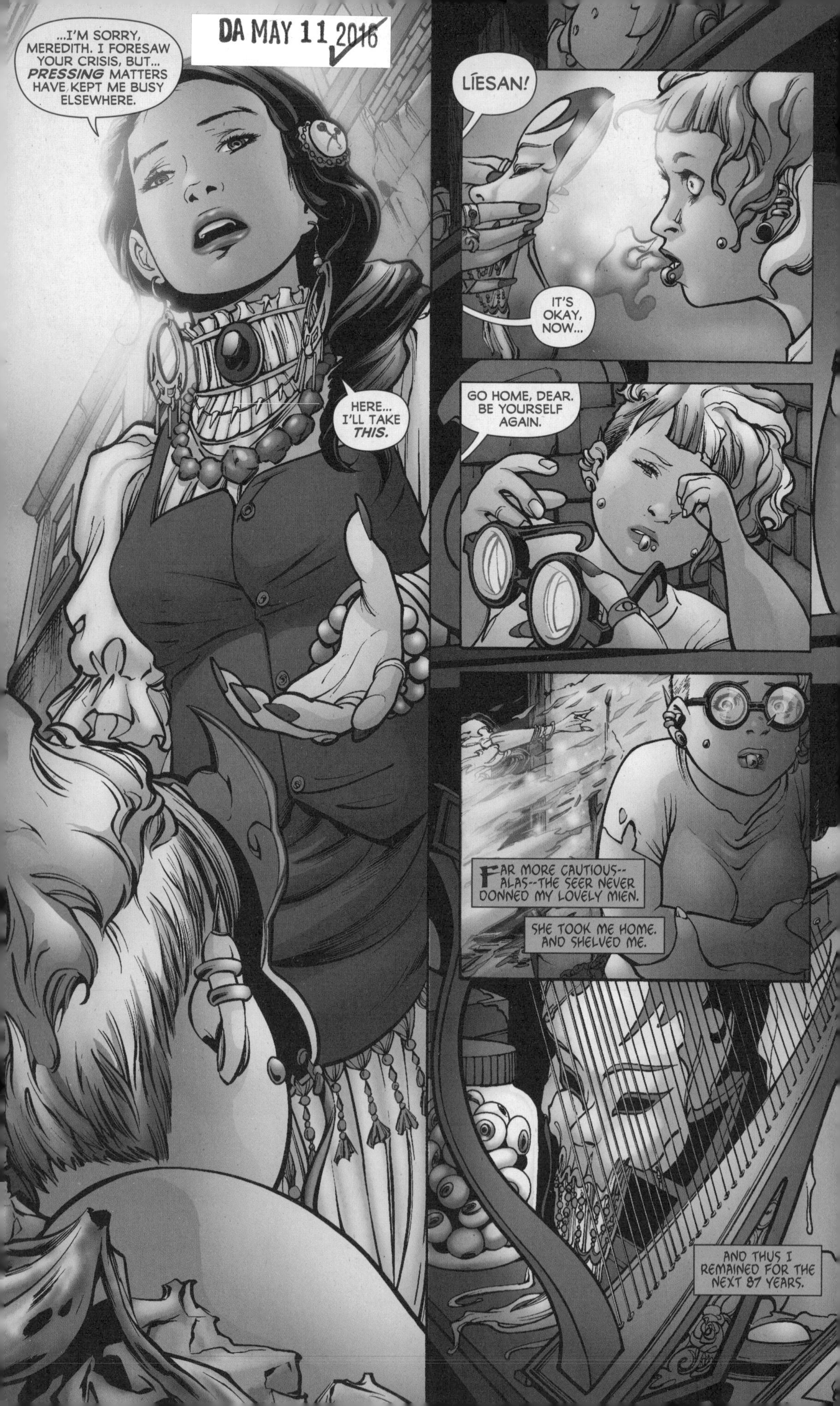

...I'M SORRY, MEREDITH. I FORESAW YOUR CRISIS, BUT... PRESSING MATTERS HAVE KEPT ME BUSY ELSEWHERE.
DA MAY 11 2016
HERE... I'LL TAKE THIS.
LÍESAN!
IT'S OKAY, NOW...
GO HOME, DEAR. BE YOURSELF AGAIN.
FAR MORE CAUTIOUS--ALAS--THE SEER NEVER DONNED MY LOVELY MIEN.
SHE TOOK ME HOME. AND SHELVED ME.
AND THUS I REMAINED FOR THE NEXT 87 YEARS.